DANCING AT ARMAGEDDON

Dancing at

Armageddon

SURVIVALISM AND CHAOS IN MODERN TIMES

RICHARD G. MITCHELL JR.

THE UNIVERSITY OF CHICAGO PRESS • CHICAGO AND LONDON

RICHARD G. MITCHELL JR. is professor of sociology at Oregon State University. He is the author of *Mountain Experience: The Psychology and Sociology of Adventure* and *Secrecy and Fieldwork* and the coeditor of *Exploring Society.*

The University of Chicago Press, Chicago 60637
The University of Chicago Press, Ltd., London

Printed in the United States of America

10 09 08 07 06 05 04 03 02 11   1 2 3 4 5
ISBN: 0-226-53244-5 (cloth)

Library of Congress Cataloging-in-Publication Data

Mitchell, Richard G.
Dancing at Armageddon : survivalism and chaos in modern times / Richard G. Mitchell, Jr.
p. cm.
Includes bibliographical references and index.
ISBN 0-226-53244-5 (cloth : alk. paper)
1. Survivalism—United States. I. Title.
HN90.R3 M55 2002
301′.0973—dc21

2001027814

♾ The paper used in this publication meets the minimum requirements of the American National Standard for Information Sciences—Permanence of Paper for Printed Library Materials, ANSI Z39.48-1992.

For the three Anns

When the instruments are broken and unutilizable, when plans are thwarted and efforts useless, the world appears with childlike and terrible freshness, unsupported and pathless. . . . [D]efeat restores to things their particular reality. . . . [D]efeat when considered as the final end is both a challenge to, and an appropriation of this world. A challenge because man is *worth more* than what crushes him; he no longer challenges things in their slight reality, like the engineer or the captain, but, on the contrary, in their excessive reality, by his very existence as a victim. . . . The defeat itself turns into a salvation.

—Jean-Paul Sartre, "Art and Action"

CONTENTS

ACKNOWLEDGMENTS

Years ago I had the good fortune to publish an earlier book with the University of Chicago Press. In those days, undue institutional modesty forbade mention of press staff members in acknowledgments. But a debt I owed. So now, tardy but undiminished thanks to John McCudden, patient editor, tutor, and guide to the mysteries and detail of our published language.

For the present volume, I owe my thanks to Jenni Fry, who helped me transform this volume from a gaggle of notions and notes to tempered text; Mike Brehm, who gave comely looks to the typography and covers; and Erin Hogan, who provided the project visibility and attention. To Jenni, Mike, and Erin go all praise for a presentable publication. I retain credit only for the bumps and stumbles. Two reviewers, continuing the professional tradition of anonymous modesty, must of necessity be praised impersonally, but well and thoroughly, for their patient readings and much-valued suggestions. Doug Mitchell, with the able assistance of Robert Devens, defines the Chicago tradition of excellence and is of course behind all of this and all of us, our mentor and muse.

I'm indebted to Michelle Grismer, Chuck Brown, Mary Ann Naylor, Lanny Lumondier, Chris Curry, Jurg Gerber, Gordon Sievers, Ann Yoders, and Ed Johnson for assistance with content analyses of relevant periodicals and correspondence. Thanks, too, to Christopher Schmitt, Dan Glaser, Marc Betz, Gary Tiedeman, and the members of the Beanery coffeehouse community for their honest interest, longstanding friendship, and good counsel throughout.

To those who shared their survivalist lives and times, Hank and Penny, Tim and Nic, Thomas and Percy, and the rest, masked and unmentioned though they be, the greatest thanks. Without them, there would be no survivalism to recount, no stories to tell. And without the encouragement, patient ear, and camaraderie of Kathy Charmaz, there would be no storytelling, no joy in nudging language about, no search for craft in writing.

This work is dedicated to three Anns: Vera Ann, my mother, fifty-two years my inspiration and conscience, now gone from this world but not forgotten; Eleen Ann, twenty-seven years my spouse and companion, now gone her own way in the world; and Katharine Ann, age ten, my daughter and brightest hope, for whom the world waits.

1 PROSPECTS

HANK'S OPINION

"Who's that?" Hank asks, pointing to one of the old news clippings in my notebook. Hank doesn't recognize the name in the headline, but the circled word "survivalist" catches his eye. After all, Hank is a survivalist, leader of the Mount Rainier Rangers. I read him the story, editing together bits from clippings and notes of other media coverage, which he appreciates. Hank reads a lot, at least an hour each day. "Research," he calls it. But he reads slowly, moving his fingers and lips as well as his eyes. The fingers are not so important; Hank has a keen memory. But the lips help sound out words not encountered during his eight years of formal education, finished nearly four decades ago.

The clippings tell a lurid tale. Just before 4:00 P.M. on July 18, 1984, James Oliver Huberty pulled on a pair of camouflage pants and a maroon t-shirt and headed for the door of his San Ysidro, California, apartment. "Where are you going, honey?" his wife asked. The things he carried suggested the answer: a 12-gauge pump shotgun, a Browning 9 mm semiautomatic pistol, an Uzi carbine, and a bag of ammunition. "I'm going to hunt humans," he replied (Horstman 1984).

"To hunt *what*?" interrupts Hank, slightly hard of hearing and clearly disbelieving.

"Hunt humans," I repeat.

Next come the facts of slaughter. It took Huberty only a few moments to drive the one-quarter block to a nearby McDonald's restaurant. Once inside he tuned his pocket transistor radio to a pop music station and opened fire. Two hundred and forty-five rounds and one hour and fifteen minutes later, forty people had been shot. Nineteen lived. Twenty-one died. At 5:17 P.M. officer Charles Foster of the San Diego PD Special Weapons and Tactics team strained to hear the orders of his superiors as two television station helicopters roared overhead. The command came. Foster held a short breath, squeezed lightly on the trigger of his scoped sniper rifle, and as a fellow officer described it, "put one right in the 10 ring" (Freed 1984). Huberty's chest exploded from the impact of the .308 caliber slug. He died, gasping, in seconds. The killing was over. Now journalistic explaining began.

First, biography. Huberty was ordinary in many respects, the stories said. He was born in 1942, raised in Canton, Ohio, married in 1965 to his wife, Etna, and had two children, ages ten and twelve. He attended but did not finish college, worked as a welder, mortician, security guard, and in January 1984, moved to the Southwest in search of new opportunities. But one attribute set him apart and gets Hank's attention. The papers call Huberty a "survivalist."

"What do they mean by that?" Hank demands.

I continue to narrate.

Huberty saw signs of growing trouble in America. Government regulation and meddling caused business failures and unemployment; he was forced to switch from job to job. High interest rates stifled economic growth; his real estate investments proved unproductive and hard to sell. These were not accidents, Huberty complained. International bankers were purposely manipulating the Federal Reserve System to bankrupt the nation. Soviet aggression was everywhere. Economic collapse, perhaps nuclear war, a complete breakdown of society were near, yet when he tried to warn his coworkers they would not listen. It became clear that only strong, independent individuals would survive. He vowed to be among that chosen few. He purchased thousands of dollars worth of nonperishable food and a half-dozen guns to provision and defend his home. The guns were especially important. He knew what they could do and how to use them. When Huberty left Ohio the food stayed behind, but not the guns.

The clippings end with dark warnings. Survivalists do not know precisely when or even how today's world will end, but they talk as if one thing is sure: the slide toward chaos has begun. For James Oliver Huberty it was later than he thought. He found his own chaos on a California summer afternoon in 1984. Other survivalists across the country are still waiting.

That was the story of survivalist Huberty, the news media creation—a stark, simple, senseless horror, malevolence larger than life. I never met

Huberty or most of the characters who would hold the headlines in the name of survivalism in the years to come, but I had to live with the expectations—public and professional—that kind of storytelling creates. So did Hank, the enigmatic, everyday survivalist next to me on the overstuffed sofa, sitting stiff and silent in uneasy confusion.

I always had a notebook in those days, full of news clippings and photocopies, as well as a camera and a tape recorder—a regular fieldworker's toolshop. Hank and the other Rangers called colleague Eleen Baumann and me the "college teachers" who were "studying survivalists" to "write a book." That's what we told them, over and over: name, department, research design, objectives—the whole obfuscating story. I was not about to repeat my earlier mistakes. No secrets with Hank and the others. Full disclosure, nothing hidden. Life is too short, I had learned, or could be. Everyone knew who I was, I thought. In fact most did, except me.

Eleen and I were also the Rangers' "cold weather survival instructors" (our previous mountain climbing experience was useful here), editors of the "Survival Times," the group's occasional newsletter (I owned a computer), and we had been regulars at meetings for a year and a half.

Slowly Hank begins to stir, shaking his head in negation, regaining his voice. He thanks me for the read, then sums Huberty in a phrase.

"Sure was messed up, that guy. Nothing like us."

"Yep," I agree. "Nothing like us."

Enough of Huberty. It is time for lunch. Hank and I put down our guns and head for the kitchen.

INTRODUCTION

This is a book about troubles that might be coming to America, the people looking forward to them, and the aspects of modernity that condition both. These enthusiasts for trouble have been dubbed many things: citizens' militias, tax and antigovernment protesters, racial separatists, survivalists, and others. I use *survivalist*[1] in reference to the whole for practical and theoretical reasons: because participants themselves often do, and because one sort of survival, the creative transcendence of calamitous cultural change, lies at the root of seemingly diverse events.

Anticipated troubles vary. Environmental catastrophe, economic collapse, seditious insurrection, widespread civil strife, internecine race war, thermonuclear holocaust, invasions from within, abroad, or above, and other calamities hold a place in survival discourse. In a dozen years of correspondence and participant observation at group meetings, public conferences, and clandestine training camps in eight states and two Canadian provinces from British Columbia to Tennessee, the survivalists I met varied, too.[2]

Retired contractor George Kassner built a $700,000 fortified retreat in the foothills of Montana, replete with bulletproof shutters, alarm systems, and an entry hall that could be flooded with poison gas and destructive sound waves. Tim Constance lived out of the back of his twenty-three-year-old Volvo station wagon, subsisting on food stamps and pigeons snared in public parks while squirreling away rusty guns, tools, and bits of food in abandoned buildings, buried tin cans, and with friends up and down the Atlantic seaboard. Frequently unemployed Nic and Leanne lived in the basement of her parents' suburban Pacific Northwest home, saving money to enlarge their stash of fourteen guns, six thousand rounds of ammunition, five goats, three sheep, a peacock, and five acres of retreat investment property. In central California, "Reverend" Gale sermonized about killing Jews and overthrowing the government but was careful not to jeopardize his generous military pension. Uncle Terry was trained by Gale to kill Jews but had other aspirations. Mostly he wanted to trap more coyotes to earn money for chocolate cake. Tim wanted to leave rural Washington and return to school to triple-major in English, history, and diesel mechanics. Once-wealthy, retired Canadian engineer Thomas Sands wanted five hundred volunteers to join him underground, learn to speak a new language, and breed the next generation. Some had simple wants. Palo Alto resident Tom simply didn't want his income tax audited. Louis was simply wanted—by the FBI.

Mensa, the society for persons with IQs demonstrably above the norm, had a survivalist-oriented subgroup of computer programmers, engineers, dentists, writers, and other professionals. Survivalist-theme writers like Mel Tappan, Thomas Clayton, and William Pierce boasted of doctoral-level graduate training. Usually unemployed tree planter Tim Dalkins, like Hank, was a survivalist organization officer who dropped out of high school years before graduation. During the week, Hungarian émigré William Udvary repaired appliances in California's San Joaquin Valley. On Sundays "Reverend" Udvary urged his small church congregation to begin armed resistance against the "terror squads of God-hating, communist henchmen and dupes," his term for the federal government of the United States.

When I first moved to Oregon in the late 1970s Huberty was in Ohio, Hank was in Alaska, and survivalists had attracted meager attention. I had just finished writing a book and was looking for a new project. Survivalists seemed a possibility with practical appeal: accessible to a

Pacific Northwest academic on a budget, not yet fully exploited by competing researchers, sufficiently distinctive to hold readers' attention yet easy enough to explain with ready theory, and perhaps providing a place where Eleen and I could use our outdoor skills. We were wrong on nearly all counts, but that was where we started.

The book just completed was on mountain climbing and "the psychology and sociology of adventure," as the subtitle read (R. Mitchell 1983). The study of mountaineering had taught me an important lesson. Explanations of human behavior based on presupposed "needs" for public recognition, deference, or control of material resources have limits. Climbers, I discovered, gained little profit or prestige from their avocations. Nor did climbing offer much as a psychological balm to bolster weakened egos or to provide isolates with senses of belonging. Mountaineers appeared neither deprived nor despairing. They reported no pressing urgency for increased status, stability, security, certainty, or material assets. Although diverse in background, climbers were distinctive in one respect. They evinced strong attractions to ambiguity, uncertainty, and puzzlement. They perceived themselves as capable, even exceptional persons, with affinities for challenge and complex problem solving that extended well beyond work and other primary roles. At the outset of my study of survivalism, mountain experience seemed distant and irrelevant. Wrong again.

SURVIVALISM AND MODERNITY

Exploring survivalism is the subject of this book but not the sole object. Survivalism is both a consequence of modern times and a means by which modernity may be understood. My intent is to examine both the phenomenon of survivalism and contemporary social life together.

Simmel suggests that since emerging from medievalism, humanity has sought answers to two vexing questions regarding the moral order of social institutions. The eighteenth century answered the question "Who shall rule?" against the unjust and inequitable bonds of religious, political, guild, and agrarian traditionalism in favor of participatory democratic forms. To this the nineteenth and twentieth centuries added "Who shall work?"—that is, how shall opportunities for individual achievement be allocated—and answered with universal education and inclusive efforts to eliminate barriers to participation based on race, gender, and other ascribed statuses (Simmel [1903] 1971, 339).

Survivalists ask the next question: "Who shall create?" Who shall have a hand in crafting culture for the twenty-first century? The question has been raised before and answered with discouragement.

Rational Legacy

At the beginning of the twentieth century Simmel foresaw that the "deepest problem of modern life" would lie in the "attempts of the individual to maintain independence . . . of his existence against the sovereign powers of society, against the weight of historical heritage and the external culture and technique of life" (Simmel [1903] 1971, 324). Not everyone accepts Simmel's priorities in these concerns,[3] but there is wide agreement on the form and direction of contemporary change.

Industrial civilization is now in the throes of a historically unprecedented, meteoric realignment of social, economic, and cognitive patterning Max Weber called "rationalization" and more generally is referred to as "modernity." Institutions and relationships are being permeated by an urge toward logical planning, structured management, measurement and calculation on all fronts.

Some argue this Enlightenment-spawned project goes well enough. Rational economic organization combines capitalism, machine process, and cybernetic control to produce goods and services in unprecedented abundance. Technology, rationalization's concrete manifestation, provides the leverage to pry away the Earth's crust, capture the power of the sun, and fling men to the moon. It brings within grasp the abilities to suppress polio, reattach retinas with tiny blades of laser light, and restructure the genetic foundations of living organisms. Reason in law continues to enfranchise and even opportunities, increase tolerance for diversity, and broaden the range of peoples included in self-determination (Parsons 1951; Nisbet 1980; Kolakowski 1990; Callinicos 1989). These are the benefits claimed for rationality. Others point to the deficiencies.

In the French tradition the rate of change in opportunity structures outstrips the normative order, leaving persons "separated from the social substance" as Hegel put it,[4] anomic in Durkheim's terms, confused, destabilized, disoriented, cut off from the collective conscience (Schacht 1970). The rationalized world increasingly becomes an artificial product of mechanical manipulation, estranged and separated from conquered nature. Modern science replaces primitive superstition, but with new ways of knowing comes a vast new unknown. The pantheon of ancient gods, the mysterious animation of ever present spirits and sprites have vanished. The once-sacred stream is channeled and dammed, the sacred grove measured for board-feet of timber. Astronomers and astronauts reach out into the expanding universe and discover humanity's insignificance and solitude. Instead of the surety of God's grace there remains only the ability to reject null hypotheses, to reduce the probability of error. Knowledge of material things is gained, but encompassing, spiritual understanding of life is lost. The residuum is the sparse legacy of Democritus: atoms, empty space, and "mere opinion."

Rationality begins to set its own agenda. Expanding scientific inquiry, commercial applications, and the burgeoning affairs of state demand ever larger and more specialized organizations, further dispassionate management and refined calculation. Late-stage capitalism and monolithic governments reduce persons to objects and objects to commodities, occasioning what Hegel called a "separation from self,"[5] an estrangement Marx labeled the alienation of labor. Workplace loyalty and tradition are replaced by meritocracy and cost-benefit analysis; craft and skill are subjugated to the depersonalized routines of automated mass assembly. Personal worth is increasingly gauged by the control, display, and consumption of material goods and visible services rather than one's role in producing them (Veblen [1899] 1967).

How are these intrusions met? Not well, according to many accounts. Faced with the growing power and complexity of modern institutions, the diminishing individual no longer hopes to comprehend or control even a fraction of the forces that surround her or him. Bloated, sclerotic social structures, amoral inconstancy, powerlessness, purposelessness—these too are the legacies claimed for rationalization. In response, the human condition declines in two directions: toward frenetic hyperconformity, the "one-dimensional," "other-directed," "organizational," or "protean" marionettes of modern bureaucratic life[6]; or toward disintegrating deviance—suicide, crime, mental illness, political apathy or extremism, and other destructive behaviors and beliefs.

So goes the standard account of modern times. But is this an accurate picture? And if so, what are its implications for survivalism? These are the questions that structure this book. We begin with the latter. How do survivalists fit and fare in the contemporary social order? Chapters 2, 3, and 4 explore their aspirations, adaptations, and discord with three elements of cultural experience: economic valuation and exchange, material function and resourcefulness, and evocative persuasion, with entrepreneurship, bricolage, and charisma in words and deeds. Chapter 5 shifts focus from survivalism as phenomenon to be explained to survivalism's utility in understanding modernity's emerging forms and influences. New instances of survival action are introduced and used to test the limits of rationalization and its antitheses in the bureaucratic state, dissident rebellion and corporate influence. Chapter 6 looks back over what has been learned of survivalism and modern social life and reflects upon the futures of both.

At the outset this much may be said. It would be convenient to lodge survivalists among beleaguered company, to add them to the list of modernity's ostensibly disadvantaged, explained away as one more confused, disheartened, embittered minority on the margin of relevance, left behind in the real or apparent march toward progress. It would also be wrong. A few fragments of survivalism might be explained in these familiar terms, as consequences of social-structural strain, interest conflicts, or the confusions of bemused and befuddled isolates; as expressions of collective ire, personal despair, and contrarian fitfulness (as in Aho 1990, 1994; Dees 1996; Coates 1987), but this book explores an alternative. Across a wide range of settings and behaviors the practiced survivalism I observed was less reactive than proactive, less a retreat from or renouncement of social life than a novel exploration of its possibilities. Therein lies a truth about survivalism and a hint regarding modern times.

The Self in Social Life

Much of the critique of modernity and its sequels sets volitional social action over against the institutional order. The self is presented as an entity apart from and in opposition to structured social life. Simmel and Weber reflect this view in their concerns regarding social experience in the rational future. In times ahead the omnipresent rational institution "becomes the frightful leveler," Simmel warns, "it hollows out the core of things, their peculiarities, their specific values and their uniqueness and incomparability in a way which is beyond repair" (Simmel [1903] 1971, 330). Weber concurs. Amid the pervasive disenchantments of rational society, the "shell of bondage," the "basic fact" of "the irresistible advance of bureaucratization," he asks, "How can one possibly save *any remnants* of 'individualist' freedom in any sense?" (Weber 1958b, 1402–3). In more recent commentary even the inner sanctum of personal identity comes under assault. The self is reformatted to the place and pace of the assembly line or the corporate subculture, saturated to overflowing in pressing waves of incoherent, disconnected demands for relation-work (Gergen 1991) or rendered public, left "up for grabs" (Sica 1993, 17) as commodification invades even to the essential core of subjectivity, to emotion and feeling (Hochschild 1983).

In all these cases the institutional order is the villain, the enemy of individualism, the antithesis of integrated selfhood against which persons must resist to retain their identities or be "swallowed up in the socio-technical mechanism" (Simmel [1903] 1971, 324). But as Jay Gubrium and Jim Holstein (2000) make clear, this is a narrow if not naive view. In the pragmatist tradition of George Herbert Mead (1934) and the symbolic interactionism that followed (Blumer 1969; Stryker 1980; Fine 1996), the self unfolds within social contexts, not in spite of them. The self is not cloistered and private but a structure arising from and flourishing in social experience (Gubrium and Holstein 2000). Modern life offers a thriving landscape of identity options, a myriad of "going concerns" (Hughes 1984) that "provide more occasions than ever before for constructing who and what we are" (Gubrium and Holstein 2000). "The self is always crafted in relation to institutional preferences and the biographical particulars of one's life" (Gubrium and Holstein 2000). So, too, is survivalism. Survivalism is not a rejection of or a protest against ordered social life. Rather, survivalism arises from the interplay of contextual restraints on the one hand and self-constituting social actions on the other, from the interaction between biography and circumstance, perceived capacities and constraints. This point deserves emphasis.

Survivalism accompanies the changes in modern times but in distinctive ways. Consider the negative case, what survivalism is not. Survivalism is neither a retreat from modern social life nor a search for privilege within it. Survivalism does not derive from want, perceived scarcity, or privation. Survivalism is not pragmatic effort to redistribute resources, rearrange status hierarchies, or reorder public agendas for personal gain. Survivalists are not principally wayward protesters dissatisfied with their share of the goods, services, and deference at hand (cf. Lipset 1960; Lipset and Raab 1978). Nor are they underclass authoritarians prone to fundamentalist rage against the conditions of modernity (cf. Hofstadter [1965] 1996). It is not diminished possessions, prestige, or sense of autonomy that motivates survivalists. In most instances survivalism begins with perceptions of relative choice, surplus, safety, and comfort: when the larder is at least part full, the neighborhood quiet, the electricity on.

The factual particulars of the contemporary institutional order, the organization of the state, the structures and means of corporate power and profit, or of scientific knowledge generation interest survivalists only a little. The attractions of survivalism lie in imaginatively reforming the totality of social life, not by changing institutions but through discovery and reinterpretation of the cultural assumptions and intrinsic practices that undergird the institutional order. Here is the key to understanding survivalism.

Survivalists do not, metaphorically, covet a larger share of the cultural pie. They want something more and different. They want to express creativity, not achieve control. They want a job at the pie shop, writing the recipes, mixing the ingredients, and watching the oven. It is the imaginative work of *culture crafting* not the artifacts of culture to which survivalists are attracted. Survivalists relish inventing new narratives, new primal means and fundamental meanings by which the world may be known. Survivalists seek to reinterpret the wisdom of science, not obedience to its laws. They want to reformulate the social contract, not the privileges of citizenship. They desire a hand in economic production and exchange, a voice in valuation, not ownership or consumption. In this process survivalists deconstruct fixed and formalized notions such as "politics," "economics," "science," and "religion," transforming these from social "facts" to talking points and plot structures for dramaturgic invention, adding their own yeasty, emergent, evocative turns and tones on their ways to cultural genesis.

To find places of consequence survivalists fashion discourses of pending need, speculative circumstances of crisis and concern wherein major social institutions face imminent serious erosion or total dissolution and in which survivalists themselves play central roles in reprioritized revisioning, recovery, and renewal. Survival discourse tailors widespread rancor and disorder to fit schemes for maximizing personal competence, actualization, and relevance. Troubles draw near, but with them come opportunities to celebrate humanity's full élan vital, to achieve a sense of belonging, not to the comfortable mass at the center of stability but among the novel few of the cutting edge of change on the new frontier.

The New Frontier

In modern, monolithic, rationally ordered industrial society, formalized in bureaucratic routine and driven by the ebb and flow of global capital, it would seem that Weber is correct. There are few apparent means for modern men and women to fully express their individualism, invention, and imagination in broad and meaningful ways.

Omnipresent modern culture comes ready-made: finished, sized, sorted, packaged, priced, and on the shelf. The creative work of visionary individuals is over. Little is left to do but acquire and arrange possessions and perspectives at leisure—passive leisure, inconsequential leisure. All around, a predictable plethora of general goods, standard knowledge, regularized relationships, and reasoned order. Only a few find cracks and chinks and unfinished places in this structure. Some of these we call survivalists. Kai Erickson knew them well enough even though he and they likely never met.

When the American Sociological Association held its annual meetings in San Antonio, Texas, in 1984, the convention center facilities were shared. Through the closed but unlocked doors fifty feet from the association's conference booth was a large regional gun show and survivalist gathering. Kai Erickson did not know Hank or the Rangers, and I doubt he visited the survivalists before preparing his presidential address, but he spoke directly to an understanding of survivalism.

> It may be one of the ironies of the modern workplace that people who rank lowest on any index of alienation are almost sure to be those who install machinery when it is first put into service and those who repair it when it begins to fail. Virtually every study of job satisfaction I am aware of suggests that repairers enjoy work more and derive more from it. They set their own work pace, command a wide range of skills, exercise a considerable amount of autonomy, and retain a secure sense of craft. It is dirty work, often, but creative, challenging, full of variety. *Breakdown, then, may be the surest antidote for feelings of alienation in the modern workplace.* (Erickson 1984, emphasis added)

Not all challenge-producing breakdown need be mechanical. National boundaries, ethnic identities, political and economic structures, knowledge systems, and other elements of culture may weaken and need refurbishment or deteriorate and require rebuilding. Crises, chaos, even doomsdays have latent allure. Along with uncertainty and danger come opportunities for creative engagement in meaning-filled, concrete work that matters, honest tests of character in contests with the fateful forces of a new age. Survivalism is a celebration of these changes in imaginative narrative and rehearsal.

One frontier remains: the doubtful future. Survivalism finds its niche in dramatic doubt, in a rhetoric of radical skepticism toward the prospects of contemporary institutional orders. Doubt progress. Dramatize alternatives. Treat modernity not as the irresistible advance of bureaucratization but as a failing project near its end. Recast modernity's formal systems as outmoded organizational straw men full of foibles and flaws primed for revelation and correction, as dull and dysfunctional contrasts to survivalists' discoveries, innovations, and adventuring. Ask difficult questions.

While opportunities for culture crafting may be few in present conditions, are those conditions immutable? What if there were troubles ahead, cataclysmic troubles? What if things broke down? What if Jim Jones, president and founder of Live Free, Inc., a nine-hundred-member mail-order survivalist organization, is right? What if highly specialized, interdependent society is ripe for internal strife or systemic failure? What if "the dinosaurs are dying. The big, all powerful, centralized institutions that past generations have come to depend on for their security are all near the end of their days. We can see in the near future the dissolving of the great corporations, the ruination of old political institutions, the end of many nations as we have known them, and the breaking up of almost all current economical and power structures. These dinosaurs of the industrial age prove more and more unable to cope with a changing world, and their efforts to retain power only lead to more catastrophic results."[7]

Doubt creates possibilities in profusion; portents invite creative planning, prioritizing, research, rehearsal, study. Suspecting what might happen later suggests what might be considered now: invest in precious metals, cultivate organic gardens, establish the aryan nation. Construct fallout shelters, fortify retreats, stockpile food and camping supplies, amass munitions and armaments. Try to organize mail and phone networks. Dream of forming communes, militia training programs, or revolutionary cells. Develop strategies to protect against future predators, against radiation-crazed bomb victims, rapacious government agencies, the have-nots of the post-apocalypse. What can go wrong? Alternatives abound, and not all are new.

PRECEDENTS

While the survivalism recounted here is a recent phenomenon, anticipating cataclysmic transformations of society is a venerable American tradition. Puritan settlers worked toward the establishment of a Holy Commonwealth in urgent expectation of the second coming, a soon-to-be-realized heavenly kingdom on earth (Persons 1958, 89–90). Early sectarian communes such as the brethren of the Woman in the Wilderness (f. 1694), the Ephrata Cloister (f. 1735), the Shakers (f. 1785), and the Rappites (f. 1804) were inspired by millennial visions, with the brethren said to have "scanned the heavens every night for signs and portents [confidently awaiting] the angel with the flaming sword" (Linder 1982, 54). While the invading heavenly hosts did not arrive on the brethren's timetable, millennialism has continued to play a dominant role in American sectarian Christianity for more than two centuries. From the Great Awakening of the 1740s and '50s and the Great Revival of the 1830s and '40s to contemporary Baptists, Pentecostals, Seventh-day Adventists, and Jehovah's Witnesses, there has been ongoing agreement. Literal interpretation of scripture reveals abundant signs of the coming "last days." For many of faith, the end is near.

More recent apocalyptic scenarios come from science as well as religion. The Club of Rome constructed formal models of population growth, industrialization, and resource utilization (Mesarovic 1974). In a series of reports beginning in the early 1970s they concluded that catastrophe is to be expected soon unless unplanned development, energy and resource gluttony, pollution, and the burgeoning of human masses is not curtailed (Center for Environmental Quality and Department of State 1980). In seeming confirmation of these warnings, famine has grown chronic in regions of Africa. Apparently innocuous Styrofoam cups and refrigerator coolant are indicted in a global depletion of the ozone layer, threatening crop failures and mutations, cataracts and cancer. Coal-fired electrical generators power conditioners to cool and cleanse office and home air, while outside the water and land are sterilized by acid rain (Tinker 1985). Digit-frugal programmers of the 1980s send businesses and governments scrambling to avoid Y2K computer system crises at the century's end. Social scientists (Catton 1984; Peachey and Learner 1981) warn of the collective violence likely to accompany widespread food and fuel shortages in the environmentally disrupted near future. Even the usually noncommittal *National Geographic* offers cautious pessimism in its millennium series (January 1998–December 1999). The Big Bang theory (Hubble 1936; Silk 1980) provides at least one arguable scientific precedent for a universal cataclysm.

Elsewhere fantasy moves toward fact. A real-life *Andromeda Strain* (1969), the mutated Ebola virus, is found lurking in Africa's *Hot Zone* (1994). The greenhouse effect is out of the pages of William Goldman's *Heat* (1985) and into the weather reports (Oppenheimer and Boyle 1990). North American croplands are seared by the summer drought of 1988; the coastlines creep inward. Nevil Shute's *On the Beach* (1957) is indirectly credentialed by scientific hypotheses of a post-atomic war global nuclear winter and underscored by the effects of El Niño and in the aftermath of Mount Pinatubo's 1991 eruption (see NOAA 1992; Fiocco, Fua, and Visconti 1996).

There are yet other hazards to contemporary life. International tensions pose perennial perceived risk grown acute in the atomic age as nuclear weaponry proliferates among smaller nations, even following the collapse of the Soviet Union. Daily, airplanes and automobiles crash, politicians are corrupted, bankers embezzle, terrorists bomb, and physicians make mistakes. Forests burn, rivers flood, ships sink, bridges collapse, and elevators get stuck between floors.

Survivalists draw color, arguments, and examples from these traditions, scientific reports, and common concerns in their search for delicate optimism.[8]

Delicate Optimism

Survivalism is centered on the continuing task of constructing "what if" scenarios in which survival preparations will be at once necessary and sufficient. This is a tenuous process. Survivalism depends upon scenarios built on middle ground, delicately fashioned to fall between the extremes of disbelief and despair: secular in cause, of concern to many, amenable to individual solutions, and employing practical means.[9]

Among themselves, survivalists more often narrate than debate the cause of coming cataclysms. Assorted calamity stories may coexist without discord, to be retold and tailored as individuals see fit. Constructing a cataclysmic tale personalized to one's circumstances is a survivalist prerogative and pastime. Once constructed, these tales accrue respect from survivalist others *as stories.* Quality is judged, as in Hellenic poetry contests of old, on the bases of artful drama, clever plot twists, and especially refinements in technical detail, not on the basis of correspondence to the empirical. Stories need to be believable, not provable; evoke imagination, not reveal first principles or primal truths.

Survivalist scenarios are akin to contemporary legends told in future tense. Paraphrasing Fine, they are accounts of happenings in which the narrator has not yet been directly involved, presented as *propositions for belief,* events that *could* occur, told *as if* their probability is high. They are notable happenings of the kind that are "strange but true" (Fine 1992, 2), but only if they achieve the balance of delicate optimism. Problems ahead must be defined as both urgently compelling and manageable in scope, neither trivial improbabilities nor certain destruction. This is challenging, creative work.

Despite the plenitude of potential horrors and hazards predicted by authorities, imagined by artists, and experienced in everyday life, impending doom is not obvious to most members of modern industrial society. Daily life does little to substantiate survivalist stories. All around, the appearances of order, not chaos, predominate. Institutions continue to adapt and function with stubborn durability. Stocks are bought and sold, votes are cast and counted, the police are on call if not always on time. There are goods on the store shelves, entertainments to watch, and planes and trains are more or less punctual. Credible scenarios of coming disaster must be crafted from anomalies and exceptions to this pervasive stability. Broadcast and print media and Internet sources help by dramatizing deviance and disaster, but hinder by the very dependability with which untoward events are promptly if not always accurately reported.

Some pessimistic futures are more easily substantiated than others. There are historical precedents for earthquakes, tornadoes, crop failures, urban rioting, currency fluctuations, foreign invasions, meteor strikes, and even return of the plague. But the relative infrequency of these events is also a matter of record. Other hypothesized events—millennial endings, heavenly vengeance, race war, and the subtle workings of entrenched subversives—are less amenable to prediction but also less credible. Survivalists seek a place in between, pending and probable, according to their interests, opportunities, and imaginations. But the specter of Huberty hinders their efforts.

The Huberty Problem

Huberty is a problem for Hank and the Rangers. Huberty is no Ranger, likely no survivalist at all in their view. So why is he granted a place in this narrative? Because Huberty and stories such as his have come to define survivalism in the public mind. Therein lies competition to Hank's scenarios and confusion for analysts.

Except for the rarest of instances, survivalism is not a present-day achievement. The satisfactions of survivalists are found in what-if wonderment, exploration, tinkering with tools, exchange of ideas and techniques, and above all artful, balanced storytelling. Huberty upsets the balance, diminishes the wonderment, and distorts the salience of certain techniques and tools. Yet part of this Huberty problem is understandable in practical terms. Huberty is simple and handy. Hank and the survivalists are not.

Survivalists are neither convenient nor convivial subjects. Organizationally, survivalism is a shifting cloud of loosely linked events, discourse, commerce, sign equipment, and erratic gatherings lacking obvious form, regularity, or routine. Survivalists for the most part do none of the things that make for easy writing or research. They do not meet or recruit regularly in public, ally with established associations, respond to focused leadership, or recognize a shared agenda. They have no long-established haunts and hangouts, no favored street corners, lodge halls, lunch counters, fixed headquarters, public phone numbers, or representative spokespersons ready to answer questions, provide mailing lists, or offer official opinions. Indeed privacy, secrecy, and seclusion are moderate survivalist concerns. Some are uncomfortable with strangers, offering only aliases, nicknames, or CB "handles" at first contact. Mail from one survivalist to another may be laundered through anonymous letter exchange services.[10] Home phone numbers are unlisted. Street addresses seldom given. This decentered, polyvocal, uncooperative, shifting mist of survivalism is not ready for prime time. Huberty is.

While Huberty's notoriety arises from a single outrage spanning no more than a city block and half an afternoon, his frenzy was widely announced on police scanners, videotaped from every angle, and generated a bounty of law enforcement and eyewitness interviews, all in time for the evening news. Huberty was a ready-made media occasion needing only a label for completion. So he became a survivalist.[11] Modern broadcast journalism favors events that are encapsulated in time and place, visually explicit, and readily understood in conventional terms. Accordingly, the media over-report unrepresentative but accessible confrontations, shootings, bombings, standoffs, and tragic Huberty-esque characters associated with them by the name survivalism. In consequence, hard-to-find Hank and the other survivalists acquire stigma and perhaps prurient allure unjustified by their own mundane action. And with stigma comes marginality.

"They" are removed from "us." Survivalists are set off from conventional life as an aberrant fugue, enveloped in what Joseph Gusfield calls the "aurora of consensus" (1989, 434). In this realm of public troubles the likes of missing children or elder abuse,[12] problems are seemingly so obvious and urgent that analysts need not be unduly reflective, concerned with examining all sides of the issue, or attentive to details. The notion that survivalists might aspire beyond practical politics for personal gain or grievance is discounted. Survivalists are allowed anxiety but not curiosity, desire to improve their own circumstances but not interest in larger change, confusion and *mens rea* but not aesthetic or humane sensibilities. The possibility of survivalism as a symptom of more pervasive cultural trends is disregarded.

We might expect scholarship to correct these misrepresentations. But survivalists do not accommodate themselves readily to favored methods of social science research—surveys, systematic standardized interviewing, and subsequent enumeration. Those who have sought to impose these approaches onto survivalism have been disappointed.[13] Other analysts forgo the observation of lived survivalism in favor of passive texts, scrutinizing news and magazine articles, public speeches, handouts, and the like without sufficient concern for the ways these materials are produced or interpreted. There is value in survivalist texts, but advertisements for products and services must not be read as destinations, only signposts, not as evidence of survivalists' interests, only of survivalist-oriented marketeering. Speeches and handouts must not be judged without attention to their dramaturgic intent and subsequent interpretations. Huberty stories must not be taken for concrete conditions but as constructions of concern (see Best 1990). Those who disregard these cautions may miss survivalism all together.

Any study of survivalism must confront the tension between sentiments and acts, words and deeds, what survivalists say (or are claimed to have said) and what they do (see Deutscher, Pestello, and Pestello 1993). Ungrounded representations of survivalism in the media and elsewhere are duplicitous; discrediting survivalists' delicately balanced scenarios while magnifying the threat of survivalists' actions. Survival discourse is on the one hand dismissed as preposterous and on the other treated as a literal description of foreboding intent. What survivalists *say might happen* in the future is of no account; what they *say they might do* about the future is reified into explicit description of pending action. In such reporting the subtlety of survivalism is lost and we are left to ask: Where is the line drawn? Within what limits and by what means is culture crafting pursued? Survivalists know there has been no apocalypse. America is not yet in the grip of alien invaders, economic failure, or civil turmoil. For all its apparent calculation and utility, survivalism is no practical readiness for uncertainties but a celebration of imagination, an encompassing compelling game of make-believe. But with what urgency is this game played? How far will actors go to find a place in culturecraft? And are there times when the line is crossed, when audiences are so small there are none to disconfirm the tale or when stories are so well told even the tellers are convinced? If an unknowing public takes Huberty as a sample of genuine survivalism, what outsider attributions might survivalists themselves come to accept? To find out we turn to survivalism in practice, to time with the Rangers, to talks with Hank and Tim and Thomas and others like and unlike them, to texts in context, and to ongoing participation and observation, questions and answers.

In the stories ahead most of what interests survivalists—gun grease and real estate, books and booby traps, campfire conversations and Sunday sermons—finds a proportioned place in the account. I say proportioned because certain topics we might preconceive to be salient such as "politics" and "religion" may seem underrepresented. This is no oversight but a reflection of survivalists' demonstrated interests. Throughout, I seek accord with symbolic interactionism's attention to emergent meanings within institutional limitations (see Fine 1996) and the need for lucid reporting and candor regarding the researcher's role in fieldwork and storytelling (see Mitchell and Charmaz 1996; Charmaz and Mitchell 1996; Richardson 1994; Ellis 1995). My concern is to find ways of reporting that survivalists would recognize as full and fair, and from which both they and we might learn something about contemporary social life. There are many ways to create such reports, some traditional, some innovative. After this introduction and some basic groundwork in the next chapter, nonexclusive preference is given to showing over telling, to bringing the reader along to survivalist gatherings and outings to meet members and share their puzzlements and my own as we seek to make sense of each other and of the changing world. For this purpose attention is paid to the details, to description as thick as events warrant and records allow. For dialogue, I depend upon tape transcripts and field notes; for recollection of setting, photographs and sketches. These in turn are offered whenever appropriate, as they were experienced, as tales of the field (Van Mannen 1988) in which survivalist meanings emerge. No doubt there are errors in these retellings, but there are no intended fabrications. The events and deeds, words and scenes to follow are as I found them; sometimes strange, but as representative as my skills and resources permit.[14]

There is selection. Not all stories are told. Many would prove redundant; survivalism does take predictable forms. More important, some might prove harmful. Names of people and places have been changed, and time has been allowed for events to defuse, actors to move on, away, or out of sight.[15] Not all stories are complete. This is lived ethnography, not imaginary fiction. Plots are rough-edged, unfinished. Characters leave with improper exits. Actions begin but go unconsummated. So it was in the field. So it is here.

Enough of introductions. I have had my opening say and Hank has borne more than his share of scrutiny for as yet so small a part. He will have more to tell us in chapter 3. For now I ask what Gide might in my place. Understand these survivalists. But please, don't understand them too quickly.[16] I learned this and other lessons even on my first interview.

THE FIRST INTERVIEW

Recalling my first interview brings to mind the March 1983 issue of the white supremacist publication *National Vanguard*. It was a gift from my first informant. It came at exactly the right moment.

I had just finished reading "Survival Treasure Chest: Today's Pieces of Eight Make Sterling Investments" in my new subscription to *Survive* magazine (Kogelschatz 1983). Gold and silver were the things to have in times of crisis, the article advised. No survivalist should be without a good supply. If this was the case, I reasoned, then my hometown precious metals dealer, John Nixon, might be in contact with local area survivalists and therefore was perhaps a good place to start my research. I called him for an appointment. As it turned out I was right, and I was wrong. Nixon knew about survivalists, but not about the ones who hoard gold and silver.

I armed myself with a notebook and a list of naive questions: "How many survivalists would you say visit your shop in a typical week?" "Approximately what proportion are males, females?" "What would you estimate the average age of these survivalists to be?" Feeling a bit insecure about my reception, I concealed my already running tape recorder in a light fabric bag. I had forty-five minutes before the recorder would reveal itself by a loud end-of-tape click. I walked into Nixon's shop, shook his hand, and accepted the chair he offered at one side of his desk. Arranging my papers, and setting the concealed tape recorder on the desktop, I was ready to begin.

I introduced myself. I explained that I was a sociologist working on a book about survivalism and would like his help. I showed him the *Survive* article on investments. He had never before seen the magazine. After looking the article over without much interest, he said that to his knowledge no survivalists of the sort the article described came to his shop. Fifteen minutes passed in unfocused talk. It seemed Nixon thought little of gold and silver stockpiling as a survival strategy, or of my writing project. Then the conversation took an unexpected turn. Our roles reversed. Nixon began to ask me questions—about my wife, about the nationality of our parents and grandparents. When he learned we were both university faculty and of German and Norwegian descent, he grew excited. "You talk about survival," he said, "I've made an in-depth study of that. . . . You and your wife would be prime candidates to be taught the realities of the last hundred years of United States civilization and what's going to happen to us if we don't wake up!"

Nixon had his own apocalyptic vision. And he had something else I just then noticed. On the desktop to his right, partially covered by a few sheets of paper, lay a .38 caliber revolver pointed my way.

The future looks grim, Nixon asserted. "We are living in a collapsing civilization. It's like an implosion." The cause of this failure? "The cultural bearing stock, the Anglo-Saxons and northern Europeans that are the problem-solving peoples of our civilization, are being displaced." The presumed best of this lot, the "Nordics" who "fought the Mongol hordes in Europe" and later "got in covered wagons and came west and survived in the wilderness," are at special risk. According to Nixon's reading of census publications, "Nordics are only having about 1.2 children per family." He added, "White people instinctively know things are wrong, particularly the Nordic because he is very sensitive to his surroundings. Even though he may not be able to verbalize this distinctive feeling he stops reproducing, especially in the big cities. It was the Nordics that built New York City, but it's a fact that the ones who live there now have literally stopped having children." His prognosis: "If you project over a 150-year period in the United States, the Nordic will be extinct!" And elsewhere, worse. "It's worse in Sweden, Luxembourg, in France, even Russia and the white Communist countries, Poland, Czechoslovakia, Hungary." Other hazards are more immediate than extinction, Nixon warned. "We were 90 percent of the population up until the Civil War, now we are probably only 60 percent. When we become less than 50 percent of the population, then, living in a democracy, the other groups are going to completely dispossess us. We will be the dispossessed minority."

Nixon added details and examples, citations from Charles Darwin and George Orwell, Marx and Hitler. The tone of the conversation changed again. He began to speak of "us" versus "them," to include my wife and me in his cause. He moved his chair closer, leaned forward. His tone became conspiratorial, as if secrets were being shared. "I'm not interested in giving you this information just so you can write a book," he clarified, "but for your own information. Then you can do with it what you will, because you might become a recruit. Then you will go out and want to proselytize." He seemed anxious to incorporate me into this hypothetical fate, to stress the personal seriousness and urgency of the aryan's problem.

At that moment I had another worry. I saw another problem, serious and urgent. I glanced at my watch. In nine minutes, more or less, Nixon would discover I had been recording this conversation. The trust he seemed to imagine between us might suddenly end.

Right then I wished I knew more about this man. A few things were apparent: his clear blue-gray eyes, thick dark hair, athletic build, and clean, delicate hands. Some facts about him, had I know them, might have put me at ease. At the time, he was forty-four, married, and had two teenage children. He held bachelor's and master's degrees in music and had done some work toward a Ph.D. He had been a schoolteacher and a one-time unsuccessful congressional candidate. Other information, also obtained later, would probably have made me less comfortable.

As it turned out, Nixon was well known to area journalists and local government officials for his frequent, unsolicited essays, phone calls, letters to the editor, and speeches at public meetings. The timing of these expressions of opinion was unpredictable but the themes were consistent: international Jewish conspiracy, growing government repression, impending "patriotic" rebellion. Nixon was on record as having claimed, among other things, that the "Illuminati hired Marx to write the *Communist Manifesto*"; the United States military is preparing to quell a "nationwide tax rebellion of six million people, maybe more, who aren't even filing any tax returns"; the government has readied "Operation Cable Splicer," which will "isolate various areas of the country" by creating "power blackouts and various communications breakdowns, then move the military in," confiscate guns and property, and "arrest those people they consider dangerous—like myself." But "when they try it," Nixon bragged, "we will kick their butts right out of the country. I don't know what's going to happen, but there's going to be bloodshed!" Nixon predicted that at the head of this "patriotic rebellion" will be the Posse Comitatus, in which he had long been active. The Posse Comitatus, I was to learn, advocates armed resistance to what they view as illegitimate taxation based on personal income or property, and to any governmental authority superordinate to the county sheriff. In retrospect this would have been relevant background material and certainly would have helped me understand what was going on, but I knew nothing of it at the time. Instead I could only continue to listen, unsure of the interview's course or outcome.

The tape recorder kept running.

From a file cabinet next to his desk Nixon brought out the latest edition of *National Vanguard.* He was quiet for a moment, glancing through the issue as if to remind himself of its contents. Then, placing the magazine on the desk between us, he continued. "They talk about racism," he said. "Well I'm a racist. I believe in preserving all the races, but not mixing them together."

Nixon argued some social science, wittingly or not, contributes to this denigration of racial purity. "One of the great misconceptions that the American civilization has been under since World War I has been the egalitarian or the equalitarian philosophy which is spread through the Franz Boas and Margaret Mead school of anthropology. . . . When he [Boas] came to the United States he was thoroughly imbued with Marxism, and the whole basis of Marxism is egalitarianism. In other words you cannot admit to racial or individual differences if you are a communist."

This ideology of egalitarianism, while not part of the Constitution, has come to permeate educational curricula and governmental policy. "What you have here is Marxism. It goes from the very highest echelons of our federal establishment right into the school system." But Marxism is only a symptom. It is not an end in itself, Nixon explained, but the means by which international Jewry seek to gain control. "What the Jews want to do is reduce us to the lowest common denominator, not just socially but biologically. They want to destroy the cultural bearing stock." Current social policies further this end, Nixon argued. "That's what integration does, it mixes the gene pool. It destroys the cultural bearing stock. And look at the manipulation in this "zero population growth" idea. The only people that have cut back on their population are the Europeans, especially the Nordics. Your Blacks and Mexicans and Vietnamese and other ethnic groups keep right on breeding."

Both Nixon and I had become agitated. Nixon seemed to care very much about the issues at hand. As he had told an earlier interviewer, "Once you get into this, if it piques your interest, you'll never get out of it. You just dig and dig and dig until it consumes you." Nixon seemed to be enjoying himself. Here he had, at once, an apparently receptive audience, perhaps a potential recruit, and the chance to unveil what he saw as a fundamental but overlooked principle of social science to a credentialed sociologist. In contrast, I felt confused and disoriented. Nixon was an obviously intelligent, widely read, articulate individual, a resident of my own community, yet he was espousing racism of a sort I had believed would be found only among bucolic bumpkins or the genuinely demented. The interview had drifted far from my intentions or control, my liberal sentiments had been summarily rejected, and my ability to withhold judgment was growing frail. Fieldwork was proving to be more than I was prepared for. In my uncertainty, I said little. While Nixon was eager to reveal what he knew, I was trying to keep a secret. And frankly, I was frightened. If another's ideas could be so contrary to my expectations, what then of his behavior? How would revelation of the tape recording be received?

As Nixon spoke I thought of the time and of his impending discovery, now no more than a minute or two away. Nixon grew even more animated. Leaning forward again, forearms on the desk, his right hand strayed toward the revolver, brushing the papers away. Like an engrossed thinker stroking his chin, he began to rub his palm back and forth idly across the gun's cylinder. A sliver of afternoon sunlight breached the shutters and glinted off the gently swaying barrel. From my muzzle-on vantage point, and in this direct light, I could see the chambered bullets were a copper-jacketed, hollowpoint design.

It ended as T. S. Eliot predicted the world will, not with a bang, but a whimper. As a final punctuation to his discourse on yet another topic, the misrepresentations of Black History Month, Nixon picked up the *National Vanguard.* "If you want to find out what is really going on, read this!" he enthused, slapping the publication down on top of the concealed recorder. The "whap" of the descending magazine, and the "click" of the ending tape coincided. Almost exactly. The whimper was mine, a partially suppressed, involuntary cry of fear, and relief. Puzzled by my utterance, Nixon offered reassurance. "You can keep it if you want," he said, tapping the journal. I thanked him, assured him I would look it over carefully and consider what he had said, and gathered my things to leave. The first survivalist interview was over. I had come, confident of my will and skill, to "win" respect and "acquire" information. (These were the terms I used in preparatory notes to myself.) My presented self, or so I imagined, was that of the competent, objective, purpose-filled researcher. I left in ambivalent confusion, titillated by flirtation with apparent danger, befuddled by my naivete, and frightened by my potential new identity, by what I had been taken for, and might become, if this study continued—a racist.

Chapter 4 reconsiders some of Nixon's notions and more of his motives for participating in survivalist discourse. There were hints of things to come in his storytelling that I did not see at first. Race was Nixon's topic but not his principal interest. Storytelling was. Race was not the end of his argument but its beginning, a theme around which to order stirring narratives, tales about the origins and causes of the human condition, tales unraveling the mysteries of history and demography, migration and evolution, a starting point for the grand and heady work of culture crafting.

HANK'S HOUSE

By the time Hank Wentworth's invitation to the next monthly meeting of the Mount Rainier Rangers arrived, Eleen and I had met many survivalists. Still, the smudged, handwritten note was intriguing. Here was opportunity: a chance to meet survivalists on their own territory, in a member's home, not in the woods amid gunplay and war games. But what would it be like? Would our way pass along little traveled rural roads? Would our approach be watched by surly, sleeveless extras from the film *Deliverance,* leaning against fenceposts, shotguns cradled in their arms? And the home itself, would it be a hillside burrow or a bunker, bermed and barricaded, surrounded by barbed wire, a snarling Doberman straining at his rusty chain in the front yard? Perhaps not, but whatever might be the case, Eleen and I planned to be prepared. No surprises this time. We would go early, check out the surroundings, get the lay of the land, familiarize ourselves with the kinds of places survivalists live before the gathering started.

It was a two-hour drive from our place to the city. From there we followed Hank's instructions north along the interstate and into the unexpected. The route did not lead out to the country as we had anticipated but into the prosperous suburbs. Malls and grocery stores, automobile and tire dealers, fast food outlets and convenience marts—all were busy with late-morning shoppers. Successive turns led us away from the boulevard into the quiet back streets of a middle-class bedroom community. One more corner and we were on Hank's street. Smiling women tended flower beds while children biked and triked over rounded curbs on protected cul-de-sacs. Open garage doors revealed men puttering with implements of domestic leisure—cleaning barbecues, repairing small boats, and straightening tool benches. The uniformly neat lawns suggested conformity to local norms. Confused by the neighborhood's appearance, we drove slowly, feigning nonchalance, parked a half a block past Hank's house, and sat for a few moments wondering how we might have so misjudged survivalism. Other things would prompt our wonder several times more before that day was finished.

Were survivalists more conventional than we thought, perhaps nothing more than eccentric hobbyists interested in refining a few scouting skills among sympathetic friends? As the meeting time neared we walked back to Hank's. The impression of commonplace middle-class American living grew stronger. Later checking and observation would add to this impression. Hank's home was part of a ten-year-old housing development on the periphery of a metropolitan area of 1.5 million people. His house, like others in the area, had three bedrooms, two baths, about 1300 square feet of living space, an attached double garage, and an assessed valuation 10 percent above the regional median for single family homes. In the driveway we saw two unremarkable vehicles: an eight-year-old, three-quarter-ton Chevrolet pickup truck in good repair and a two-year-old domestic subcompact sedan. The rye grass lawn was a healthy dark green, the junipers neatly trimmed. Only a few details of this scene reminded us of why we had come. There were adornments on the truck's rear window. At center-height on both sides of the glass were ten-inch-high decals—stylized eagles clutching olive branches and arrows, wearing breastplates of stars and stripes and with "E Pluribus Unum" banners in their beaks. At the lower left was a membership sticker from the National Rifle Association; on the right, the corporate logo of Hank's current employer. The sticker on the front door was less obtrusive but more explicit. It was a small sticker, perhaps five inches square, at the top of which was a drawing of three crossed guns—a rifle, a pistol, and a revolver. Below the drawing there was a warning:

> This property is protected by
> An Armed American
> Exercising Freedom of Choice
> To Protect Life Liberty and Property
> THERE IS NOTHING INSIDE WORTH
> RISKING YOUR LIFE FOR!

We exchanged glances, acknowledging the merit of this message.

In the years ahead, until he lost the house, Hank's front door would open for us many times. There would be more meetings, informal visits, group-related errands, and often people to meet: family, other survivalists, and guests. Regardless of the event our reception would be the same as that first day's.

I rang the bell. Smiling genuinely around false teeth, and to our relief unarmed, Hank opened the door. "Afternoon," he mumbled. "Com'on in." For me there was a muscular, four-pump handshake, animating Hank's forearm tattoos. Eleen only got an uncertain two-pumper and quiet tattoos. At five feet, eight inches tall and 160 functional pounds, Hank was a proportioned "medium" man. Much of Hank was straight.

His posture, gaze, and speech were straight. So were his combed-back, thin black hair and trim, combed-down mustache. Penny, Hank's spouse and partner of twenty-seven years, was more generous in speech and proportions and less linear. That day she came beaming from the kitchen, aproned, spoon in hand, repeating welcomes and gesturing nonspecifically about the room. Shortly we were all seated and awaiting the other guests. I looked around and at our hosts. The door sticker had been partially misleading. Comfort as well as safety was a concern in this home.

Hank and Penny were dressed for plain comfort. He wore Levi's, a white t-shirt and white socks, and Kmart training shoes. Penny needed bifocals, and more coverage. Her five feet, five inches and two hundred pounds nearly overfilled her large polyester slacks, argyle sweater, and cheap tennis shoes. The living room offered fancy comfort. Textures, patterns, colors surrounded us. Home-knit afghans, throw pillows, and doilies protected all conceivable wear and glare spots on the overstuffed neocolonial furniture. Yellow-brown floral upholstery, green shag carpet and crocheted area rugs, tasseled fringes on scalloped lamp shades, mirrored wall panels, and striped wine wallpaper combined into an aesthetic of amiable miscellany. Penny's warm chatter and Hank's deferential agreement filled ten or fifteen minutes of acquaintance time until the doorbell rang. The Todds, John and Deborah, had arrived, then came Nic and his girlfriend, Leanne, then Ron Goodman, and soon others. Penny and some followers returned to the kitchen to tend the three-bean casserole, her latest "healthy" recipe. The Todds introduced themselves and their outlook.

John and Deborah sounded like the survivalists about whom I had read in the *Survive* article Nixon had ignored. With John's new job as an emergency medical technician and Deb's work as a buyer at a department store chain, they could afford a new, midsize Honda sedan, a riverfront apartment close to downtown, and a hobby: survivalism. With financial success came the luxury of creative worry about the future and the cash to enjoy preparing for it. The previous month, for their third wedding anniversary, each had bought the other fifty dollars worth of silver coins and a commemorative gold piece from South Africa. They were going the following Sunday to look at a parcel of rural land seventy miles to the east. They had other investment plans. Investments were the key to the Todds' survivalism. Deb and John spoke of entrepreneurial protection and adventure. Over the years, in many places, I encountered this kind of survivalism.

• • •

In the beginning Eleen and I found survivalism as we expected and as we didn't. Nixon's dark intensity and depth surprised us, as did Hank's good cheer and welcome. But neither was difficult to locate. Useful signposts were as near as the local newsstand. We would learn more of Hank and Nixon and their sorts of survivalism later, but the newsstand items helped frame survivalism's first characteristic form from the outset. The message was not in *Survive* and the other magazines we found. Indeed, magazine content proved misleading. The message was the magazines themselves. Finding survivalism was not hard because non-survivalists with practical motives had already been there. Survivalists were seen by some as potential consumers, a market, whatever else they might be. So marketeers set out exploit them.

Survivalists meet them halfway, not with the anticipated desires to consume but with curiosities regarding the marketplace itself. Markets interest survivalists, as signs of the times and sites for invention and craft. This mix of outsiders' would-be commercialism and survivalists' own inquisitiveness about value and exchange requires careful sifting and becomes our task in chapter 2. Data are plentiful. Marketeering maximizes visibility. But for survivalists the meaning of the marketplace is less obvious.

2 THE CRAFT OF VALUATION

THE COFFEEHOUSE

At Smith Barney, we make money
the old-fashioned way.
—advertising slogan

I got Tide, Charmin, Cheer,
Brawny—all the best stuff!
—Major Sudzmann

Friday night, 11:30. The trendy coffeehouse near the beach in Santa Monica is packed. The after-something crowd turns out to critique Los Angeles' performing arts over lattes and cappuccinos. I'm working on this manuscript in the corner. Two movie industry executives take the table next to mine. Both are fashionably thin and tanned (it is December). She: late thirties, wearing a short, fur-trimmed vest, a silk blouse with little holding it together in front, boots, and a long velour skirt, slit from ankle to mid-thigh. He: forties, wearing designer-wrinkled olive linen pants and a matching jacket over another designer's sweater and accent scarf. His beard looks as shampooed and permed as their hairdos. They have just come from a preview screening of their studio's next action moneymaker (Bruce Willis does something violent and heroic).

They talk shop, drifting comfortably back and forth between English and French. He jokes. She coos. They discuss distribution and marketing, the nutty flavor of soy milk in their lattes, the script revisions that should have been made. Then comes accounting, percentages and bonuses, how and how much they stand to profit. With money imaginarily in the bank, it is time for survivalism.

They speak of their stocks and options. Then with cheery pessimism they concur: the stock market can't last much longer. Yes. Oui. Agreeing nods. It is probably time to sell, to protect themselves.

Both: A crash is coming.
He: Perhaps it's even planned.
She: The insiders will know.
He: There is a priority list of those who will be told, who can get their money out before it all goes under.
She: We should buy a little place, some land we could live off.
He: There isn't any left. All the land is too expensive.
She: I heard about this place, just across the bay from where we stayed at Puerto Vallarta.
He: What's it like?
She: It's a little island. Practically no one lives there. They don't have electricity, just candles and kerosene. We could grow our own garden and catch fish. It never gets cold.

PARABLE

It is a brave new world. Decades of stifling government regulations are finally gone. Business opportunities flourish. Inflation is low, growth brisk. There is uncertainty of course, but the possibilities seem vast. Marketeers with modern savvy and methods, and glittering offers, reach small, rural, working-class investors. Little bits of capital, together, will create big leverage, big profits, high returns and solid futures, they say. Even the government approves, or seems to. People listen, dig into their savings, invest. Profits begin to pour in—for some. The rest wait their turns, encouraged by the marketeers' testimonials and small payments. Months go by. Real jobs diminish. Real prices soar. There are flaws in the plan. Capital does not capitalize production but is consumed by the marketeers, the top of the pyramid. The schemes begin to collapse, first privately then in public announcements. The government freezes the marketeers' remaining assets but little is left and few care. The schemes have failed. The government that encouraged them has failed.

In the south, protesters take to the streets, raid government arms depots, blockade roads, call for the president and his government to resign. In the capital, riot police beat back rebellious throngs, killing dozens, wounding hundreds. Enraged bands take control of regional governments. Federal jets bomb insurgent villagers in their homes. The president announces his government is stepping down. The next day Congress declares a national state of emergency and imposes curfews and media censorship. The day after that, Congress reappoints the president.

Rebellion spreads from the rural south to populous centers throughout the country. The military effectively collapses. Armed vigilante squads roam the streets, unleashing indiscriminate automatic weapons fire. Rescue helicopters attempting to evacuate foreign nationals are hit, shoot back. The loose opposition finds a name: The Organization for Security and Cooperation. Those without allies or allegiance or guns flee. Thousands pour across the borders. Thousands more head toward the coast in hopes of escaping the looting and violence. A haphazard flotilla of leaky fishing boats, luxury yachts, and commandeered government ships takes to the open ocean to escape the chaos. Some sink in storms. Some are blown back to the mainland. Some are repelled or sunk by warships of surrounding nations. A few craft slip through, reach relative safety across the fifty-mile straight. Survivors plead for asylum. One of these is the fleeing former Minister of Defense.

The president, now with little authority or power, tries a desperate ploy. He orders police stations in the north to hand out guns to citizens willing to proclaim allegiance to his government. Hundreds, then thousands respond. By nightfall of the program's second day a new sort of vigilante, men wearing civilian clothes and ski masks and brandishing machine guns, sets up checkpoints on major roads, searching cars and busses for opposition members and stolen weapons.

Violence escalates. The streets of one coastal town fill with corpses of secret police murdered by antigovernment crowds. Inland, near the capital, another city rebels. Mutilated torsos of special forces troops fester at curbside. The government responds, turning armored vehicle guns on a hospital filled with rebel wounded, beating staff members, taking hostages.

Unlikely international forces assert themselves. Greeks send troops to evacuate Chinese, Jordanian, and Syrian diplomats and their families from embattled enclaves near the capital. The Italian navy exercises its might, intercedes, provides a neutral diplomatic meeting ground aboard one of its warships off the coast. The major European powers act; they arm, embark, and land an international military force by sea and air to restore order. Calm settles over an occupied nation. The rebels retreat into scattered countryside strongholds. Some talk of elections. Some talk of all-out war.[1]

Survivalist fiction?

No.

Springtime in Albania, 1997.

COMMODITIES AND CREATIVITY

Imagine that the coffee house couple are right. Imagine what happened over there happening here, a kind of Albania in America. Imagine inflation, depression, devaluation of stocks or bonds or the dollar, shortages of food or fuel or other resources. Breakdown could follow, then violence, civil strife, even nuclear war. Now imagine there are ways to prepare, material ways, economic ways, prophylactic prudence in the American tradition. Anticipate these events. Preserve capital, invest strategically, maximize market advantage. Emulate the Boy Scout, the busy summer squirrel. Stockpile necessities, guard them against dangers. Begin with two maxims, one applicable to all survivalism, the other specific to marketeers' efforts to persuade survivalists. What you have is what you will need. What you will need is for sale.

What You Have Is What You Will Need

One premise is common to all survivalism: trouble is coming, but manageable trouble. The talked-of cataclysm ahead may destroy, confuse, destabilize, but only selectively. Necessities now available from traditional sources—retail goods, military security, government services, church leadership—may dwindle. But prepared survivalists can fill the gaps, for themselves and perhaps for others. In the disrupted future, survival readiness will neutralize institutional and systemic failures. No matter what the future may hold, what you have will be the foundation for what you need. As such, survival readiness is relative and tenable, not absolute and tested. Preparations are not evaluated against benchmark standards. Calorie consumption rates or roentgen shielding capacity, the number and distribution of enemies, the strength of their faith and firepower—all should be known. But pertinent facts do not make programmatic imperatives. They serve other purposes: as punctuations and embellishments to survival storytelling; as evidence that scenarios crafted to fit individual circumstances are grounded in reasoned practicality. Consider a few short examples built on premises of economic troubles.

New Yorker Kirk Schmidt, twenty-nine, is married to an engineer. His scenarios hinge on "economic collapse" and its consequences. Early evenings he attends college, working toward a degree in business administration. Late nights he devotes to his hobby, making survival plans to suit his lifestyle. "My hobby is investments to build a secure future," Kirk says. "If a bomb hits New York City I am doomed, but I don't think that will happen, really. New York City is a stimulating place to live and is great for investment and the future. I live in a condominium and advocate them for all to save money and energy." Kirk emphasizes energy dependence as the weakest link in our economy, but he has a plan. "I am investing to make big money so I can build a solar house in the country and pay cash for it." Away from the city things will be safer. Meanwhile, Kirk makes a living. "I manage a store that sells insulated windows and doors, and I see how interested the general population is in saving energy."

Dr. Ronald Smallfield and his wife live in Los Angeles. They describe themselves as Anglo-Saxon Episcopalians in their early sixties whose politics are "conservative, hard money, Republican but not radical right." Their interest in survivalism grew out of their "concern about the deterioration of the monetary system and breakdown of the social structure of the country, especially the large cities." Dr. Smallfield feels his horticultural expertise developed through thirty years of orchid cultivation will complement his medical background as an essential postdisaster skill. Mrs. Smallfield runs an interior decorating business and has a lifelong interest in "sewing, designing, stitchery," and related crafts, which she views as her contribution to family survival preparations.

Carol Kennworth, like Kirk Schmidt, illustrates a survivalist corollary: what you plan for now will be what you will need later. Good intentions, backed by a good story, count as action among survivalists. Carol, thirty-five, attorney-at-law, lives with her spouse and children in urban New England on a comfortable six-digit income and belongs to Mensa's roughly one-hundred-member survivalist "special interest group." The obviously intelligent members hold no meetings, recognize no leadership, and share only the "Survivalist SIG Report," a six-page monthly mimeoed newsletter compiled from the contributions of the most active participants. Carol describes herself as a political conservative with a Protestant background and distinctive tastes. Likes: "classical music, opera, and playing the piano." Languages: fluent "French and German, a little Spanish and Hebrew." Enjoyments: international travel, "acquiring knowledge about history and other cultures," and "a good debate and free exchange of ideas" with "healthy, self-confident, uninhibited" people. Prospects: "I have become a 'survivalist,'" Carol reveals, "mostly because I do not believe most people have an objective standard of values, which should be a common ground for all. This lack of objectivity has infected our government and our people." She can see the possibility of "shortages and riots due to economic pressures" and the "ensuing military effort to control same, eventually leading to a wartime economy and possible nuclear resolution." Her plans: a joint retreat venture with "six or seven families who might wish to purchase with me a large tract or farm, put vacation houses on it (now a tax shelter and when needed a fallout shelter)." But these partners should be compatible, "well-educated professionals," preferably "atheistic or agnostics, persons who have successfully completed psychoanalysis, and . . . who adhere to the principles of Ayn Rand in *Atlas Shrugged*."

While these snapshots do little justice to the subtlety of the valuation issue, they immediately make obvious both the relativity and intrinsic attractions of survivalist scenario building. Survivalism fits lifestyles and budgets.

What You Need, You Can Buy

Marketeers promote a streamlined survival. There are troubles ahead but ways to cope. It is a matter of being in the right place at the right time with the right stuff. And acquiring the right stuff seems simple. In the gospel folk song "All My Trials," faith trumps finances. Salvation is not for sale. "If religion was a thing that money could buy," the song proposes, "then the rich would live and the poor would die." But they cannot and do not, claims the song. Marketeers claim differently. Religion does not matter much, but the song's null hypothesis is reasonable. Protection can be bought. Survival is for sale.

What is for sale? Shelter, security, staples, implements, accessories, and anything else expected to sharply accrue or preserve value when disruptions occur. Full coverage of all survival-for-sale items would make for a daunting volume in its own right. To illustrate I'll sample the stock in a limited arena, products and services offered to secure goods and people in safe havens, nooks and crannies, shelters and retreats, and other locales theoretically resistant to harm or removed from trouble. Stroll through the survivalist market. Consider the offerings. Note their diversity. But remember, appearances are not meanings. Commodities are not culture. Not everything advertised for a purpose serves that purpose. Not everything for sale is sold.

CONCEALMENT

One can "learn how to hide almost anything" in *The Stash Book*. Use *Hidden Doorways* to build sequestered nooks and crannies "in houses, cars, motorcycles, bicycles—even one's own body."[2] Keep valuables safe from government inspection (or FDIC protection) in Swiss Security Vaults (located in Aurora, Colorado).

SHELTERS

What about the bomb? While the Reagan administration recommended shovels and dirt,[3] the Todds showed us more detailed plans, working drawings of a "Blast-Upgradable Hazard-Resistant Earth-Sheltered Residence" (see also Chester et. al. 1984, 24), just purchased for twenty-five dollars from the American Civil Defense Association, publishers of the *Journal of Civil Defense* and the *TACDA Alert* since the Kennedy era. Off-the-truck handy havens can be had, too. In the 1980s "The Egg," Underground Shelters' cement box, Stormaster Shelters' concrete ellipse, and Survival Center's quonset provided 60 to 120 square feet of back-yard-buriable shelter for up to five persons for two weeks of radiation- or mayhem-induced encapsulation. Sans freight, installation, water, food, air, or toilet facilities, these shelters ranged in price from the cost of a quality compact car to a luxury sedan. By the late 1990s fiberglass and thermoplastics put Radius Defense's "P10 Disaster Shelter" at the head of the ready-made shelter field. The P10 provides space, nutrition, and hygiene basics for a family of four for two months (or twenty visitors for a long weekend). The P10 offers air and water filtration systems and keeps undesirables out with bulletproof portal covers and multiple entrances disguised beneath fiberglass rocks "almost impossible to detect," displaying "no thermal signature, little or no metallic . . . or radar signature."

FORTIFIED HOMES

Unitized shelters sound dark, dank, odoriferous, crowded, or worse, a bad investment? How about a fortified home? Architect Joel Skosen's firm, Survival Homes Corporation in Portland, Oregon, specializes in residences with camouflaged, hardened interior strongholds and redundant heat, light, air purification, and alarm systems. If the customer insists he will add bulletproof windows and machine-gun ports, but Skosen recommends against them: "You never want to make a house look like an obvious fortress. Those who want in can always move up a bigger gun. There is no way you can design a home to withstand RPG rockets and tanks. That's why I design these homes so you virtually cannot tell inside or out that they are any different from a conventional home."

Fortified homes are more comfortable than underground shelters but quadruple the cost of conventional construction. The land and Skosen's fees are extra.

RETREAT PROPERTY

Retreat properties offer alternative attractions as vacation or retirement destinations, rental income, or tax write-offs. Amenities now, security later. The area around Grants Pass in southern Oregon is periodically depicted in popular rumor as a hotbed of survival retreats.[4] These rumors are exaggerated but not groundless.[5] Southern Oregon has qualities appreciated by survivalists and others alike. Small, picturesque communities are scattered sparsely among the forested mountains. Local government, by citizens' intent and fiscal necessity, is laissez-faire. Being located far from major population centers fosters provincial isolationism and perhaps diminishes the risk of mass immigrations in times of crisis.

Rainfall is adequate to green the rolling hillsides and nourish crops without irrigation. The prevailing winds keep temperatures moderate year round and, some say, minimize the risk of radioactive fallout. The southern Oregon scenery and greenery are attractions enough for some. Richard Bach, author of *Jonathan Livingston Seagull,* and Russell Meyer, cartoonist creator of the comic strip *Broomhilda,* moved there in the '80s, along with Steve Miller of the Steve Miller Blues Band, who purchased his own large farm.[6] Widely read survivalist-author Mel Tappan lived in Rogue River during the 1970s and '80s while writing *Survival Guns* (1976), his numerous articles in *Guns and Ammo* and *Soldier of Fortune* magazines, and editing the "Personal Survival Letter." At Tappan's urging a few joined him in retreat, but of these Tappan was demographically disappointed. "Too many doctors and lawyers" retreated to Oregon, he complained, but "not enough plumbers, electricians, or carpenters." Bob McQuain, a former TV bit-part actor from southern California and 1982 Grants Pass Realtor of the Year did not complain. Retreat properties then and now are his specialty: expensive, but in chronic undersupply. During the 1980s "the really big ranches—five hundred to eight hundred acres"—were in high demand, "but there were just not that many around." "Imagine what it's like," he reminisced, "when a client calls me who has a million dollars or more to spend, and I don't have anything worth that much to sell him."

DEVELOPMENTS

By the end of the 1990s, with the continuing scarcity of large ranch properties, wealthy buyers began building 4,000–6,000-square-foot homes on smaller lots with Skosen-style sophisticated shelter systems and even congregated in walled subcommunities—"survivalists' suburbs," of sorts.

The commercial retreat community idea is not new. In 1977 Peg and Larry Letterman acquired 1,089 acres of semiarid range land in southeast Washington and began developing Ponderosa Village, 202 plots with the promise of "increased security from possible economic and social deterioration" but without water or sewage treatment. By century's end 170 lots had sold or resold and 47 were owner occupied.[7] Perhaps the most ambitious of all commercial retreat developments was the Terrene Ark, a subterranean condominium complex in the southern Utah desert proffering both security and comfort: independent power generators and water and air filtration, but also "an attractive retreat residence" with "furnishings anyone would be proud of." The Ark promised central air conditioning, an underground recreation hall, jogging track, library, and even a kennel for the family pet.[8] For those willing to remodel, a Sacramento-area realtor began offering perhaps the ultimate in secure real estate in the late 1990s: decommissioned Titan I missile complexes. These circa 1965 facilities sited on roughly fifty-acre plots featured 160-foot-deep silos for three Titan I missiles (not included), *really* strong hatches, subterranean power generating, command and communication domes, antenna silos, utility elevators, living spaces for 150, honeycombs of personnel tunnels, a helicopter pad—priced for quick sale in the new millennium at under two million. Equally secure Atlas missile sites were cheaper but came with only five acres of land. Locations and availability varied.[9]

GETAWAYS

Planning "getaway" vehicles, routes, and schemes is a perennial topic with potential for survivalist-oriented commerce. Emergency jacks, auxiliary lights, chain saws, winches, tools, spare parts, maps and navigation gear, and performance upgrades are commercially available to outfit the family car, truck, trailer, 4 × 4, or motor home for unsettled times. Less common are more stout terrestrial transport. Used armored military vehicles can be purchased as mobile fortified homes (Lee 1997). Joel Skosen recommends frailer but more lithe alternatives. He outfitted one customer with an ultralight aircraft for reaching his reinforced seaside retreat from his workplace in the urban center. For upscale offshore retreats, Alain Bories, a French marketeer, promoted two models of motorized sailboats, the Arche de Noé and the Voilier de Survie. Each had a steel hull, electromagnetic pulse shielding, a deck washing system to remove fallout contamination, bulletproof ports, and all-electric controls operated from the sealed master cabin.[10]

Some scenarios are built around a single, key item. A student of mine, Mary Ann, who knew I would be interested, showed me her recently purchased car. It was twenty-three years old, plain but well cared for, a no-frills 1971 Mercedes four-door sedan featuring efficient diesel power, a manual transmission, manual windows, cloth upholstery, rubber floor mats, no air conditioning, no tape player, and a distinctive accessory. In the trunk, purchased from a survival supply catalog, sat a forty-gallon auxiliary fuel tank. The retired couple who sold the car warned Mary Ann. The economy could collapse at any time; fuel will not be available at any price. But the couple had a plan: relatives to help, rural property, some stored food, security measures. The car was the key to it all. It was their "getaway vehicle." With care and adequate warning they figured the fuel-frugal diesel would make it nonstop twenty-two hundred miles from western Oregon to their retreat in southeast Texas.[11]

BAD NEWS

A wealth of bearish advice, pessimistic projections, and "secrets" are available from self-proclaimed experts, in periodic flyers, newsletters, and books. When the Todds came to Hank's house for the first time, they brought along well-used copies of some classic recommended reading: Jerome Smith's *The Coming Currency Collapse* (1981), Douglas Casey's *Crisis Investing* (1981), and Howard Ruff's 1979 bestseller, *How to Prosper during the Coming Bad Years*, as well as recent copies of Ruff's newsletter, "Ruff Times." Many more publications of like kind can be had. So popular (and inaccurate) are these dire projections that entire careers have been built around forecasting fiscal failures, then explaining why these predictions are only marginally off timetable. Spin-offs and imitations of Ruff's work have appeared annually for more than two decades.[12]

• • •

Survivalist-oriented commodities are more obvious than markets, markets more conspicuous than the meanings of the marketplace. Concealment, shelters, retreats, getaway vehicles, commercial forecasting services, and a myriad of other attention-getting items are on the figurative shop shelves. But these are the symptoms, not the substance, of survivalism. Inventory is not analysis. The meaning of the marketplace does not reside in items for sale but in the ways survivalists act toward and interpret the whole—the products, the processes of marketing, and their own roles therein.

Economic Troubles, Participation, and Modernity

Survival scenarios may begin in tales of economic trouble and culminate in economic participation, but participation takes varying forms, more and less desirable. Marketeers may indeed provide protection for sale, but buying security over the counter is of little survivalist value. Security is not the point.

What matters most to survivalists is not the utility of their possessions, the firepower of assault rifles or the overpressure ratings of bomb shelters, the capacity to provide emergency nutrition or electricity, hide the family jewels, avoid enemy hordes, or predict downturns in the stock market. The necessities of material security are relevant to credible tale telling, to be sure, but more fundamental is the part survivalists themselves play in the economy of security, in the production and distribution of security resources.

Here is survivalism's first conflict with modernity, with rationalized economy, monetization, mass production, and mass consumption. Goods and services abound: armored cars, subterranean condos, oversized fuel tanks, miniaturized radios, packaged food and powerful weapons, camping supplies, health aids and a legion of accessories line the market shelves. Multitudinous goods for every taste, in every color, for every budget, bar coded, board certified, shrink-wrapped, use dated, sized, weighed, credentialed, and guaranteed to perform, function, and please, if used as directed. But survivalists want something else. They want a part in creating the marketplace, in fashioning economic culture, in crafting rituals of appraisal and exchange, a place in the fundamental mediation of value.

Certainly, what you have is what you will need. Come the crisis, survivalist set-asides and savings, provisions and stores, tools and supplies will revalue upward, perhaps to scarce and vital necessities. So too will present-day professional knowledge, hobby skills, and practiced play forms: Dr. Smallfield's medical know-how, Kirk Schmidt's understanding of energy conservation. Herein lies opportunity. What you have now is not only what you will need later, but also what others will want. How is this opportunity exploited? Not for profit and power. In biblical prophecy the "first shall be last, and the last shall be first."[13] But this reversal is not the objective of survivalists. The purpose of survivalism is not predominance, supremacy, or triumph, but the achievement of a hypothetical balance between the imagined hazards and hardships ahead and the resources, skills, and knowledge at hand or within reach.

Survivalist action is not aimed at market domination or monopoly, is not ultimately profiteering, does not seek maximum gain for minimum cost. Frugality is honored, as is sharp bargaining, and the tales survivalists tell position them at advantage in times ahead. But mere wealth or control of goods, tools, or knowledge earns little respect. Rather, survivalism serves as a rhetorical means of transforming depersonalized consumer society, rife with mass commodities and mass marketing, a place where survival is merely for sale, into an aesthetic discourse of valuation where survivalists are adventuresome architects of new economic orders. The discourse of valuation brings survivalists imaginatively from the sidelines of passive consumerism to the center of economic culture crafting. It does not bring them to the top.

Survivalism as "Irrational" Commerce

The possibility that economic participation might mean more than probabilistic cost-benefit analyses, might manifest in "irrational," affect-filled, cathected, social experience, has been largely ignored by neoclassic economists. But this disregard is neither complete nor correct. The vitality of aspects of survivalism by another name has venerable roots in economic scholarship.

In 1755 Cantillon wrote of *entrepreneurs* (see Casson 1982); Say ([1803] 1964) accorded them a place in economic theory; J. S. Mill popularized the term in English; but it was Schumpeter who gave them their full due. Schumpeter's *Theory of Economic Development* ([1912] 1934) compares what he calls the "static-hedonism" of managers who maintain the status quo and capitalists preoccupied with costs and benefits to the "dynamic-energetic, creative" action of the entrepreneur: "Modern industry was created by 'real men' [and women]; they were not wretched figures constantly asking themselves fearfully whether every effort to which they had to submit would promise enough surplus. . . . They were barely concerned with the hedonistic fruits of their actions. Such men [and women] create, because they cannot help themselves. Their activity is the greatest, most splendid moment that economic life presents . . . and the static-hedonistic explanation appears quite pitiful next to it" (in Dahms 1995, 13). For the entrepreneur, "economic action is motivated by the joy of creative expression and the impulse to action as an end in itself." Such "economic creativity resembles the creative activity of artists, thinkers or politicians" (Dahms 1995, 5).

Stockholders, bankers, and factory owners are not, by simple virtue of their control of capital and the material means of production, entrepreneurs. The entrepreneur, Schumpeter insists, "is never the risk bearer" merely in a fiduciary sense ([1912] 1934, 137). The entrepreneur risks more than material resources. She or he puts identity on the line, risks reputation, prestige, respect in the community of peers. However, not all risks are the same. Entrepreneurship among survivalists takes strong and weak forms. In its weak form survivalist entrepreneurship is unremarkable, sometimes no more than an excuse for nominal consumption or petty dabbling. But in its strong form, the very bases of the marketplace itself may be transformed. Consider first the weak form.

TOKEN ECONOMIES

To be at the heart of economic action with a respected say in the worth of things is a survivalist ideal; to be a mute consumer, dependent on monolithic systems directed and constrained by others, anathema. Survivalists point with derision to an indifferent majority (and those among themselves) whom they judge willing merely to consume and conform, to accept passively the course and consequences of modernity. Though barter and home craft offer honorable alternatives, they are at times judged impractical. In such cases survivalists may consume. But when they do so, it is with managed impressions, reluctance, and excuses.

Survivalists seek to skirt the stigma of bald consumption by redefining quotidian economic activity as strategic commerce and preparation for future survival marketeering. Kirk Schmidt defensively insisted his dabbling in equities was "survival investing." The Todds turned their storage supply purchases into figurative "business opportunities" by becoming "dealers" for Yurika Foods, one of numerous pyramid schemes selling bulk, prepackaged, storage-ready survivalist consumables. Hank and Penny offered us deals on the "wholesale" wheat supplies they purchased. Nic could get both ammunition and herbal medicines at "dealer discount."[14] By the late 1990s distributorships were available for survivalist-packaged powdered protein cocktails, whey-based beverages, edible seaweed, dehydrated, freeze-dried, and irradiated meals and side dishes, vitamins, mineral supplements, water purifiers, and a panoply of other components of the survivalist food chain.[15] While such opportunities abound, they do not necessarily appeal to survivalists. Hank and Penny and Nic offered their purchasing services in private asides, not public pronouncements. Claims to "dealer" status are widely available to survivalists but infrequently invoked. Being a "dealer" is a fragile account, capable only of diminishing the undesirable taint of direct consumption, not of eliminating it. Whenever possible survivalists avoid association with any unmediated cash-for-commodity exchange. But how?

One form of entrepreneurial action discussed by Schumpeter appears frequently in survival scenarios: the pioneering of markets for articles no longer produced or in short supply, where "price is determined without regard to cost of production" (Schumpeter [1912] 1934, 135). It is easy to imagine a postcollapse world where safety pins and soap, 9 mm ammunition and saw blades might be produced, if at all, in small numbers, of low quality, and at considerable effort, yet continue to have substantial use value. Survivalists well supplied with these merited goods would position themselves at the center of future markets. Major Sudzmann has such a plan.

Major Sudzmann, a friend of the Todds', lives near Hank in an upscale suburban housing development. His wife teaches third grade, and they have two children, ages seven and ten. As a civil engineer for the county he knows sewage and drains and plumbing codes. He knows how important cleanliness and personal comfort could be if things began to break down. And he is ready. Sudzmann buys wholesale, by the station wagon full, case after case. Major showed Eleen and me his cache one Saturday afternoon. Stock arranged on neat, narrow aisles of floor to ceiling shelving filled his two-car garage. The station wagon and the compact sedan sat outside. Everything was accounted for on his computer:

purchase dates, costs, deterioration rates, rotation schedules, sources. For Sudzmann, it is an investment worth taking care of, one sure to go up in value. He has what people will need after the collapse, and the best brands, too: Charmin, Tide, Cheer, Brawny. Two months' salary worth of toilet tissue, detergent, and paper towels—the Sudzmann household's form of survivalism.

Entrepreneurs are economic adventurers in search of new combinations of productive means and consumer markets. Most count on one thing: an uncontested medium of exchange. A dollar is a dollar, a yen is a yen. But what if that foundation, too, came into question? In its strong form, survivalist entrepreneurship does just that.

MAKING MONEY THE OLD-FASHIONED WAY

In the early 1990s the brokerage firm of Smith Barney began a new advertising campaign in which they claimed, "We make money the old-fashioned way." The claim was misleading. No one at Smith Barney cast ducats or florins, pierced cowrie shells or formed salt blocks, printed notes or bills. No one made money the old-fashioned way at all. Instead, Smith Barney's methods were thoroughly modern. They rearranged digits and decimals on accounting entries in exchange for labor or the profits of risked capital. They merely earned money. No one gave a thought to making it.

Who makes money? In the economies of modern industrial society the question seems irrelevant if not ludicrous. Money is taken for granted, a neutral, transparent medium by which quality is transformed to quantity. Money is impersonal, the ultimate manifestation of rationalization in human experience (Weber [1946] 1971, 331), transforming "the totality of existential interests" into "the purest reification of means" (Simmel [1907] 1978, 211).

In normal times, few question the origins of money, its worth, or its meaning. Money is colorless and indifferent, to borrow from Simmel ([1908] 1950, 414), worthless in its own right, yet the technically perfect instrument for the transfer of worth (Simmel [1907] 1978, 373). Monetization levels subjective differences, providing a common standard for the measure of value in objects, ideas, and emotions alike: price. In the ideal-typical market economy, everything has its price and there is a right price for everything (Zelizer 1987). In this radically homogenized social order, meanings are reduced to sums. Living a monetized life becomes "an arithmetic problem" (Simmel [1908] 1950, 412).

Opinions on money vary. Classic economists see benefits. Money contributes to the common good, promoting efficiency in exchange, obviating barter's dependence on coincidences of reciprocal wants (see

Carruthers and Babb 1996, 1558). Humanists see problems. Marx damned money as the ultimate fetish, a "god among commodities" (Marx [1858] 1973, 221) and "the transformation of all human and natural qualities into their opposites, the universal confusion and inversion of things" (1963, 000).[16] For survivalists, money and its alternatives offer one more means of moving toward the center of economic action.

What if money were not taken for granted, not transparent, neutral, generic? Economists claim money is evolutionary, developing from direct barter of consumable goods and services through commodity-based specie to pure warrants of exchangeability. But is all evolution progress? Some survivalists envision an atavistic future economy of barter on a wide scale with a few money-objects of mixed merits emerging, less liquid than modern cash or coin but sufficiently in demand to be exchangeable for other goods or services. Economic life is less rational but also more complex, engaging, amenable to innovation and self-expression.

A dollar is a dollar, but is a handful of nails a fresh fish? Is a pair of wool socks an old file? Is a chicken a hatchet? Is a bottle of penicillin tablets a quarter of venison? To make such determinations the discourse of valuation must expand to include not only consideration of goods and price, but the needs and wants of exchange partners, their present and projected circumstances, community expectations of reciprocity, and a range of other sedimented meanings. Exchange emerges as a primal social ritual by which community solidarity is formed and through which the collective conscience finds voice.

Some survivalist scenarios imagine future lives permeated with entrepreneurial economic activity: finding, fixing, and selling, trading and bartering, saving, scrounging, collecting, gathering, recycling, repackaging, and swapping. A few live that life now.

BEN AND MARIE

Ben Thompson and I traded letters a couple of times then agreed to meet on a Sunday at his stall at the fairgrounds flea market in the next county. He and his wife, Marie, lived in a small town on the coast, over the mountains, so they had to start early to set up. I came later, an hour's travel south through the valley. By late morning the Pickwick Flea Market parking lot looked half full. About fifteen hundred admission tickets sold that day at $1.50 each. On a busy day, four thousand come to this once-a-month event, management claims.

Pickwick also profits from the sellers, who pay fifteen dollars each to display their wares on one of the market's three hundred folding tables. "Thompson's at number 84, west building," the ticket taker told me.

"What do people sell here?" I asked. "Anything you want," she said, "except guns and food." But visitors do not go hungry. The "food stands sell stuff to eat: spaghetti, chili, and such," she added. Later I learned guns are sold in the parking lot, from car trunks and pickup campers, while management looks the other way.

The residuum of an overabundant material culture tends toward two fates: one, ignominious interment, first in attics and garages, then as discards to Goodwill or detritus to dumpsters and trash heaps; the other, metamorphosis, from consumer goods to tokens in the ritual discourse of valuation. At swap meets, gun shows, and garage sales of interest to survivalists, items are seldom bought and sold in simple exchanges of currency for commodity. That is shopping mall behavior. Survivalist commerce is a dense web of negotiations regarding goods' functional utility, scarcity, authenticity, and the relative needs of buyer and seller. Merchandise is of the sort that invites this dialogue. It is, variously, used and therefore has history, surplus and thus originally expensive and of high quality, or miscellaneous and therefore offering maximal potential for a coincidence of interests between buyer and seller.[17]

At table 83, a sixty-ish woman offered coins, stamps, and buttons from well-worn, professional-looking display cases. Two rare pennies and Los Angeles mayor Sam "Yorty for President" buttons were the stars of her stock. Table 85 featured several hundred used LP records, '60s and '70s pop and country, audio tapes, and rock concert posters. In between, the Thompsons.

Ben and Marie, both in their forties, were smiling, chatting with customers when I arrived. Marie: stout, strong, with thick red hair bristling from under the de rigueur baseball cap, plaid cotton flannel shirt, genuine Levi's in a large waist size with short legs and folded cuffs. Freckles mixed with age spots in her Irish complexion. She was born and raised in Tennessee. Ben: comparably proportioned, similarly dressed, but bald on top and with a bushy gray-brown beard and side fringe under the obligatory cap. The Thompson merchandise was typical: a dozen hand tools, a rack of German wool army pants and jackets, khaki Vietnam-era shirts (all too short for most American men, Ben agreed), a few used board games, books, multipurpose pliers in leatherette holsters (new, made in China), folding utility knives, a rusty entrenching tool, bits of electronics, one of a pair of citizens band walkie-talkies, a camera with a good Zeiss lens and a broken shutter, cigarette lighters with enamel emblems, a used metal detector, and three plastic tubs of odds and ends. (Out in their car was a small stock of guns: two used Czech pistols and a Japanese army rifle.) The customers chatted, moved on. We said hello. The Thompsons sat down to rest, eat plates of spaghetti, and talk survivalism.

It had been a busy week for Ben and Marie. Most weeks were. They had their usual chores running their seaside pizza parlor and home-based gun shop. The first of the month was collection time at their three small rental units. They sold two other properties last month. But this week their boats received most of their attention. Ben explained:

> We have three [boats], well, four. We have a thirty-four-foot cabin cruiser and a twenty-six-foot tugboat, and a thirty-eight-foot motor sailer—that's the one we just launched. And I'm caretaking, actually partial owner of, a salmon trawler.
>
> All last year we crabbed commercially but our tugboat, that's our crabber, froze last winter and damaged a lot of stuff. Basically, we're junking it out and going to salvage the parts and work on the other boats.

Some work was recent. The four-decade-old motor sailer, which Ben bought for fifteen hundred dollars and a "pretty good" twenty-year-old truck, had just been launched, after some necessary repairs. Very necessary, according to the salts down at the dock. The salts predicted it would sink—rotten ribs, leaky hull—but Ben went to work. He fit sister ribs, new planking, covered the whole thing with a quarter-inch of cheap fiberglass and resin. Heavier that way "by tons," Ben admitted, but "stronger, too." In any case Ben liked fiberglass. "If you make a mistake, you can grind it down, fix it up, no problem." He and Marie put it in the water early Thursday afternoon, then went home. It sank around sunset.

Just a little problem, Ben said, a hull fitting not properly seated. It was an Oregon day. Rain accumulated in the hold, the deck load of timber shifted, bringing the leaky hole down to the waterline, then in came the ocean. Kindly neighbors at the harbor who saw it going under put a dockside hoist and all the pumps they could find to work for salvage. By noon Friday, when Ben and Marie returned, it was coming up again, awash if not afloat. "We have too many boats," Marie opined. But boats seemed to keep coming and going. Boats were part of their plans now. But they had not always been.

For ten years Ben and Marie had a "survival retreat" in Arkansas, near Little Rock, where Ben worked as a policeman. Then they hit the road: Montana, New Mexico, California. "We had a bus then. Still have it. It's not fancy or anything. When we were on the road, traveling around, we were camped in Carlsbad, New Mexico. And where we stopped was in the middle of some little land war. So we stacked sandbags on the roof. Then they took a picture of our bus, and it was in a picture book on busses people live in. It was captioned, "Survival Bus." Ours was the only bus with fortifications! [laughs]."

In the '70s the Thompsons settled for a while. Ben went to work for the Los Angeles police department. He was proud of the education that got him that job. "I'm always going to school. I was one of the first, maybe the first, in California, to have a two-year degree with a major in police science. Up until that time you could get a major in sociology and minor in police science. But by going to three different community colleges, I had enough credits to get a *major* in police science. I think Berkeley was the first to offer a degree in police science. Till then it was catch as catch can."

Later Ben got temporary work in Alaska, near Ketchikan. The land was providential.

> In an hour two people could fill a five-gallon bucket with clams. In an hour with a dip net we could dip up eighteen big Dungeness crabs on an average. Blackberries grew all over. Gardens grew great. Rained just like it does here, steady, not too much, never gets real cold. When I'd catch a halibut we would trade with our neighbors, they had a big garden. The guy at the Chevron [fuel supply dock], we took him crabs and halibut, and he'd give us oil for our outboard.
>
> After that, we decided that for survival we would like access to the ocean. We were going to move all the way up to Alaska. Live off our boat. Do a little scuba diving, fishing, and subsistence hunting. But this is as far as we got.

"It's been an interesting weekend," Ben reflected. "We had some other survivalists drop by to see us." "That guy from California," Marie confirmed, "and the other one from Portland. He had some good books."

Ben and Marie read "all the time." "We've got a lot of survival books, history books, some 'escape' fiction, too." "What sorts?" I asked. "She reads romances," Ben offered. "I read everything from just basic adventure to sci-fi." "Do you have a favorite book?" I queried. "Well, my favorite is usually the one I'm reading. But I do have one that is interesting. I think it is called *Applied Science,* written 1807 or something like that. I bought it at a flea market on the coast last year. It has all sorts of useful information about how to do things before they had electricity." Survivalist knowledge is valued, too.

Flea-market denizens sell and swap goods, but intangibles may also figure in the deal making. Information—sources, resources, techniques, demonstrations of simple skills—is of worth. The survivalist economy mixes goods and applications, commodities and know-how.

Ben and I had gone through his stock of surplus shirts and found one with sleeves long enough for me. We bargained.

"How much?" I asked.

"$5.00"

"How about $3.50; see this hole in the elbow?"

Ben's response was unanticipated. He ignored the shirt, moved closer, spoke clearly and slowly so I would get it, and threw something in with the deal: a technique, know-how. "Something I found out about maybe fifteen years ago: if ever you have a situation, someone is bleeding bad, even an artery, take some regular wheat germ, open the wound, and put it right in. Close the wound and the bleeding will stop. Then the body absorbs the stuff so you don't have infection." He pointed to chain saw scars on his forehead, remnants of a wound that had received this treatment, then looked at me for a decision. I paid him five dollars.

Ben continued his enthusiasm for education: "You've got to read, learn things on your own. People aren't taking care of themselves anymore. Lots of things you can learn without hard knocks. Read, get education. It helps a lot. Like how important it is to wear seat belts. People can be educated on that issue if they would just read." A bystander entered the dialogue. "Seat belts. More danger than they are help," he muttered.

MAKING MONEY, AGAIN

Monetization is a pervasive feature of modernity but not a universal one. All money may be created equal but it is not treated as such. On the macro- and micromargins of society, economic rationalization meets resistance. In spite of Simmel's claim for its "unconditional interchangeability" and "internal uniformity" ([1907] 1978, 427), not all money is the same. Mary Douglas (1982) notes that modern money, while consistent in form, is normatively, not rationally, controlled in at least two circumstances. On the borders of nations in international exchange and within the boundaries of private affairs in families and other primary groups, money is vested with extraeconomic meaning.

The World Bank, the International Monetary Fund, and the U.S. Agency for International Development, as examples, all loan, allocate, or buttress monies only with strings firmly attached. Such grants, loans, and guarantees as these agencies provide are not fungible assets, interchangeable for any and all marketed good and services. Instead these funds bear their own zweckrational, their own internal purposes. They are irrigation-project monies, or road-building monies, or munitions-purchasing monies, or loan-repayment monies. The application of one money-form for another, building roads with irrigation-project money, buying foodstuffs with weapons funds, is untoward—graft, mismanagement, malfeasance.

Within households and other nuclear units, at home or on the farm, "special-purpose" monies (Polanyi 1957, 264–66) proliferate and are imbued with differentiated sentiments. Thomas and Znaniecki ([1918–1920] 1958, 164–65) observed that for the Polish peasant, monies obtained from selling a cow are qualitatively different from a dowry or wages. Zelizer (1987) draws attention to a range of specialized domestic monies (for example, husbands' and children's allowances, wives' "pin" money) socially constructed in U.S. households from wages, including children's wages, during the 1870–1930 era.

On other occasions, monetary tokens become valued objects in their own rights. The business owner frames and displays her first earned dollar. Spanish pieces of eight exhumed from the holds of ancient shipwrecks are put on exhibit in museums. Coins or bills in limited circulation are sought and prized for their rarity, not face value.[18] Yet these are the exceptions.

Most places in modern life a dollar is a dollar, a yen is a yen. Ben and Marie, working around the economic edges, bargain and trade and fix and promote and move merchandise about, but they hardly can be said to have circumvented the institution of money itself. Nor can the Polish peasant or the American housewife or even the International Monetary Fund. Perhaps Smith Barney is essentially right. They make money the only way imaginable. But a few survivalists do not agree. They can imagine alternatives. Sometimes they put imagination into action.

Consistent in the recommendations of investment "experts" is the advice to shun paper in favor of "hard" assets: Krugerrands, silver bullion, diamonds, and other presumed buffers against economic downturns (see Cipollini 1983; Kogelschatz 1982; Kogelschatz 1983, 38, 39, 42; McAlvany and Sellers 1982; Souchik 1987; Nichols 1992; Carr 1996).[19]

The Todds bought a few gold and silver coins. John Nixon was disinterested in this aspect of survivalism, but in a later interview he did admit having steady, small-time customers for gold commemorative coins and metal-by-weight in $25 to $100 denominations, customers who talked of coming crises and the coming new money, based on the durable worth of precious metals. Most talk of this sort is inconsequential, but not all. In Texas three brothers talked about the same idea, took their talk seriously, and shook the financial markets of the world.

SILVER HUNTS

In late August of 1988 a federal jury found the Texas multibillionaire brothers Herbert, Bunker, and Lamar Hunt guilty of conspiring to corner the world market for silver. Their protagonists in the trial portrayed the brothers as insatiable deal makers overcome with avarice and heady with the power their great wealth gave them. These protagonists won the case but missed the point. The Hunt brothers were not greedy capitalists. They were survivalists.

The Hunts had a family tradition of conservative political activism. The patriarch, H. L. Hunt, underwrote anti-Communist radio and television programming and supported Joe McCarthy. Bunker contributed to the John Birch Society and a fundamentalist Christian organization. However, political conservatism does not a survivalist make. The Hunt brothers did more than complain about government. They tried to create a branch of their own.

Bunker was said to have been obsessed with silver since the mid-1960s when he discovered a vast oil field in Libya then lost control of it to nationalization by Muammar el-Qaddafi (Hurt 1988). Bunker was bitter over this loss and even more so at the U.S. State Department's unwillingness to protect what he viewed as legitimate business interests (see Williams 1995, 20). In the Hunts' view government was not to be trusted in business matters, especially the most fundamental matter of exchange media, of currency. Government monetary policy was particularly disturbing. The brothers did not trust paper money. By the end of the 1970s they were convinced a major economic crisis was drawing near (see Hurt 1981). Paper currency had lost its worth. The nation, perhaps the entire free world, could be on the brink of monetary collapse. So they made plans.

In the autumn of 1979, U.S. and world inflation rates were indeed on the rise. The Soviet Union invaded Afghanistan. The Ayatollah Khomeini seized power in Iran and American hostages in Teheran. It was time to act. The Hunt brothers made an all-out effort to buy silver, acquiring it in bullion and other forms by the tens of millions worth wherever they could find it, at prices from as low as nine dollars to as much as fifty dollars an ounce. Price was not crucial. Speed was.

In classic market-cornering efforts the object is to gain monopolistic control over a commodity, drive up the price, then sell and convert the profits to cash. The Hunt brothers were not interested in cash, profits, or selling. They wanted silver—shiny, hard metal. The brothers acquired nearly \$200 million worth of bullion and coins and stashed them in vaults around the world. Then they bought over \$1 billion more on margin and made plans to warehouse the lot and leverage further purchases. They wanted to control as much of the world's silver as they could. But not for profit.

Three months later, on March 26, 1980, they announced their stunningly ambitious plan. They intended in essence to unilaterally privatize the U.S. Department of the Treasury. Paper backed by faith alone would soon be valueless, they argued. To save the country, and with it democracy and the free world, an alternative was needed. If the federal government would not act, then the Hunts would. To maintain the solvency of the nation, they offered to provide a new trading currency in the form of bonds of their own issue, secured by their vast and growing store of precious metal. The Hunts were prepared to underwrite America.

Then prophecy came true. In February of 1980 the U.S. Commodity Futures Trading Commission imposed buying limits on silver, making it impossible for the Hunts to continue amassing more metal by borrowing against the bullion they already controlled. Prices began to edge downward from fifty dollars per ounce to thirty-four dollars by mid-month. The day after their bond-offering announcement, the market crashed. Silver fell to eleven dollars per ounce. The brothers were forced to sell hundreds of millions of dollars in oil properties and real estate to make margin payments on their bullion. The scheme to rescue America had failed.

In all, the notoriously frugal Hunts lost an estimated $4 billion dollars (Hurt 1988). They acquired no worldly possessions, lived no glamorous lifestyles. Instead they pursued a survivalist vision. Bunker summed up the brothers' feelings. They had few regrets (and no remorse at their trial). The Hunt's lost money, but not conviction. "Money never meant anything to me. It's just the way you keep score in life." Investments, economic maneuvering were just the means for acting on a hunch, a vision, a way of making a difference if you can. You win some and you lose some. What matters is being in the game (Hurt 1988).

• • •

Again, survivalism is found where it is expected, and where it is not. The image of survivalists as down-and-out losers, disgruntled with their share of material gains and bent on fomenting radical correctives or expressing their frustrations in Huberty-esque mayhem, must be set in balance against an observed cast different in both character and conduct. Upper-income professionals, Mensan intellectuals, and eccentric billionaires craft survival scenarios. Most dabble and fantasize, network and debate, telling stories to zest the late night coffee, or to justify hobbies and pastimes. A few back their talk with effort and funds, investing surplus resources, building fortified homes, stockpiling rural retreats, preparing sailboat and motor home getaways.

Self-actualization manifests in entrepreneurship and creative adventuring in the lived economy, but almost always stays in bounds of imaginative rehearsal, what-if storytelling, and sidebar preparations. Almost, but not always.

Three brothers in Texas crossed the line. Steeped for a generation in traditions of distrust, insulated from contradictory ideas by their elite status, commanding potent means, and confronted by what they perceived as genuine crisis, the Hunts acted. Preparation time was over. The brothers' time to matter in the world had come. For the good of all, in deep conviction and at great personal risk, on their own initiative, they set out to recraft a foundation of culture, to reframe the discourse of valuation, to replace the coin of the realm and undergird Western civilization.

Valuation themes reappear throughout the chapters to follow, but one part of the telling is finished. There has not been much difficulty assembling the story so far, mostly "indoor work, no heavy lifting" as Joel Best aptly puts it (1997). My reported role as researcher has been distanced from survival action, limited to an interview here and there, some weekend visits, the comforting review of mute books, articles, and news clippings. That soon must change.

3 THE CRAFT OF FUNCTION

Clever beyond all dreams
the inventive craft
that Man has
which may drive him one time
or another to well or ill.
—Sophocles, *Antigone*

I got a axe-handle pistol
with a graveyard frame.
It shoots tombstone bullets
wearing balls and chains.
I'm drinkin' TNT.
I'm smokin' dynamite.
I hope some screwball
starts a fight,
'cause I'm ready,
ready,
ready.
—Muddy Waters, "I'm Ready"

CALL TO ORDER

Nic handed out flyers to all of us gathered at Hank and Penny's for the meeting of the Mount Rainier Rangers. The flyers were sure-fire attention getters and talk soon turned to the group's recent media exposure. Eleen and I listened.

The previous month Hank had organized a "training exercise." The exercise wasn't much, the participants admitted, just an overnight car camp at a nearby state park and a kind of hide-and-seek game after dark. In this game the "defenders," Nic and Sasha, sat quietly hidden in the tall grass at one side of a large field next to the "objective," a footbridge over an irrigation ditch. The "attackers," Hank and Ron and a companion, tried to creep across the field and reach the bridge without being heard and verbally dispatched. The grass was dry and noisy, so careful creeping took a long time but made no difference. The defenders won. Twice the attackers were surprised with a shout of "Bang! We gotcha!" from the defenders' unseen hiding place.

Sasha even made the second "kill" by herself. By 10:00 P.M. everyone was back in Hank's camper, crowded warmly together, sipping hot chocolate and talking about the evening. Nic was congratulated for his clever tactics and Sasha for her maturity. Hank and Penny especially praised Sasha. She had been levelheaded and alert the whole time, they said. She had been patient and acted with good judgment. Their praise was perhaps expected. After all, Sasha was Hank and Penny's granddaughter. She was ten years old.

None of this evening would have been newsworthy except for the presence of Hank and Nic's companion. Much debate had preceded his invitation; much consequence would follow from his participation. Like most survivalists, Hank and Nic were ambivalent about publicity. They realized that a degree of secrecy would protect them from the ridicule of disbelievers but also understood that isolation diminished opportunities for recruiting new members and exchanging information with others of like minds. They did not need Simmel to remind them that enemies have their uses. Hypothesizing predatory enemies from whom information and resources must be protected serves to bring members together, provides collective purpose, and elevates the apparent worth of the group's existing knowledge and skills. In practice, Hank and Nic were like other survivalists. Their security measures were a compromise. They made efforts to deny the least sympathetic of other people access to personal information about themselves and their activities while at the same time attempting to create interest and favorable impressions with potential recruits (see Mitchell 1993, 12–22).

Hank, Nic, and Penny argued about distortions and misinformation in the media, but in the end Hank called the local newspaper. He told the news editor about the Rangers' formation and of the upcoming exercise. An enterprising reporter joined the evening's maneuvers in search of a story. What he didn't find he fashioned. Two days later, three-quarters of the first page of the newspaper's community section was devoted to the Rangers' exercise and to survivalism. The eye-catcher was a three-column wide, eight-inch high, sunset photo of Nic, with rifle and face paint, in a scout-on-patrol pose amid a clump of bushes by the campsite. The text was headlined "The Survivalists" and punctuated with bold subheads and pull quotes: "They Drill for Postwar Chaos," "Local Group Sharpens Skills to Live," "Nuclear war is survivable," and "We will be ready."

Hank and Nic capitalized on this exaggerated image. They put this fabricated news drama to work, making recruiting posters by photocopying the newspaper pictures and headings onto legal-size paper along with a quickly fashioned group logo and a contact address. Hank and Nic handed out these makeshift posters to a few curious workmates and to everyone who came to the group meeting. They were also pinned to the walls in Hank's garage and office-den.

A camp-out with family and friends had become a media-manufactured social movement. The Mount Rainier Rangers gained visibility and a reputation. All this was heady stuff for the members, who had to this point led unobtrusive lives. It kept the living room talk moving briskly and accounted for the presence of several newcomers at the meeting. Only a few, including Eleen and I, knew there was a bigger story brewing. Another article would soon appear in print featuring some of the Mount Rainier Rangers. Nic and Hank had not been idle since that first outing.

Nic helped Hank and Penny host the meeting. He made his way through the busy room to offer a personal welcome to Eleen and me. "Glad you could come," he said and seemed to mean it. "We hoped you would accept Hank's invite." The greeting was different than when we had last met, less formal, more relaxed. Today, he was just "Nic," unarmed, out of uniform, friendly. Last time we were together, he had been "LT," the lieutenant, our commanding officer.

OPERATION AURORA BOREALIS

After my interview with Nixon, I went looking for more survivalists. I continued to read the papers and each new issue of *Survive,* where after a few months I found a small ad for Live Free, Inc., an Illinois-based organization claiming to have branches nationwide. I became a mail-order member and soon received a letter from Live Free's local contact, Tim Dalkins. We exchanged correspondence and phone calls. Then this notice arrived.

> Wapalosie Mtn. National
> Survival Association
> Group Icefield Operations HQ.
> [Address]
>
> Dear survivalists and patriots:
>
> Oct. 1–2 the American Pistol and Rifle Association in coordination with Live Free, Inc. will be holding a defense operations seminar on its permit in the Bakerville National Forest. Bring firearms. If you don't have anything more than a .22 bring it. This is a school, it is important you come, the instructors are good. Classes will cover map and compass problems, code, patrolling, ambush and counter ambush, recon and scout, night

perimeter ops. Equipment: OD green clothing or cammies, canteen, small pack, rifle or shotgun. Rules: a. All participants will respect the flag and the U.S. Constitution. b. There will be no profane language during the program. c. There will be no illegal weapons. . . .

Six more rules followed, then a hand-drawn map, an invitation to "bring your friends," and sketches of two fire-belching rifle barrels labeled "RAT TAT!!" and "LIVE FREE!!" It was signed "Tim Dalkins." Eleen and I talked about it. At least the rules seemed reasonable. We called for final permission and directions. With trepidation, new camouflage clothing, and a borrowed shotgun, we went. It took thirteen hours of driving across two states to reach the dirt road junction designated as our rendezvous. Saturday, 7:45 A.M., worn from sleeplessness and active nerves, we did as we had been told: pulled to the roadside in plain view, shut off the engine, remained in the vehicle. "Someone will come for you," Tim had promised. Who or how he had not told us. We watched the mirrors and road ahead and bolstered our courage by ridiculing our unseen subjects.

Rumors exaggerated survivalism, we were sure. Survivalists were probably nothing to worry about, nothing really strange. We made nervous fun of them: "weekend wannabe warriors," I called them, and "characters out of dime-novel Westerns." With mock seriousness Eleen dubbed them "free-rovin' anarchs, beholdin' to no man."[1] But name calling did not help much. We were still nervous, so we made fun of the nearby countryside, too. "Yesterday Land," we called it, a forgotten Disney attraction. The area through which we had driven since dawn did seem a piece of America out of time if not place. Dirt roads connected tiny towns set amid pine and fir forests, bluffs and hills, separated by clear streams. Road signs, gate posts, and the few people we saw suggested a sparse population of cattle ranchers, ever hopeful miners, out-of-work loggers, and ostracized Indians. Even the names on the map fit the Old West theme: Bear Mountain, Cougar Mountain, Quartz Mountain, and Iron Mountain lay in the cardinal directions around us. The road ahead went down Refrigerator Canyon along Rabbit Creek and around Gold Hill, just south of the all-American town of Liberty. At the general store and gas station a few miles back, we got orange juice and directions from a proprietor who, it seemed to us, wore his holstered revolver as casually as his cowboy boots. "Good fight at Rosie's [bar] last night," he confided, nodding toward the two bruised and disheveled coffee drinkers on the front porch.

At 8:15, amid dust and loose engine noises, a car pulled in behind us.

I soon met my second survivalist. Like a member of the displaced gentry of industrializing England, Tim Dalkins was a man of many titles but few possessions. In his correspondence he called himself the "Wapalosie Mountain National Survival Association, Group Icefield Operations Director," or "Sergeant Major Tim Dalkins, Member, Survival Base Board of Directors," or "Regional Director of Live Free, Inc.," or "Director of Affiliation—American Pistol and Rifle Association, Group Leader Icefield Unit." Today, he was just "Tim."

Tim's eighteen-year-old Chevrolet sedan leaked fluids and fumes as we watched, and was corrugated on three corners. "That's my Mexican APC," he joked. "APC" is military shorthand for Armored Personnel Carrier. The back seat was filled with plastic buckets, tools, blankets, camping gear, odds and ends of army surplus, and his "battle rifle," a World War I bolt-action British Enfield .303. Tim was in his early thirties, trim, stood about five feet, ten inches tall, and wore a "uniform" of assorted Vietnam-era surplus garments. After some mutual identity checking, he told us that the exercise was about to begin a short distance away. "You'll meet Hank there," Tim told us. "He runs the Live Free group in your area." Hank and the other members of Live Free were real enough, but for much of the weekend were not sure about Tim. He headed back toward his car. Then to our surprise he stopped, turned toward us, came to military attention, and started to salute. The gesture was interrupted only when his hand was above his shoulder.

"Follow me," he instructed out of the open passenger window as he drove by, jouncing down the hill toward the assembly point three miles away. We followed and in a few minutes found ourselves in the middle of an isolated clearing in heavily timbered forest. We were surrounded by survivalists. None of them were like Tim.

The clearing was ringed with primer-spotted domestic pickups and four-door sedans with blackwall recaps and six-digit mileage. Men with guns—large and small caliber assault rifles, sidearms, grenade launchers, and submachine guns—stood about chatting, smoking, loading ammunition magazines, and examining each other's weapons. They wore well-used military camouflage over modest denim and polyester readywear. Their billed caps and the buckles of their necessarily ample belts proclaimed allegiances to brands of trucks and farm machinery. Two men performed the survivalists' toilette, sharing a truck side-mirror as they painted their faces, ears, and necks with dappled green and brown makeup. These two and others looked martial. The man squatted before us across the smoldering campfire looked primeval. This apparition was wearing a ghillie suit, the ultimate in portable concealment, a handmade hood and cloak of dark fishnet through which uneven earthtone rag strips had been woven and tied. Twigs and leaves were added for accent. Imagine a Sesame Street Big Bird pelt, darkened, tattered, and soiled.

As we watched, he carefully poured a half-cup of water from his canteen into a pile of ash at the fire pit's edge. Then with both hands he began kneading this slurry into a loose paste. Small amounts of dirt and spittle were added. The paste stiffened. He looked up from his work and gave us a steady glance. Then to our amazement he lowered his face into these handfuls of mud and began smearing the mixture carefully into the creases and hollows and over all the exposed skin on his head. For several moments only the rustling ghillie suit was visible. Then he again looked up.

Only the eyes reminded me of humanity. The rest was transformed into a kind of filth-covered, primitive man-thing. I stared at it. It stared back. The thing fastidiously wiped its hands on a patch of grass, rose from its haunches, stepped around the fire, and stood square in front of me. It extended one hand and, almost to my surprise, spoke.

"Hello," it said. "I'm Hank."

We had tried to prepare for this moment. We had followed directions, arrived on time, and brought what we could of the required gear. We wanted to be unobtrusive, to "blend in." Hank's direct stare now joined the others we had received since our arrival. We had not been overlooked. Into this circle of camouflaged men riding battered Detroit iron and armed to the teeth we had come, nearly empty-handed, driving a late-model, diesel-powered Peugeot station wagon, "disguised" for the occasion in freshly pressed, discount-store duck hunting outfits over preppy L. L. Bean pants, Patagonia jackets, and Nike trainers.

In a short while ambush maneuvers and gunplay began. Over the next two days we learned how to whisper and creep, how to handle weapons, how to shoot at people. And something else. Our attempts at "disguise" were a paradox: successful failures. Instead of hiding us they made us the center of positive attention. After all, who else but naive enthusiasts would wear such ludicrous costumes? We were accepted, treated with gentle respect, even praised. But we never went unnoticed.

With rough courtesy, Hank introduced us to Nic, then went off to his car. Nic explained the first and most frequent order of the day: wait. Recruitment for Operation Aurora Borealis had been typically inclusive. Any friend, associate, or interested party known to Tim was invited and encouraged to bring others who met muster. As Tim's networks were limited the results were groups of loose acquaintances from two geographic areas a full state apart. From the west, "Hank's" group, which nominally included Eleen and me. From the east, "Macy's" group, for whom we now waited. We soon heard vehicles on the approach road.

Macy's personal sedan arrived, followed by a flatbed truck carrying the weekend's mobile command and control center, the Badger. At last, Eleen and I thought, survivalism in action.

Macy and his companions called themselves the Nighthawks. Commander Major Terry Macy, U.S. Army (reserve), was only five feet, seven inches tall, but he did what he could to improve his stature. He stood in the doorway of his five-year-old Chevrolet subcompact surveying the camp, wearing mirrored aviator glasses, beret, silk cravat, and pressed fatigues tucked into the tops of shiny black combat boots. His cap and lapels bore the insignia of an armored infantry officer. The four Nighthawks with him were similarly dressed and all had custom "Nighthawk" insignia patches on their sleeves. Tim had seen the Nighthawks in action before and held them in high esteem. He had worked hard to get them to take charge of the weekend, and take charge they did. Order fell upon the camp.

Paperwork

As I look back over my notes and mementos of Operation Aurora Borealis, there is evidence of bureaucratic organization and structure in the weekend's events. Like much of survivalism, the exercise was rich in plans and complex design. On paper, and there was plenty of paper, survivalism looked serious and substantial. Even before the Nighthawks' gear was unloaded, Tim began circulating among the participants, distributing some of the eighty-seven pages of handouts, directions, and rules we would eventually receive.

First came "The Order of the Day," an hour-by-hour agenda covering the entire weekend. The impression of rigorous forethought heightened when next we learned that our weekend performances would be carefully graded on eleven separate skill criteria. Tim distributed scorecards on which the instructors would mark our credits: "confirmed kills—1 point," "disassembly of a large mine—1 point," "capture of enemy alive—5 points, dead—1 point." There were credits to be earned for decoding messages, proper radio use, first aid, and so on. Rifle marksmanship tests included "20 rounds fired at 200 meter target." For pistols and shotguns there would be a test of "20 rounds at 100 yard target." Demeanor counted, too. "Disrespect toward commanding personnel will result in loss of 1 point per offense or 5 push ups. Anyone receiving 3 reprimands will be sent home for THE GOOD OF ALL." At the end of training regular troops would receive a "Letter of Completion," while outstanding performers would be awarded certificates of "Individual Commendation" and "Platoon Commendation." So much for schedules and scoring.

Next, we received instructional materials. The largest of these was a thirty-four-page packet of professionally illustrated pictographic directions for constructing lethal snares, traps, and deadfalls. Some featured three-hundred-kilo logs studded with sharpened twentypenny nails and perched over roads and trails. Others detailed pits lined with excrement-tainted spikes, delicate trigger mechanisms, and other impromptu technologies to crush, impale, dismember, and strangle enemies. We also received a handy pocket guide to Russian mines and a grid of random letters for generating radio code. One obviously plagiarized document, "Task Number: 071–326–0502–Move under Direct Fire," outlined prescribed military instructions for crawling, rushing, and selecting battlefield positions. By contrast, "Techniques of Foot Movement for Small Units" was apparently part of a book in progress, twenty pages of know-how on ambushes, kill zones, assault team distribution, and mine placement replete with editorial corrections and hand sketches.

These plentiful texts, structured plans, and detailed instructional guides gave the weekend, and survivalism, appearances of order and pragmatic organization. They offered plentiful opportunities for theorizing, "reading," and textual analysis. They were also quite misleading. Survivalism on paper and in practice are only slightly related. As Macy and his helpers busied themselves creating a rustic teaching tableau, Tim was creating other impressions. He carried a camera as well as a rifle. Published survivalism is even farther removed from reality.

Centerfold Drama

Four and a half months after Operation Aurora Borealis took place, the leading commercial survivalist magazine, *American Survival Guide,* featured a full-color, eight-photo, four-page centerfold article describing the weekend's ostensible activities under this heading:

> Allied Families: OPERATION AZIMUTH BEARING "Cupcake Stomper, look for position 172–249. Proceed there and set up an ambush against the enemy . . . "

The article makes no mention of handouts, schedules, paperwork, or grading. Instead, *American Survival Guide* gives its seventy-thousand-plus readers survivalism packaged as bold adventuring and decisive deeds. The article begins

> "DUNCAN ATLAS! Velvet Ashcan command post requesting radio check and patrol position. Over."
>
> "This is Duncan Atlas. Affirmative radio check. Our grid coordinates are 165–253. Over."

> Picking up their equipment, the heavily armed, camouflaged patrol moves into the sweltering woods. Switching radio frequencies, the drill instructor at Velvet Ashcan calls out to the opposing patrol, the marauders. . . . Look for position 172–249 on your map. . . . Proceed there and set up an ambush against the enemy. . . . The marauders grin at each other and start out through the brush. . . . There is a sense of voluntary discipline. All realize they are here for a definite purpose, to learn evasion survival. . . . Given the signal to move out, the pointman takes off, followed by LT, Sarge and a radioman in the middle. The remainder bring up the rear. The patrol moves cautiously forward, climbing a steep, wooded draw. Eyes constantly circle, watching the pointman's actions as he uses the timber for cover. Camouflage clothing blends effectively with the tree covered terrain. . . . The men begin to feel the worry that is common when men are forced to pursue the most dangerous of animals, man. . . . Coming to an opening near the knoll, the patrol bites the dirt. LT gives the order, "This is it. Let's go in!" No choice, low to the earth, troopers scatter and move for cover. Suddenly the quiet ends with the stuttering crackle of HK91 and AR-15 fire.[2]

On and on the magazine warriors go, day and night, mile after mile, over hill and down dale, gritty, grim, determined—for three more pages. "Operation Azimuth Bearing" offers a dramatic view of survivalism. Frontline men of action face night-long enemy attacks, capture prisoners, undertake a daring two-thousand-foot mountain climb and navigation exercise, and march with full packs for miles through trackless terrain, sniper fire, and land mines. There is plenty of sweat, a little blood, and no tears. No less would be expected of such an elite force. "The marauders are very good at ambushes, all are ex-Army or Marine Corps vets." They are "a rare breed in a society where honesty and patriotism are disappearing rapidly. They see a possible cataclysm in the near future. Free men, Americans, they are determined to do something to defend the cause of freedom and to prepare their families to weather disaster on a national and global scale. They are true survivalists."[3]

This is how our weekend adventures were eventually represented to the public. The rhetoric is typical of survival publication feature articles. So is the accuracy of the reporting. To judge how "true" the survivalists and the rest of the published accounts might be, consider some on-site observations.

Marching on Survivalist Time

That Saturday morning in Bakerville National Forest, the *American Survival Guide* article was months away, but the other paperwork was already making us nervous. About guns and such we knew little, but Eleen and I were veterans of the teaching business and the short course ahead looked tough. For openers there were the eighty-seven pages of on-the-spot reading, then the stress of earning credits and receiving instructor rankings day and night when everything was foreign to us and much of it frightening. I began to sympathize with my first-year students. We signed our score sheets as instructed and started skimming the handouts, making margin notes, turning diagrams this way and that, whispering help to each other. Macy was taking longer than I expected to get things going, so we had some catch-up time.

After hurrying through the booby trap instructions, I looked up for a moment, eyeing the nearby trees and downed logs for suitable limbs and deadfalls. We had no twentypenny nails. Then I noticed the other survivalists and nudged Eleen. She saw what they were doing as quickly as I. Our anxiety grew. Most were doing nothing. Upon receipt of each new handout they nodded thanks, then either flipped through the pages briefly or set them aside uninspected and went back to chatting and coffee. I worried out loud to Eleen. "My God, they already *know* this stuff!"

Hank shuffled back from his car with something for me to use. Eleen had borrowed a duck hunter's gun for the weekend, but word had gotten out that I was without a firearm, so Hank loaned me his "street sweeper." This loaner was a Remington model 870, 12-gauge pump shotgun modified for combat with a sawed-off barrel, high-capacity magazine, sling, sights, and a flat, olive-drab paint job. It looked sinister. It was. I later learned this was one of the most lethal forms of portable ordinance in the survivalist arsenal. Here was a weapon that, with Hank's special reloads and in skilled hands, could fire the rough ballistics equivalent of ninety .357 magnum rounds in six or seven seconds. Hank showed me how to load it and disengage the safety, then returned to the comfort of his log backrest and his conversation with Nic. I fired a practice round into the air across the road, flinching at the roar. No one else seemed to be bothered by or even to notice the blast.

As Macy's rustic classroom neared completion, the students gathered. I counted fourteen participants in various poses on the ground near the fire pit. Macy and his second, Art (whom everyone called "Doc"), a Spokane-area dentist, sat on folding chairs behind the instructors' table. The table held Macy's notes, a pointer, and stone-weighted stacks of extra handouts (lots of extra handouts). Nearby, on a tripod easel, stood a three-by-five-foot white board with four colored pens. Tim circulated with the last handout, a "Course Evaluation Form," then saluted Macy, orated a short welcome to the Nighthawks on behalf of the "Wapalosie Mountain Region United Forces of Live Free," and sat bolt-upright in a third chair behind the table. The first class of the weekend, scheduled for 8:00 A.M. sharp, began punctually on survivalist time at 10:40.

"The Order of the Day" listed lessons in "radio and code," "troop movements," "map and compass," "concealment," "fire team coordination," and other handout topics. As a courtesy to Hank's group, Macy turned over instruction in basic crawling and concealment to Nic. Nic was twenty-four, intelligent, unassuming, complex, and utterly without Nighthawk pizzazz. Instead he was short, round, bespectacled, and had a high whiny voice. He stood before the group wearing far-from-natty, thick, olive-drab wool pants and jacket—practical, inexpensive, Cold-War surplus from the German army. Nic worked part time as a foundry hand with Hank at Specialty Design Cast Parts, and was in his second year of junior college. His aspirations? "I think my job will be automated pretty soon. What I really want to be is a high school civics and drama teacher." He helped his hometown police auxiliary as a "search and rescue" adviser, and he had six years of military experience in the Marine Corps Reserve, where he became a lieutenant and a combat engineer. "What's a combat engineer?" Tim asked. "Well," Nic replied, "I can either build you a bridge or I can blow one up." Nic told us he had been "into survivalism for two years with LFI." "I got excited about the idea when I was a kid. I read the *Guadalcanal Diary* in the fourth grade." This was probably correct. Nic proved to be voracious reader and presumed that everyone else was. He seemed puzzled when I asked him if his fourth-grade classmates were reading full-length nonfiction books on their own. "I don't know. I guess they did. I liked to read. My dad helped me some." He modestly gave full credit to Hank for organizing the Mount Rainier Rangers but was openly proud of one of his own recent accomplishments. "I've been volunteering for a year and a half but this time they are *paying* me [a total of $150]!" he enthused. The job? Lighting and set design for a community theater production of *The Glass Menagerie*.[4]

Nic's class in camouflage and creeping was simple, clear, and brief. "Concealment keeps you from being seen," Nic explained, "cover keeps you from being shot. . . . Know the difference and use them both." This seemed good advice. He began with a short discussion on visual perception—relative movement, contrast, backgrounds, profiles—then he outlined the hazards of various kinds of small arms fire and explosives. This took perhaps ten minutes. It was time for a "rest break." Next Nic persuaded Ron, a seventeen-year-old, athletic, Live Free acquaintance, to demonstrate military-style crawling.[5] Then Hank showed off his ghillie suit, which was much admired. Commercial makeup was discussed and a small flyer distributed. Perhaps twelve minutes passed in this class segment. Time for another break.

In hindsight Eleen and I had already seen enough to evaluate the weekend's instruction. Teaching could be summarized this way: no lesson lasted longer than a quarter of an hour, camouflage was understood, and crawling had been demonstrated. And the rest? The list of topics and objectives: maneuvering, traps, radio code, and other subjects so prominent in handouts and in the Order of the Day? Simply ignored. After the handouts on booby traps, Russian mines, and troop movements were distributed and acknowledged, no one, students or instructors, ever mentioned them. Months later at Hank's house we would learn why. But there was instruction on one topic. For Macy to command and control he must also direct. There could be no giving of directives without knowledge of directions. Orders to "proceed to coordinates 172–249" would be meaningless without a way of locating that designated place. So the weekend's lecturing boiled down to the crucial topic of navigation.

While Eleen and I were naive militia members, we did have experience in wilderness travel. We had crossed California's Sierra Nevada range and the Oregon Cascades a dozen times in winter on skis, climbed over seventy-five peaks in the Sierra Nevada, and twenty more in the Cascades and British Columbia's Coast Range including some first ascents. For more than ten years we taught basic mountaineering courses through the Sierra Club and university sports and extension programs. At Oregon State University I'd been hired for five terms to teach wilderness survival to auditorium-size classes. Map and compass skills were key to all of these courses, and in expert opinion, to all travel in undeveloped or remote terrain. To teach navigation I prepared a twenty-six-page packet of materials in support of four hours of lecture, six hours of field exercises, and two assigned textbook chapters. In my experience all these were necessary to achieve reliable navigation proficiency. Apparently Macy agreed with my priorities. He put navigation first on the program. Therefore it was with professional curiosity that I watched the Nighthawk commander in action.

Macy began his lesson by drawing black dots on the white board, then intersecting lines between them, and finally arrows pointing to and from the dots and the intersections. He gestured north and south, up the road and toward the center of the earth. He quoted assorted passages verbatim from a short stack of advanced armored infantry training manuals. His talk was impressively complicated. He used military slang and acronyms without elaboration and technical terms without definition. He punctuated his talk with pointer thrusts, paced to and fro with one hand clasped in the small of his back, and preceded nearly every sentence with an outline point number. The lecture sounded like this: "One. Compass. The military lensatic compass has seven parts. One-eh, hinged baseplate marked in scale increments. One-bee, integral sighting wire. One-cee, liquid dampened magnetic needle." "Read UTM grid points bottom to top and left to right. . . . You civies, ignore those USGS refs." He spoke of baselines, shooting sights, azimuths and back azimuths, true north, magnetic north, declinations, and the need for rigorous precision. With concentration and ten years' experience teaching this topic, I could follow most of what he said.

As Macy spoke the students took out their compasses. I looked over their equipment as I routinely did in my own navigation classes. This class was ill prepared. Only three had instruments mechanically capable of reproducing the manipulations Macy was describing. Four had no visible compasses at all. Another four had ersatz copies of the military model on which essential "moving" parts had been cast into the plastic housing in a fixed orientation. These looked real enough but were good only if one wished to sight perpetually northward. Rex had other troubles. His compass was an unusual version with degree markings ascending counter-clockwise. Macy's instruction assumed a clockwise layout. Two participants had "compasses" consisting of only a magnetized needle in decorated circular holders. These incomplete instruments required that nearly everything be pictured in the imagination of the user. Direction of travel, baseplate orientation, correction factors, and the rest must be simultaneously fantasized—a situation about as realistic as a Lamaze class exclusively for single men. I'd seen these problems before in numerous classes of my own. Equipment check was the first order of business in my navigation classes. But not in Macy's. He soldiered on with the lesson material, disregarding the students. Most participants tried to follow for a while, then twirled sticks in the dust, scratched, yawned, and otherwise filled the time. Nic and Hank sat against the same log. Nic seemed bothered. As an officer in the reserves he had learned navigation before. He should know this stuff. He followed Macy's talk with knit brows, note taking, and agitation. Hank apparently expected less of himself that day. He had only been an enlisted man, a stateside army warehouse worker—no navigation required. In the comfort of his ghillie suit, and now warmed by sun, Hank's muddy chin settled comfortably on his chest. He did not snore.

With the usual breaks, Macy took an hour and a quarter to finish his presentation. The participants were then divided into two groups that later, in Tim's article in *American Survival Guide,* would be imaginatively called the "Cupcake Stomper" and "Duncan Atlas" patrols. Right then we were only groups A and B. Rex from the Nighthawks was put in charge of the A's and told to pick his troops. Tim, Hank, and two others made his group. The leftovers—Eleen and I, Tim's friend Jake, young Ron, and Will from the Nighthawks—were assigned to Nic, the "LT" as Macy and soon everyone else called him. It was test time.

Macy handed the leader of each group a slip of paper on which were written grid coordinates and instructions. Rex didn't look at his paper nor did he even have a map. He just asked Macy, "Is this at the end of the meadow where we stopped this morning?" When the Major responded, "Right, that's it. Set up your ambush there," Rex wadded the instructions into his pocket, gathered his gear, and began hiking slowly along the level, mid-valley dirt road, talking to another Nighthawk in the A-team. As an afterthought he called "Come on, let's go" to the rest of his troops, who followed at various intervals. It was now afternoon and hot, so after about one hundred yards of hiking, it was time for a break. Rex stopped in the nearest shade, where the patrol united, rested, then ambled off to its assignment: prepare an ambush for group B. The B's remained at the camp, waiting for directions.

Just before he left with the A's, Tim took a photograph of the B's preparing for action. What would happen now? Eleen and I wondered. The photo told the story.

Months later, in the "Operation Azimuth Bearing" article in *American Survival Guide,* Tim's photo would be featured in the center of page 42, above a bold type pull-quote that read, "They are the true survivalists." The picture revealed much about practiced survivalism and its media representation. In it, three people are huddled on the ground. The caption reads, "LT and members of the Duncan Atlas patrol review topo map coordinates before moving out, perhaps to engage the enemy." The "true survivalists" in the picture were the only three, as it turned out, who knew where they were much of the weekend: Nic, the Marine Corps Reserve officer who wanted to be a high school drama teacher, and two sociologists.

After watching the confused B's stare and mutter at their maps for a quarter hour, then realizing their predicament, Eleen and I volunteered to help Nic figure out the patrol's destination, and we were soon accepted as skillful navigators. But as it turned out, navigation mattered little. The problem, we discovered, was simpler. Macy was an armored infantry officer, a "road" man. Group A was down the road, waiting. He expected the B's to follow along, on the look-out, then get ambushed. The idea of avoiding the ambush by going off-road had occurred to no one.[6] But as we readied to depart, Jake made a novel proposal. Jake was more a friend of Tim's than a survivalist. A lean local logger in his mid-twenties, he wore worn OD clothing and cap, carried a single-barrel shotgun, and possessed the easy strength of a long-time woodsman. We were weekend visitors; Jake lived there. "Why not go that way?" he suggested to Nic, pointing to a grassy ridge running parallel to the road. Nic eyed the ridge for a moment. It was neither steep nor far away. "OK," he affirmed, and then to Will: "Take the point." With elaborate caution, as if checking each step for enemy hazards, hunkering down and hiding behind each bush, tree, and grass clump along the way, Will lead the patrol uphill. From that moment on, nothing went according to plan.

Chaos in the Pines

We stopped often, first so Will could "clear the way" of suspicious obstacles, then at each opportunity for shade. We marched on survivalist time: creep-walk ten minutes, wait for stragglers, rest ten minutes, repeat, always in slow motion. An hour and a half after we received our orders, we had progressed only three hundred yards from the classroom clearing. On our second rest, the radio on John's backpack squawked. On the third break it broadcast voices. After some fiddling, Nic was able to speak with Macy, who was calling. Radio procedures and message coding had been part of Macy's morning instruction, presented with the same befuddling blend of technical jargon and in-group shorthand as his navigation lecture, but with fewer consequences. While map-and-compass procedures had no everyday analog, radio talk could be treated as phone conversation. "Hello? Hello? Command? Are you there? This is group B here. Can you hear me? Are you there? Hello?" Unmilitary and uncoded, but workable and quickly adopted. Macy wanted to know where B-team was. Some of us were amused by this question.

While group B worked its unhurried way up and along the ridge, Macy and Doc had gone to get the Badger. The Badger was a one-of-a-kind device, a homemade ATV Macy hoped someday to market. It was assembled from a bits and pieces: eight small wheels, two seats from golf carts, a lawn mower motor, and a go-cart-type transmission, all mounted in a fiberglass basin much like a small, mobile hot tub. The Badger was supposed to climb mountainous terrain, ford streams, and carry stout loads in the backcountry. That weekend it did not like steep hillsides, water, or much weight in the tub. But the barely muffled engine made a terrific racket, it steered with levers like a real World War II tank, and it carried Macy, Doc, their gear, and the command radio. Remember, Macy was an armor man. He did not walk much. Doc's generous stomach made him an armor man, too.

As Nic and Macy began their radio conversation, the Badger's engine roar filled the countryside, but it soon had carburetor problems and died. Peace was restored to the valley, and its excellent acoustics were revealed. Macy called asking Nic for the coordinates of B-team's present location, and when he did, we all heard him. The Badger was parked on the road just below us, only a short distance away. Doc and Macy's conversations were clearly audible. Coordinates were not necessary. Nic could have radioed Macy to look uphill, then waved a handkerchief. Our patrol was in plain sight, albeit spread out on the ground in the available shade. Or Nic could have put the radio aside and simply spoken loudly, "We're up here, right above you on the hill!" and raised his arms. But we were on patrol. Patrols did not announce their whereabouts and wave handkerchiefs. They used radios, usually in hushed tones lest the enemy hear. Nic seemed nervous about this contradiction but maintained appearances. Coordinates it would be. These required calculations, approximations, assistance from sociologists, and about fifteen more minutes to estimate. Meanwhile, communication deteriorated further. Judging from Doc and Macy's talk, the Badger's radio had joined the carburetor in malfunctioning. The scene then became one worthy of Pirandello. We lounged, watched, and listened to the senior Nighthawk trying to call our patrol on his dead radio. "Group B, do you copy? This is Command. Come in and report your position," said the voice on the road just below us. "Group B, do you copy? Come in." Macy's natural voice was clearly audible, but the B-team's radio speaker remained mute, so Nic continued to play his role. Dutifully, repeatedly, in a muffled voice, he called into the microphone: "Command, come in. This is B." "Command, come in. This is B, ready to report."

After a half-hour of ministrations, the Badger came to life, lurched another fifty yards along the road, and died again, dislodging the radio antenna for good measure. We listened as Doc and Macy discussed the situation. One patrol had presumably been in position for nearly two hours without action and was probably restive. The other patrol was lost entirely. It was time to reassemble the forces.

Neither Eleen nor I will ever forget the way that punctilious little major faced defeat. Without the radio he could no longer control, but he could issue one final command. Macy straightened his beret, climbed up to stand on the Badger's front seat, and struck a Patton-like pose. Then he cupped his hands around his mouth and recalled his troops in the time-honored manner of children ending games. He yelled, loudly, over and over: "Olli-Olli-oxen-free! Olli-Olli-oxen-free! Olli-Olli-oxen-free!"

The afternoon shadows were growing long when we all finally reassembled at the Badger. Another maneuver had been hastily planned.

This time, group A would get a ten-minute head start on its way back to its former position. The B's would rendezvous there ASAP and engage the enemy. It would be dark soon. We were told that preparations were underway for the night action. The Badger and the radio were working again so Macy, Doc, and Rex climbed aboard and scooted up the road, leaving the rest of the departing A's leaderless and the B's on their own.

Jake had another idea. He was no keen map reader, but he did notice the lay of the land and had spied a fresh logging track through the woods a short distance away. He guessed it would keep us off the main road and take us to our destination undetected. By this time Nic was feeling the strain of leadership and simply waved point-man Will off in the suggested direction. The exaggerated creep-walk began once more and continued at the usual pace for half an hour, until we encountered another surprise.

While Will and Nic led, Jake and I had been assigned to bring up the rear. Our patrol was not fast, but to our credit we were quiet. The Badger had been put to rest somewhere, so as we worked our way along the logging road all we heard were birds and an occasional squirrel, until the voices. It was Macy, Doc, Rex, and the rest of the A-team, laughing, moving about, setting up camp, and talking about the upcoming evening assaults. Jake and I listened. There they were, the enemy, immediately below us in a small bowl screened from the road by thick second-growth Douglas fir and apparently unaware of our presence. I hurried to tell Nic. Jake, Eleen, and I figured the action would really start now. We had them surrounded on three sides. They would be totally surprised. We would turn the tables, ambush the ambushers, and probably earn lots of points. We figured wrong. Nic was exasperated by this interruption. Jake's course deviations had been uneasily tolerated, but this proposal to alter the script was out of the question. Our orders were to proceed to the ambush point and be ambushed, and that is what we would do. But we never made it.

It was now late dusk. We turned onto a road headed down into thick timber. Within a short time visibility was reduced to tree-filtered starlight. Nic could only hope we were headed in the right direction. A radio check with Macy was long, confused, and unsatisfactory for both parties. Macy inquired about our whereabouts and we about his, but neither party had more than vague descriptions to offer. Then each group fired shots in the air to fix locations and, after a time, Macy issued new orders: continue along the road until we came to a stream, then wait. A stream showed on the map, sure enough, but these orders sounded suspicious. Would there be enemies waiting? The Badger belched to life in the dark behind us and headed our way. One thing was sure. Enemies were coming.

There were enemies ahead, too. Even deep in the woods, Hank's lookout post was easy to find. Everyone could hear him snoring comfortably in his sleeping bag under the big pine tree. We tiptoed past without disturbing him, but we soon heard the A's, now on foot, in close pursuit. They came upon snoring Hank. In the near total darkness, he was what they were looking for: an audible target. Firing began. Hank was attacked by his own troops. The B's joined the fray, firing on the attackers. Muzzle flashes and explosions filled the woods. In the dark there were no command and control, no tactics, no orders, no plans. At last there was action.

Guns were everywhere but not what they seemed. Take Nic's for example. He carried a Colt M-15, the civilian version of the U. S. service-issue assault rifle, the M-16. This rugged weapon is capable of rapid, reliable, and sustained semiautomatic fire of high-velocity .223 standard military rounds from forty-round magazines. Nic carried six of these magazines. With the exceptions noted, Nic's rifle was typical of those carried by the outing participants. These firearms were commanding in appearance and potential, but on this weekend they were by no means lethal weapons. All had received mechanical vasectomies of one sort or another and were loaded with blank cartridges—still capable of noisy banging but in reality, impotent. Many such as Nic's had little prophylactic caps on their ends to prevent the discharged blank residue from being spewed toward others.

Up the dirt road, tittering A-team marauders prepared the weekend's real weapons of choice. "Grenades" and "artillery" made from tennis balls split and primed with a spoonful of hobby shop black powder and fitted with a short fuse. Some were lit and thrown in our direction. Others were launched from "mortars" made of tennis ball cans with a pinhole in the bottom through which a squirt of lighter-fluid propellant was ignited. The B's organized a hasty defense. The A-team's attack pressed forward. Missiles arced toward our lines to kaboom or fizzle in the underbrush. The B's responded with massed rifle and shotgun fire. The woods sparkled with flashes like the stands at the opening of a nighttime Olympic event.

The background darkness between flashes was so complete that recognizing friend from foe was not easy. B-team had a password system. "Bravo" was the challenge, "strongbox," the response. Leaves crunched on the roadside. Eleen, the only woman on the operation, challenged the unidentified walkers. "Bravo," she said. Silence. Then from the road, whispered recognition of Eleen's voice, and more creeping. Foe! The

B's who had heard the password exchange opened fire, then came general engagement. Lines collapsed, sides disintegrated. Melee. Us versus Them fragmented into individuals and pairs defending some personal refuge or on predatory prowls, and all in a range of moods. Macy and Doc, without troops to command, drove the Badger back to their camp. Nic, the reasoned daytime strategist and educator, lost his authority and his composure with the first fusillade. His orders unheeded, he dissolved into uncharacteristic and untoward profanity. Easygoing Hank, his hearing damaged from years of exposure to high decibel industrial work environments, was able to maintain his composure throughout the encounter. We were sure of this because we could still hear him snoring whenever the firing stopped.

Tim was in melodramatic thrall of the moment. Darkness had transformed him. Gone was the parade ground sir-and-salute soldier act. The new Tim was an all-purpose hero, a leader without followers, a wellspring of gratuitous advice and meaningless but creative threats to the enemy. "I'll take the point!" "This way!" and "Watch out!" he called to no one in particular. Crashing through the underbrush and downed logs, he delivered his favorite line. "Yankeeeeee! Toooonight yooou diiiieee!" he crooned, over and over, in his most creative Asian accent. Tim and the meandering marauders drew closer. So did real harm.

Eleen and I heard steps nearby and joined the fray, adding our shotgun fire to the pitch-dark din. Suddenly the game changed. After my third shot a voice called out in apparent pain, "I'm hit!, I'm hit!" from about the spot at which I'd been aiming. "Retreat!" Tim called. No game this time. The firing ceased. Footsteps hurried out of the nearby brush. What happened? Was this cry and withdrawal just good war-game sportsmanship, a kind of fair-play admission that an A-team member probably would have been struck in a real gunfight, and the B's, therefore, should be credited with a "kill"? Or was it more serious? No other such cry had been heard in all the commotion. We listened as the victim was examined nearby.

"Where did it get you?"

"Ow! On the leg. Ow!"

A flashlight shone briefly.

"Sheeez! Look at that! Wad got him. Watch out for those shotguns!"

"Shotguns?" I thought. "My shotgun?"

I had meticulously followed Macy's instructions during the morning breaks, prying open each shell I was given and removing all of the lead pellets with care. But there is more in shotgun shells than lead. Inside each round, the pellets are carried in a stiff plastic cup, or "wad." When the round is fired, the wad itself becomes a missile, achieving high velocity for short distances and having an impact similar to a rubber riot-control bullet.

Here was a new possibility. Eleen and I, with our ludicrous getups and low-tech weapons, were no longer background players. Our basic firearms gave us primal advantages. We could hurt people. The next morning I would remember that possibility.

The assault continued sporadically for another hour, with a bizarre intermission toward the end. On one vigorous charge, A-team pushed the B's back across the small creek and down the darkened road into the vicinity of a previously unnoticed travel trailer. Suddenly the trailer lights went on, the door opened, and a burley hunter (it was bear season) stood backlit in the entrance, looking sleepy and asking, "What's all this fussin'?" Gone was the willing suspension of disbelief. The teams mingled together apologetically at the trailer's stoop. Feet shuffled in embarrassment as Tim explained that we were "practicing for war." The hunter seemed amused. He complimented Tim on his blotched face paint: "Nice Halloween outfit you got there." "You boys have a good time," he told the rest of us, then closed the trailer door and turned off the light.

From then on, enthusiasm dwindled. Hungry, tired troops went AWOL back to their packs and sleeping bags, munching candy bars, hanging shelter tarps, and settling in. A few diehards continued to slink up and down the roadside, firing occasionally. Not certain how long these interruptions would continue, Eleen and I retreated up the slope and spread our bags behind a large sheltering log. Soon night prevailed. By 10:00 P.M. Hank's sentinel snoozing was the loudest sound in the forest.

The next morning the pattern of "normal" exercises emerged. Macy at last had his ambush. After a leisurely breakfast and late start, the B's were sent creeping up the road where, as planned, they were annihilated by the A's in hiding. Macy was quite pleased with this bit of action and gathered us all together for a lengthy debriefing, explaining how much we had learned and how these experiences would prove vital in "the future." He detailed radio procedures for calling in fighter aircraft support or helicopter attacks and artillery bombardments. No one mentioned avoiding ambushes. No one asked from where the aircraft or artillery would come.

By late morning there was time for just one more maneuver. As usual the Nighthawks and their A-team allies were pitted against the hapless B's. To add some spice the Badger was designated as a "tank" and assigned to the A's while the B-team's consolation was a single blank shotgun round labeled an "antitank rocket." This was issued to B's "bazooka team," Jake and me. We two hid in the roadside brush while the rest of the outgunned B's waited at a bend nearby. The A-team attack was as expected, swift and lopsided (though no one kept score). The victorious A's headed back toward our hiding place, laughing and congratulating themselves. Several rode aboard the laboring Badger. Macy drove. Rex sat beside him, closest to the road bank. The "rocket" round was still unfired.

• • •

Of all the characters Eleen and I met that weekend, Rex stood out in our minds as the darkest and most disturbing. Rex and Will were brothers. Both took pleasure in taking life. Will, younger by two years, was single, lean, self-confident, restrained, and a more conventional life-taker. He was an all-season hunter. Pheasant, duck, geese, grouse, deer, and elk were his game of preference, although "Pheasants are too easy," he told us, and "Elk are not much of a challenge." Lately his interests in firearms had expanded into the paramilitary. The previous summer he had completed a private two-week mercenary training course in southern California. He spoke in technical detail about a range of international assault weapons and accessories he had learned to service and fire during that course. He wore faded fatigues, a Nighthawk beret, and carried a well-worn Ruger Mini-14 rifle and the ubiquitous Colt .45 pistol. Will, the man of action, seemed most comfortable on the move, on maneuvers. In class he sat by himself and on breaks, with his brother or amiably with the sociologists. With us he was quietly talkative, giving us background on Macy and elaborating on task-related themes: the best way to scout, spot traps, walk silently. In action, he took the pointman's job seriously, took the troops' ineptness in stride, obeyed orders, and offered no opinions.

Rex was different: unathletic, fleshy, an "armor" man of much opinion, criticism, and complaint. Both brothers' childhoods were filled with violence. Their father beat them frequently on spontaneous occasions with different results. Will was beaten into toughened stoicism, Rex into distrusting vengefulness. Rex's distrust was catholic. Politicians, Indians, and black people, those who are too wealthy and those without property, the uneducated and overeducated, many men and most women were not to be trusted. Women had always been a problem. Rex found them "dirty and lying" or "stuck up" (an exception being German prostitutes, who, he insisted, were "really clean and checked up . . . no diseases"). Rex had served two years in the navy but was discharged before completing his stretch. His drinking binges led to blackouts and incapacitation, leaving him incapable of performing his duties. However, he was successful in other pursuits. "I used to steal stuff all the time," he told us. "I had fifteen pounds of [plastic] explosives in my locker. Stealing was the only way you could get things you needed." He also ran a profitable shipboard loan-sharking business, providing cash to his shipmates at 20 percent interest—per week. By his account the highlight of this business was accompanying his two strong-arm collectors to "teach a lesson" to loan payment delinquents, especially "niggers." The "niggers" ran less scrupulous enterprises than his, Rex told us. "All the niggers were pimps or hit men," or worse. One bunch he claimed to have known hated an officer, "so they grabbed his legs and arms and shoved him in a metal locker and locked it. Then they threw the locker out a fourth-story window." This crime was never punished. Another crime was, but inadequately, Rex thought. A "bunch of niggers" from another ship hated another officer, so "they raped and killed this officer's wife. She was a librarian." But "they only put 'um in jail. They got life." Rex's opinion? "I would've killed 'um all." Rex probably did not need the extra income from loan sharking. His father owned substantial real estate and construction businesses as well as the fourteen hundred acres of timbered land in northeast Washington on which we would conduct another exercise months later. Other family members controlled the remaining four thousand acres in the valley.

Following his post-navy alcohol detoxification, Rex decided to wed. Cleanliness was important. The woman he married had to be clean. He assured us he always had been. But finding such women was hard, so Rex signed on with a dating service that cost him "a lot of money" and provided "only clean women that had been thoroughly checked out." After half a year of mismatches and a five-week courtship, Rex married last year, at age twenty-six, to a woman nine years his senior who had a seventeen-year-old son. Parenting was not going well. Rex disliked people who took drugs and his new stepson seemed a likely user. When he suspected his stepson had taken hallucinogens "I just wanted to kill him. . . . I've seen so many people ruined with drugs. . . . I just wanted to blow him away." His new wife intervened, showing what Rex judged to be a "lack of discipline." According to Rex, his sister, too, lacked parental discipline. Her son "got into her live-in boyfriend's Blazer and kicked off the brake." The Blazer rolled backward into another vehicle, breaking two taillights. His sister's response? "She just went down and got the kid out of the car and didn't do anything to him—just carried him back to the house. . . . I would've beat the tar out of him." "How old was your sister's son?" I asked. "Oh I don't know," Rex replied. "It doesn't matter. . . . He was four or maybe five. . . . I would've beat him good."

Rex was a creative life-taker. He told of hunting exploits, like Will's, and of other killing. He told us how, in years past, he had fashioned a stick with a sliding string loop on one end for snaring frogs around their middles. After capturing his prey, Rex would tighten the loop slowly until the frog was bisected. Then he would shoot the gaping heads and twitching abdomens with his .22. He taught Will how to use that stick and another one with a nail in it, which they used to impale frogs and crawdads. He spoke nostalgically of the long summer days of his youth spent looping and impaling and shooting.

Rex shared these opinions with Eleen and me at the lunch break, and with Jake who sat silently nearby, eating, listening. "I can kill a person easy," Rex told us, "but it's harder for me to kill an animal because they're trustworthy and they understand discipline. With people you can never trust them."

Rex had a dog named Ding, a gentle, scarred black Labrador we met months later. Rex described disciplining Ding. "One time I called Ding and he wouldn't come," Rex recounted, "so I grabbed my [baseball] bat and hit him a good one that picked him right off the ground." Another time, "I shot at him a couple of times because he was running around the house," but "I just nicked him once." Lunch was over. Rex left, and Jake finally spoke a few tightly compressed words: "I've got a dog, too."

• • •

Jake and I lay low, flattened into the earth behind obscuring brush, shotguns ready, as the Badger laden with A-team troops crawled near. My assigned job was to "cover" Jake; his was to launch the "rocket" at the A's "tank." In reality he had one round to fire. Hank's shotgun that I carried held eight. The Nighthawk-laden Badger was now only a few feet away, its overworked engine geared down, howling. I watched Jake take steady aim on the creeping vehicle's sidepod like any good bazooka man. Then his gun barrel rose—one inch, two—to a new target. Jake fired.

Rex was hit by the shotgun wad dead center in his protruding roll of waist fat at a range of no more than ten feet. Rex shrieked and pawed at his side as if he had been stung by a wasp. The Badger stopped abruptly. Macy warned, "Shotgun!" No one moved, except me.

Rage! Right then I hated that place, those people. I hated Rex's cruelty. I hated Macy's placid followers and puffed-up leadership. I hated Tim's silly salutes and his celebration of authoritarian rule and a war that a generation, my generation, had lived through and opposed with so much sacrifice. Had all that been for nothing? And I hated myself. I hated my tiredness, my fear. I hated my hands that now held too tightly a shotgun pointed at other human beings after a lifelong commitment to pacifism.

The roar of repeated shotgun fire filled the roadside followed by other unforgettable sounds. Chambering a round in a pump shotgun like Hank's requires two motions: one hand slides the forestock back along the barrel until the action opens and the spent shell is ejected, then slides it forward, bringing a new round into battery. The other hand holds the buttstock against the shoulder and pulls the trigger. Each end of the cycle produces a distinctive sound: "clack"—open, "slick"—reload and cock, "click"—fire. These sounds are unmistakable to those familiar with firearms and feared in close combat. I now heard these sounds close to my ear, repeatedly. Clack-slick, click; clack-slick, click; clack-slick, click. I had emptied my gun at the Nighthawks. Then, uncontrollably, over and over, I continued to work the action and pull the trigger.

"Jeeeeze!" was all Tim could say as he sat on the back of the Badger, staring point-blank into the still wobbling gun barrel.

Every shot had missed.

It was a little past noon. Macy said a few loose words about the use of armored vehicles in an assault, then dismissed us. Operation Aurora Borealis was over. The troops headed back to their vehicles in pairs and strings. Nic walked with us. Relieved of command, he was again talkative and friendly. Hank reclaimed his shotgun at the cars, admitted "You guys did all right," and invited Eleen and me to the next meeting of the local Live Free branch, the Mount Rainier Rangers. We thanked him for the loan, accepted the offer, and hit the road. Five hundred and sixty-five miles and thirteen and a half hours was a long drive home. We used most of it trying to make sense of the survivalism we had seen, and of which we were now a part.

NEEDS FIXING

> After the riots and the bombing of the city, all was destroyed. There were bits and pieces of machines everywhere amidst the ashes and dead bodies. . . . In the early light, the town seemed an enormous jewel box, lined with the black and gray of velvet flyash, and filled with millions of twinkling treasures: bits of air conditioners, amplidynes, analyzers, arc welders, batteries, belts, billers, bookkeeping machines, bottlers, canners, capacitors, circuit breakers, clocks, coin boxes, colorimeters, computers, condensers, conduits, controls. . . .
>
> A faint hubbub came from around a corner, from where the railroad station had been, where it still was after a fashion. Finnerty turned the corner for a better look at the celebrators.
>
> In the station's waiting room, carnage was everywhere. But around

one machine a group had gathered. The people were crowding one another excitedly, as though a great wonder were in their midst.

Paul and Finnerty left the car to examine the mystery, and saw that the center of attention was an Orange-O machine. Orange-O, Paul recalled, was something of a cause célèbre, for no one in the whole country, apparently, could stomach the stuff—no one save Doctor Francis Eldgrin Gelhorne, National Industrial, Commercial, Communications, Foodstuffs, and Resources Director. As a monument to him, Orange-O machines stood shoulder-to-shoulder with the rest, though the coin-box collectors never found anything in the machines but stale Orange-O. But now the excretor of the blended wood pulp, dye, water, and orange-type flavoring was as popular as the nymphomaniac at an American Legion convention.

"O.K., now let's try anotha' nickel in her an' see how she does," said a familiar voice from behind the machine—the voice of Bud Calhoun.

"Clunkle" went the coin, and then a whir, and a gurgle.

The crowd was overjoyed.

"Filled the cup almost to the top that time; and she's nice and cold now, too," called the man by the machine's spout.

"But the light behind the Orange-O sign didn't light up," said a woman. "Supposed to."

"We'll fix that, won't we, Bud?" said another voice from behind the machine. "You people get me about three feet of that red wire hanging out of the shoeshine machine, and somebody let me borrow their penknife a second."

The speaker stood up and stretched, and smiled contentedly, and Paul recognized him; the tall, middle-aged, ruddy-faced man who'd fixed Paul's car with the sweatband of his hat long ago. The man had been desperately unhappy then. Now he was proud and smiling because his hands were busy doing what they liked to do best, Paul supposed—replacing men like himself with machines. He hooked up the lamp behind the Orange-O sign.

"There we are."

Bud Calhoun bolted on the back. "Now try her."

The people applauded and lined up eager for their Orange-O. The first man up emptied his cup, and went immediately to the end of the line for seconds. (Vonnegut 1952, 291–94)

WHAT HAPPENED IN THE WOODS?

What happened on Operation Aurora Borealis? We had our weekend of paramilitary thicket crawling and gunplay, to be sure, and we met survivalists. But the action bore little resemblance to the media images of martial virility and revolutionary fervor we had been led to expect.

Aurora Borealis seemed, well, a flop. The elaborate lesson plans and scoring schemes came to nothing. No one walked far,[7] took the initiative, learned much, or read the handouts. Most of the group had only sunburn, bruises, broken equipment, and memories of a cold night out for their trouble. Yet the participants seemed buoyant enough. Returning to the cars they joked and chatted. Hank and Tim shuffled along, lightheartedly debating mortality. Tim (who had bushwhacked his own team member earlier that day): "I got you good with that mortar!" Hank: "You missed by a mile." Tim: "You were dead!" Hank: "I was not!" Tim: "You were! I got you!" This childlike banter was full of ah-shucks smiles and lasted for a hundred yards of road. In conclusion, Hank warned Tim to watch out "next time." And there would be next times, on future field actions. "Operation New Moon," "Operation Frostline," "Operation Lava Fields," all lay ahead. Eleen and I would join in these as well, with many of these same survivalists. Later I would attend training sessions and field exercises in Tennessee, Missouri, and California. The groups and locales would be different, but the formats and results similar.

As the homeward miles accumulated Eleen and I grappled with the weekend. Immediately we realized something was missing: political talk, ideological talk. We had gone on Operation Aurora Borealis expecting to hear talk about looming disasters and enemies on the horizon (or under the bed). Yet there was nearly none. No one said much about the Communist Threat or the New World Order or the machinating Illuminati. No one had much to say about the causes of nuclear war, civil strife, economic collapse, or any of the other themes often represented as permeating survivalism.

Participants were not mute. Indeed, a subdued but friendly banter went on in classes, on the march, and even while attempting to ambush enemies. Mild gossip, gibes, and above all, tech-talk filled the day. Over the weekend we heard and were invited to join animated discussions concerning tent weights and carburetor efficiency, sleeping bag warmth and raincoat permeability, CB radio range, cable winch torque, flashlight brightness, camp chair comfort, and much about the care and performance of guns, ammunition, and accessories. The Aurora Borealis survivalists were manifestly full of opinion, conviction, and perspective, and shared all with generous frequency. But not political opinion. Instead they sounded like hardware or sporting goods store employees or handymen, arguing the merits of their favored merchandise from positions of enthusiasm, knowledge, and long experience. Judging by the weekend's talk, the fix for cataclysmic doom lay in mastery of mechanical details and routine techniques, in some elaborate craft of function.

In retrospect the problem was not that politics was "missing" but that we were missing the subtle complexity of the survival action all around us. Vonnegut understood. The struggle is not literal, not a fight to regain control of the podium or ballot box, but figurative, to find enough Orange-O machines to go around, enough things that need fixing. Fixing requires skills and the right tools, not votes, to leverage impromptu invention into practical solution. As Kai Erickson made clear, there is pride in such work. Ben Thompson hinted at this interest in self-expression through mechanical means in his choice of favored literature, *Applied Science*. Newton, Franklin, even Rube Goldberg are the ideologues nearest to these survivalists, not Marx, Mao, or Adam Smith. Social scientists, perhaps, need notions like "politics" and "ideology" to do their work, but some survivalists manage well enough without either. What these survivalists do seek are opportunities and purchase: crucial junctures of events and circumstance where select tools, applied with skill, magnify effectiveness. But consider that not all skillful tool use necessarily restores. Not all crisis-time effectiveness is in repair. Other functions may take precedence.

Eleen and I discussed the weekend's logical puzzlements, too. How would it be possible, we wondered, for participants to hit targets one hundred meters distant with shotguns and pistols, as was suggested by the evaluation score sheet? We knew in general terms that shotguns and pistols were short-range weapons, unsuited for use at such ranges. Some tactical assumptions also strained the imagination. Under what scenarios would a small group of amateur survivalists, defending family and community, be in a position to "call for indirect fire" from supporting "artillery" or "tanks" or "aircraft," as Macy's lecturing implied? We also wondered why, with the exception of nonsurvivalist Jake, the participants were so passive, at least until darkness collapsed command and control. The disregard for teaching materials and procedures bothered us personally, for we were teachers ourselves. Why did no one seem to care about the handouts and directions or even the navigation lessons, the weekend's essential topic? Were Hank and the other nonlearners simply dull? Fundamentally we wondered how the participants could be satisfied with a weekend so apparently confounded, disorganized, and contradictory? But participants used their own standpoints to evaluate the weekend. They were survivalists, not sociologists. They attached their own meanings to the weekend's events and their satisfactions varied.

By his own report and others', Hank had a good time. The weekend pace was relaxed by comparison with his work week, the outdoor air cleaner than the factory's, and his ghillie suit led the weekend's fashion parade. It even looked as if he had recruited two sociologists (whatever they were) for the Mount Rainier Rangers. Nic, too, sounded content, now that the weekend was over. I spoke with him on the phone early the next week. He confirmed Hank's enthusiasm and answered several questions.

I asked Nic about Tim's rigid ritual formalities. Throughout the weekend Tim saluted nearly everyone on some occasion and the Nighthawks almost continuously. No one else saluted at all. At first we thought he had served in some exceptionally strict branch of the military. Nic set us straight. "Tim has never been in the service," he told us, "but he reads a lot of books. The only thing he knows about the military is what he reads"—a steady diet of war novels and histories. According to Nic, this reading was influential. Tim was infatuated with a caricatured militarism, with swashbuckling adventure and disciplined formality. In the presence of what he judged authority, he played the "good" soldier, saluting, standing at attention, and calling people "Sir!" (often while smiling broadly). On his own, he made complicated plans and rash Audie Murphy-style charges on imaginary enemy positions. That was Nic's opinion of Tim. Tim had more to say.

Tim

I didn't speak with Tim right away. After Operation Aurora Borealis we exchanged a couple of utilitarian notes over the next few weeks, then had a long talk. Tim was discouraged and alone. "Are you married?" I asked. "No," he said. "I was, but it didn't do me no good." His wife had left him, he told me sadly. "I'm real monogamous. Once I love somebody it takes a long time to think about anybody else. I'm a real spiritual person inside." His work was also going poorly. Seasonal, part-time tree planting jobs were the only wage-labor he could find in his area. At off-times he cut and sold firewood. These were meager and irksome means. "I'm sick and tired of going uphill five foot every summer, then losing six foot during the winter." But Tim had a plan. "Next summer I'm going to Alaska," he confided. "I can work on a fishing boat . . . make some good money . . . and they've got real wilderness up there. You can live right off the land."

He talked for a quarter of an hour about conquering the wilds and high earnings, then the frontier machismo began to fade. Quietly, plaintively, another topic emerged. Tim confessed that he had other aspirations. Most of all he wanted an education. "I work in the woods but I want out of it. I want to go back to school. I want to take marine diesel mechanics and welding and major in English and history." This eclectic curriculum made sense enough to Tim. Degrees mattered little. "I just want to study and study and learn." There were personal reasons for this urge to scholarship that I would not fully understand for some time. He had a tradition to uphold. At the time, however, he was a high school dropout. He was also a writer.

"Operation Azimuth Bearing," the article in *American Survival Guide* that described the weekend's action in such vivid and fanciful terms, hit the newsstands five days before my talk with Tim. I asked him how he became involved in cowriting the article. "I'm sort of friends with the editor," Tim bragged. "He's the one that got me into writing and I'm going to keep it up." We discussed Tim's part in preparing the article. "Well, I had a lot of help putting that one together," he admitted. I was the "idea man" and the photographer. "What about the content?" I asked. The action described in "Operation Azimuth Bearing" seemed far removed from the events I'd observed, and I told Tim so. After a few filler remarks, Tim changed the topic, confirmed Nic's opinion, and told the truth.

Tim was unconcerned with the accuracy of the article's technical details. It was the feeling of the thing that mattered, its link to larger themes. For Tim, the article "felt right," it was consonant with his other reading. "Well, you know, I'm a fluent reader," Tim explained. "You've got to read about history and the wars we've fought to know what's going on." Reading inspired Tim. "Reading gets me thinking about writing, you know, plots and sentence structure and everything. It plants itself in you after a while. Then when I write, it just works itself out."

"Operation Azimuth Bearing" was not a field report but a "working out," as he called it, Tim's deconstruction of his experiences, a figment of recent history, a lively, stirring tale, rich in color and free from cloying empiricism. Tim already had three published articles to his credit in nationally circulated magazines. Even then, he was a recognized survivalist author across the country. But at home, nobody knew him.

For all his titles, his directorship of the "Wapalosie Mountain National Survival Association," his seat on the "Survival Base Board of Directors," his position as "Regional Director of Live Free, Inc.," and the rest, Tim had few close survivalist friends. In his area of the state survivalism was not popular. When I asked him directly what groups were active nearby and with whom he trained and cooperated locally, he seemed uncomfortable. He changed the topic to his participation in a larger, abstract moral community. Tim described his survivalism as a vocation, a calling. "It's not just for me and my family you know. It's not. We have a moral responsibility towards freedom. It's been dumped on us since birth, because we're the only people in the world guaranteed by the constitution the right to keep and bear arms and the freedom of speech. As far as free people of the world goes, we're the leaders. And we're losing it."

This sounded like the ideology talk Eleen and I had expected to hear at Operation Aurora Borealis. But there was no conviction in Tim's words, just the impression that they covered up something else he did not want to talk about. "But what about your local groups?" I persisted. Tim dodged again, to a new problem, security, and surprised me once more. Another Nixon-reversal occurred. Eleen and I were accorded in-group status while the existence of shadowy others was hinted at, then darkened with distrust. "I think a lot of things are coming up that will demand a lot of security. Don't trust everybody that comes along just 'cause they say they're into Live Free, and all," Tim warned. "The only man down there that I trust, other than you, is Hank and his family, and that's it. He found me after I'd been active about a year, and he's the one that put a group together."

The cover-up dissolved. Tim was disappointed in himself. He confessed organizing survivalism had proven cheerless and elusive. After years of work he remained a phenomenon unto himself. Operation Aurora Borealis showed him as he often was, a lone voice in the dark. "I'm still an active integral movement. But I failed, you know. I mean I failed to actually put a group together here. I've got hundreds of man-hours in helping LFI get on its feet. I'll never give up. But do you realize that of all that time, other than you and Hank and a couple of other people, do you realize that after three years, you're the only ones. I mean really. There's no group in Liberty. There never really was. There's a couple of others that are allies, Macy and those guys out of Spokane. But nothing ever really worked. I've just seen a lot of, I'll be blunt, phony crap!"

Tim the survivalist was a character apart from Tim the part-time tree planter. Tree-planter Tim was well known and clearly defined by his neighbors of twenty years as an affable, quirky, unskilled woods worker of little import in a rural timber town. Survivalist Tim took less substantial form in the weak social bonds of irregular correspondence, the author's imagined readership, and the vicarious adventures of his fictive and historic heroes. Survivalist Tim, the center of practical action and effects, was a fragile fabrication at constant risk of dissolution by others' disregard and his own personal disappointments. But survivalist Tim had resources. At his disposal lay an array of symbols and arguments that made his position less tenuous and more attractive than nonsurvivalists might realize. Tim could read and imagine, tell and publish stories that included a provocative place for himself. And he could invite others into the storytelling. He could master a few skills with a few implements and, like the Dutch boy by the leaky dike, accomplish much with one digit, perseverance, and good timing. Survivalism was not all Tim did, but a part of his life that added animation and an alternative to humdrum times.

Survivalism as "Warrior" Resourcefulness

We draw examples of Thorstein Veblen's contemporary relevance from instances of consumer behavior, in "pecuniary waste and personal futility," because that behavior is made obvious for us by marketeers. Research material is as near as the TV remote or the airplane seat pocket. But if we look in less obvious places such as survivalism, we find other sorts of emulation. Historically Veblen's leisure class did more than control community wealth and industrial capacity. They were more than economic predators. They also monopolized martial prowess, the means of organized force. They were the military as well as industrial elite. What if some group set out to emulate this leisure class in all its forms, to imitate the full spectrum of elite prerogatives? What if they played at being warriors as well as masters of economic production and distribution?

Operation Aurora Borealis introduced us to survivalism with new emphases, cataclysmic outlooks and "warrior" discourse. As with all survivalism, warrior discourse optimizes disorder. Back at the cars, as Eleen and I prepared to leave, Tim bid us goodbye and recommended some of his recent reading. "Look it up," he urged. He could not remember the reference, but he quoted a few lines and endorsed the author and the topics. Nietzsche. Hammers. Hardness.

> And if your hardness will not flash and cut and cut to pieces: how can you one day—create with me?
> For all creators are hard. And it must seem bliss to you to press your hand upon millennia as upon wax,
> bliss to write upon the will of millennia as upon metal—harder than metal, nobler than metal. Only the noblest is perfectly hard.
> This new law-table do I put over you, O my brothers:
> Become hard! (1888, "The Hammer Speaks")

Hammers break. Hammers build. So did Vonnegut's rebels in *Player Piano*. So can survivalists.

In his epilogue to *The Twilight of the Idols* (1888) Nietzsche gives voice to a survivalist vision: Hammer-man, the tough, self-directed instrument of cause and consequence. The warrior's cataclysmic outlook uncomplicates the world, gives Hammer-man a place to work. Inexorable, profound change approaches, and with it, fateful opportunity.

How is the survivalist to both break and build? How is Nietzsche's new law-table to be laid upon the land? What work must Hammer-man do? Can Sophocles' chorus in *Antigone* sing of humanity's cleverness on the same stage as Muddy Waters's brutish boast, "I'm ready"? Survivalists, too, may brag of being clever and ready, but how and for what?

The logic of warrior survivalism proceeds in three steps. First, modernity is revisited and redefined as mechanical, technical, material processes, endangered by its own excessive scope and complexity and on the verge of collapse and chaos. Next, crisis-time coping strategies, the essential means of production of social stability, are imaginatively distilled to spartan tools and toolcraft. Finally, mastery of these simplified means is claimed for survivalism, not in demonstrated use, but in displays of inventive use-skills, bricolage, adaptations of what you have to what you will need in postcrisis contingencies.

Materials, Skills, and Modernity

Again, survivalism confronts modernity and finds trouble, but trouble with possibilities. Massive, monolithic, hyperrationalized, interdependent systems of production and regulated order have failed. Specialization has gone too far.

Jim Jones, founder of Live Free, echoes Weber and Durkheim as he issues this warning: "The Achilles heel of modern Man is his growing inability to provide life's essentials on an individual, family or small group basis. . . . The typical modern man may be master of the computer, builder of the skyscraper or Vice President in charge of what-nots, but knows nothing about how to provide food, shelter, medical aid or protection for himself or his family without 'the system.'"

Without "the system" survivalists must provide their own means of production, their own essentials of life. But which are the most essential essentials? All-terrain vehicles? Rural property? Toilet tissue and soap powder? Perhaps in time. But in warrior world scenarios, a more urgent essential must be produced: security.

From Conflict to Chaos

Many warrior tales begin but do not end in dialectic conflicts between existing systems of order: cops vs. criminals, natives vs. newcomers, communism vs. capitalism. For eight years, off and on, the president of the United States told his own tale of fulfillment through virile confrontation.

Ronald Reagan was fond of repeating the story of a young optimist who once received the dubious gift of a large pile of horse manure. Undaunted by appearances, this plucky lad set about to sift the offal, confident that with so much horse odeur in evidence, a pony must surely be near. Reagan often claimed for himself a similar though more grandiose optimism, a vision of a transformed America rising from the mire of contemporary social ills. But Reagan's optimism was not independent, not sufficient to itself. It was relative, dependent upon harsh dialectic confrontation with contravening forces. His utopian fantasies grew from distopian roots; his optimism was linked to pessimistic fears. The imaginary citizens of Reagan's Shining City on the Hill drew their figurative strength and sense of community from their mortal and profound opposition to other phantasmagoria, to the reified Hollywood notions of a Dark Force emanating from the Evil Empire. Without these antitheses the Shining City was unmanageable, even unimaginable. The proffered benefits of the Reagan vision were obtainable only in a world radically simplified, polarized, and homogenized, only in a world far removed from the obdurate present.[8]

Entertainment industry versions of warrior survivalism reiterated these Reagan-esque fantasies in "foreign invasion" films like *Red Dawn, Invasion U.S.A.,* and the ABC miniseries *Amerika.*[9] These films entertained but missed the point. In warrior scenarios grand polarized confrontations do not last. Invasions, as well as comet strikes, crop failures, shortages and riots, civil uprisings, currency collapse, and other cataclysmic instabilities, are not met by survivalists coordinated to fight chaos, repel the invader, restore the status quo, and return control to vested legal or economic authorities. That is Hollywood storytelling, not survivalism.

In warrior scenarios, initial dialectic conflicts do not escalate into two-sided efforts at mutual annihilation but disintegrate into random fractious strife sliding toward total disorder. The economy fragments and falters into shortages and want. Warrior world systems of security disintegrate: the military, national guard, and police collapse, disband, fall back to protect their own homes and families. Soon the opposition follows suit. Enemy forces lose touch with their commanders, are cut off amid unfamiliar terrain, defect, or fight among themselves. Ravaging pillagers fanning out from the starving city after the food riots fracture into smaller and smaller bands as they reach the hinterlands, losing direction, leadership, objectives. The contesting forces are no longer monolithic, organized, or of homogeneous will. The distinctions between communism and capitalism, haves and have-nots, foreigner and native blur, contract, lose relevance. Ultimately all overreaching patterns of regulation and social control, all complex forms of exchange and procession rupture, bankrupt, and rust. Systemic ruin is complete. Hobbes had the idea, as did Weber.[10] So did Yeats.

> Things fall apart; the center cannot hold:
> Mere Anarchy is loosed upon the world,
> The blood-dimmed tide is loosened, and everywhere
> The ceremony of innocence is drowned;

> The best lack all conviction, while the worst
> Are full of passionate intensity. (1920, "The Second Coming")

Here is a world that needs fixing.

The age of automation, rational bureaucratic order, civic continuity, and overreaching regulation falters. In its wake, havoc, discord, and challenge. With ruination new priorities arise and with them new opportunities. New merit is found in the special talents of people like survivalists, those on the margins of modernity and beyond, in "primitive" consciousness. The name of this talent? The heart of practiced warrior skill? Lévi-Strauss, in *The Savage Mind* ([1962] 1966), calls it bricolage.

Bricolage

Bricolage is nonstandard work, an inclusive process of make-do, juggling the modalities of perception, assemblage, and craft in creative problem solving. The bricoleur is simultaneously scrounger of parts and materials, designer, artisan, and craftsperson. English is a poor vehicle for expressing this concept, offering only the jack-of-all-trades, the odd-job worker, the handyperson; but the meaning is more comprehensive. "Consider him at work and excited by his project. His first practical step is retrospective. He has to turn back to an already existing set made up of tools and materials, to consider and reconsider what it contains and, finally, and above all, to engage in a sort of dialogue with it, and before choosing between them, to index the possible answers which the whole can offer to his problem. He integrates all the heterogeneous objects of which his treasury is composed to discover what each could 'signify' and so contribute to the definition of a set which has yet to materialize" (Lévi-Strauss [1962] 1966, 18).

As lived experience, bricolage unifies fragments of opportunity, material assets, self-management strategies, contingent knowledge, emotional reserves and sensitivities, hunches and curiosities, and the dexterities of eye and hand. Bricolage calls forth the whole of the corporeal self in tests of honest skill and clear objectives wherein success or failure, praise or blame, are earned on merit alone.[11]

Kurt Vonnegut's *Player Piano* (1952) is a fantasy novel of repressive rational society torn apart, not by greed or malice or material inequities, but by a shortage of things to do that matter, by want of conditions calling forth the bricoleur's dialogue with the material world. Doug Harper's *Working Knowledge* (1987) is an astute ethnography of bricolage, the tale of Willie the all-purpose repairman in his conversation of gestures with old Saabs, hothouse heaters, grain transport devices, and the rest of what is missing, bent, or broken in rural Potsdam, New York.

Paul Theroux's fictional protagonist Allie Fox, in *The Mosquito Coast* (1982), employs bricolage as cultural critique, abandoning silicon, plastic, and fast food to bring locally made ice blocks to Central American jungle dwellers. MacGyver, the 1980s TV series hero, escapes evil-doers and metes out justice with the bricoleur's resourcefulness and his trusty Swiss Army knife.

Willie, Fox, and MacGyver are not survivalists, but they would likely be admired in survivalist company. Each is deft and ingenious. Each achieves notable results. Each is magnified in consequence by tool use. What of survivalists? What tools magnify their consequence? On hand are many items: chain saws, pickup trucks, axes, hoes, generators, grain and tool grinders, knives, wrenches, first aid kits, and other aids to motor vehicle upkeep, carpentry, household chores, gardening, and construction. These find their ways into the warrior collection of ready implements and figure in crisis-time scenarios. But one device stands out from the rest. One far exceeds the others in potential dramatic potency for the warrior world.

MEANS FOR THE OCCASION

One survivalist implement is distinctive in its ease of use, transportabililty, nominal cost, traditional acceptance, and frequent application in popular culture as a favored means of conflict resolution: firearms—symbolically and literally the most bang for the buck (see Gibson 1994, 81–100).

In much nostalgic and popular lore, America is a land of guns (see Wright 1975). Cop guns, robber guns, squirrel guns, buffalo guns, kill-the-Indian and conquer-the-West guns. Guns to defend family, country, and honor. Colt, Remington, and Winchester are as familiar to many Americans as Franklin, Bell, or Ford. Grandpa had a 30–40 Krag, dad a 30–30. Your brother got his .22 on his tenth birthday. They are part of our heritage, a constitutional right, some say, a daily necessity, claim others. For two terms of office the president's wife had a little one in her nightstand. Four in ten American households have firearms; six in ten survivalist homes do. But firearms are not all the same.

Fancy European hunting rifles show off Old World crafting in burnished steel, finely tooled wood, and expensive optics. These kill with a silent elegance, even respect. Death comes like service at a fine restaurant, unseen, unheard. Precise projectiles arrive ahead of their own sounds, delivering death from a deferential distance. So-called assault rifles are different, American, just good solid machinery. Some are made in Germany or Israel or Belgium or even China or Russia, but they are still essentially American: mass produced, efficient, tough plastic and gray stamped metal, easy to understand and handle. They dispense quick, clattering, noisy death like apples at the Automat, reliably, for pennies per death in one popular caliber. Just the thing for a practical man or woman with a lot of killing to do.

Survivalists do not do a lot of killing. In practice they do none at all. Gardening, auto repair, and carpentry tools get real use. But as *sign equipment,* props to buttress imaginative self-presentations (see R. Mitchell 1983, 117–34), firearms, particularly high-potency, accessorized, military weapons and the combat costumes and accessories that go with them, are without peer. Tom Mix and Humphrey Bogart got by with simple, over-the-counter handguns and strength of moral character. But no more. Contemporary Hollywood action heroes and survivalists alike create their best impressions with weapons of spectacular performance: bristling with gadgets, gushing lurid gouts of flame at mercuric rates of fire (see Gibson 1994, 81–100).

OCCASIONS FOR THE MEANS

As instruments of lethality, tools for killing, firearms require no further packaging. But as symbolic adjuncts to personal competence, as centerpiece stageware in survivalist scenarios, guns alone will not do. They must be set in suitable contexts, surrounded by what-if circumstances where hostility and martial strife, not starvation, disease, injury, or other debility, are the preeminent problems. Paradox worlds must be constructed where "defense" looms paramount, *where the core cultural product, the essential means of production, are the means of destruction.* As the institutionalized social order fails, restoration of order (though not institutional order) ascends in salience. Here survivalism can flourish, not in authentic contention, in armed battle with capable adversaries, but in the artful dramatizations of technical readiness, in displays of relevant tool-skill, in bricolage.

To put defense in the foreground, a little "luck" is built into the script. Chaos has limits. One candid but uncharacteristically crude warrior put it this way:

> If the next war goes full nuke, we're fucked, we're all screwed. The U.S. Government can't even protect the military very well, what chance do we, the civilians, have? Sure I have all the finest NBC [nuclear, biological, chemical] gear: the M17A1 gas mask, the medicines, the plastic suit, the pocket dosimeters, and all the other nuke paraphernalia. I train with it, but it's merely academic. In a biological or chemical attack, I may have a fighting chance. But nuclear—forget it. There is no way a person is going to have time to jump in a car and head for some bomb shelter somewhere

> in northern Michigan, or wherever, under a nuclear attack. The mentality is ridiculous. The big boys aren't talking about the firecrackers that were dropped on Japan, they're talking *megatons*; bombs equal to millions of tons of TNT. To tell you the truth, if they're going to drop a bomb on me, I'm going to make damn sure that I have a beer in one hand and a dame in the other. (quoted in Conti 1983, 69)

In warrior scenarios, full-scale nuclear war hardly ever happens. The omnibus horror of thermonuclear decimation is transformed into limited, mano-a-mano contests with susceptible human adversaries. Perhaps U.S. leaders, faced by an enemy with far superior strategic nuclear forces, will have no alternative but to accept an ultimatum of surrender and subsequent occupation. Alternatively, limited nuclear strikes could disable communications and the governmental infrastructure, and in the ensuing confusion foreign troops invade. In either case, global holocaust, the scourges of radiation, pestilence, disease, and climatic destabilization, are neatly exchanged for more conventional conflicts on familiar ground with warriors playing the part of Rambo-esque guerrillas. And Rambo is no Dr. Strangelove. Life remains possible but complex social organization does not.

Other luck comes from a division of labor. In crafting warrior scenarios survivalists segment action into discrete tasks. Not only is nuclear oblivion skirted in survivalist stories but the remainder of the cataclysmic effects are divided into problems of manageable proportion and negligible covariance. The first order of business, defense, is called for only during business hours. Marauder attacks come only when defenders are ready, boots laced, pants up, socks and ammunition dry, women and children safely sequestered.[12] In times of hunger, wild game abounds, unaffected by chemical or biological warfare agents or other possible side effects of systemic collapse and conflict. Nuts, berries, and edible roots are in season and easily distinguished from harmful counterfeits. Battle wounds to the enemy are humanely and quickly fatal; to self and compatriots, painless, neither lethal nor debilitating, aseptic, and conveniently inflicted on nonvital extremities in the company of attentive companions at locales close to long-term, safe shelter stocked with plenty of nutritious food and clean water. There are problems to be solved in disrupted times ahead but problems encountered on the survivalists' terms, turf, and timetables.

These were the basic assumptions behind Operation Aurora Borealis and the rest of the field training action in which I would join over the coming years. It was all there at the beginning but I could not see it, could not understand. Eleen and I focused on the manifest action, the maneuvers and commands and classroom exchanges. We listened for "politics" and "ideology," read the handouts, studied the lessons, watched the exercises, and tried to imagine how these could improve the odds of citizen-warriors facing an aggressive foe. We were quick to spot what we took for poor organization, passivity, and slow learning. What we missed was the subtler authentic action in the details all around.

Operation Aurora Borealis had little or nothing to do with preparations to repel real enemy hordes. It was an artful animation of sign equipment, a cooperative endeavor to bolster alternative identities. Why didn't anyone show any initiative beyond the assigned plan of action? Because the willing suspension of disbelief was hard to build and easy to break, as the episode at the bear hunter's trailer demonstrated. There were initiatives aplenty throughout the weekend, but they were technical and aesthetic, not tactical. What we took for a sloppy assemblage of equipment and clothing oddments was more than it seemed. This was no standardized army.

Everywhere among the participants' accoutrements were innovations, combinations, incremental modifications, improvements. Some alterations were the result of personal craft and effort. Hank's ghillie suit, hand sewn and decorated with much patience and ingenuity, was one example,[13] as was his mud facial camouflage. Tim suspended his hunting knife with plastic ties, upside down on his left pack strap, explaining that this was "commando style . . . for quick draw." Nic lectured about commercial camo makeup but wore his own concealment creation, a face covering fashioned from an old t-shirt, tie-dyed in a junior college art class to his interpretation of "Northwest forest" brown-gray-green. The shirt was knotted at the top to form a hood, then pulled over his head, leaving his thick corrective lenses protruding froglike through cutout eye holes. Over this went an elaborate webbing harness of suspenders and belt, from which were hung canteens, food packets, ammunition containers, and other supplies, dispensers, and gadgetry. On his right hip he carried a budget sidearm under reconstruction, a World War I British officer's Wembly .45 caliber revolver, complete with lanyard and canvas holster, a pawn shop bargain. Other firearms were modified in more and less obvious ways, not stripped for action but dressed for the occasion, for showing off to friends as well as holding off enemies. Hank's shotgun with its spray-can paint job, sawed-off barrel, and large firing capacity was the "best weapon for the point man in heavy brush," he claimed, and most agreed. Will's pistol looked like a conventional Colt .45, but by his account it had been extensively modified by the installation of a stronger recoil spring and high visibility sites, reworking of the trigger, and the addition of a larger safety-release knob, special grips, and other "combat" upgrades. In sum the modifications made the pistol "lots more accurate, no jams in a firefight." Doc's Ruger

Mini-14 rifle was replete with numerous after-market add-ons: a pistol-grip-equipped plastic and steel folding stock for "off-handed [one-handed] shooting and brush work," custom sights, a massive "flash suppressor" on the end of the barrel, and a "combat sling." Tim boasted humorously that we could have seen a pair of home-dyed camouflaged undershorts had we watched him at the right times. Other participants' packs, combat equipment harnesses, and belts featured various quick-release pouches, waterproof compartments, hidden pockets, attachments for water bottles, binoculars, first aid kits, ammunition magazines, weapons cleaning kits, compasses, energy bars, and at least one rosary.

Each selection, arrangement, combination, and accessory was explained by its creator to be the "most" rational, efficient, multipurpose, adaptable system one could devise, ideally suited to its owner's special survivalist needs. Participants had little to say about politics, but when it came to their equipage they were quick and eager to explain and recommend, at length and in detail. During the many breaks, rest periods, and interludes, participants passed equipment back and forth, showed and told, demonstrated, and gave credence to their firearm improvements and accoutrement choices with justifying stories. Everywhere, modest but concerted bricolage.

What of the skill tests listed on the score sheets? There were tests of skill, day and night, but they were different from what we thought they would be, different from what was listed. Not knowing what abilities really mattered, we could not judge or even identify the real questions or answers. Months afterward, at Hank's, I'd undergo some of that same testing and fail clumsily.

But that would be later. Terry Macy had already failed, or so he hinted. He was disappointed with the weekend. When he explained why, his meaning of survivalist action made more sense.

Macy

Disappointment was familiar to Macy. He had been disappointed before. He was disappointed on Aurora Borealis. He would be disappointed on Operation New Moon, the next "united" outing. The Badger, the radio, and command and control would break down, again. No one would keep score, again. There would be only one ambush, again. The handouts would go unread, again. Not very many people would show up. Just one person would get captured. Doc's twelve-year-old son, Eric, and Hank's granddaughter Sasha would cause trouble by being themselves—kids.

Macy was philosophical about these disappointments. As he prepared for the next outing we discussed his modest expectations and the good times when things "worked out" the way he wanted them. Tim liked to bring people together. Macy did, too. But he liked scattering them apart best of all.

If Tim was a one-man organization, Macy was a stand-alone holiday, the Fourth of July. The real war, Vietnam, was long over and real munitions were far from reach, so Macy improvised both. While Tim networked, Macy rigged connections and measured powder and fuse. For Macy, survivalism was a do-it-yourself fireworks show with gadgets and an attitude.

Operation Aurora Borealis was not Macy's best effort. "I've put on several operations, but the one up in Liberty was not near what we usually have." Thinking he was concerned about the classroom part of the weekend, I commiserated, one teacher to another, about inattentive students and unread assignments. "Yea, I guess," he affirmed weakly. But as Macy saw it, the real problem was the action, not the education. Not enough things blew up. "Usually I have lots of pyrotechnics, like mortar rounds coming in on ya and hidden stuff going off everywhere, so you've got flour and dust in the air and everybody's running for cover. I set up ambush ranges where targets pop up when you shoot at them. Some have rifle grenades—that's a tennis ball that shoots up, and it sounds like gunfire. It has firecrackers behind it."

He described electrical control systems and battery chargers, ways to hold a funnel while pouring gunpowder and tricks for maximizing explosion noise. I complimented Macy on his gadgeteering ingenuity and asked how he had developed these devices. He had learned as part of his Army Reserve assignment.

> That's what I was training in, putting together [simulations for troop practice], see, and we had all these survival manuals and stuff, and all I did was duplicate the stuff out of there only limit the pyro to just downcoming. I set up this range on Doc's property.
>
> There was this one day when, Hal, another friend of mine, he was running his [Army Reserve] platoon through [our rifle course], and they were knocking all my targets down. They knocked this one target down, and Rex, who was helping me, he fired up a rifle grenade and it landed about eight foot behind Hal and had a long fuse. So it started rolling downhill, and Hal doesn't see it. His lieutenant is about six feet away, and the other guys are close. He looks back and goes, "Aw, heck!" just as it goes "Poof!" . . . It was perfect! You know I didn't aim it. It landed right behind him. It got all five of them!

Like Tim, Macy imagined a popular survivalism. "So what happens is when the weather gets nice people start coming to me, they start beating on my door wanting an outing." But when pressed for attendance figures Macy admitted the uncertain popularity of his outings. As

Operation New Moon took shape I asked him how many participants he expected. He answered obliquely, wistfully, with a retrospective on an earlier operation. "Well, it depends. I'm not sure exactly. On [Operation] Deep Woods we were trying to limit it to fifty. Then we had about thirty people say they were coming, and about eight people showed up, so I've learned to be real skeptical. Maybe none. It does get a little discouraging. We went up there with enough pyro one time to send through sixty people, and we only set the range up one time. And it takes just as long, almost, for seven or eight as it does for fifty, except to rearm it. See all of our stuff, like I said, has firecrackers behind it; it has tennis balls, stuff for mortar attacks."

While Macy charged a small fee for participation in his exercises, he absorbed most of the costs. Doc, Macy, and the rest of the Nighthawks were better heeled than Tim or Hank or Jake. Doc had a thriving dental practice, Macy a substantial reservist's income and his own successful appliance store. They had property and health plans, steady incomes and assortments of survivalist equipment and supplies. Still, Macy's expenditures were not trivial. "I spend a lot. I've got hundreds of dollars tied up in wire to run down into the valley so all this pyro can be hooked up. And without a certain number of people I can't break even, not even for the powder and stuff like that."

We chatted about radios and ammunition, cleaning solvent and do-it-yourself survivalist gadgets. Making and fixing and invention were Macy's favorite survivalist pastimes, and weapons were his favorite object of attention. "Yeah, I love weapons. I rebuild them. I've got a lathe; I can make parts."

There was more to this remark than an enthusiasm for tinkering. The man or woman with know-how, a lathe, and another tool or two has expanded possibilities. Only a few small parts are needed to turn ordinary firearms into fully automatic weapons. Silencers, too, can be fashioned and fitted. But Macy didn't talk about that.

For Macy, the core of survivalism was not improved weaponry but the opportunities Operation Aurora Borealis and the other outings offered to wire and prime, sequence and choreograph, to put on a show of things that go "Poof" and "Swish" and "Bang" in the day and night. Sometimes the fuse was too short or the crowd too small, but when it all worked together, that was survivalism at its best.

PLEDGE OF ALLEGIANCE

With a nod and a hand signal from Penny, Hank called the September meeting of the Mount Rainier Rangers to order. Hank led the members and guests in the pledge of allegiance, facing the portable flag stand by the kitchen door. Penny stood up next with an opening prayer and visitor introductions.[14] Group business followed: the minutes of the last meeting, a progress report on the membership cards (logo redesign still in progress),[15] plans for a winter outing, a note and newsletter from the North American Patriots (a six-member Seattle-based group who read about the Rangers in the paper), the treasurer's report, (+$25.55), and an announcement of next meeting's topic, date, and time ("Caching Supplies," Hank and Penny's place, the twenty-second). All this took twelve minutes.

Next the main program, "Food Storage." Hank replaced the flag with an easel and a hand-drawn poster. Penny presented. "If the woman is gonna have to learn how to use guns," she instructed, then "the man is gonna have to learn how to cook." Smiling, she added, "Now pay attention." Penny's firing range performance could stand improving but at the easel she was an expert. She hit the points on her poster in rapid fire. "Get hard red winter wheat, it's got 11 percent protein, shouldn't have more than 10 percent moisture; rotate once a month; put in a bay leaf to kill the bugs." "Buy noninstant powdered milk; keep it in cans off the ground." "Store honey; use half as much as sugar." "Keep your salt in jars." "Boil water twenty minutes . . . six drops of Purex; wax the lids shut." "Dry pineapple, apples, pears, bananas in the oven, lowest setting, leave the door open; put them up in Seal-a-Meal bags." Sticky, sweet, dried banana samples were passed around the room for taste testing. "Read *Just Add Water* by Barbara Salsbury. It tells you how to dry practically anything." "Check those dates careful when you buy army surplus." "Keep a notebook with dates for everything you store." Total time for this lesson: nine minutes.

Hank and Penny ran clipped, efficient meetings. Two months later Hank would cover "Firearms" with a six-minute excerpt from a borrowed commercial video (Lieutenant Colonel Bruce Bissett's "The Armed Patriot," three-tape series, $49.95 each) and this advice: "You gotta treat guns with respect." "Check to see if it is loaded first." "Watch that muzzle." "Be sure the barrel and action is clear." "Be sure of your target." "Never point a gun at anything you don't want to shoot." "No horseplay with firearms." "No alcohol before or during shootin'." And when reloading ammunition, "Be sure to use small base dies, original factory size." Nic spoke up to remind us, "The best weapon to have is the one you have in your hands. Never leave it more than an arm's length away." To which Penny added, "Hank and me, we sleeps with ours close." Total class time, with reminders and additions: thirteen minutes on my tape recorder.

The following spring, "Organization and Leadership" went this way: Hank propped another hand-drawn poster on a chair in front of the room, this one showing boxes connected by lines, then pointed to each of the boxes, reading the job title and assigned name, if any, then pausing for comments. "Leader" and "Assistant Leader" topped the chart. "Recruitment Officer" appeared one rank below, followed by a lateral listing of other tasks: "Transportation," "Supplies," "Communication," "Training," "Security," "Intelligence," "All-out Defense." A few names were already pencilled in—Nic for recruitment, Penny for supplies. Hank modestly left himself off the list. Participants' comments included "Nice chart," and "Good idea," but no one volunteered to fill a position or suggested modifications. A long meeting: fourteen minutes. That was the last ever said publicly of group structure. Hank and Penny went back to running things, with Nic giving advice.

With the day's lesson complete, Penny invited the group into the kitchen for supper, the three-bean special (with too much salt) and potluck contributions from the rest of us. We squeezed around the kitchen table and countertops.

News: Penny was taking a course at the local Mormon church, she told us, "Cooking the Natural Way." "Sasha is getting celery and carrot sticks in her lunch and won't touch sugar now."

Rumors: Kermit mentioned that "concentration camps" are being readied on military bases around the country to contain dissident survivalists "soon." Hank heard from a workmate that remnants of Rajneesh Purim in the Antelope [Oregon] area had recently purchased "thirteen M-60s [large caliber machine guns] and fifty M-16s."

More correspondence: Hank passed around a letter he had received from Washington Senator Slade Gorton regarding activation of a "state militia" in times of emergency. Hank had urged the idea; Gorton was equivocal.

Aside: Hank told Eleen how to camouflage her blond hair with a nylon stocking.

Brag: The Wentworth garden was bountiful and all organic this year, Penny beamed. They canned twenty-three pints of carrots and sixteen of green beans last weekend, and they were drying forty pounds of apples from the backyard tree.

Hints: Penny handed out flyers featuring recipes for beef jerky, a trick for using baking soda solution to remove fish odor from hands and utensils, and a method for extracting excess salt from stew by adding raw potato (which didn't work with the three-bean dish).

Social events: The Todds get together on Thursdays with Paul and Susan Cervino to talk about retreats and the Constitution. All welcome.

Announcement: The Christian Patriots Defense League will be meeting in Missouri, gathering all the patriot survivalists in the country. The American Pistol and Rifle Association will hold a "Survival Training Seminar" for "Patriots—Marksmen—Survivalists for God, Family, Country, and Freedom" at that group's "academy" near Benton, Tennessee. Plan ahead. (I did. I went to both. No one else in the Rangers left the state.)

Invitation: Dale, an engineer turned contractor, offered the use of a medical office building he owned for meetings. It had comfortable foyer seating and was "easy to secure" on weekends when his wife, an anesthesiologist at the local hospital, was not using it to see patients. His wife was "not much interested" in survivalism, Dale admitted, but added that "he was in charge of plans" in his household.

Congratulations #1: Hank did it! After thirty years smoking cigarettes, a pack and a half a day, he had kicked the habit for two weeks so far thanks to Penny's herbs and haranguing. Penny, aside to Eleen: "I still give him his cigarette money with his allowance." Addendum: The smoking ban would last a month, the coffee, sugar, and red meat that went with the cigarettes would come back in two months.

Congratulations #2: Hank won first prize for best costume at the neighborhood Halloween party. He went as a survivalist—ghillie suit, rifle, gas mask, and all.

Item: Nic still does not have a car, but his Wembly .45 is back from the gunsmith, freshly blued.

"Got the Wembly with you?" Kermit asked. "Lemme see it." With that, another ritual began. The women (mostly) tended the dishes and leftovers. The men (mostly) headed for the living room to circle on the floor and sofas. It was time for show and tell. It was time for testing.

Testing

"Hank, why don't you show them your birthday present," Penny invited. Hank grinned, disappeared for a minute down the hall, and returned with a paper sack in one hand and a quiz item in the other. Taxonomy was the first test: What was Hank holding?

RM: [silently] "Phew! What a nasty looking little gun!" Grade: F.
Deborah: "That's a cute gun, Hank!" Grade: D.
John: "Nice. Colt . . . the paratrooper model." Partial credit. Grade: C.
Dale: "Say, a CAR-15, short barrel, looks like the welded flash hider [obvious] with pistol grip [obvious]. Where did you get that?" All correct but no extra credit. Grade: B.
Kermit: "Did you get it in .223, too?" Grade: A+.

The bricoleur knows his tools and materials, is able to categorize and type, classify and order, from a few subtle details. Cabinetmakers can tell walnut from mahogany, cherry from red cedar, at a glance. Mechanics know if the bolts are standard or metric, galvanized or stainless, recognize their thread pitch, width, and socket size by quick inspection. Kermit knew survivalist tools. Kermit knew guns.

Kermit could ask, "Did you get it in .223, too?" because he was able to identify Hank's rifle precisely by noticing its barely discernible idiosyncrasies and because he was broadly familiar with the weapons industry. It took me nearly a year and much study of firearms to understand the skill and reasoning behind Kermit's question.

Kermit recognized Hank's rifle as similar to the Colt CAR-16, the compact, folding stock, short-barreled assault rifle issued to elite U.S. military units. Similar, but not identical. Kermit's practiced eye noticed a difference, a slight variation from standard, in the fluting pattern on the sides of the protruding ammunition magazine. What could this mean? If it was not a standard Colt magazine, what might it be? To judge correctly, Kermit needed to know a good deal about the global small arms business. He did. He knew that Olympic Arms was the only manufacturer in the world making a Colt-framed weapon that could utilize nonstandard magazines. Kermit knew that as accessories to their model OA AR-15/CAR-15, Olympic Arms sold interchangeable barrels, receivers, and magazines. He knew these were available in three calibers: 9 mm, .223 (5.56 NATO), and the Russian 7.62 × 39 mm. As the weapon was obviously a Colt frame design, and the magazine showing was not the standard Colt type for .223 U.S. military round, nor anything like the much smaller, straight-sided 9 mm magazine, it must be the Russian 7.62 × 39 mm.

Now a strategic judgment. As Russian 7.62 ammunition is less common in North America than standard-issue .223, and assault weapons are intended to be practical instruments, it is possible Hank had barrels and receivers in both calibers. Hence the question, "Did you get it in .223, too?" If you were good at this, like Kermit, you could do taxonomic assessments from across the room.

"Yep," answered Hank, pulling the .223 barrel and receiver out of the paper bag.

While Kermit basked in the group's admiration for his keen analysis, Hank's rifle system began its rounds of inspection. Soon it was joined by weapons brought along by other show-and-tellers. Usually three or four newly acquired or upgraded firearms circulated among six or seven active participants at each meeting. This passing, too, was full of meaning. As a circulating weapon was taken up for examination, another test began: anatomy this time.

Bricolage depends not only on knowledge of instruments and material types but familiarity with the kinesthesia of tool use, the handling of materials and execution of standardized procedures. The arms and back and rooted legs know the strengths and motions necessary to heave and haul. Fingers know the compass and heft of tools, their friction and grip on surfaces, where things go and fit, the sequences, the points of delicacy and needed forcefulness, the tensions of parts properly aligned.

Firearms elicit such sensitivities in two circumstances. Most obvious is marksmanship, a skill rife with evolutionary contradiction. Proficient combat firearms use requires behavior in stark contradiction to the instinctive responses of fight-or-flight. In moments of danger, the firearm user must overcome both responses, limiting all physical movement to gentle incremental pressure on trigger mechanisms while holding the rest of the body—legs, trunk, hands and arms, and most critically the eyes—in firm alignment facing the enemy hazard. Novice firearms users are frequently overcome in such moments of stress, discharging their weapons quickly without careful aiming, or without any aiming at all, even using long guns as clubs or throwing handguns at adversaries. Firearms use in movies of the Old West is often depicted in conjunction with other vigorous action: running, jumping, riding horses, leaping from or to objects, and so forth. In reality, most of these secondary movements, while cathartic, would put an end to practical marksmanship. To shoot straight you have to hold still, sight carefully, and squeeze, not jerk, the trigger. This is one manifestation of the bricoleur's kinesthetic sensitivity in the realm of firearms, but the lesser one for survivalists. Few have faced real enemies in battle and none do so on a routine basis. The enemy is not here yet. Shooting takes place at the range or in the woods, at innocuous and usually stationary targets. So a survivalist's aptitude in combat marksmanship remains unknown. But there is another side to firearms competency, more obvious and common.

Firearms must be periodically serviced, cleaned, lubricated, and inspected for wear. In this process, patterns of powder, copper, lead, and brass residue are diagnosed, then removed. Points of metal-on-metal contact are inspected for burnishing, shine, burrs, rust, and other patterns of wear, stress, and alignment. Inspections and cleaning require disassembly, "field stripping," to disengage and separate those parts accessible to cleaning and service without special tools. Each firearm comes apart a different way, requiring knowledge of the type and of standard procedure as well as experience in the dexterities involved.

Another test. Dale handed Nic his pistol. Nic glanced at it briefly and then started his test. First, taxonomy. "Stainless Randall. Hummmm," he mumbled, indicating he recognized the weapon as a high-quality reproduction of the 1911 Government model Colt .45 manufactured in stainless steel by Randall Firearms. Nic's words returned to what he was saying before Dale passed the pistol, discussing the sorts of retreat vehicles he preferred: motorcycles, mountain bikes, small trucks. But his hands also spoke as they fieldstripped the weapon, answering questions about his skills and knowledge.

First, unload. Dale left in a full magazine and "one in the pipe" (a round chambered), so first remove the magazine, then pull the slide back to eject the live cartridge. Next, cock the trigger. Prop the pistol vertically, barrel upward, on a hard surface. Use the cartridge magazine to depress the edge of the recoil spring plug until it comes even with the slide and the slot in the recoil spring is exposed. Now use the index finger of the other hand to turn the barrel bushing out of the slot. (At this point the recoil spring is held in place with only thumb pressure, and if released, will send the spring and plug flying across the room or into the face of the disassembler.) Next, position the slide stop in a small disassembly notch, and push it laterally out of the frame, allowing the barrel link, recoil spring guide, then the barrel and slide themselves, to come off in succession.[16] I saw Nic glance down only twice during this process, and he never stopped talking about getaway vehicles. With all the parts spread on the table, he picked up the recoil spring and guide and commented, "Wilson Combat" and "Nice beavertail," referring correctly to the manufacturer of the spring assembly and the quality and design of the hammer—taxonomic extra credit. Then resuming his monologue, but again without looking, he reassembled the pistol and handed it to John, loaded, but without one in the pipe.

There is a subtle adroitness derived of thorough understanding that allows a survivalist bricoleur to pick up a weapon, perform routine but not always simple weapon disassembly, comment upon the condition of submechanisms, maintenance regimen, and likely firing characteristics, then put it back together and pass it on. The object of this action is not merely to separate the parts and reunite them in proper sequence. The object is style, performance with a studied nonchalance indicating familiarity and experience. The ability to roll cigarettes by hand (or one handed) and the card-handling skill of a practiced poker player are similar ritual authority claims. Those observed in casual, accurate field stripping and analysis of weapons are accorded expertise in broader, unseen realms of survivalist prowess. The part stands for the whole; field stripping skill substitutes in good measure for combat marksmanship. This is not all status work.

In the usual sense, who we are derives from our interpretations of the behaviors of referent alters toward us. Identity arises in a conversation of gestures with social actors. Mead intended this, certainly. But he intended more. In *The Philosophy of the Act* (1938) he extends the notion of alter to the inanimate, to objects with which we may interact as embodied as well as socially abstracted selves.

Mead located human corporality, our senses of selves as bodies, in just such work, the "kinesthetic sensation" of objects embraced, grasped, fingered, pressed upon, wherein the experiences of physical objects and physical selves coderive. The self "become[s] a physical object over against the physical thing," in the same manner that "in social conduct . . . we stimulate ourselves to act toward ourselves as others act toward us and thus identify ourselves with others and become objects to ourselves" (1938, 428, 429). We touch and turn and weigh in hand, and from these textured resistances, derive senses of our own physical scope and attributes. Bricolage, utilitarian eroticism, extends self-discovery into the material realm.

We watch the impression management, as well we should. The weapons go round and round, are taken apart, reviewed, reassembled, passed on. Others scrutinize, judge, rank. This process is a central part of survivalism, but not all of it. There is also a quieter conversation of gestures, in the subtle talk of arms and palms and fingertips with the objects of nature and culture at hand through which survivalists come to know themselves.

The emphasis on weapons among warrior survivalists is common but not exclusive. Other tools, materials, or implements applicable to the bricolage of survival problem solving are amenable to dramatized skill displays. In a year and a half of meetings I saw two chain saws, a knife sharpener, a grain grinder, ammunition reloading equipment, hand tools, and even a pair of hiking boots and items of clothing circulate in this fashion. When an item could not be disassembled for inspection it would be described as to function and performance potential.

The information thus provided was always appreciated but did not always appreciate the provider's status. As an ex-mountaineering gear salesman my explanation that the boots circulating at one meeting were of poor quality, "rough-out, split-hide construction, Littleway welted, with a plastic midsole," were correct but advanced my standing little, as the facts of boot making were far outside the group's common information pool. Still, warrior gatherings were tolerant and inclusive of novel ideas and implements. Skill demonstrations of all sorts were granted polite attention. Nic occasionally displayed his survivalist prowess in diverse ways. At one meeting he brought books instead of weapons to pass around; a vintage *Boy Scout Handbook* and a *Red Cross Canoeing Manual,* but also Freud's *Civilization and Its Discontents* and the *Complete Works of Shakespeare.* He patiently introduced and explained each volume as to its interests and survivalist merits while the books circulated in the usual fashion, each respectfully examined if not thoroughly read.

In retrospect, there was testing aplenty on Operation Aurora Borealis. Taxonomy tests. Anatomy tests. Tests of skill and knowledge regarding weapons, accessories, equipment. What is it? How does it work? Do you know how to handle it? What is it good for? What are its limits? How has yours been improved? Can you help me with mine? Much of this questioning and answering was object mediated, demonstrative, and part nonverbal. All of it was unwritten.

Questions, answers, innovations, applications, praise, criticism, astonishment, learning, day and night, everywhere. Staring at our score sheets and handouts, waiting for the paper-and-pencil exam that never happened, Eleen and I missed it all.

Allies

Hank had one more announcement. The Rangers had received another letter, this one from a Dave Ringman, leader of the Cascade Valley Force (or CVF, as they came to be known), another nearby group. It was an urgent, pompous invitation. The Cascade Valley Force members had seen the local newspaper article, the one in which Sasha and Nic hiding in the grass yelling "gotcha" had turned into "They Drill for Postwar Chaos" with the spiffy posed picture. CVF met several times, argued, weighed risks, and finally decided to break their "secrecy" and contact outsiders. Their worry? Somehow, in a time of crisis, the Cascade Valley Force might run afoul of the (fearsome) Mount Rainier Rangers when both groups went "operational" and were maneuvering toward their respective retreats. A "leaders" meeting was arranged. Within three weeks, Eleen and I were promoted to the "leader corps" and went along. A Cascade Valley Force ally, Freedom Brigade, also attended. Including the two children under twelve, it was the largest gathering of survivalists I ever saw in a private home: nineteen people.

Technical, functional discourse is found throughout survivalism but is concentrated in some settings. Imagine a small group built around a dozen or fewer unrelated males, their primary group affiliations being workmates, neighbors, and friends. High school education, noncombat military service experience, and technical or skilled labor employment in an urban area are characteristic. They salute the flag, vote with the union, and mow the lawn or go hunting on Sundays. Wives and children are often active practical participants but are rhetorically iconified into hapless dependents, justifying preoccupations with "defense" preparations.

The Cascade Valley Force shared barbecues and fence lines on a suburban cul-de-sac. All members had other things in common: camouflage uniforms, distinctive shoulder patches, .45 caliber semiautomatic pistols, military assault rifles, and a twenty-eight page manual of operating procedures. Consider the manual. Again, texts belie action.

Eight manual pages related to leadership, promotion, meritocratic skill-testing, duty assignments, and organization of a complex, nine-tiered hierarchy of ranks from "commander" to "infantryman." So the manual said. Actual behavior? No member of the Cascade Valley Force had ever passed any of these tests; none had ever been given. The ranking scheme contained nine strata; Cascade Valley Force had only seven members.

The members of Cascade Valley Force also shared CB radio frequencies, occasional outings, target practice, inspections, and the last part of the manual—a detailed crisis-time escape plan of Olympian scope. If the day-to-day peacetime actions of the CVF need be circumspect, their plans need not be so. Adventure was to be had, at least in bold and heroic imagination. Seven they were, but seven with a plan. When the time came, they would move east to their retreat area in the forested mountains 150 miles away. The move required several key actions. There was a plan to attack and loot a food warehouse and a plan to assault and sack two police stations for additional weapons. But these were minor plans. The crux was uniting the troops, two from the north, five from the south, across the great river. Some time later I made this trip myself, to look at the place where the crucial action would take place. The proposed crossing had been used before.

Bridge of the Gods

Geologists tell us that a thousand years ago the mighty Columbia River was blocked by a great landslide 120 miles from the ocean, forming a vast freshwater sea stretching across the inland prairies as far as Idaho. In time, the river grew tired of confinement, burrowed under the slide blockage, and flowed once again to the sea, leaving a great stone arch that spanned the river from shore to shore.

Native peoples called this place the Great Cross Over, and later, the Bridge of the Gods. The Bridge of the Gods was important to the people, so the Great Spirit Manito sent Loo-Wit, the wise woman, to guard it. He also sent his son Klickitat (Mount Adams), the totem maker, to stand on the north shore, and his son Wyeast (Mount Hood), the singer, to hold the south. The Evil One played upon the sons' youth and virility, luring them into jealous quarreling over beautiful Squaw Mountain. In their intemperance, they growled and grumbled and shook the earth.

Loo-Wit tried to stop the fighting and did what she could to save the bridge. She bravely stood her ground, though battered and burned by the white hot rocks the giants hurled at each other. The brothers belched forth clouds of black smoke, which hid the sun and darkened the snows. The forests were scorched by fire, the earth shaken to its foundations. In the end, even Loo-Wit could not hold the bridge against the sons of a great god. The arch split, collapsed, and carried her to her doom.

Today another bridge spans the same shores, upstream from a modern day obstruction, the Bonneville Dam. The new steel and concrete cantilever structure stretches 1,858 feet across the Columbia Gorge, 135 feet above the water. Loo-Wit and the sons of Manito have been replaced by a twenty-four-hour tollhouse and regional police relay stations on both sides of the river.

The Cascade Valley Force had plans to capture this key interstate highway bridge with purloined police munitions and crafty tactics, a pincer action, five from the north, two from the south,[17] followed by dynamite to prevent the hordes of crisis-spawned refugees from following. It was all detailed in the manual. The CVF members talked about the plan with satisfaction, showing us pages of maps and lists of supplies, timetables, radio frequencies, and sketches of troop deployment. "It should work OK," said Dave. "It could work," offered Ron. I wondered aloud how so few could persevere against so many, how they could succeed amid the likely crisis-time chaos and strife and turmoil of the region's million and a half fleeing, crazed, wounded rioters, roaming bands, disintegrating army and national guard units, and the police forces of two states. Dave's answer was simple. While the masses might be many, they would be disorganized, in disarray, unfocused, a clot of confusion. The Cascade Valley Force had a plan, was ready, proactive. The Cascade Valley Force were survivalists, a singular node of rationality and disciplined foresight amid breakdown. The plan, their skills, and the right tools would see them through. Homer could devise no more heroic drama nor fanciful fiction.

The joint meeting also featured a potluck meal, and as conviviality grew, a surprise show-and-tell. By ice cream and coffee it was clear that the groups would get on well enough. One by one, amid friendly smiles and let-me-show-you-mine talk, the Cascade Valley Force members pulled out their weapons, the tools needed to make their plan work: eight assault rifles similar to Hank's prized new CAR-15. Rifles emerged from closets, from behind chairs, from beneath the living room sofa, and from other close-by sequestering places. Dave's eleven-year-old son brought his from his room. The sound of an ammunition magazine being stripped from a weapon, then the rattle of a dechambered .223 round bouncing on linoleum, came from the kitchen, as did Dave's wife, JoAnn, waving her rifle amiably in a greeting reminiscent of Penny and her spoon. All weapons had been stored loaded. The Cascade Valley Force had been ready for trouble from the Mount Rainier Rangers. Eleen and I were white knuckled and speechless as this hidden arsenal came into view.

It was agreed that the CVF and the Rangers would share planning information. Hank was appointed the joint "intelligence officer," Dave, the CVF leader, was charged with developing further "plans." The Freedom Brigade would handle "training."[18]

Many persons at this meeting were previously unknown to each other. Names and faces were not firmly linked across groups. Dave moderated the formal discussion, calling upon people in turn and by name for opinions and suggestions. But the name of one Freedom Brigade member obviously escaped him. Sensing Dave's predicament, the member smiled and offered help. "Just call me 'Blackie.' I'm the only one here."

Just then, Dave remembered the member's name, John. But John's remark disturbed him. He grew stern, forceful, and turned to speak to the group at large. This was a policy issue. "John, *we do not treat people like that*! Never! We are a united force. We are all the same!"

The message was emphatic. John carried an expensive HK93 German assault rifle with quality optics and had handled the pass-the-weapons test with élan. That was enough. The detail that John was, as Maya Angelou might describe him, of a "plum blue" complexion, while the rest of the room was Pacific Northwest pale white, was neither relevant nor admissible. Survivalism was all about enemies and allies, not black and white, and Cascade Valley Force would tolerate no overt racism.

The meeting adjourned, having reduced tension between the groups and set a vague cooperative agenda. Hank left pleased with his new assignment as "intelligence officer." Eleen and I had already seen a sample of his intelligence work at our first meeting with the Rangers.

Intelligence Report

After the guns had made their rounds at Hank's place and the kitchen had been put in order, the Todds, then Dale, then the rest started drifting out, thanking the hosts, exchanging final bits of information, tips, sources, and contact numbers, then bidding good-bye. By four o'clock Eleen and I were again on the living room sofa, alone with Hank and Penny, looking about.

On the wall by the kitchen, mementos: A hand-painted plaster of paris eagle holding a shield, over olive branches and arrows. Beneath the eagle's left wing, a picture of Sasha in her Girl Scout uniform. Beneath the right wing, Sasha's baseball team. At the east end of the room, a large free-standing woodstove of the type popular in the Pacific Northwest, where coniferous wood is a cheap fuel supply (and a serious source of air pollution). "It's for heat and cooking when the power goes out," Penny told me. I had two doubts about how often the stove was needed or used in this modern, all-electric home. First, I checked with the local power company. They reported no service interruptions of note in Hank's neighborhood within the past five years. Second, the incendiary potential of the full kerosene lantern on the floor a few inches away from the stove suggested that the stove had not been lit at least recently. Against the south wall, the television—top clean and knobs dusty—another little-used appliance. While the television is on one-third of the day in a typical American household, Hank and Penny were survivalists, not typical Americans. They watched little television, "maybe three, four hours a week" by Hank's estimates. Favorite shows? None. They watched the news sometimes or kids' shows with Sasha. But for the rest, for sports, game shows, soap operas, and other "entertainment," they had no time or interest. "Watching TV, you just sit and do nothing. It's all make believe," Penny offered. Survivalism is more compelling, more real.

HANK AND PENNY

I asked Penny and Hank about their backgrounds. Penny, then fifty-four, was born in the isolated logging hamlet of Valsetz, Oregon, at the height of the Depression. She was athletic and self-assertive as a child, taking over her brother's paper route when she was eight, and when the family moved to Salem during her high school years, becoming active in sports. She ran sprints and hurdles on the track team, joined the swim team, and was captain of the girls basketball team. Married at age eighteen, she had one child, then separated from her husband. A second marriage lasted "three or four years," and she was in the process of divorce when she met Hank—by accident.

Hank had gone to visit his ill mother in the hospital. In the next bed was Penny, recovering from a near-fatal car crash. The car in which she was riding had driven off the road. She had been thrown through the windshield and then, incredibly the doctors said, had continued *through* an aluminum panel fence. Shredded abdomen, ruptured bladder, fractured pelvis, compound fracture of left femur, fractures of both forearms, nose flattened onto left cheek, and a right Achilles tendon severed were the main injuries. "I was in the dying room, I remember that. They put me in the dying room." She had kept the hospital bill and police reports as mementos and showed us both. She required 135 stitches and twelve and a half weeks in the hospital, lost five feet of intestine, and had to pay $586.27 in medical bills. The fence was destroyed.

Hank was smitten but shy. Penny was vivacious but invalid. The hospital evened the odds for wooing. Hank could always find her "in," and with his mom in the same room he had an excuse for visiting. He began bringing flowers for both ladies in his life and spending long hours with Penny in quiet bedside talk. His mother approved and encouraged. He and Penny were married within the year and soon had a daughter of their own.

Hank, six years younger than Penny, was born in a small town in Oklahoma but moved with his mother, at age four, to the Sacramento, California, area. He never met his father in person, only through a single Christmas time telephone call and his mother's accounts. Dad and the call were surprises, Hank said. Dad turned out to be likable and caring. He also turned out to be something else, something his Mom had not told him and which Hank did not tell us for many years. Hank dropped out of school at age fifteen, moved north, and worked in the Oregon logging industry. Then he joined the army and for three years during the Korean War served stateside as a warehouse worker. Returning to civilian life, he married Penny in 1957 then went to work as a welder for a large logging firm.

These were some the word-facts Hank and Penny spoke. But speech, especially targeted, "answer-my-question-please" speech, is not always the best way of knowing. Penny's served well enough. Her speech was robust, full-sentenced, enthusiastic, and easily heard down the hall. She had a warmhearted way with children and animals but could also get the church volunteers organized and keep the meeting on schedule as effectively as she used to call for a full-court press in high school basketball. Hank was quieter, less certain with words.

If you listen long enough to Hank he will talk of technology (admiringly), common sense (occasionally), religion (uncertainly), children (happily), women (respectfully), and other things. If this talk is taken out of context, in parts and bits, in question-answer interviews or other occasional snatches, much of its sense is left behind. Hank's speech is neither long nor eloquent. Less than a decade of formal education and thirty years of manual labor have left him with only a small vocabulary and practical grammar. Excerpts and quotes from Hank's speech show only the technical weaknesses, not the merit of his whole discourse. But give him time. Listen for more than and hour, more than a day. Come back later, next week, next month and listen again. Listen with tender ears to talk on the edges, around the campfire, late at night, over coffee. Put the pieces together.

At our third meeting Hank exclaimed with pride, "Sasha played 'Happy Birthday' for me on her computer!" An accomplishment indeed for a self-taught ten-year-old with only a beginning programmer's manual and a crude tone generator on her ancient CP/M-based machine.

Reflections on grandchildren and loss: "Sasha and Adele [Sasha's thirteen-year-old sister] will be with us all the time now," is all he said at one meeting. Later we learned why. Twenty-six years after Hank met Penny following her near-fatal auto accident, their daughter was crushed to death in a car when her drunken husband struck a power pole. The father lived but cared poorly for Sasha and Adele. First Sasha came to join the Wentworth household, now Adele, too, needed a new home. More sadness: The home was not perfect. Adele's stay was short, her delinquencies frequent. Next meeting: Adele went "back to her father." By the meeting after that, she had moved to a church-run, supervised foster facility because she "wasn't following the rules. She was flunking school, too."

Hank's voice did not break when he told of this grandparenting failure, but there was the no-sound of emptiness in his words. To hear Hank, listen to the whole speaking, to the meaning woven of short stout threads of simple words and strong feeling. Patience is as important as a tape recorder for this task.

Penny took us on tour about the house, showing off the garden, the food storage pantry, canned goods, wheat and barley and rice and other foodstuffs sealed in plastic buckets, stacked in the back hall and along the garage wall. Then, to Hank's room, his den and study, the intelligence center for the Mount Rainier Rangers.

FACT FINDING

Information of sorts was everywhere at Ranger meetings. Likely to catch the eyes of newcomers were the glossy commercial survivalist publications, some brought by visitors, some from Hank's subscriptions.

In the early '80s local newsstands began to fill with survivalist publications. Venerable *Soldier of Fortune* was joined by *New Breed, Survive*[19] (later called *Guns and Action*), *Survival Weapons and Tactics* (*S.W.A.T*, later titled *Special Weapons and Tactics*), *Survival Guide* (formerly *Shooter's Survival Guide*), *Commando, The Combat Survivalist,* and other short-lived periodicals. By the early 1990s this group had been transformed and winnowed to three, and ultimately to one principal publication, the again-renamed *American Survival Guide,*[20] at century's end the survivalist staple, along with a half-dozen gun magazines.

The success of these publications depended upon their ability to interest readers while serving as vehicles for the advertising of technical aids to survival enterprise. An analysis of a seven-year sample of *American Survival Guide*[21] revealed that about half the magazine's content was devoted to infomercials, "staff articles" and "product reports," thinly disguised promotionals for merchandise advertised elsewhere in the issue.[22] About half of this merchandise was weapons related. The product mix among these types of magazines has changed over the years and continues to evolve (for example, "assault" weapon articles were replaced by "sniper" rifle reviews after passage of the Brady Bill). Style has remained more consistent than content: florid, sensational, conspicuous.

Readers might learn that "Ultra Shock" bullets produce "greater wound cavities with more penetration," that the Nighthawk carbine offers "firepower, fast and furious in 9 mm Parabellum," that the "Foxfire high-tech crossbow reflects silent lethality," and that the features of the "Urban Skinner" push dagger "make it possible to sever major muscle groups in a single slash . . . and easily pierce the rib cage." There were articles and ads for custom hollow-handled survival bayonets costing up to two hundred dollars each, umbrella and sword canes, and other knives and daggers disguised as lipsticks, fountain pens, belt buckles, and credit card holders. Defensive paraphernalia, available through mail-order catalogs as well as magazines, included "bulletproof" vests, caps, clipboards, and even umbrellas. For stealth there were camouflage-patterned shirts, pants, jackets, walking sticks, and caps. Of less obvious utility were camouflaged handkerchiefs, pens, Bic lighters, hiking shorts, boots, shoelaces, suspenders, dress ties, footlockers, underwear, cardboard folding personal commodes, and diaper covers. The response of airport security personnel to a passenger carrying an "airline proof" jungle-pattern camouflage attaché case "that can fit easily under the seat" may only be imagined. These, along with tear gas projectors, GI-style dog tags, blow guns, night-vision gunsight systems and goggles, used armored personnel carriers, and booklets on "Secrets of the Ninja," "How to Avoid Electronic Eavesdropping," "How to Find a Girl to Love You," and "Torture, Interrogation, and Execution" were all offered to the interested reader.

Dramatic stuff. And the rest? Magazines advised as well as advertised. Approximately one-quarter of the total articles were contributed by nonstaff writers and pertained to adventures, outings, destinations, hazards, and remedies pending and possible: group dynamics of assault teams, natural disaster preparedness, and knife design; currency collapse, home power generation, and herbal wound treatment; insurgency, invasion, maximizing sniper effectiveness, and making soap at home.[23] Again, plenty of drama. What sense do survivalists make of all this?

Should we read these articles as convenient samples of characteristic survivalism? Only if researcher convenience outweighs survivalists' actual behavior. After all, Hank and the others participated in Operation Aurora Borealis and read "Operation Azimuth Bearing." They could judge firsthand the accuracy of *American Survival Guide* journalism and, by implication, the worth of the other survivalist magazines. They knew what "true survivalists" were. Gathering intelligence was not so easy as taking a trip to the newsstand. It required research, a culling of sources, and help from one's friends. Many helped.

At Ranger meetings nearly everyone brought something informative to share: handouts, advertisements, news clippings, finds on bargain supplies, letters from other groups, or personal correspondence. At one meeting twenty-eight pieces of material comprising 161 photocopied pages were shared by the nine persons in attendance. Kermit brought literature from the American Pistol and Rifle Association: "Communism vs. Gun Ownership," "When Will it Happen?" (the Russian ultimatum, that is), "Will the Government Confiscate Your Guns?" "The Right of the People," and four more. The Todds handed out a guide to building solar stills at retreats entitled "Water!" and a "Personal Survival Equipment Checklist." Ron passed out copies of a flyer he had received from a friend in Spokane describing the "Countelpro Sting," in which the CIA infiltrates survivalism by using the phony "Mountain Church" in Cohoctah, Michigan, and the "Secret Underground Army of God" to lure patriot survivalists into committing crimes, then launches a national crack down on survivalism and employs repression tactics across the country.[24] Ron had not read the whole flyer but had copies for everyone. Dale came with a six-page "research paper" on "The Right to Bear Arms" that defined various forms of constitutionally legitimated militia —"Organized Militia," "Unorganized Militia," and "Militia of the Residue" (see Mitchell 2000)—with quotes and sources from George Washington and Alexander Hamilton. Dale also brought ammunition reloading hints, though he did no reloading himself. Nic brought a must-have medicine list. And so it went.

The sociologists were at first fascinated by all of this material, the lurid magazines, the conspiratorial flyers, the odd advisories and warnings. We asked for copies, borrowed others, started our own subscriptions, and at home pored over our bounty. Here was text, the written word, the "facts" of survivalism, quotable material that was sensational, stationary, ready for sociological analysis. Again, we missed the point.

Hank's room was full of information and the means to obtain more. Printed matter, the handouts, flyers, brochures brought and sent to him, the commercial magazines, and the private newsletters from other groups were stacked by type and date on brick and board shelves, on Hank's small pine desk, and in labeled piles on the floor along the walls. He had read some of these but remained uncertain. Personal correspondence, from Tim Dalkins, Kermit, and Jim Jones, was valued and given more attention but never totally accepted at face value. Hank, like other survivalists, wanted to discover for himself. The "intelligence officer," and every survivalist is one to a degree, is less an arbiter of final fact than a librarian, an archivist, an organizer of data and themes others may choose from and make sense of in their own ways. The ritual of passing along interesting tidbits of information brings the group together in a mutual tolerance of diverse views. Sharing data is good survivalist citizenship, not a way of asserting one truth over another. Much passing along, pamphleteering, and redistribution is done as a courtesy, relatively independent of content.

The object of survivalism is never the discovery of new authorities to replace old ones, the supplanting of one superordinate metanarrative with another. It may appear so from the outside, when only one voice is heard or when deanimated texts are considered out of context. But always survivalism is a way to accomplish the creative renarration of the self and often one's companions into tales of aesthetic consequence. The actions of gathering and disseminating, of passing along, photocopying, mailing, handing out are essential manifestations of survivalist identity. Survivalists have information to share and the generosity and will to share it. But they don't have the ultimate truths, the final facts, the last words. What the handouts and copies say is not what they mean. Content is not so important. Sharing is. As intelligence officer, Hank had a particular responsibility to share. He exploited all the means he understood for gathering information, and some means he did not understand.

On the bookshelf next to Hank's desk was what he judged to be an important tool, a Bearcat scanner complete with a large external speaker that at high volume could be heard throughout the house. He explained its benefits. With this instrument he would have an edge, early news, early warnings from foreign broadcasts, especially Radio Moscow, Radio Beijing, and Radio Havana. They would give him information the television news would not report, perhaps information our government would not publicly reveal. Hank had acquired the scanner at a garage sale two months before and spent twenty minutes or more every evening listening, trying to hear the Russians and the Chinese and the Cubans. But something was wrong. Though he had mounted an external antenna on the roof and tuned carefully through each band, the broadcasts he wanted never came through. They never would. The Russian and other broadcasts are elsewhere, in the shortwave bands, not among the local police, fire, ambulance and air traffic communications the Bearcat was designed to receive. But Hank did not know this.

For Hank, the scanner did not help, television reporting was dubious, and computer-facilitated communication the realm of young people. That left the flyers, the handouts, the correspondence, and imagination. Lately Hank had used his imagination. He noticed some consistency in the reports he uncovered, a trend, perhaps a pattern. He began to compare one detail with another, track events. It was his job as intelligence officer to find hazards, so he found some.

Above the shelves, the west wall of the den was filled with a map of North and Central America, from Alaska to the Panama Canal, with the United States projected large in the center. Hank had annotated the map with findings and facts, with notations in permanent ink and erasable pencil. Major military bases were marked (including the ones Kermit said held concentration camps). George Washington's prophetic triangle (another of Kermit's stories about end-times and likely salvation of southern states) was drawn in, as were strategic points and routes of supply and transport. Numerous notes filled the margins: upcoming dates, troop distributions, capacities. Last were population centers, circled in black and yellow, the centers from which the trouble would come. These were not always where one would expect to find them, not always near cities. Some were hidden in unlikely places. Pointing here and there on the map, Hank told us what might be going on.

NEWS

Read carefully. The following report, Hank's intelligence report, is recreated from notes, not a tape recording, but Eleen and I agreed on all significant points after poring over our notes in disbelief late into the night. The places and nationalities, the people, animals, and numbers below are not typographic errors. Seeing that we were taking notes, Hank spoke slowly, repeated key points.

Hank gave us the intelligence report.

Hank's scenario began typically, with vague references to disturbances in the Middle East or Africa or Central America that will draw away our prime military forces. Americans at home will be left on their own. When we are at our weakest the attack will begin. Preparation has been taking place for months. Hank provided details.

In the North . . .

> Ten thousand Russian troops are training with eight divisions of Red Chinese troops on the Mongolian border. They will attack the Alaska oil pipeline across six hundred miles of the Bering Strait on specially bred

Mongolian ponies that can carry five hundred pounds each. The attack will come as soon as the strait freezes over in February. Then the troops will push south toward Seattle, where they will be joined by Cuban troops hiding in the rain forest of the Olympic Peninsula.

Meanwhile, in the South . . .

The "Mississippi Pincer Action" is ready. In Chicago, one million Mexican, Cuban, and Haitian illegal aliens have been armed and organized and will head south at the signal. In Miami three million illegal Cubans and Haitians (just revised from one million) will move north and west toward the Mississippi Delta. (Alternatively Cuba may invade Miami directly.) In the Mississippi Delta itself, half of the 640,000 Vietnamese refugees relocated there are actually long-time Viet Cong communists, supplied by sympathizers in the U.S. government with surplus high-speed naval patrol boats for "fishing." These boats are still equipped with mounts for the .50 caliber machine guns and light cannon that have been secretly warehoused and will now be remounted. These twin-diesel-powered attack craft can reach speeds of fifty knots and will easily outrun the Coast Guard. The Vietnamese will cross the Gulf of Mexico to pick up seventy-five thousand Mongolian troops (two divisions) hiding in the jungles of the Yucatan Peninsula, then return for an assault up the Mississippi River, where they will be joined by troops from Cuba and the illegals from Miami.

As the Chicago force heads south and the delta forces head north, they will cut bridges across the Mississippi, isolating the East Coast from its vital food supplies, which all come through Kansas City. Without food, there will be riots up and down the Eastern Seaboard. Police and state troopers will abandon their posts to protect their own homes. At this time Russia will threaten a nuclear strike, the U.S. government, disorganized and powerless, will acquiesce, the Russian and Chinese troops near Seattle will take over the west coast, join the Cubans now arriving in force, assume control of the country, declare martial law, and confiscate all weapons, food, and medicines in civilian control.

That was the intelligence report.

Hank's story was not complete. He did not have all the facts and he knew it. It was a hunch, a might-be, based on what he could gather and guess. Every night he read the mail, listened to his scanner, and sometimes watched the TV news. He also made plans to act and sought information from other sources.

In the top right desk drawer lay a blued Smith and Wesson 9 mm semiautomatic pistol, clean, loaded. It went under his pillow at night. On the opposite wall, by the window, sat the center of survivalism in the

Wentworth household, Hank's chair, an old Naugahyde recliner, and other items. The corner was a comforting spot. For inspiration, the wall behind the chair was decorated with a movie print of John Wayne in marine corps garb at the flag raising on Iwo Jima's Mount Serobachi. For quick response, Hank's ready-to-go camouflage backpack leaned against the wall next to his guitar case. Guitar case? Hank was no musician. The case held his assault weapons, extra magazines, and ammunition for unobtrusive transport to his truck. From his chair Hank could look across the room at his map or his beloved Penny, who often napped on the nearby sofa in the early evenings. Or he could use the other two items he kept on the chair for predicting coming events. He tried to be diligent, to use both, like the scanner, at least twenty minutes every day.

In a black synthetic leather case, binoculars. He watched out the window: the neighbors, the traffic, the kinds of cars going by, and in the distance to the south, airplanes and helicopters from the Air National Guard base. Was there unusual activity? There would be when trouble came. When might that be? Hank had another way of knowing frequently recommended to him.

In a black cover, worn from much carrying if not use, a Bible. Hank read each day, here and there among the stories. The language was harder than most of what he was used to but he tried.

Though Hank and Penny were church-goers, recently Mormons, their spiritual faith was less strong than their basic humanism. Penny had worked many years as a practical nurse in the critical burn wards of two local hospitals, with a deep sympathy for her afflicted patients. When she and Hank were appointed heads of the church food-aid program, they promptly solicited what church leaders called "astonishing" amounts of cash to feed the hungry peoples of sub-Saharan Africa. Neither Hank nor Penny were sure what the Russians or the Chinese or the Cubans were up to, or even if they were real enemies like Kermit said. But they both had read and heard enough to know that famine and hunger were already upon distant lands. People were suffering now. They did what they could to help. Later, after Adele and Sasha had both moved out of the house, they would turn their home into state-certified foster care facility. Nurturance and practical support they understood well and dispensed generously. The Bible is a good book, but others knew it better than Hank or Penny did. Eleen and I went elsewhere for Bible study.

4 THE CRAFT OF PERSUASION

You have to choose: live or tell. . . . While you live, nothing happens . . . but when you tell about life, everything changes.
—Jean-Paul Sartre, *Nausea*

I'm telling you *we are at war*!! . . . The whole world is in a great upheaval. The evils of Godless-Atheistic-brutal terroristic Jewish Communism are on the rampage, out of control and beyond men's solutions. Satan is running rampant in these latter days. We are at war with the hordes of Christ-haters. *We* are God's race, the true Israel, we are all involved whether we like it or not! . . . Your Caucasian race, your white skin is your I.D. You can hide it not, just like your enemies are marked also.
—William Udvary, Hungarian émigré, Identity minister, and Mariposa's other appliance repairman

BRICOLAGE REVISITED

The improvisation of material culture, the synthesis of the repair and recombination of metal and wood, nails and boards, wire and cloth, palm fronds and woven grass, worked with simple tools in skilled hands—this we understand as bricolage. And functional forms of material culture are certainly part of survivalism, but not the whole of it. Survivalist-bricoleurs work in more than one medium. Hank oils his guns and sews his ghillie suit then conducts "research" and provides "intelligence." Broken bits of nonsense, disconnected data and details, rumor and hearsay are culled and curried and woven into narrative bundles of cause and consequence, tales of what-if and might-be. Here again is bricolage, improvised invention, primal culturecraft. But now the results are given symbolically in words and stories, in "facts" and predictions of current and future events. This storytelling part of survivalism, like the process of material acquisition and adaptation, must be subjected to scrutiny.

This chapter explores the possibilities of wordcraft and consumption of texts in the form of an extended example, a story about one aspect of survivalism, presented as a short history. The chapter's message is in both its structure and its substance. Structurally the chapter is assembled in the manner survivalists themselves fashion scenarios, as a plausible mix of observations and reports, events, characters, and scenes, linked and connected and set in line. The plot of this story is conceivable enough, and the facts and quotes and characters are real, but in the end one crucial question remains unanswered. What of the substance of this account? What are the consequences of telling survivalist tales? Do lectures and reports, sermons and books merely entertain, or do they move some to action? In short, do words matter? As the chapter progresses consider two possibilities. Wordcraft may be the vehicle for manipulation and control, an instrumental tool with teeth and grip to hold and twist, or it may be an expressive, autotelic end in itself, an actualizing opportunity to play in a show-off game of creative conjuring and dramatic performance.

Wordcraft As Power

Some analysts set words before deeds, dividing survivalism into two classes: willful word-wielders above, submissive word-consumers below. Theorizing of this sort begins not with the behavior of social actors but with the content of passive paper and other "texts." Excerpts from survivalist books, magazines, tape transcripts, even advertisements are assembled and typified according to analysts' "readings," their senses of implicit themes, latent messages, and authorial intent (see, for example, Daniels 1997; also Zellner 1995, 47–75; Rempel and Green 1983; Churchman 1984; Starr et al. 1985; Kifner 1995; Read 1995; Bates 1995). The content of discursive samples is taken to be self-evident, sufficient, and compelling.[1] To know survivalists' words is to know survivalism. To control survivalists' words is to reduce the word-consumer to Garfinkel's "judgmental dope" (1964), uncritical and unknowing, powerless to do more than respond to the imperatives of metonymic tyranny.[2] Like Langston Hughes's "powerful drop" ([1953] 1994, 201), words reach out to contaminate those exposed to them, transforming word-consumers into the instruments of underlying "ideology" (Goldhammer 1996). The long, rocky, faint, contested path from document to interpretation to intent to action is straightened, narrowed, and plastered over. The survivalist word-consumer is denied ambiguity, doubt, conscience. The question "What does it mean to them?" goes unasked, is presumed unnecessary. The story that follows may be seen in this light. Look carefully for the influences of word power. Entertain the idea that word-wielders manipulate and control. But hold open a space for alternatives.

Wordcraft for Itself

Twice in our discussion survivalism has come to grips with modernity through creative accommodation, first by entrepreneurial invention in the marketplace, then through bricolage amid material culture. In each approach, survivalists find ways to relocate themselves and their at-hand resources from the periphery of relevance to the center of vital culture-craft by means of artful storytelling. Sartre understood this process well enough. "For the most trivial event to become an adventure," he observes, "all you have to do is start telling about it." Then speaking directly to survivalism, he continues: "A man is always a teller of stories, he lives surrounded by his stories and the stories of others, he sees everything which happens to him through these stories; and he tries to live his life as if it were a story he was telling" ([1938] 1949, 56).

Survivalist entrepreneurship and bricolage are narrative creations with touchstones in concrete circumstances, in flea market swaps and stockpiled goods, equipment upgrades and adaptations. Survivalism in these forms shifts back and forth between show and tell, from scenario building to sign equipment, skill demonstrations, and the exchange of real goods. These touchstones, these goods and skills and equipment, give survivalist stories and their authors authenticity and empirical foundations. But they also set limits. Imagination ultimately is bound by common sense. Assault weapons do not stop atom bombs or penetrate tank armor. Camouflage does not protect from disease or napalm or infrared detection. Warehoused soap powder is not impervious to deterioration or suitable for all occasions of economic exchange. These practical facts largely limit survivalist scenarios to optimistic plans for defense or retreat, modest in scope and probability of success.[3] The best that can be expected is local stability and freedom from want amid general disorder.[4] It is only when survivalism is decoupled from material culture of any sort, only when plotlines no longer hinge on the distribution or function of goods and tools and equipment and techniques, that survivalism achieves its most grandiose visions. Unfettered, survivalist stories may soar to the distant boundaries of rhetors' imaginations, interpreting biblical intent, historical trends, evolutionary processes, and the primal mysteries of undisclosed science. Narrative horizons shift outward to encompass the totality of human efforts at knowing and being.

Discourses on reason and faith, religion and politics now may be salted into scenarios without the threat of empirical disconfirmation, standing only tests of aesthetics, style, and emotional resonance. The survivalist's success is now measured in terms of audience appeal, size, and attention span. Storytelling becomes an end, not a means. Survivalists take on the role of colorful melodramatists, not intent on moving the masses or convincing their companions so much as savoring time on the stage and otherwise exploring their own abilities to compound and expound grand encompassing narratives. Wordcraft for itself aims to evoke images, not provoke action.

We will return to these alternative views of wordcraft and its consequences in chapter 5. For now, listen to a story of books by disgruntled professors and sermons by retired colonels, of murderous revolutionaries and chocolate cake.

GHOSTS

Before shipping magnate Wentworth Bateman and his wife, Gloria, could move onto their new vacation property, they had to wait for the completion of government business. The FBI, the sheriff's office, the courts, and of course the coroner had work to do. They all took their time. They all took something. They took pictures and measurements, spent rifle cartridge casings and a handful of firearms. They sifted and sorted the soil and ash and wood bits and took samples of these, too. They took records from nearby houses and all they could find of the corpse. The bureaucratic details seemed slow and tiresome to the Batemans, but they waited hopefully for their new dream home to be realized. Robert Mathews, the corpse, had not been willing to wait for his.

When I visited a decade after the fire, things at the Bateman place looked peaceful, almost normal if you didn't know, almost like they had when the property belonged to its former owner, a professor at the University of British Columbia. After their purchase the Batemans made improvements, some desirable, some necessary, some irritating to the neighbors, some recommended by the police. Discreetly set back in the mature timber, on the site of Mathews's fire-gutted cabin, they built a grand new home with many rooms, many amenities, fine crafting, and rich comforts. A thirteen-million-dollar retreat on five and a half secluded acres of exclusive Whidbey Island in Puget Sound, arguably the Martha's Vineyard of the Pacific Northwest, went well with the area's country inns and small farms, wooded valleys, and views of the Olympics and Cascades on all sides. The neighbors—successful artists and writers, well-heeled retirees, and wealthy business people—generally approved, but the helicopter pad and the noise of the Batemans' private aircraft flying overhead caused objections. A local antihelicopter ordinance passed. Wentworth and Gloria went back to commuting by car and slow ferry from the mainland. The island's quiet resumed.

The King County coroner confirmed that the teeth were definitely Mathews's and that the rest of the remains were probably his, too. Robert Jay Mathews, age thirty-one, was dead, certainly dead. But the sifting of his memories had just begun. Others followed the Batemans from the mainland, first just a few, then dozens, bus loads, hundreds. Pilgrims and protesters came, and with them the police, the media, and a new, greater clamor over Mathews's ghost. The Batemans installed a seven-foot, steel-barred, electronically controlled gate, barbed wire, and a remote security system. Each December, on the date of the fire, pilgrims would hang memorial wreaths on the gate while protesters chanted denouncements, undercover agents circulated in the police-cordoned crowd, and national leaders offered solemn warnings for and against Mathews's memory.

WARNINGS

Eleen and I had heard our own warnings. At our first Ranger meeting, Kermit White arrived at Hank's house an hour after we did. He came alone and stayed that way, aloof, grim, unlike the others. Penny gave him a short, nervous greeting. Hank shook his hand, then grew quiet. In time I learned that Hank and Kermit did not agree on some things. Hank had investigated Kermit's brand of survivalism and found parts of it distasteful. Hank was for recruiting, gardening, sharing "intelligence," and woodsy adventure. Kermit was for security. Hank and Penny liked working on concrete if impractical plans for daily disaster living and neighborhood defense. Kermit had dark visions of malevolent enemies and pending pogroms. In the kitchen, Penny told Eleen he also had status as a "high official with APRA," the American Pistol and Rifle Association. "It's a real honor to have him here," she said flatly.

Knowing nothing about Kermit's differences with Hank, I offered him a cheerful hello. Cheer and my introduction were cut short. "I'm not saying anything about Hank. He is a good man. But things are a lot more serious than you know." Some serious things about which Kermit knew: The income tax is unconstitutional. Communists control the government. Our guns will soon be confiscated. Jews are behind it all. He didn't elaborate these themes but neither did he seem to have doubts, as Hank did. He promised to send some materials in the mail, recommended membership in APRA, and put us in our places. "Just remember, I don't know you really," he clipped, "and you don't know me really." In the organizations that mattered (hinting that Hank's group did not), "We let people join but they never know more than two or three other members. They never get to the top till we check them out personally." By the time Kermit's mail packet arrived, we had heard similar warnings from closer to the "top" and understood why Penny felt nervous and Hank held back.

After making some false claims regarding our creeds and seeds, we received another invitation. This time no score sheets, grading schemes, or handouts. The participants brought notebooks, not guns. No time for games. No use for guns. There were other methods to learn and plans to make. No one mentioned respecting the flag or the Constitution, but only those "born of the Caucasian race and professing the Christian Faith" were allowed. We went anyway.

A SHORT TIME IN A DARK PLACE

Again we drove, one-third the height of the nation, but on this trip south. No public forest and open entrance at our destination this time. A barred gate, a sentry box, and a guard who looked like he knew what he was doing blocked our way. He didn't have fancy face paint or firearm gadgets, just an M-15 on safety, two spare magazines of live ammunition, and a phone line directly to the main building. He called. We were on the list. OK. As the bar closed behind us, I remembered the acceptance notice: "Approved applicants must arrive at Manasseh Ranch prior to 7 A.M. Friday and not depart until 3 P.M. Sunday. You must remain on Church property for the entire training period." Apparently we had no choice. Past the gate, up the slope, on 110 acres of dry foothills on the west side of California's Sierra Nevada range sat a double-wide trailer, the Ministry of Christ Church, the site of the three-day National Identity Survival Training Seminar. Reverend Colonel William Potter Gale, preaching, presiding, instructing.

Roxanne, Gale's spouse, met us in the parking area behind the assembly buildings and assigned us accommodations in one of the six small trailers scattered nearby. We and a few others were lucky. Our ten-foot trailer, without wheels, windows, or water, at least had bug screens and some privacy. The two larger barracks trailers separated men from women, provided all with iron bunks, and shared a single toilet. By day these dormitories became unbearably hot. At night they filled with mosquitoes. Yet their occupants did not complain.

Most of the twenty recent arrivals shuffling back and forth to their vehicles were strangers to each other but not to suffering. Bent, bespectacled, slow, and worn looking, many had had both long drives and hard lives. A majority were older, in their fifties and sixties, stolidly married with three or four grown children. Their unsteady work careers in agriculture, construction, and other semiskilled labor had begun before graduation from small-town high schools.

We came to know these people over the weekend and in the years ahead as both abstainers and participants. They abstained from alcohol, tobacco, strong language, national elections, nonprocreative sex, and television. They participated in theological debates and pamphleteering, local elections for the sheriff or school board, and in networks of correspondence usually centered around a "church" of one to three dozen visible members and twice that number of subscribers to mail-order sermon tapes. The dorms and trailers held the mail-order members. Others from closer by, the Mariposans, came later, left earlier, and were less infirm, or reflective, or temperate.

The rough dozen Mariposans provided the church core. Some had migrated from southern California when the Ministry moved north in the '70s. Others came to the area for different reasons and were recruited to the cause. In an hour the participants from near and far mixed and mingled on the patio behind the main building, then the assembly bell rang. It was time for church. Gale called us to order.

Identity

> Reverend Marrino, will you do the honors? We are going to start this service the way we should start everything, with a request to our Commanding General to bless this meeting. Slim, come on up here.

They called him "Reverend" and "Slim" but he was neither. Antonio Marrino, a Mariposan, the weekend's distant second in command, was tall, handsome, gray haired, beefy, impassive—Stonewall Jackson in OD fatigues. Marrino and Gale's lesser assistants, Jack and John, were Mariposa immigrants, dropouts, "early retirees" from the Los Angeles County Sheriff's Department. All three resigned after confirmation of some of the many complaints lodged against them for excessive violence against minorities. They were bitter about these charges. They admitted the violence, even joked about it. For them, violence against "niggers and spics" was normal and necessary, not "excessive." Now they lived in the Mariposa hills, far from Los Angeles minorities, close to Gale. Marrino's house was better appointed than Jack's or John's, more secure. It was surrounded by a high-powered electric fence. Marrino claimed the fence was lethal.

For ten years Gale had been grooming Marrino to assume leadership of the Church when he was gone. Some of the grooming showed.

Marrino prayed woodenly but worked in the weekend buzzwords: "strength," "courage," "fight," "Christian," "Republic," and so forth. The right words for now. Later, in betrayal, with other words, Marrino would abandon a disillusioned Gale to a slow, choking death.

At sixty-eight, Gale's decline had already begun, though not all knew it. He looked the part of the senior soldier: brusque, spry, open collared, self-confident. He stooped down only slightly from six feet. His flat-top haircut still stood at attention as it had for the thirty years it took his hair to change from black to white. His trim figure and fine features at first suggested fitness, then something missing, twenty pounds in the past two years, each breath a wisp of oxygen short. In spite of the emphysema, he still smoked. The physicians were now guarded. But just then Gale was invigorated. He had what he wanted: an audience willing to suspend disbelief, a podium and props, and a long-familiar script. The show went on.

When revolutions are complete, charisma is absorbed, normalized, set back into everyday routines. This is the endpoint of revolution. Beginnings are different. Charisma infuses the familiar. Rituals are dramatized. Even a simple act, a commonplace rite, given charismatic consequence, can provide a starting point for reformulating the whole. Gale started simply.

> Thank you, Slim. Now our pledge of allegiance. Remember, we don't pledge allegiance to any form of government. We pledge allegiance only to God Jesus Christ, the original Constitution, and the Christian Republic of the United States.
>
> [congregation together] I pledge allegiance . . .

The weekend curriculum would cover three topics: religion, politics, and practical survival skills. The first two, the indoor part, came in the form of sermons, morning, afternoon, and evening, fourteen hours in three days. The participants were accustomed to sermons. Gale gave them what they expected, and some surprises—religion with political purpose, prayer with literal punch lines. He began the surprises with a lecture on heraldry.

> Look behind me. You know what that flag is [U.S. flag, stage left]. But what is that other one? It flies over the capital of the state of Mississippi, over Alabama. What do they call it?
>
> [audience member] The Confederate flag.
>
> Right. What else?
>
> [audience member] The Stars and Bars.
>
> Well I have news for you. Big news. That is *not* the flag of the Confederacy or the Stars and Bars. That is the flag of your *race*!

> "What race?" you're asking. The Adamic race. The race of Adam. How is that defined? The race of ruddy, reddish complected peoples, capable of blushing upon anger. Think about it. Did you ever see a nigger blush? Or another race? They can't. Only you can. 'Cause you're Israelites!

Forty-two ruddy, reddish faces perspired in the springtime heat in the west half of the double-wide trailer, the church half. The church held a piano, a small organ, 17 assorted back issues of *Spotlight, Shotgun News,* and *National Vanguard,* 140 unused blue hymnals, and 57 well-used steel folding chairs. Padded folding chairs, thankfully.

Sermonizing has limits. Not every argument can be carried forward on the force of personal enthusiasm and theatrics alone. Gale mixed the bases for his claims, sometimes depending on longstanding institutional practices, sometimes on personal prescience, reasoning from facts and deductions then discerning from holy writ.

> My buddies in the navy remind us of an important rule. If you have a problem, you go to the manual. They've got one in the navy, and we've got one, too. It's called the Holy Bible. That's where you'll find out who you are. Read the manual.
>
> I know those other preachers and politicians have told you that Israelites are the Jews. That's a lie! That's another bit of misinformation you've been given. And those preachers told you there were ten Lost Tribes of Israel, right? More lies! God didn't "lose" those tribes. Those tribes, who were called Israelites, were your ancestors. And they were *red* skinned, not white. Are you shocked? I don't mean Indians. Columbus didn't discover India. But some of the people he found were Anglo-Saxons who came over thousands of years before Columbus did. In Florida they were the Seminoles and in Oklahoma they were called Cherokees. On the East Coast they were called Algonquins, and the Algonquins today speak the language we call Hebrew. In Maryland they were blond haired and blue eyed. Pocahontas, who married John Smith, was blue eyed. If you go to the place where the Cherokee nation had its councils you'll find the records there and pictures of all the chiefs, and it proves they were actually Scottish princes from Scotland.

The ruddy faces looked curious, interested at these revelations.

> If you study the subject of heraldry—heraldry involves flags and standards—you'll find that all the standards or flags of the tribes of Israel, all *thirteen* of them, had only three colors: red, white, and blue. Now look at this [Confederate] flag. See the same colors: red, white, and blue. You will see the cross of your Christian faith on this flag in blue. You'll see thirteen stars in exactly the same positions that Moses put the tribes of Israel when

> he brought them out of Egypt. The three tribes on the north are these three stars . . .

Gale was no rigid, tight-lipped Macy, boring the likes of Hank into somnolence. He was an orator of experience and skill, attuned to his audience. The fragments quoted here should be understood in context. Gale's presentation was much longer, filled with asides and personal commentary, varied in cadence, tone, and content. Whimsy preceded startling revelations, correlations, and conclusions. His points were repeated for emphasis and style. He kept themes simple and used illustrations the audience understood or were willing to consider.

> Do I have to say it again? This is the flag of your race, of God's people, Israel, not the Confederate flag. There were only eleven Confederate states, right? Look. This flag has *thirteen* stars. Why? Because there were *thirteen* tribes. And the manual says the tribes would be given a *New* Jerusalem, not the old Jerusalem. What else does it say? It tells us those *thirteen* tribes, the descendents of Abraham, were to become a great nation. *Thirteen* colonies, *thirteen* stars, *thirteen* tribes, all united.

When we sit next to a stranger in public we seldom look them over from head to toe without invitation. We look down at our own hands, at a notebook perhaps, then glance sideways. The stranger comes obliquely into view. We notice things.

The large man on my right breathed through his nose, slowly, rhythmically. He smelled of automobile oil and some kind of candy or medicine. (It turned out to be cough lozenges.) His hands looked oversized, red, and hard worked, recently on machinery of some kind. (The universal joint on his friend Cliff's car had broken on the way up the hill that morning.) From the top edge of his dog-eared Bible bristled a myriad of plain and colored paper bits marking sections of import. As Gale spoke the man flipped from one marker to another, ran his index finger slowly over a line or two, and shifted breathing to his mouth. His white shirt was partially untucked from brown, permanent-press polyester slacks too short in the legs. He wore clean white socks inside work boots scuffed down to the midsole on the inside. A pronator. He could use orthotics.

> *E pluribus unum*. Ever hear that? Where do you find those words? On the Great Seal of the United States. And what else is on that seal? On the other side is the great pyramid of Aesop—*thirteen* levels on that pyramid. And photographs prove it, that before Jew-archaeologists destroyed them, on the base of that great pyramid were the Roman numerals "1776," one-seven-seven-six, carved in the stone. That's right. "1776" carved on a

> pyramid built twenty-three hundred years before the days of Noah. And where? According to astronomical measurements, in the exact center of the earth, Egypt. And on the other side of that seal are the wings of a great eagle. Two nations or tribes of Israel have that great eagle as their symbol. Only two have it. The United States and the nation called Germany!

People called the man beside me "Uncle Terry." He made his living as a bounty hunter, killing coyotes wholesale for the Bureau of Land Management and retail for an occasional rancher. Uncle Terry would practice killing me in the afternoon.

The cars parked outside were a familiar assortment of Detroit products, most into their third decade of use, dull and dusty station wagons, pickups, even a stake-bed truck with wisps of hay still on board. One was different, foreign, expensive, barely four years old. Gale called it his "mobile home," and his "command car." Gale was proud of this vehicle for practical and political reasons. He later showed us its single-sideband radio and bragged, "We've got much better equipment than the sheriff has. All our vehicles [the Mariposans'] have two-meter equipment [long-range radios] and all our houses, too. We can put thirty or forty armed vehicles, radio equipped, on the road in two minutes. The sheriff only has two cars."

Gale's vehicle provided transportation, communication, and a statement of allegiance. A Volkswagen Westphalia camper is efficient, reliable, and declaratively German.[5]

> Now you can see why the anti-Christ Jews, who are the communists, who financed [World War II], backed it, and supported it, still hate Germany. And Germans. Because they know that's the Royal Tribe of the House of Israel! Those communist Jews hate Germans, they hate Christians, and they *hate you*!

Through all this some looked quizzical. Brows furrowed. Pencils tapped on notepads and scribble reminders. No eyelids drooped.

> All the tribes of Israel were to become nations. All these nations were of one tribe that was called, according to the manual, the Royal Tribe of the House of Israel, the tribe of Judah. Now I didn't say "Jew." I said Jud*ah*! They went up through the Caucasus and migrated up into western Europe from the Middle East. That's why we're called Caucasians. That pass between the Black and the Caspian Sea has a monument there today that says "Pass of Israel" on it.
>
> The manual says that 2,520 years exactly from the time each tribe went into the wilderness or into captivity, they would become a nation. And each nation would come from the tribe of Judah. So what happened? Well,

> look at the tribe of Zebulon. We find that to the day, 2,520 years from the time it went into captivity, France had its first king, Louis, who was of the tribe of Judah, a German. And Asher? 2,520 after they went into captivity Sweden had its first king, Hornsorns, of German stock. The tribe of Dan, in what we call Denmark, had its first king, Dansmark, of pure German descent, 2,520 years . . .

Next to Eleen sat Carol, bouffant freshly bleached, a yard and a half in lower circumference, wearing flannel OD pants and a bright pink, sleeveless blouse. Her arms would sunburn during combat training but few would notice. We watched the fingers. Each nail was at least an inch and a half long. There was consensus on this and on her waist measurement among the mealtime gossips. Each nail was decorated, not just with plain polish, but with enameled subdivisions and ornate appliqués. A thin diagonal silver stripe divided the maroon tips on each digit from their purple bases. Atop the fields of maroon and purple, twenty contrasting floral decals. She wore rings on five fingers, including a seven-diamond wedding ring with the stones set into the mouths and backs of two entwined snakes.

"What about Russia?" Carol asked, when Gale finished his migration lesson.

> I *hate* to hear you say Russia! Russia doesn't exist anymore! Russia, the nation of White Christian Germanic stock people is gone. Russia is dead. Ever since the tsar was killed it has been under the command and control of Jews! All the way down the line, every communist country that's been taken over has been headed by a Satanic Jew! Don't let anybody tell you there's anything but Jews in charge in Russia, or any of her satellites. In fact you have the communists right here! Their gestapo is the Internal Revenue Service, a collection agency for the international banks under the Federal Reserve System which is run by those Jews!

And so it went, hour after hour. With arguments and anecdotes, doubts and details, bombast and crude humor (but temperate language), Gale mapped the geography of history, analyzed the logic of faith. The whereabouts of the Lost Tribes, Christ's ethnic origins, God's plan for white America, and Satan's counterproposals on these matters were made clear. This was an old story with variations.

In brief, Identity Christians (called Identity "Christians," by some) continue a theological line of argument begun by Edward Hine in nineteenth-century England and rejuvenated in post–World War II United States by Wesley Swift and his followers. Distinctive Identity tenets are few but stand in dramatic contrast to mainstream beliefs. In Identity doctrine the biblical Lost Tribes migrated from the Middle East to settle the "Anglo-Saxon, Celtic, Scandinavian, Teutonic" nations of western Europe and North America. The United States, not Israel, is the genuine promised new Holy Land. White aryans are the authentic Israelites. Jews are said to be descended from Cain, the literal spawn of Eve and Satan, and are the mortal enemies of Identity Christians. Blacks, Hispanics, Asians, and other nonwhites, the "mud peoples," are said to have branched from the evolutionary tree long before Adam, the first "white" Homo sapiens appeared, making them spiritually soulless and culturally and intellectually on a par with higher animals.[6]

Some of Gale's listeners expressed doubts about his claims, asked pointed questions, insisted on more evidence. Others nodded at familiar points during the sermon. Rhonda, a young local woman, apparently tired of background material, interrupted a Gale homily with a practical request: "When do we learn how to kill people? When are we going to do some killing?" For Gale, the question was out of time and place, but not by far. Politics and organization were on the program, then fieldwork. Rhonda would get her request.

We took a break, ate lunch, rested, stretched, and strolled about the church and nearby grounds, saying hello, visiting with participants, listening to snippets of talk. Then the assembly bell rang again. It was time to organize, for afternoon church and for other things.

Organization

For those who might still wonder what lay ahead Gale had one more sermon, less abstract than those before, more imperative. It was time to prepare for action, time to organize forces, assess the adversary, and clarify events to come. He began with basic survivalist fare, the hazards ahead, an overview of the enemy's military might and strategic foresight compared with the United States' inadequacy and ineptitude.

> The take-over is coming! The communists any day can give us an ultimatum to surrender, or else they will employ their nuclear first-strike capability against this country. And we will have to accept it. All military intelligence indicates the Russians have this first-strike capability. We have no defense against it. None. Ever since McNamara was Secretary of Defense in the '50s, there has been a program of destroying your capabilities to defend yourself or your country from a communist first-strike nuclear attack.
>
> For twenty-five or thirty years your government was in what they call détente while the Russians built up their forces. All the Russians' production, all of their factories, all of their cities are completely underground.

> They have civilian defense for all their people. We have nothing! But they don't plan to kill people. They plan to knock out our defenses, our air force, our strategic air command, our naval forces, and in the meantime create a chaotic condition and emergency with government agencies such as FEMA . . .

There was an edged vehemence in Gale's telling of these familiar tales. He added embellishments: conspiracy, internal corruption, and behind it all, vile Semitism.

> The communist commissars are already here with their Asiatic troops to take over the capitals of all of your states, even down to the county level, under national emergency conditions. They have the concentration camps all ready. One up in Oakdale, one at Camp Chafey in Arkansas. They've got 'um all over. "Military bases," they say. No. They are concentration camps. They have control of all of your intelligence capabilities through the CIA, which is controlled by Jews! Don't you remember what happened just a few years ago? That Jew Kissinger, Kiss-ass-inger, whose code name was Bor, B-O-R, an agent of the Russian KGB, was made adviser to the president of the United States for national security!

Those were the problems. What about solutions? Gale next began the crux of the weekend's arguments. This was new ground for the mail-order members and tenuous territory for the Mariposans. Gale played the two-part charismatic, Zoroaster and Mohammed in one. As Zoroaster, he riled against Christianity's cult of ecstasy, the comforts of New Testament humanism—tolerance, beneficence, love. These were traps, he warned, false ministrations. As Mohammed, he set forth to prepare the followers for battle in defense of the faith.

> They say Jesus came to bring peace. That's *not* what he said! Jesus Christ said, "I come to bring war and division! I come not to bring peace." And he didn't send us here to make peace with these heathen devils! He sent us here to kill 'um!

Excited by his topic, Gale was in fine dramatic form. His breath no longer seemed labored. He paced to and fro across the stage, hurling forth chunks of molten sermon he seemed unable to contain.

> Don't chicken out on me now! The book of Revelations says God's kingdom is gonna be brought in with *violence*! And that's how you're gonna do it, with *violence*! And I can guarantee you sometimes you're gonna enjoy it! I can guarantee it. You're gonna *enjoy* it! Don't think bad of it. It's fun! You ever go rabbit huntin'? It's the rabbit that has the problem, doesn't he? Not you. There are some traitors in your government

who have a problem right now. And that problem is God's people waking up. And when God's people wake up they're gonna cleanse the land. And those government traitors? There won't be enough telephone poles to hang 'um on!

Gale pranced and twirled like a boxer, his feet light, his head loose on his shoulders, his hands punching out their own message. The clenched fist shot up, shaking with outrage; the rigid index finger jabbed, first at one audience member, then another, accusing, challenging.

> *You* can't be a milquetoast Christian preacher's boob who wants to "love" everything. *You've* got to prepare yourself for combat! That's what this seminar will do for ya. How many of you, right now, if I told you the communist Jews had taken over your local government, and they *have* taken over, how many of you would have the guts to go up and kill that sucker? You would, huh? Well, we'll find out!

Suddenly, Gale stopped behind the pulpit, his voice quiet, his hands mute. The sermon turned from motive to means, to matters of organization and tactics. He began with history. The model to emulate was the German army between the wars, he said. Limited to small numbers by the Treaty of Versailles, the Germans trained a leadership cadre of 150,000 staff officers. That's what we were, he told us, officers in training, the nuclear staff of the army of New Israel. Having outlined this objective, Gale moved on to organizational principles.

> We're trying to get you to think of yourself as an area guerrilla commander. Now you need to know there are four functions of general staff. Remember *functions*—[counts on fingers] one, two, three, four. One is personnel, people, administering personnel, billeting, where they sleep, where they are quartered, the routes they take when they move. That's G1 or S1. Number two function is intelligence . . .

We were assigned homework.

> As soon as you get home from this seminar, get in your community and find out who a good G1 is, who is a good G2. Get your operation going. What can you do? There is plenty to do! Get a dossier on those communist-Jew suckers in your community right now! Find out where they live, where they work, what kinds of cars they drive. Where do their kids go to school? You can use that later.

This will be hazardous, Gale warned.

> If you even indicate you're anticommunist the ADL's gonna threaten you, the JDL's gonna come after you. But that isn't all. So you better be

> able to defend yourself. Small, hardcore teams is what you want. You're not gonna vote 'um out, you're gonna blow 'um out! If one of your team starts sayin' "Let's stick to the middle of he road," watch 'um! Put security on 'um! You *will* be infiltrated! Count on it! And if you give an order, say, "Go to such and such a place and dispose of so and so," and somebody starts arguing about it, there is going to be a burial. You follow me? I'll *bury* 'um! Even if he is a member of my own family! There's no room for disobedience of command in guerrilla warfare. Those who disobey become casualties. Wipe 'um out. Wipe 'um out! *Bury* 'um!

Gale began to pace once more. Defense, from within and without, should be proactive.

> Form your own BUG groups. You know what a BUG group is? Make a note of that, "bug," B-U-G. It means Belly Up in the Grass. Law enforcements know that. [Slim and Jack nodded.] You're gonna put 'um belly up in the grass about two o'clock in the mornin'.
>
> You gotta get yourself mentally prepared. Start thinking in terms of being a warrior race. You are warriors! You're not chickens! You're not slaves! You're free men!

Momentarily the audience was distracted. Roxanne and her friend Mary, a little too loud in the adjacent kitchen, clattered pans out of the oven and onto the cooling racks. The pleasant smell of fresh-baked chocolate cake filled the church. The blender whirred as they mixed frosting. Survivalist women at work. Gale had jobs for women, too. Jobs with another odor.

> Start using your women. Do I have to tell you what to do? The book of Esther, that's a Christian book. Esther was not a Jew you know. But Hyman was a Jew, and Esther got Hyman hung! So a lot of women can go out and get a lot of Jews hung. It is a fact. Women are *good* for intelligence.
>
> We had a good example in the Philippines. There was over four hundred Japs in this valley—it was on Leyte—and we only had about eighty men, and we had to get those Japs out. So we took the Philippine women—they liked our cigarettes—and for each set of Jap ears they brought us, we gave 'um a pack of cigarettes. In two weeks we had hundreds of ears. They went down and slept with 'um at night and then slit their throats, and they come back with their ears in the morning—for a pack of cigarettes. Remember, women can do a heck of a job in this area of intelligence.

The heat and Uncle Terry's pressing bulk intensified the smell, the fetid wind of ears and women and dead Japanese discharging past Gale's wet lips. Revulsed, like several others, I sought distraction, studying the mundane details of the church interior. The details seemed unreal, too.

Many churches embellish their interiors with paintings or frescoes or stained glass. The Ministry of Christ Church was decorated differently. Large framed pictures adorned the church-trailer walls. Each one was labeled: "Jesus," "Westminster Abbey," "The Georgetown Flag," "The Jamestown Flag," "The Union Flag of 1609," and others. But there was something else. None of these pictures were simple prints. None were originals. Each picture, under glass, in a gilt frame, was an assembled jigsaw puzzle.

The sermon was nearly over. Discussion turned to practical matters. Gale listed parts of the afternoon agenda—unarmed combat, ambush and patrol formations, and so forth, then emphasized the objectives of this training.

> It's not quantity we want here, it's quality. When you go into the type of action that's comin', you're going in with a few good hard-core killers. And when you leave this seminar that's what we're gonna expect you to do. "What's this guy talking about?" you ask yourself. Well, ask Jack, ask John, ask Reverend Marrino. They know. The only reason they were in their jobs, in law enforcement, being peace officers, keeping the peace, was to kill 'um! Right, Jack? [Jack nods in affirmation.] Now *you* have to be ready to do that.

In matters of combat and killing, most of us believed what Gale said. He had compelling credentials. At meals and breaks the Mariposans spoke of his background with deep respect. Gale had authored six monographs on guerrilla warfare, they said. I'd seen some of these, and I owned one and could attest to its professional appearance and organization. But Gale did more than write, they said. These books were based on firsthand experience. According to locals' knowledge, when Douglas MacArthur pledged "I will return!" to the Philippines in World War II he left someone behind, his subordinate commander of allied insurgency operations, U.S. Army Lieutenant Colonel William Potter Gale. For three and a half years Gale lived by his wits and cunning among the Japanese enemy, waging guerrilla war. That was Gale's background, the Mariposans told us. With those qualifications, no one doubted the utility of his methods. No one doubted he was a professional and practiced killer. Even when he contradicted the popular faith in firearms, everyone paid attention.

As we prepared to head outside for field practice, several participants began asking questions about guns. What calibers did Gale recommend, what ammunition design, what manufactures? Gale answered a couple of these questions listlessly then snapped:

> You're gonna have to learn some things about being a *warrior*! Oh, everybody is gun-happy. I'm not! I don't like guns much. Not in a guerrilla war. You don't need 'um. But I'll show you what I *do* like! And I'm gonna show you how to use it before this seminar is over. That's a knife. That's what I like. Or a little piece of wire, or a little piece of rope. We are gonna show you how to put that Jew, that nigger away quiet-like, with no noise at all. Does that make sense? You bet! It's much better than shootin', much better! Do your killin' with a little wire, quiet-like.

Field Training

Quietly, subdued by this chastisement, forty of us, thirty men and ten women, filed out to the freshly mown grass training field in front of the church. Four other women watched from the sidelines. Just before exercises began, "Doc" Sanchez, a dentist from San Francisco, left for home, and Tex, a trucker from Visalia, arrived. We stood in a loose circle while Gale distributed a handout. The handout was atypical—only a single page. No nail-studded tree trunks and fancy rope work described in this one. Just low-tech advice for hand-to-hand guerrilla warfare, basics on how to crush insteps, break wrists and arms, tricks for choking and deoculation.

When everyone had a copy, John Briggs, our chief instructor, read each item aloud then demonstrated with air moves and pantomime. "One. 'The Body Grasp and Eye Take-Out.' Now pay attention. Move in quick! Grab the enemy with one arm behind his waist, like this. Pull him towards you, then strike quickly upward with the palm of the hand, *hard*, up under his chin. Now reach your fingers up to his eyes and DIG with those fingers! DIG!"

The handout read just like John's instructions, ". . . now reach your fingers up to his eyes and DIG with those fingers! DIG!" As John worked down the list we practiced each maneuver in arbitrary pairs. A majority of the group were clumsy and slow, a few were eager, and fewer yet, able. The Mariposans, especially the ex-policemen, had the most experience and served as models and assistant instructors. Todd served as victim.

For Todd, twenty-two, a geology student at Southern Oregon State College, the weekend seminar was a personal Operation Azimuth Bearing, a search for direction. Todd came looking for places to take himself in the world, and places to put others. Todd was a methodological boon throughout the seminar. He arrived early Saturday morning, looking younger and even thinner than he was, road weary from twelve hours of driving "pedal to the metal," as he put it, with a long list of questions written on lined paper and folded into his pants pocket. Todd and the list appeared everywhere people gathered that weekend, and when they did, answers were provided. He knew little but wondered at nearly everything, sometimes cynically, sometimes with youthful enthusiasm. The latter showed. For what he called "combat training" he'd come prepared, wearing a concert t-shirt, Levi's, and something he bought just for the occasion—a cheap, cumbersome, enormous Bowie knife, complete with synthetic, fringed buckskin scabbard, strapped to his right leg like a femur splint, from waist to knee.

Jack, one of the Los Angeles County Sheriff's Department rejects, dressed the part of his former adversaries. He was burly armed and shirtless and wore an open denim jacket without sleeves, the arm holes frayed as if the sleeves had been ripped off in some manly contest. A street-thug warrior. Jack seemed to relish the hands-on work of bending, twisting, and choking his slight and inexperienced partner, Todd. I think part of this demonstration was for an audience. One of the four women looking on was Jack's daughter Maryann, about twenty, who had been watching Todd with interest ever since he arrived.

Practice-pair matching ranged from even to odd. Eleen went toe to toe with Laura, a friend of Carol's, who looked reasonably fit but who took unreasonable precautions to guard her fingernails against harm. Two young men about Todd's age, but more muscular, tussled together equitably. Bob the welder and Carl, Barbara's husband, looked a fair match. On the other hand, Barbara and an older woman named Zillah were separated by thirty-five years of age, nine inches of height, and one hundred pounds of weight. As it turned out, obesity in one and arthritis in the other offset these differences, and neither was able to do much. After forty-five minutes, we had practiced each exercise on the handout. We moved on to Gale's favorites, the knife and the "little piece of wire."

Garroting must be done in a proper way, Gale insisted. The wire—any piano wire in the upper register is good—should not be held in the hands directly but wrapped round wooden handles, else the killer's fingers be lopped off before the enemy's head. While approaching from the rear, form a loop in the wire by crossing the arms as if warding off anticipated blows. Once the loop drops in place around the victim's neck, turn and hunch down, as if to run away, thereby uncrossing the hands and drawing the loop tight. With practice, full decapitation is possible, Gale assured us. We practiced.

Uncle Terry was my partner, a big man of six feet four inches and 230 pounds. Our garrotes were rolled bath towels. Our victim-partners were expected to stand passively as we crept up from behind and dropped towel-nooses into place with the proper motions. I missed. The towel hooked under Uncle Terry's nose, and when I pulled the result was a series of muffled mumbles, not a garrote victim. Gale stopped practice and drew others' attention to my errors. "Now you do it," he ordered Uncle Terry. Uncle Terry, looking nervous under this close scrutiny, spat neatly in the dust then took his position. I faced away, into the sun, and waited. Footsteps. Suddenly I was off my feet, bent backward over Uncle Terry's broad shoulder, semithrottled by the towel. As I wriggled, held high, Gale walked about us as if we were mannequins, slowly reviewing the proper elements of garroting form. Finally, he released Uncle Terry from his obligation: "You can put 'im down now." A bit blue and bruised, but breathing, I sat on the ground. Uncle Terry hunched over me, fanning with the towel.

Todd seemed to find this exciting stuff. "Should we work in pairs?" he joked, in what he viewed as the spirit of the day. "One of us can garrote and the other carry the basket to catch the head?" Smiling, Gale came right back. "Yea," he agreed, "but be careful when that nigger head comes off. You don't want to get yourself messed up with that nigger blood."

During garroting lessons one woman asked, "Well, what do you do when it happens to you?" referring to having one's neck noosed from behind. "Well, you just don't get in that situation" was all Briggs could offer in reply. The woman pressed. "Yes, but *how* do you 'just not get into that situation'?" Briggs ignored her, but Gale interrupted with an explanation of sorts. "A guerrilla fights only when he can win. He withdraws when he cannot. When there's five niggers comin' down the trail, and you've got ten men, then kill 'um and go ahead and strip the bodies. But don't forget the "Flop Squad." Put a round through the head of any one of 'um that's still floppin' and all the rest to be sure."

With knives, form mattered too. "Pull the head backward quickly, kick the legs out, slice *twice,* once across, once back again. Now on the ground, push his face into the dirt. They often make gurgling sounds. Thrust down past the shoulder blade into the heart." First Briggs repeated these instructions, then Gale, as we paired off again to practice with our old partners and new rubber bayonets.

During knife demonstrations Briggs recommended literature. Jenks and Brown's *Bloody Iron* was the one to read, he claimed. "These guys are ex-cons and street fighters. They learned how to use a knife in prison and on the streets of L.A., fighting niggers and spics." They have "lots of experience slashing niggers" and know their stuff. "You do like we'll teach you today," and you can "slice 'um open from one side of their belly to the other and drop their guts right out," if your knife is sharp. This was John's promise.

When the knife fighting lessons had gone on for twenty minutes Gale interrupted, gathered us together, and explained guerrilla strategy. Our job was psychological as well as technical. "Don't just kill 'um. Terrorize 'um! If you ambush seven of 'um, don't just leave the bodies. Cut their heads off and line 'um up across the trail. Then when one of their buddies comes along and says to himself, 'There's Joe. I was drinking beer with him last night,' and he sees how you messed him up, he's gonna be mighty scared and mighty careful."

As the sun began to set an assistant showed us how to build 12-gauge zip guns with plumbing pipe, nails, and rat traps mounted on small planks. To demonstrate, four of these were rigged in trees and on the ground. Nearly invisible monofilament triggers stretched ankle high above a path through the brush. An old auto tire played the part of a strolling enemy. As it rolled down the trail, crossing the monofilaments, blast after blast of buckshot ripped through the rubber and steel cords. Gale recommended these devices for perimeter defense and assassinations. They were cheap, he assured us. About four dollars each.

Gale told us to sit on the cooling grass and explained his own attitude toward the enemy. A real warrior had more than skills. He had a perspective, a style, a sense of "vengeance" he called it.

> My old man was a cavalry man in the army, thirty-eight years, fought with Teddy Roosevelt at the Battle of San Juan Hill. When I was a kid the preacher used to tell us Moses was a Jew, Jesus was a Jew. I didn't understand. It didn't make sense. But my old man told me different. He told me these preachers were lyin'. He told me Jews were no good. He told me those Jews were stinking, crummy scum. And he was right! Jesus wasn't a Jew, he was an Aryan, and the Jews killed 'im!
>
> So when you get the chance, when you catch a Jew, use your bare hands. Take that Jew and break his arms, break his neck! But don't kill him. No! Let him suffer. Make him go to the doctor every week of his miserable life, but don't kill him. Sufferin's better.

Medicine

The day's work done, but not the night's, we filed back for dinner. Many seemed relieved the combat training was over. Talk among participants was cheerful, unfocused. We sat in chairs pulled to the rear of the sanctuary and scattered about the kitchen. In half an hour we were up, stretching and strolling about, chatting and serving ourselves seconds.

Cliff and his wife, Sue, played the good hosts, making us feel comfortable with survivalist small talk about things we presumably had in common, like guns. "I *always* carry a .38," Sue beamed. "I do too," agreed Cliff, "except when we feel *really* secure, like here with Reverend Gale." Cliff, six feet tall and two hundred pounds, about sixty-five, with gray hair and glasses, wore a sort of survivalist leisure suit, a one-piece getup with a waist belt, homemade by his wife out of camouflage flannel. He also walked slowly and with a noticeable limp across the kitchen to refill his punch. Gale noticed. Gale, the would-be full-featured charismatic, also practiced the laying on of hands.

"Cliff's got a problem," he announced to the kitchen audience. "I'll show you how to fix it." "Get on the floor," he instructed Cliff. Somewhat painfully, Cliff complied, sprawling face down on the linoleum. A dozen onlookers crowded around. Gale circled his patient, prodding Cliff's appendages, lifting a foot, pulling an arm, pushing a leg over a few inches until, he claimed, all the limbs were "exactly" parallel. Now the diagnosis. He studied Cliff's form for several moments then drew our attention to Cliff's hunched shoulders and the placement of the toes of his splayed out shoe. "His back's out of align," Gale concluded. "See, the left leg is nearly two inches shorter than the right." I didn't see, but apparently Gale did, and he proceeded with corrections. He bent over Cliff, pressing forcibly on his spine in various spots and pulling his legs. Gale sat Cliff in a chair and cracked his neck back and forth audibly, then told him to lie on the floor. After Cliff was again prone and his limbs readjusted, the splayed toes and hunched shoulders looked the same to us as they had before, but Gale proclaimed everything "all straightened out" and the treatment a success. The onlookers nodded approval. Two people applauded. Gale smiled. Cliff smiled too, gamely, from the floor. But he was unable to get up this time without Uncle Terry's assistance.

After helping Cliff to a chair Uncle Terry shuffled in our direction, stuffing his mouth with a roll as he came, excusing his delayed speech. Uncle Terry, bearish, shy, disheveled, had something uncomfortable to say. But he arrived ahead of his speech. The words were not ready yet. He stood before us, preparing in darkness, squinting his eyes closed, chewing slowly, searching the darkness for words. With the last swallow of roll, his defenses gone, he gathered what words he could find, opened his eyes, and blurted "Sorry!" Then came a long string of apologies: "I'm sorry . . . I didn't mean to . . . I'm sorry . . . Are you OK? . . . Really, are you?"[7]

Uncle Terry didn't like garroting practice, he said. He didn't like hurting people. Hurting people is bad, he said. Hurting animals is bad.

You should never leave an animal to suffer. Never. He began apologizing again. When finally I convinced him he had done me no permanent harm he beamed, shook my hand solemnly, and offered meaningful amends.

Uncle Terry was a big man with a big appetite. The part of dinner he had been looking forward to all afternoon was dessert, the chocolate cake. He had two pieces; he gave them both to me, placing each one carefully on my paper plate with his large bare hand. He seldom got cake at home, "'cause I got a bunch a kids," he explained, and "being a trapper, we just get by." "How many kids?" I asked. One for each year of his formal education, as it turned out.

After dinner there were vespers, then ambush practice and maneuvers in the darkened hillside brush. We were in bed by ten.

Departure

Sunday morning the camp was up early. As we packed, preparing to depart, Eleen and I heard sounds outside our trailer. Terrible sounds. The sounds of children playing.

One child, about five years old, darted among the dormitory trailers, chased by two others, two or three years older. The pursuers threw curses and stones as they ran. One stone struck our trailer, another hit the youngest child. He took refuge below our window, sobbing quietly.

"Don't hurt me!" he pleaded upon being discovered. Laughing, the older boys pushed him to the ground, forcing his face into the dirt. The biggest sat on him, twisting his arm painfully up behind his back.

"I'm here to break your fingers!" he taunted. "Then I'll break your legs!"

"Put him in pain! Put him in agony!" encouraged his partner.

"I want to kill him!" said the biggest.

"Yea," the other agreed.

"Slit his throat! He's a Jew! He's a Jew!"

The breakfast bell rang. Then it was time for church, for a special service, to rejoice and give thanks.

It was Easter.

• • •

When we left Gale's ranch Sunday afternoon, I drove slowly for a half-dozen miles, my mind in jitterbug confusion. Had all this been real? Did we hear correctly, did we see? It seemed not possible, not believable. Could there be with us on the same planet, in the same time and place, such an affliction of spirit, such cruelty and loathsome corrosion of what I believed it was to be human? No. Of course not. In a few more miles, as Freud promised, walls began to build.

It was all absurd I was sure, a colossal joke, an embarrassing bit of social flatulence. I began to chuckle, then laugh down the road. And what a joke! Funny! Very, very funny!

Eleen sat beside me. A stone. Silent.

My mirth increased, became shrill. How hilarious it all had been! Those sermons, those exercises. A real good one!

"Shut up," Eleen said, simply.

"Hee, hee. Hee hee hee," I continued.

"SHUT UP!" she insisted.

I pulled the car to the edge of the road, turned off the engine, and still smiling, turned to her. When she saw the sardonic rictus on my face, she was gentle.

"Shut up," she soothed quietly, "please."

I looked at her over my hunched right shoulder, my torso still facing straight forward, arms held stiffly at ten o'clock and two o'clock, tightly gripping the steering wheel as if we were hurtling down a twisting mountain road at high speed. Life and death in my grip. Don't let go. The corners of my mouth strained to reach my ears, pulling, pulling, cracking my lips, straining all the muscles of my face into a rigid, twitching grin-mask. There was pain from this and I welcomed it. My front teeth began to dry. I wanted to rip my face in half and throw away the eyes and ears that had seen and heard this weekend, the mouth that agreed and asked.

Then I wept, bitterly, uncontrollably. Eleen drove for twenty minutes to a small town and found a phone. I was forty-two years old and a male but no man. Not for this. I regressed, became childish. I called for help to one who was stronger than I, who had been face to face with homelessness and concentration camps and McCarthyism and had kept his humanity intact. "Please, Dad," I asked, "what does this mean?" How can we hate each other so much for so little, for a sliver of faith or a shade of skin or our way of making words?

THE NOVELISTS

Gale was not the only storyteller. Seymour Levine and Earl Turner never met. Bold and well-paid Earl, the electrical engineering researcher from Los Angeles, would probably have had little in common with Sy, the New York transplant, an insecure assistant professor of English at a western agricultural college. But they never met for another reason. Neither existed. Sy and Earl were figments of imagination, the creations of two authors who came close to meeting, and who did have things in common. Both shared an employer, a period of disillusionment early in their careers, and subsequent recognition as writers of consequence.

In the century and a third since its founding as Oregon Agricultural College, Oregon State University has been home to two novelists whose work in the long term has proven significant. Both novelists began at the university in obscurity, both left after years of dissatisfaction, and neither was encouraged much by his colleagues. Bernard Malamud came to Oregon State's English department in 1952 and remained for nine years. *A New Life,* published in 1961, chronicles his experiences of small-town academic life. He went on to receive the National Book Award and the Pulitzer Prize for his novels and short stories.

The second novelist, William Pierce, who wrote under the pen name Andrew Macdonald, came to Oregon in 1962. Born in 1935 in Atlanta, Pierce moved to Colorado as a child, earned a bachelor of arts from the Rice Institute in 1955 and a doctorate in physics from the University of Colorado in 1962.

Like many young intellectuals of that time, Pierce was caught up in America's growing political angst and soon learned Malamud's lesson—Oregon State was not a comfortable setting for idealists of any stripe. Even his department, theoretical and visionary physics, stood in the long, literal shadow of its more powerful and practical cousin, engineering. His scholarship was of high quality, but he had recurring frictions within his department over his stringent grading. (In Malamud's novel, Sy Levine had the same problems.)

In the summer of 1965 Pierce resigned and moved to the Washington, DC, area to put effort directly in service of his convictions. He went to work as the editor of a little-known activist publication aimed at intellectuals and the academy. His employer, who would later be murdered for his own outspoken political views, praised Pierce as an "idealist," and someone "working for what he believes in rather than money." (Anti-Defamation League 1983, 120). After his employer's assassination Pierce drifted through various administrative and editorial positions with obscure political organizations, producing seldom-read tracts and position papers. Seldom read, but not never. One young man from Idaho read them avidly, was much taken by Pierce's arguments, and traveled east to aid the cause and find direction in his own life. He did both, helping Pierce for a time, learning much, and returning to the West with a renewed sense of duty and a plan. The plan came from Pierce's best-known work, a brand new piece at the time and in a genre new for him, a historical fiction novel. The novel, written as a set of diaries unearthed by future archaeologists, chronicles the day-to-day events of a cell of revolutionaries in their fight against oppression and long odds. They are Earl Turner's diaries, the story of apocalyptic race war in America, *The Turner Diaries.*

SPAWN

William Potter Gale left the army in June of 1950. Under the pay regulations of the time he was entitled to a retirement promotion to full colonel with commensurate pension and benefits. At the age of thirty-three, financially secure for life, Gale became what he called "one of those patriots with nothing to do" in the heyday of conservative activism: McCarthyism in Washington, the John Birch Society in Orange County, blacklisting in Hollywood, and on the margins, Identity.[8] Gale took interest in Identity and found things to do.

He went to work, first for Hughes Aircraft in inventory control and accounting, then for Waddell and Reed selling mutual funds and other securities. He got a friend of his hired at the same firm, but soon the friend was in trouble, "got trapped in an illegal weapons deal with the FBI." Both were fired. Unemployed, but with his generous retirement pay, Gale drank and golfed, then opened a securities firm of his own and closed a chapter in his life. His wife and two children left him after a decade of rocky family life. Above ground, Gale dabbled in politics.[9] On the side he studied briefly for the Episcopal ministry then began "teaching the Constitution and the Bible" (Seymour 1991, 86) to small groups of conservatives in the Los Angeles basin and on occasional speaking tours of the Midwest.[10] In the shadows, Gale formed the "California Rangers," what he called a "volunteer civil defense organization." California's attorney general called them "a threat to the peace and security of our state" (Seymour 1991, 94). He did fund raising, encouraged others, and took credit for everything he could.

"Tom Metzger will tell you that I was the guy who introduced him to the race question," Gale bragged. Perhaps he did. Metzger, a southern California TV repairman, won the 1980 Democratic congressional nomination from the Forty-third District. He would go on to become a leader of the state's Ku Klux Klan, pioneer the use of public access television by separatists, form W.A.R., the White Aryan Resistance, and be found guilty of inciting a skinhead gang to beat an Ethiopian immigrant to death with a baseball bat.[11]

Gale had less to say about Hungarian émigré William Udvary, an avid Gale follower both in southern California and on the move to Mariposa. Udvary, who had narrowly escaped Russian tanks in Budapest and the troops that pursued him to the border during the ill-starred Hungarian uprising in 1956, was ripe for an anticommunist crusade. Gale used

Udvary as a model victim, repeating his tales of Russian repression, displaying him at meetings as a sample of the degraded aryan soon to receive his due. But there were differences between them, mostly theological. Udvary went his own way, but not far.

Udvary worked hard at his trade, repairing TV sets and appliances, and at Identity. He collected a few followers and wrote prodigiously: newsletters, pamphlets, and the omnibus, ever growing, loose-leaf, three-hundred-page Identity Bible. Udvary ordained himself and started an open-air church of his own down the hill from Gale's, the New Harmony Christian Crusade, interpreting God's will regarding organic gardening and vegetarianism (Mrs. Udvary's interests) and the exulted purposes and prophetic ends of the coming race war.

When I asked Gale about Udvary, all he would tell me was "There was only one appliance repairman in Mariposa before I set him up. I sent him plenty of business." Then vaguely, "He just doesn't get it." Get what? I asked. "These foreigners come over here and think they know everything, but they don't. They've got to learn to act like Americans." Gale did influence two others to "act like Americans."

NO POWER ABOVE

The broken muffler on Thomas Cove's Yamaha announced his arrival at Hank's. Thomas was alone on the motorcycle today but not always. Thomas brought his hard-of-hearing dad to one meeting and an immature fifteen-year-old neighbor to another. Neither Dad nor the teen returned, but Thomas was a regular. Bald by thirty-four, Thomas was dour and curved shouldered, tall and loose limbed. When he spoke, a rare event, his thin lips barely moved, but his long pale fingers wagged at his sides. Thomas was a Freeman. He campaigned for the United Sovereign Party, pamphleted for citizens militias and arms bearing, and was taken by the work of Hank Lamont Beach, a local retired dry-cleaning executive. In the late '60s Beach and Gale began promoting a doctrine that intrigued Thomas. They called it Posse Comitatus.

Posse Comitatus, "power of the county," has reasonable roots. The notion derives from congressional legislation passed just after the Civil War specifically barring the federal military from intervening in local police matters. When Richard Nixon's aides suggested use of federal troops to suppress and round up left-wing protesters, J. Edgar Hoover, certainly no friend of dissidents, told Nixon that such action would violate the Posse Comitatus doctrine. Later, the principle was interpreted by tax protesters and the like to mean that no citizen is legally bound to obey governmental authorities higher than the county sheriff. It is not obligatory, therefore, to pay income tax, make social security payments, or even obtain state-issued licenses and registrations from "illegal" supracounty entities (see Coates 1987, 106). Some even argued it is a duty to oppose these entities, and with force, in defense of the law of Posse Comitatus.[12]

Thomas Cove lived by part of the Posse doctrine. He had no driver's license. He didn't pay taxes. After years of legal wrangling, he no longer contributed to social security. His motorcycle was unregistered and had no plate.[13] These declarations of independence posed recurring difficulties for a government employee, such as he (a city meter reader), and eventually cost him his job.

Gordon Kahl lived more of the Posse doctrine. It cost him more than his job. It cost him his life.

Gordon Kahl knew the Posse message well. The retired Texas oil-field worker had heard Gale's tapes and read Beach's proclamations. For a decade he had spread the word himself to friends and a few followers. Then he informed the government of his sentiments.

In 1969, instead of filing an income tax return, Kahl sent the IRS a letter declaring "the progressive graduated income tax is the implementation of the 2nd plank of the Communist Manifesto" and he would no longer be giving "aid and comfort to the enemies of Jesus Christ" (Seymour 1991, 150). The jurisdiction of federal courts is invalid, he claimed, and he was not responsible for taxes because no statute creating the Internal Revenue Service was ever passed by Congress.

The IRS responded routinely to Kahl's protest letter: reminder letters, minor charges, and a summons followed by a short trial, conviction, a mild suspended sentence, probation, and an admonition to file tax returns in the future. All of this, step by step, Kahl publicly protested, disregarded, or denied while continuing to advocate Posse principles. Three years after initial sentencing the IRS bureaucracy ran out of options. Proceedings began for the revocation of Kahl's probation. Nine months later, in Midland, Texas, a warrant was issued for his rearrest. Kahl moved. The warrant lay dormant for two years. Then, on February 13, 1983, patience ended on both sides. Three Posse members returning from a local organizing meeting in North Dakota faced six marshals with the warrant. In a roadside shoot-out, sixty-three-year-old Kahl killed two marshals, wounded two others, and escaped with his companions. Kahl went into hiding.

Four months later, on a besieged Arkansas farm, Kahl's commitment to the county sheriff was bravely tested. The local sheriff crossed the encircling police lines and walked directly to the farmhouse door, calling for Kahl's surrender. Kahl blew the sheriff's lungs out with a single high-velocity assault rifle round fired point-blank from his door-side hiding place. Kahl died spectacularly when large quantities of ammunition cached on the farm were ignited in the firefight that ensued. The contest to control petty bureaucracy had exacted a heavy price.

NO PEACE BELOW

During the late 1950s Wesley Swift became the center of Identity in California, attracting crowds of several hundreds to his Friday night political meetings and Sunday services of the "Anglo-Saxon Christian Coalition" at the Hollywood Women's Club. Gale fell in and out with Swift several times, but he did help Swift's effort in one crucial way. He recruited Swift's successor. "There was this anticommunist activity going on with the state legislature," Gale recalled, "and the state coordinator for the Assembly Bill being proposed was Richard Butler from Whitier" (Seymour 1991, 82). Butler came to visit. "Well, one afternoon in Hollywood, I got a knock at my door and it was Mr. Butler. He was with a fellow from Chicago who was working with him on this legislative attack on communism. And the fellow was a blond Jew! Right away, that triggered me, because I was alert, but Butler wasn't. We found out later this guy from Chicago was an ADL agent, infiltrated with Butler. I said, 'Hey, Mr. Butler, you got something to learn! Sit down!' and I gave him Identity—the Bible message. He was a Master Mason. Betty, his wife, was a wonderful gal, Scotch. They didn't leave until four in the morning" (Seymour 1991, 82).

"I baptized his kids, all the family," Gale claimed. "He became a member of my church; I was his minister" (Seymour 1991, 81–82). In time, he introduced Butler to Swift. Gale's apprentice became Swift's disciple. In Swift's declining years Butler assumed the full mantle of Identity. Richard Grint Butler bought land far to the north and started an oddly named Identity church of his own.

It was to a homestead near Butler's church that Macdonald's young assistant came, full of zeal, on his return from the east. The young man, Robert Mathews, the Whidby Island corpse, more often referred to the church by its secular name, the World Headquarters of the Aryan Nations.

HOMECOMING

> I soon settled down, clearing my land, and reading. Reading became an obsession with me. I consumed volume upon volume on subjects dealing with history, politics, and economics. I was especially taken with Spengler's *Decline of the West* and Simpson's *Which Way, Western Man?* I also

> subscribed to numerous periodicals on current American problems, especially those concerned with the ever increasing decline of White America.
>
> My knowledge of European history started to awaken my wrongfully suppressed emotion buried deep within my soul. That of racial pride.
>
> The stronger my love for my people grew, the deeper became my hatred for those who would destroy my race, my heritage. And darken the future of my children.
>
> By the time my son had arrived, I realized that White America, indeed my entire race, was headed for oblivion unless White men rose and turned the tide. . . . Hail Victory! (Robert J. Mathews, age thirty-one, one day before his death)[14]

Like Nic and Tim and Thomas Cove, like Nixon and many other survivalists, Mathews was an avid reader. When the FBI came, his hand-hewn home in the Idaho woods was full of books, hundreds of volumes, read, marked, dog-eared, nonfiction political, economic, and social history, political philosophy, anthropology, theological treatises, reference works. The media often talks about the guns found in survivalists' homes. They usually forget to mention the books. Usually, but not always. One of Mathews's books is often mentioned. It is an exception to his usual reading. Fiction. A story of make-believe. Some say he tried to make it come true.

When William Pierce turned his hand from physics to fiction under the pen name Andrew Macdonald, imaginary historian-chronicler of the great Race Revolution, editor of *The Turner Diaries,* the consequences were hard to predict. As literature, the diaries were not much. Just another "men's" adventure novel. Hero: soft spoken and loyal, pragmatic, ah-shucks modest, tough and self-sacrificing, quick witted, uncompromising. Enemy: vast in number and resources, morally debased, cruel, selfish, and miscalculating. Women: only a few "good" ones, and those, willing and in their place. Odds: long. Circumstances: fateful. Action: stoicism and tough-minded reasoning, violence, grand finale.

What stands *The Turner Diaries* apart as a story is not its style or characters, but the setting. If Pierce had cast his band of freedom fighters into a fray in the jungles of southeast Asia or on some mission of mercy or redemptive vengeance in Latin America, action-hero style, few would have noticed. Or he could have written about mercenaries fighting in Africa against enemy influence, or some nouvelle *Seven Samurai,* or master assassin-spies sent to destabilize a despotic Middle Eastern regime. Any of these framings would have left the diaries barely distinguishable from other pulp fiction. But Pierce brought Turner and his troubles home to North America. And at home, Mathews's home, and in Butler's nearby church, an odd handful of isolates looking for excitement read the diaries and found what they wanted: pulp fiction plots, action scenes, and a modus operandi.

The Turner Diaries appeared as a book in 1978 but was originally serialized in Pierce's *National Vanguard* magazine. Pierce admits the idea for his diaries was not original. Many years earlier Robert Welch, founder of the John Birch Society, had recommended another book to him, *The John Franklin Letters* (1959).[15] The anonymous *Letters* tells of a 1950s United States "Sovietized" by communists come to global power through domination of the United Nations, of Americans' privations at the hands of alien oppressors, and of eventual liberating revolution, all in the form of letters from patriot-rebel John Franklin to his uncle. The Franklin story goes this way:

Loss of sovereignty. The United States ratifies the World Authority treaty and soon is placed under "indefinite administrative penalty" for past war crimes by the Authority's dominant Soviet-Asian-African bloc.

Takeover. Red Chinese administrators are sent to Washington to implement the World Administrative Plan.

Indignities. The president of the United States must grant a drunkard Yugoslavian inspector from the World Health Organization authority to invade American homes to be sure water is "being properly treated with mind-sapping fluoride as ordered by the global Communist conspiracy" (70–73).

Invasion. Globalist troops occupy America.

Assassinations. The president, vice president, and many high ranking military officers are killed.

Riots. The economy decays. Fear and want envelop the land. Urban have-nots fan out into the suburbs to pillage and profane.

Holocaust. Twenty million "ordinary people of the United States," almost "anyone who protested or even looked unhappy at the Takeover" are killed, "whole towns and cities" are blasted with atom bombs. Others are "sent into slavery to Africa or China and worked to death" (123).

Rebellion. The Rangers, young, clear-eyed, patriotic John Franklin among them, have been preparing, stockpiling supplies, gathering information, selecting targets, training, hiding weapons on a remote woodland retreat. When the time is right, they strike; they assassinate, bomb, disable, and drive the enemy from U.S. shores. Rebellion spreads. Communism is defeated everywhere. The World Authority crumbles into pastoral provincialism.

Franklin's "letters" and Turner's "diaries" and their respective rebel groups, the Rangers and the Order, have points in common. Earl and

John each have a significant other named Katharine. Each uses printing presses to increase their resources. Each plays a specialized role as a communications expert in the rebel underground. Each recommends cultivating chaos to anger and realign public sentiment. But there are differences.

Franklin's enemy is an alien political economy; Turner's is the despised copresence of non-Aryan peoples. The mass murders described in the "letters" are the work of enemies; in the "diaries," they are the Order's eugenic handiwork. In triumph, Franklin's Rangers restore federal government; Turner's Order destroys it. Franklin lives. Turner dies, a suicidal domestic terrorist atom-bomber.

Earl Turner's diaries tell the tales of the Order's patriotic effort to wrest freedom and genetic simplicity from ZOG, the Zionist Occupation Government, the despotic international Jewry ruling over a future United States. The "Cohen Act" leads to the confiscation of all private firearms. The Supreme Court rules antirape laws unconstitutional because they imply differences between the sexes. This results in waves of rapes, particularly of white women by black men. Banks are required to provide low-interest loans to mixed-race couples buying property in white neighborhoods. Dystopian America decomposes into a "cesspool of mongrels and Blacks and Jews and sick, twisted White Liberals" (Macdonald 1978, 175). Then, the Order strikes back.

The members of the Order swear solemn oaths and answer miscegenation with murders. They rob banks and flood ghettos with counterfeit currency, inciting minorities to liquored revelries and sending the economy plunging. And they perpetuate a holocaust of their own in the cause of racial imperative. They direct the Day of the Rope.

> It started at three o'clock this morning . . . in a thousand blocks at once, in fifty different residential neighborhoods and every squad leader had a long list of names and addresses . . . [D]oors splinter[ed] as booted feet kicked them open. . . . If they were non-White—and that included all the Jews and everyone who even looked like he had a bit of non-White ancestry—they were shoved into hastily formed columns and started on their no-return march to the canyon . . . north of the city.
>
> The Whites . . . were . . . hanged on the spot . . . hands taped, a rope thrown over a convenient limb or signpost . . . hauled clear of the ground . . . left dancing in the air.
>
> When the execution squads began running out of rope, we stripped several miles of wire from power poles to use in its place.
>
> It is quiet and totally peaceful . . . but the night is filled with silent horrors; from tens of thousands of lampposts, power poles, and trees . . .

> grisly forms hang . . . at every intersection. Hanging from a single overpass only about a mile from here is a group of 30, each with an identical placard . . . "I betrayed my race." Two or three had been decked out in academic robes before they were strung up, and the whole batch are apparently faculty members from the nearby UCLA campus. . . . The System has already paid them their 30 pieces of silver. Today we paid them. (162–63)

That was the make-believe, the fabrication, the exceptions to Pierce's usual writing and Mathews's usual reading. But there was another Order, Mathews's Order, not a book borrowed from another book, not a neatly finished cover-bound figment, but an eighteen-month, rough-edged reign of tangible terror.

How much of *The Turner Diaries* were inspired by *The John Franklin Letters* is hard to say, but the parallels between the Orders created by Mathews and Macdonald are a matter of record—a court transcript, in excess of twelve hundred pages, from the trial of the Order's surviving members. Hundreds of magazine and newspaper articles also tell the story, as do at least two books (Coates 1987, 49–76; Dees 1996, 135–47) Here are some highlights.

Activities of the Order

Mathews recruits eight "Aryan Kinsmen" (including one woman), each of whom swears oaths of secrecy and loyalty, then goes looking for things to do.[16] Where to get money? They try the old-fashioned way—making it themselves. The printing press at the Aryan Nations headquarters produces only smudged paper. Even with help from professional forgers and a proper press, arrests are immediate whenever distribution is attempted. The gang changes tactics. Better to acquire other people's real money than make their own bogus bills.

Their robberies start small, grow large. The Spokane pornographic bookstore grosses only $369, but the Seattle bank yields $25,900. The Fred Meyers discount store job earns $43,000 and the Bon Marché, $500,000. Then they hit a Brink's armored truck in Ukiah, California, and make off with $3.8 million. Where does the money go? A little is for expenses. The FBI recovers $600,000. More is traced to the cause: $100,000 to recruit "high-tech scientists" to develop weapons for the Order; $50,000 to William Pierce for writing *The Turner Diaries*; $700,000 to Louis Beam, Tom Metzger, and others for recruitment; and $40,000 to Richard Butler for use of his church in getting started. The remaining $2.8 million? Somewhere unknown.

With money in hand, it is time for action. An adult theater in Seattle and a synagogue in Boise are bombed with little damage; a talk show host and a turncoat member are shot with fatal results. Time grows short. The government acts too, searching, finding.

In all, sixty-two are tracked, arrested, and charged; twenty-four are indicted; twelve plead guilty and testify for the prosecution; ten are convicted at the trial. And one is dead. People remember the dead one best. He died this way.

The law is closing in. On the run from a shootout and near-arrest in Portland, Oregon, Mathews and three companions retreat to their "safe" houses on Whidbey Island. Soon the FBI follows, watches, prepares. Traffic is cut off from the island; the shipping lanes are blocked. Two hundred agents surround three houses. The companions surrender. Two houses stand empty. Mathews is alone in the third.

The FBI negotiates then threatens with an ultimatum then assaults with tear gas and firearms. They are repelled with automatic weapons fire. They negotiate again then wait.

Dawn. A helicopter circles overhead, dropping white-hot magnesium flares on the cabin roof. From the highway, where the crowds have gathered, explosions and the erratic splattering of automatic weapons fire can be heard.

One reporter, closer than the rest, described the end. "The sky was turning orange. The explosions were incredible. No one could have survived that fire!" (White and Larsen 1984, 8). No one did.

Wreaths

The first wreath was laid at the gate to the Batemans' home one year later by a small group of skinheads. Over the years, the crowds grew. Butler came. Metzger came. Civil rights activists came. The media came, especially the media. Jim Larsen, editor of the local newspaper, told me of "one skinhead punk, oh maybe fifteen, with tattoos on his head and arms" who was interviewed "at least thirty times" by regional and national reporters. The county was forced to cordon off roads and close parks to keep the assemblies contained and the protesters pro and con apart. In mid-1996 the Batemans sold and moved to less hallowed ground. Few protesters come now. There have been no wreaths in the new millennium.

When it was all over, the reading and research, the organization, training, and plans, when the robberies and the killings and the trial were over, when the smoke cleared over the Batemans' homesite, when the evidence was collected and the remains identified for certain as those of Robert Mathews, William Pierce, "Andrew Macdonald," the physicist turned novelist with a cause, said this. "Bob gave us a very important symbol. He did what was morally right. He may have been a bit premature . . . and he may have made many tactical errors. But he reminded us we are not engaged in a debate between gentlemen. . . . Bob elevated . . . our struggle. He took us from name calling to blood-letting. He cleared the air for all of us. In the long run that will be helpful" (quoted in Dees 1996, 144–45).

In reflecting on all this remember four things: Robert Mathews and the Order are gone. Two hundred and twenty thousand copies of *The Turner Diaries* are in print. Timothy McVeigh had one of them. Hank never heard of the book.

Final Word

What then is to be made of survivalists' words? Will some heed Udvary's strident alarm of "Godless-Atheistic-brutal-terroristic" enemies upon the land and seek to stem to tide? Is Pierce's odd novel the countermeasure, the call to arms of true believers even now marching in force to the brink of revolutionary wrack and ruin? Will *The Turner Diaries* stand in future times beside *Das Kapital, Mein Kampf,* and Chairman Mao's little red book, the impetus of cataclysmic political change? Or is Sartre's vision more astute? Is the survivalist's real choice between mundane living and adventuresome telling? Are the pen and podium the true survivalist bulwarks against the aesthetic amnesia of commodified kitsch, the trivialized, sentimental simulacra that pass for culture in rational times?

To answer these questions in confidence we return to the theme that first framed survivalism, to the formal reason, the rationality said to permeate modern social life. Chapter 5 tests the credibility and limits of rationality, gives its antithesis name and form—charisma—and considers three possibilities for interpreting present and future society: the state emerges all-powerful if not all-repressive, insurgent zealots triumph, or corporate rationality co-opts both. In each of these trajectories survivalism is revealed for what it is: usually more than idle talk, often less than consummate action, but always a mirror of larger events.

5 SURVIVALISM AND RATIONAL TIMES

THE RATIONAL LEGACY

The reason for the unreason with which you treat my reason so weakens my reason that with reason I complain of your beauty.
—Feliciano de Silva, a poet much favored by Don Quixote

It is time for survivalism to take on new responsibilities. Grounded social science seeks utility beyond mere situation-specific description. We examine the particular in repeated detail in order to say something about the general. In this chapter survivalism is turned toward those broadened purposes. Survivalists are presented not just as a consequence, a dependent variable, a result of the conditions of contemporary social life, but as an indicator, a lens for perceiving and understanding those conditions.

In chapter 1 it was claimed that modern industrial society is characterized by a comprehensive rationalization spread to influence human lived experience in nearly all aspects. Formal reason triumphs everywhere. But is this true? With the echoes of Gale's dark oratory, Pierce's sinister pen, and Mathews's final fusillades fresh in memory, does the claim still hold? Can we in good conscience and comfort assert that rationality has indeed become the dominant means of organizing human affairs, for most the path to follow and the end to achieve? Should Weber's theory of bureaucracy be read as an accurate and intentional discourse on the omnipresence of rationality in modern life, as structuralists would have it (see Blau 1970), or do Gale and the rest point to weaknesses in this argument? Survivalist entrepreneurship and bricolage were represented, for the most part, as creative accommodations to rationalization. But is this a process without limits? When might accommodation become resistance, and resistance, rebellion? Is rationality but a thin tissue, "stronger today than when Galileo knelt before the Inquisition" but still "a minority habit of mind . . . its future . . . much in doubt," while "blind belief fuels the millennium universe, dark and rangy as space itself" (Ferris 1997)? Is bureaucracy mere belief, rationalization only repair work to taken-for-granted assumptions of order and form (Hilbert 1987)? Do survivalist rhetoric and exploits signal a breakdown of rational ordering, reveal roiling countercurrents of muddle and rancor beneath progressive appearances? And further, is rationalization itself always obvious? Is all systematic social ordering reserved for public institutions, obvious and open to review? Or are there compelling rational influences disguised in other forms, concealed perhaps in consumerism, behind specious choices among superficial preferences?

In the new millennium rationality and its venerable antithesis, charisma, manifest in forces weak and strong, admired and abhorred, private and public, wrenching in contrary directions. These forces are most distinct in three forms: nation-states, conflicting dissidents, and transnational corporate powers; rationality apparent, abnegated, and hidden. What is to be made of these trends? Which will prove most potent and durable as the century unfolds? Will monolithic governments suppress dissension? Will megacorporate commerce transcend national sovereignty? Or will rebellious malcontents defy and destroy all attempts at regulated order? These possibilities will be examined in turn, first by setting forth each in hypothetical form, then by exploring attendant survivalist accommodations. In these contexts survivalism reveals several things: the possibilities and limits of culturecraft, the importance of survivalism in effecting change, and most crucially, the scope of rationalization in modern times.

APPARENT RATIONALITY

Since World War II, rationalization is said by some to have found its most potent manifestation in Leviathan forces attributed to nation-states, painted grand and invincible as ancient Rome or mid-nineteenth-century Britannia (Lapham 1988). Election- or succession-year journalism speaks of awesome swings of fate and fortune as power changes hands. These hypothetical titans hold human social life in place and on course with Orwellian efficiency and sure-handed bureaucratic control so perfect they can make the world stand still or rumble toward oblivion. How does this image compare with observed events? Some say not well.

These titans are sometimes fragile, occasionally toothless. In the past generation the Soviet Union has splintered, China has endured at least two revolutions, and the United States has failed to impose her theory of democracy on a single Latin American state. Even the full combined force of Western nonnuclear military might loosed on a middleweight Near Eastern dictator was insufficient to induce social, political, or ideological change. After the onslaught, Kuwait's oil once again flowed westward, but Iraq's helm still answered to the same hand. Signs of the titans' internal weaknesses are also evident.

Survivalists relish fashioning antigovernment rhetoric, but this is hardly distinctive behavior. Popular culture, from contemporary radio talk shows to classic cinema, has long found ready entertainment in assertions of villainy and indolence in American government, especially federalism. Early films in this genre, such as *Mr. Smith Goes to Washington* in the late 1930s or *All the King's Men* in the 1940s, pitted corrupt political bosses on high against courageous grassroots heroes taking on the establishment with individual tenacity and superior moral fiber. Later, villains became a handful of elite politicos or military officers about to co-opt or corrode national control and security: *Seven Days in May, The Twilight's Last Gleaming, The Company,* or humorously, *Dr. Strangelove* (see Hacker 1981).

To these fictions, social scientists add other theorizing that damns federal government. During the late 1970s policy implementation studies blossomed into an academic "growth industry" (Majone and Wildavsky 1979, 177) with consistently dismal conclusions (see Desai 1992). In the eyes of many social scientists, federal policies of every sort, from pesticide control to airline safety to National Park management to urban renewal, did not work, did not achieve their objectives, or produced explicitly harmful results (for example, Downs and Larkey 1986; Kettl 1988; Weiss and Klass 1986).[1] Despite evidence that in the long term some government programs work well (Kaplan and Cuciti 1986; Schwarz 1988; Lehman 1990), pessimism remains the dominant theme in academic analyses of governmental efforts.[2]

So what is to be made of government? Are the cited policy failures characteristic or anomalous? Do Hollywood ridicule and academic dismissal reveal the state's genuine powerlessness? Consider survivalists' behavior toward public authority.

Survivalists join academic policy analysts and conservative advocates in faulting government, especially federal government. But fault-finding is not disregard. Words are not deeds. While antigovernment rhetoric is commonly associated with survivalism, survivalist action is often conforming. Reconsider Operation Aurora Borealis.

No one mentioned them by name, but there were silent forces in the woods that weekend, forces everyone heeded if not feared. In nervous humor, and to ourselves, we called this area "Yesterday Land," a forgotten Disney attraction, but the analogy was not all wrong. Like the real Disneyland, the nearby woods and hills and hamlets were not what they seemed. There were hidden mechanisms behind the facade. The romantic notion of autonomous frontier life was a popular part of the local mystique and of the weekend's war-gaming, but not the whole story. The local cattlemen did not graze their stock on open range. The loggers did not cut trees at will. Ranching, timber harvest, and survivalism alike took place on public land, government land, land overseen, studied, and regulated by the Bureau of Land Management and the U.S. Forest Service, the Bureaus of Mines and Indian Affairs. Congressional legislation and national policy played as much a part in shaping this country as the cowboy six-guns and carbines of old, or the M-15s of today. Bureaucratic rationality maintained the setting for romanticized individualism.

At first we noticed what seemed a survivalist penchant to "play by the rules" in war-gaming and attributed it incorrectly to a lack of initiative. Other conformity, more telling of survivalism, went unheeded. Revolution and mayhem might lay ahead in survivalist scenarios, but for the time being there are laws to obey and rules to follow.

In the late 1970s the Civil Rights Division of the Anti-Defamation League of B'nai B'rith took specific action to curtail survivalism, drafting and promoting model "anti-paramilitary training" legislation, state by state, across the country. By the time Operation Aurora Borealis was held, such legislation had been enacted and signed in Oregon but not Washington. In compliance, the Rangers and Nighthawks moved their activities across state lines. Later, when Washington passed similar laws, field operations were shifted to Idaho, and later still, onto private lands. Compliance with state law was grudging, but timely and complete. So too were the practices of other groups in which I participated in Missouri, Tennessee, and California as legislation was adopted in those states throughout the following decades.

Much is made of survivalist armaments in popular reporting. Many survivalists are armed. But in my experience they are armed legally, within both the relatively permissive Federal Bureau of Alcohol, Tobacco, and Firearms regulations and the often more stringent state and local statutes.[3] Of the hundreds of weapons I saw in survivalists' arsenals, only three—two M-16 assault rifles and a pistol-caliber Uzi—had full automatic firing capabilities.[4] In each instance the owners were careful to point out these weapons were properly licensed (as were the long-range UHF radio systems owned and operated by Gale and the other Mariposans). Survivalist rhetoric may emphasize state intrusions or incompetence, but survivalism in action is largely law-abiding.

Nic clarified survivalists' responsibilities to the state when we were on Operation Icefield, an Idaho sequel to Operation Aurora Borealis. Macy was again providing circuitous, windy lectures, necessitating frequent breaks. Nic, Eleen, and I sat slouched against a downed log. Nic held another Macy handout propped against the convenient reading shelf of his bulging stomach, keeping his place in the text with a well-sharpened combat knife. He told us of a recent chat with a local journalist. "[The reporter] wanted to know what survivalism was, and I told him it is just having the knowledge, skills, and equipment to be ready for anything. Then he wanted to know what we were going to do with 'all our guns,' and I told him, 'nothing.' We [survivalists] go by the same laws as anyone else. I'm not about to defend my house with an AR-15 in peacetime. . . . You don't go outside and hide in the bushes and blow away poor Mr. Burglar."

For the majority of North American survivalists the rational order of governance, the state, matters. It tempers behavior and, in the instance of military equipage and methods, even sets emulatable standards. But will this last? Others argue that the real forces of consequence in modern times lie not in the centralized state but in the decentered pockets of intransigent self-interest, amid the antirationality of corrosive charismatic fervor.

ANTIRATIONALITY

Around the world, sovereign states face the antipathy and disregard of anarchistic fragments, fundamentalist fanatics, and others with narrowed allegiances. Cabals, conspiracies, and coups d'état are no longer hatched on high but among the grassroots. In pockets and enclaves a kind of retribalization is taking place. Jihad, Barber aptly if not precisely calls it (1992, 53), the realignment of identities based on primordial divisions of clan, race, creed, and cultural practice (see Geertz 1973, 255–310). It takes form in French and Canadian movements to legitimate provincial languages and dialects (Levine 1995a, 16), in the bloody violence of Lebanons and Ulsters and the chronic warfare of Saharan and equatorial Africa—tribe against tribe, people against people, culture against culture. Jihad spreads in the name of myriad narrowly defined oppositions to cooperative interdependence and civic mutuality (Barber 1992, 53).

This separatist dissension suggests that, far from being omnipotent, governments are weak and waning. Formal public rationality has failed.

Nationalism, formerly the force of unification and integration, now rends the very nations it once brought together. Racial, ethnic, religious, tribal, and sectarian factions, offshoots, and dissident minorities seek countries not their own or smaller worlds of control and privilege within borders that will seal them off from heterogeneity. In the 1990s Tamils, Palestinians, Kurds, Basques, Québécois, Hutus, Tutsis, Zulus, Serbs, Bosnians, Croats, and Algerian fundamentalists were among those who held the headlines and sometimes the rifles. The list changes often. The trend does not. Jihad is not rational war, not Von Clausewicz's extension of policy by other means. In the face of Jihad, formal public rationality is a nostalgic fiction. Beneath the crust of apparent ordered regularity, beneath law, social policy, and international accord, seethes a pressurized magma of chaos and strife ready to flux forth through the cracks in fracturing institutions.

Some argue survivalism is the symptom of America's own Jihad. The Hubertys, Mathewses, Kahals, and McVeighs are presented as typical. Along with the Republic of Texas, the Army of Israel, and the Aryan Nations, these characters get the prime-time interviews and column-yards of print coverage accorded the most celebrated of antiheroes. We are told these are the harbingers of *A Gathering Storm: America's Militia Threat* (Dees 1996), *Armed and Dangerous* radicals signaling *The Rise of the Survivalist Right* (Coates 1987) preparing to reap the *Bitter Harvest* (Corcoran 1990), the *Harvest of Rage* (Dyer 1997).

No doubt harm has been done by, and in the name of, survivalism. No doubt there are individuals and perhaps groups primed for conflict, willing and ready to scuttle, sabotage, tarnish, spoil, and vandalize civil society. Our task is to judge if meaningful patterns may be discerned among these predations and predators, and how comprehensive their harm may become. Is survivalism the first sign of societal disintegration, of Jihad on the home front, of the primogenitive power of irrational, affect-driven outrage, overwhelming states and collective orders? Or is it less than it seems, the exaggerations of media promoters trading briskly if not too honestly in sensationalism? Let's look more closely at the process proposed to impel antirationalities, the theory and practice of charisma.

Charisma: Theory and Practice

"IRRATIONAL" CHARISMA

In the preceding chapter evocative personality and pencraft were proposed as sources of persuasive power, but neither the process nor the certainty of these influences were clarified. Do wicked words foment dire deeds? And if so, how? In the standard account, charismatic word-power provides both an impetus and a mechanism for survivalism and other organized "irrationalities." Charismatics the likes of Gale are said to craft will-sapping ideologies from the antimatter of sober society—unregulated feeling, emotion, affect.[5] These swirl out from charismatic texts and rhetoric, putting in thrall bemused and obedient followers (see Mitchell 2000).

Such charisma is located over against all forms of reflective reason in a hypothetical realm of totalizing affect. Alan Dawe illustrates: "Pure feeling . . . this is clearly the *sine qua non* of charismatic authority, which rejects all rules save the rule of intense, single-minded emotional commitment whereby separation from the world of mundane rationality is preserved and which therefore demands the 'sacrifice of the intellect.' The appeal is directly to the deepest emotional roots of individual human beings" (1978, 395).

In interpretations of this sort, charisma suppresses rationality, producing a "monolithic definition of reality, and asymmetrical solidarity between leaders and led" that "inhibit public expressions of differences among followers" (Dow 1968, 336). Under the subheading "He is God," Couch argues that charisma insulates the charismatic from judgment and censure. No matter what the charismatic's actions, bemused followers "foster conferring gratitude toward the leader . . . and the leader's position, which allows him to define reality" in ways certain to "preclude blaming the leader" (Couch 1989, 274).

How this bemusement derives is not clear. Consider Dawe's typical, tautological account. "Charismatic authority rests upon the recognition by followers of the charismatic leader of his individual possession of extraordinary qualities, by virtue of which he commands their personal devotions" (Dawe 1978, 394). In other words, charismatics lead because followers perceive in them charismatic qualities of leadership.[6] In sum, the standard intellectual account represents charismatic appeals as irrational, charismatics as personally insulated from responsibility, and their claims as immune from truth testing and depicts leaders and led alike as bound together in "single-minded emotional commitment of the charismatic community to its pursuit of its chosen values, regardless of consequences" (Dawe 1978, 394).[7]

What of survivalists the likes of Gale? His searing rhetoric is quintessential firebrand rabble rousing. What are its consequences? To answer this question, the notion of charisma must be refined beyond the standard account.

CHARISMA RECONSIDERED

The formal rationality of the modern social order is a matter of fact; whether or not this social order is substantively rational depends upon one's perspective. "A thing is never irrational in itself, but only from a particular . . . point of view" Weber writes in a footnote to *The Protestant Ethic and the Spirit of Capitalism* (Weber 1958b, 194 n. 9). Rationality is not an attribute *of* behavior but an attribution *to* behavior (see Brubaker 1984, 35). Rationality, like deviance, is ascribed to things, it does not inhere within them. And rationality is relative. Actions are judged rational or irrational from arbitrarily given points of interpretive orientation. All knowledge-based action is rational from some perspective. So is charisma.

In Weber's view, charisma is directed *against* "unthinking acquiescence in customary ways," traditional, normative, sedimented practices, and *in favor of* alternative, arguably technically superior means and "deliberate adaptation to situations in terms of self-interest" (Weber 1964, 22). Charismatics may evoke strong feelings, but only as a consequence of their novel, even revolutionary *methods for accomplishing group goals* (see Weber 1978, 25). Emotion is thus put to use, directed, sublimated, channeled. Charisma aims not to raise passions but to fulfill projects. Shakespeare's Henry V on the fields of Agincourt delivered his Saint Crispian's Day oratory not to reassure his troops but to defeat the French.[8] The charismatic's claim is to alternative rationality, not the abandonment of rationality. Action, not ecstasy, is the objective. The aims of charisma are not achieved in unified tearfulness and wringing of hands, or chorused singing of praises, but in storming the walls, recapturing the senate, or purifying the gene pool.

Far from being unsubstantiated or ascribed, the charismatic's authority, precisely like that of the entrepreneur and the bricoleur, must constantly be confirmed in concrete accomplishments.[9]

This is not to suggest that charismatic engagements are staid and dispassionate. Charismatics offer rational programs, programs that are knowledge-based, that make sense and promise results, though these offerings are by no means limited to the orthodoxies of systematic empirical science. Charismatics may propose fundamental, paradigmatic reconfigurations of knowledge with profound and far-reaching potential. Their proposals are often "extraordinary . . . unheard-of . . . strange to all rule and tradition" (Weber [1946] 1989, 23). Retellings of history elevate group members to positions of newfound legitimacy and contemporary prominence. New interpretations of natural law place mighty forces within reach and control. No doubt "distress and enthusiasm" alike derive from these revelations (Weber [1946] 1989, 23).

SURVIVALIST CHARISMA

The emphasis on immediate demonstrations of practical achievement needs tempering. Survivalism is almost always anticipatory, a negative achievement in the Bergsonian sense of the "negative," the not here, not now. For survivalists "proof" is in the coherence of telling, not the correspondence of showing.

Among survivalists charisma takes three forms partially defined by Weber ([1946] 1989, 254): the prophet, magician, and dramatist. Prophetic charisma trades in knowledge of trends and tendencies, inclinations and forecasts, ascertained from distinctive modes of perception. The entrepreneur, as a practical example, uses hunches, signs, and intuition to anticipate demand and supply. Like the alchemist of old, charismatic magicians combine extant material and technologies in exceptional ways. They do not challenge the core credence of centrist science, only its failure to examine and exploit all potentials and publicize all findings.[10] Magicians find shortcuts: unrevealed hazards in everyday living environments, vital health aids in simple herbs and foodstuffs, powerful weapons in overlooked principles. Prophecy and magic abound among survivalists, but they are the secondary forms. First is charismatic drama.

The dramatist makes a place for prophecy and magic, legitimates prophetic imagination and magical invention. The dramatist claims neither divine revelation nor special method, but opens the discourse to new possibilities, enfranchises others in their own claims to search and create. Dramatists offer unremarkable people means of acquiring remarkable self-conceptions. Dramatists derive authority indirectly, from their capacities to convince *others* of their own extraordinariness. This may be less than they intend. I suspect Reverend Gale wished to be taken as the final arbiter of grand causes, master soothsayer, divinity, knight, savior, all at once. He offered prophetic predictions, laid on hands to cure, and proposed to lead during the coming apocalypse. But he accomplished something else. The literal content of his preaching was interesting but not unquestioned. Participants interjected doubts and inquiries throughout his sermons and instruction. His prophecies had competition, from the nightly news and a myriad of alternative "intelligence" reports the likes of Hank's. And Cliff still limped on Sunday. What Gale accomplished was not the slavish conformity often associated with the metonymic despotism of charisma but enthusiasm for radical culture crafting. Gale set the stage. He did not assign the parts or write the script. Members themselves did that, while invoking their own charismatic prophecy and magic. Listen to the table talk.

TABLE TALK

At the Manasseh Ranch, Gale arranged meals that were ample, not refined. Considerable supplies were on hand. Five rust-streaked metal sheds in among the trailers contained dried and preserved foodstuffs, canning gear, garden tools, soaps, and other long-term survival supplies. Numbered freezers worked side by side against the heat in a patio enclosure at the rear of the kitchen trailer. Gale ordered forty-five steaks defrosted for Saturday dinner. These came from freezer three. Other meals of hot dogs and hamburgers came from number four. Lunch came from kitchen supplies, a spread of sandwich makings in basic colors—white bread and mayonnaise, yellow mustard, orange cheese, green relish, red bologna, ketchup, and Kool-Aid—set on the side counters. We ate outside, crowded around picnic tables, in groups of seven or eight. Gale knew the limits of listening comfort, if not credibility. Meals were unhurried and sociable.

Mealtimes brought participants together for introductions and networking, knowledge sharing and inquiry. People took these opportunities to showcase their own variants of survivalism. Topics shifted in wide compass round the tables.

Kermit had been right to combine tax protest and militia activity, conspiracy theories and fundamentalism, apocalypse and revolution. Not all the weekend participants cared about these topics, or even granted each one full credence. But taken together, they illustrate a sampling of participants' talking points. No single scenario or report of ostensible facts dominated. None were fundamental beliefs to which all participants were committed. Teleological truth was not the point. Discourse was. Few could answer ever curious Todd's questions, for example, especially his obscure theological riddles (Gale tried after-hours a time or two), but most invited his asking. Todd's inquiries and others' sparked debate and elicited opinion, and gave believers what they seemed to value most in the weekend—an invitation to participate, to have a say, put on a show, interpret, dramatize, and recast the events of the day and the signs of the times.

"Who was Tesla?" Todd asked. Bob and Tina, an attractive middle-class couple wearing matching Welders and Pipe Fitters Union t-shirts, were from Merced. They left their two preteen children with relatives for the weekend and drove to the ranch in a new, bright blue Jeep. They were discussing trading their present boat in on a larger one for fishing trips in the San Joaquin Delta when Todd asked "Who was Tesla?" Bob and Tina knew. So did others.

> Tesla . . . died in 1943 . . . was Serbo-Croatian. Albert Einstein was a Jew. He took the theory of relativity from a patent of Tesla's interferometer when he worked in the French patent offices. Recently, a paper written by an Irish scientist reveals that $E = mc^2$ was the basis of Tesla's energy

> curve, explained in his patent application, but Einstein lifted it and claimed it as his own idea. The Tesla curve is a new form of energy. Protons . . . neutrons . . . electromagnetic fields. The U.S. government knew about Tesla and took all his experiments and hid them . . . Russians used Tesla's formulas. . . . They have secret weapons. . . . If you bring these two energy curves together, there will be a huge explosion . . . fireballs over Afghanistan . . . fireballs over Africa. . . . The way to defend against this new weapon . . . Tesla's interferometer . . . put up energy domes over cities. . . . The Russians have them, nothing can get through, not even birds. . . . Russians are practicing using energy curve weapons . . . from satellites, from flying airplanes, and they melt down dogs. . . . Our government won't develop [Tesla weapons] 'cause you have to melt down dogs to test them and the Humane Society won't let 'um. . . . We all have little interferometers built into our brains. . . . That's how we do mental telepathy. . . . UFOs are just the Russians' biggest interferometers used to generate Tesla curves. . . . No, they are from another universe . . . across the time warp. . . . God is on the other side of the time warp, in another universe . . .

And so the topics changed. In times of trouble you may need to hunt and then cook some creatures of the wild, Bob and Tina and the others agreed. This lunchtime talk of game recipes seemed noncontroversial until Barbara received her warning. She was figuratively adding whole carrots and potatoes, quartered onions and peeled tomatoes to her description of a hunter family's main dish—fresh raccoon stew—when Jane blurted, "*Never* eat anything with paws!"

John Briggs, our hand-to-hand combat instructor, a Gale associate for more than ten years, agreed. "No! You can't do that! You can't eat raccoon!" Others at the table began to listen with care. Jane, after all, was the camp's chief cook for the weekend.

Barbara became defensive. "But my mom fixed it for us when we were kids. It was good. The tomatoes take away the gamy flavor."

"It's not in the *book*!" Jane insisted. I thought there must be some definitive wild-game cookbook in question. Wrong. Jane cited her authority: "The Bible forbids it!"

To this, others soon added their own recollections of biblically tabooed table fare. Creatures with cloven hooves and scales were also off the list of edibles.

"Not bear either."

"Or dogs."

"Snake meat tastes good, but it'll make ya sick."

"And don't eat camel!" [laughter]

Finally, John, in curious contradiction to the weekend's anti-Semitism, admitted, "The Jews are right. Never eat pork. It's the worst."

No one called this a Kosher diet.

Attention turned to John. Food prohibitions and other health-related matters were a topic of general interest all weekend. Todd said what others perhaps were thinking. "But I *like* to eat pork."

"I know," John agreed, "but you can't." He then gave us proof. "My dad is a butcher," John told us, "a professional butcher at a market. He says when he slices a pig in half, then he has to take his knife and wipe all the pus off. 'Cause pigs are full of pus. And they got screw worms all through 'um."

"Are you talking about *trichinosis*?" asked Zillah from the next table. John ignored her.

"And if you eat pork the screw worms in the pus will get into your joints. That's why old people's hands are clenched together. It's not arthritis, like people think, but screw worms from eating pork."

"Yea, and the United States is the only nation that hasn't gotten rid of them!" Jane accused. "Screw worms" became yet another government policy failure.

There were simple technologies for improving health, too, but you had to understand the problem. The problem was the electricity all around us in modern life had been bent and become dangerous. Ray, a near-toothless, wiry farmhand from the Bakersfield area knew electricity.

"Where there is a lot of alternating current, the electromagnetic environment has been turned from its natural clockwise orientation to a counterclockwise orientation," he told us. When that happens we "are living in a sea of electrical poison, which affects our abilities to function electrically." Nearly everything that goes wrong with us can be traced to this problem, Ray claimed. But there is a solution. "Polarize your electricity" so it "turns right again." Devices are on the market for just such a purpose. Ray had one and recommended it. "Researchers found that when an electrical system is polarized, strange things happen to the people living there." If you have polarized electricity in your house, "the wires act like a big antenna." "If your spine is out of adjustment it generally will self-adjust if you look at a polarized fluorescent light. Or you can hold something operated by an AC motor, that works too. Or drink polarized tap water. . . . If you have a polarizer," the water "gets straightened out because electrical ground wires are attached to the pipes."

Zillah, seventy years old, one inch under five feet tall, and ten pounds under a hundred-weight, dressed to impress, not kill. Some participants had bought or borrowed hunting clothes in anticipation of field training, but Zillah created her own costume for the occasion, sewed it herself according to her own design. Imagine a Joseph's coat of mottled greens and browns, lined in gray flannel, with synthetic bone buttons, pockets big enough for a Bible on one side and packet of handouts on the other, and topped by a flaring cowl. Add elastic-waist pants, a natty beret of the same material, and child-size hiking boots to finish the ensemble. Imagine Little Green Riding Hood with an arthritic left hip and a sheaf of flyers. That was Zillah. Todd had read some of Zillah's handouts back in Oregon. Zillah had ideas for political reform.

Her plan was radically democratic, unlikely, and in the usual survivalist fashion, expounded at length in her handouts. Zillah's handouts were typical of the type: utopian, long-winded, full of details about the specific ails of America, the evils of various "-isms," and a few imaginative technical solutions, all in tiny Zillah-size print, nine pages worth, double-sided.

Zillah's vision streamlined democracy to its most intimate forms, the New England town meeting or the Swiss Canton assembly writ large. No more out-of-touch politicians and political parties, no more representation by others.[11] "Freedom's Last Straw," as she called it, could be grasped by involving the electorate directly in the legislative process. A constitutional amendment allowing easily initiated national referenda would supply the proposals; printed ballots in local newspapers, free public phones, and "secret voting codes" would allow direct voting by all citizens. Given these mechanisms, all that would be needed for enlightened self-governance would be "unbiased" news coverage of important events "so voters could learn the facts and learn about all sides" of relevant issues. "Public opinion" would rule supreme and "politicians" would be unnecessary. Again, nearly all the heads nodded. Democracy was good, it seemed; only government was faulty.

Tom Hagner doubted the government was even legal, at least in one respect. The government's crime? Income tax. Tom, in his late forties, worked in the Silicon Valley as a "QC man." "I'm an electromechanical inspector, in common language, quality control." Tom was independent. "I do contract work. . . . I work for myself. I'll work one plant until they don't need me anymore or until I don't need them anymore. It's sort of a mutual thing. . . . I get paid direct and I'm not an employee." Not being an "employee" has its benefits. According to Tom, you don't have to pay income tax.

Tom, like Thomas Cove, belonged to the "American Freemen Society," referred to simply as the "Freemen" in media coverage of their Montana standoff with the FBI during the summer of 1996. Tom had handouts, too. Again the point was long in coming and the evidence detailed, disjointed, and tedious. A fragment of a Supreme Court decision used the term "shall" to mean "may," Tom's flyer noted. An IRS publication referred to the tax system's base in "voluntary compliance." Other legal texts and government documents were analyzed and interpreted, case by case, point by point. After five single-spaced pages the logical conclusion was clear, at least to Tom. Paying income tax is voluntary, not compulsory. "You don't have to pay if you're not in a certain category, if you're not an employee . . . or a resident of the District of Columbia. . . . The person who files income tax returns is subjecting himself to the IRS rules for filing." Don't subjugate yourself, he advised. Don't file.[12]

Charisma Waning

Rationality permeates even the most evocative of survivalist events. Gale's charismatic performance did not narrow listeners' interests and perceptions or benumb their reason. Rather, he opened the dialogue to alternative, survivalist-crafted rationalities. Following Gale's tirades seminar participants did not babble in tongues or run amuck but offered insights into dietary conduct and household electrical systems, political reform, tax regulations, and the history of science. Nor did either Gale or the table talkers seek to convince by evocative talk alone. Claims were permeated with rational appeals and appearances. Gale's future-casting was offered as history as well as prophecy, as fact based, trend analyzed. Scripture never stood alone. Gale cited standard military procedure, not spiritual ecstasy, as the analog of Bible reading. He tracked the lost tribes' migration with concrete data: linguistic evidence, observable signs at the top of the pass, photographs of the Cherokee chiefs, and recorded inscriptions on the pyramids. Pork and pawed creatures were off the menu, both because they were on the list of Bible prohibitions and because of the unappetizing testimony of a practicing butcher. The income tax was rejected on technical not emotional grounds, on close readings of constitutional and case-law precedents. Throat cutting, garroting, and the organization of revolutionary cells were taught according to military protocol and practical experience.

In contemporary, pluralistic Western society the power of charismatic leadership is weak when based only on personal performance, however evocative. Rhetorical theatrics alone compel no more than audience appreciation, not behavioral change.[13] Only when problems are fateful and pressing—when enemies encircle and threaten, when the nation is crushed by debt and depression, when the ship is holed and sinking—and members perceive a sure and common fate, only then may charismatic calls for practical action carry the day.[14]

Charisma's effects among survivalists are limited for the same reasons; survival is not a pressing problem, not a common fate. Many action choices remain open. Survivalists face future troubles, not contemporary crises. Today, everyday, is a time for patient planning, not urgent action. Charismatic calls to arms are muffled by the heartening hum of daily routine. Charisma acquires its greatest potency when accompanied by collective interdependence and substantial resource reallocation. Charismatic leadership in strict churches (Iannaccone 1994, 1180–211) and successful communes (Kanter 1973) is durable and commanding primarily because membership requires material and structural realignments: dietary modifications, changes in children's school curricula, residential reallocation, career displacements, and sacrifices of time, money, and real property.[15] These in turn sever ties with workmates, neighbors, even family. Outside their own small circles, communalists have few alternative associations, few places to go or means of livelihood.[16] Survivalists have many. Survivalists live thoroughly immersed in contemporary routines of kinship, vocation, and community. The bureaucratic state and other forces, not charismatic rhetors, set the tempo and direction of their daily lives.

There are exceptions. A few, already cut off from conventional life worlds, actively seek encompassing, charismatically led communities among survivalists and elsewhere, fully willing to sacrifice and join. Most are disappointed. Ponderosa Village or the Terrene Ark or southern Oregon offer no such destinations. The Mount Rainier Rangers and the Freedom Brigade, the Cascade Valley Force and the Nighthawks are only common interest clubs. Participation in these communities mellows, moderates, and postpones action in deference to the core survivalist activities—narrating what-if worlds, making plans and preparations. When violence and conflict arise, they come from outside survivalism, from individuals who have separated themselves not only from conventional worlds of association, but also from survival organizations they deem unfocused, equivocating, convocations of mere talk. Robert Mathews, as an example, was not in thrall to Richard Butler or William Pierce, but in revolt from both, frustrated by the unwillingness of either to do more than wait for the tide to turn and conditions to sour, to sponsor no more than recruitment drives, flyers, pamphlets, and newsletter mailings. He read *The Turner Diaries,* but also Spengler and the Bible. Then he *broke away* from the charismatic community of the Aryan Nations, such as it was. As a last alternative he formed his own "leaderless cell." And he died alone.

Gale nearly did, too, his charisma asphyxiated by disease and relentless rationality, by the government which had so long been his benefactor, and which he had so long reviled.

Gale's Finale

We were not everywhere on our weekend at Gale's. We did not hear every plan. There was more going on than we knew. Culturecraft was being played on a grand scale. A document was being drafted, a sixteen-page "compact" authored by Gale and ultimately signed by forty-three others, including Butler. Gale's treatise went farther than the Hunt brothers did. The compact was in essence a new national constitution. The coin of the realm remained but the present U.S. Congress was dismissed, the Federal Reserve Board abandoned, and the income tax declared illegitimate and void. As a final touch of drama, and a reminder that the state is never entirely irrelevant, Gale filed his declaration of independence from federal authority with the county recorder's office in Mariposa on July 11, 1984. This playing at constitutional authorship went by without response from authorities, but the committee's attempts to recraft criminal law did not. Gale and his partners mailed "constructive notices" to various federal agents warning them of "criminal indictments" and "warrants of arrest" to be issued by the "Committee of the States . . . sitting as the Grand Jury of the People of the States of the Union," and bearing this threat: "Any interference or attempt to interfere with the functions and the activities of this Committee of the States or its delegates by any person or agency of the government shall result in the death penalty being imposed upon conviction by said Committee sitting as Congress of the United States" (quoted in Seymour 1991, 270).

Words and deeds began to collapse inward; government tolerance wore through. After a lengthy investigation, Gale, Marrino, and seven other defendants were arrested and charged with ten counts of conspiring to kill IRS agents and federal judges as part of an alleged plot to destabilize the national government. The trial, too, was lengthy. Some of the defense tactics were curious.

The reader may have wondered about the source of the quotes from Gale's seminar, reported in chapter 4. How were these obtained in such detail? Eleen and I took volumes of notes whenever possible. We wrote during sermons, on trips to the bathroom, in our trailer at night. We did the best we could. But our records were far from complete and principally focused on the informal dialogue.

As we prepared to depart I thanked Gale for the seminar invitation and mentioned our shortfall. So much of the material had been new to us. We probably missed a number of points. Knowing that Gale did a brisk mail-order business selling copies from his fifteen-year collection of taped weekly sermons, I asked for recommendations. Which ones should we order to start?

Gale brightened as he had when Cliff agreed to a back-straightening. "Got any blank tapes?" he inquired. "Yes," I affirmed happily, thinking we might be able to buy some of his prerecorded sermons on the spot. I brought in a box of used tapes from my car trunk. Gale began loading cassettes into a duplicator behind the pulpit while we milled about, bidding good-bye to other participants. Half an hour passed. Gale reloaded the machine several times, wrote some quick titles on the tape covers, and handed us our copies. They were not old sermons. What he gave us was the weekend's lectures and sermons, a complete set, everything we had heard, all fourteen hours. He had been recording himself the entire time. We were amazed at this willing revelation. So were others.

Roxanne Gale, the colonel's spouse, sent periodic updates on the trial to the Ministry mailing list. When Gale went on trial, copies of the seminar tapes were obtained and entered into the court record. According to Roxanne the jury heard much of the material quoted in chapter 4 directly from the source, in Gale's own voice. When the tapes were played in court she judged them to be powerful evidence. She reported, "The first one was played in its entirety and upon its conclusion the entire courtroom sat in dumbfounded silence for several minutes." Dumbfounded, indeed. As Roxanne tells it, federal prosecutors knew nothing of these tapes prior to the trial.[17] The tapes were submitted as evidence by the *defense,* by Gale's own attorney. Roxanne's report assured us that the resulting courtroom silence was a good sign. Now the judge and jury would understand the problem. They did.

All guilty. At sentencing, defendants and attorneys pled for leniency. Pleading styles varied. Gale's attorney sought a reduced sentence by lecturing the judge on the colonel's military record. He concluded by shaking his finger literally at the judge and figuratively at the idea that a man of such distinction could be sent to prison, repeating "For shame!" "For shame!" Gale was sentenced to a year and a day of incarceration, a $5,000 fine, and five years probation. The Ministry's assistant pastor and favorite son, "Slim" Marrino, used a different strategy to impress the judge. The Ministry's favorite son went over to the enemy.

"Now for Slim," Roxanne reported, he "caved in and tearfully explained to the court that he was very sorry, 'I have completely divorced myself from all members of the Committee of the States, Unorganized Militia and The Ministry of Christ Church because their beliefs and methods are wrong.'" Marrino was released with credit for time served. Credit with the court, that is, not the Ministry of Christ Church. With his renouncement, Marrino abandoned his position in the Ministry, and Gale to his fate.

Fate was swift but not kind. His appeals exhausted, Gale was remanded to federal prison to serve his time. But his time was less than the state required. After half a century of cigarette smoking, Gale's emphysema took its toll. He died on April 27, 1988, leaving behind six hundred hours of dusty charisma-on-tape, an empty, leaderless church, and a defunct mailing list.

Still, Gale's protégé of old, Richard Butler, maintained a detectable profile. I went to see what Butler had accomplished, to judge what chances remained for charismatic revolt, for Jihad on the home front. Would the state have the last word with Butler, too? Or might other forms of rationality assert themselves? In time, Butler's fate would unravel in several directions. But first there was a gathering.

ARYANISM RECONSIDERED

Imagine a world congress of aryans. That's spelled "ARYAN WORLD CONGRESS" in twenty-six-point type and Gothic script. What images arise? Fasching and Carnival? Mardi Gras and the Olympics? Perhaps the grandeur of Bayreuth and Wagner's glorious Ring or the massed power of a Moscow May Day parade? Well, not quite. I'll tell you what it was like.

Countdown

It is to be an Aryan World Congress, a late-July, three-day, Idaho gathering of aryan elite from the millions of Anglo-Saxon, Germanic, Nordic, Basque, Lombardic, Celtic, and Slavic peoples around the globe.

Calls go out to all the Aryan Nations, all thirteen tribes, Manasseh, Ephraim, Ruben, Simeon, Judah, Dan, Napthali . . .

And to the thousands actively sympathetic here in North America.[18]

At least seven hundred are coming, organizers claim two weeks before the event.[19]

Three hundred will be here, Butler tells the press on Thursday.[20]

One hundred and thirty are found in the late Saturday head count. (But not all count. The twenty-two women and ten children need protection. The twenty skinheads don't care.)

Fifty-seven go to church to hear Pastor Butler preach.

Fifty-two stay through the sermon.

Forty-nine stay awake.

Then comes the alarm, broadcast over the camp loudspeakers. "Attention! Attention! Uniformed officers report to the guardhouse! Trouble at the entranceway! Aryan pride at stake!"

Thirteen Aryan Warriors answer the call, scuttle to the gate, take up positions behind the cattle fence.

Twelve wear long pants.

Eleven have both shoes on.

Seven have regulation uniforms.

The din of the six Enemy is magnified by loudspeakers and the cheers of their supporters along the roadside.

At first the warriors are stunned. How to attack? Where to defend? The Enemy is already on the move, legs kicking high, arms in unison, drawing recruits and media cameras to their side, teasing, taunting at the very gates of the aryan homeland.

There is only one thing to do. They stand in a disordered line and salute, over and over, in various styles: stiff armed, bent elbowed, middle fingered. "Sieg Heil!" "Sieg Heil!" "Sieg Heil!" "Sieg Heil!"[21] It is the salute that saves them. Here is the picture the media came for, the one the editor expects, the one that sells. I used to be a part-time photographer. I know what will happen next. Reflecting on how I would handle the shot, I watch the pros in action.

Quickly cross the road. Get closer. Use a short telephoto to pull the group together. Drop down a bit, frame them through the barbed wire fence. (Don't show the shorts, the missing shoes.) Get all the arms up at once. One photographer coaches, "Salute together!" over the Enemy's loudspeakers. The warriors hear, finally understand, more or less synchronize.

Click. Click. Click. Click. Click.

News created, expectations fulfilled, editors satisfied. Scribble notes for caption: date, time, names, suggestions. How about, "Aryan Nations Menaces Idaho Panhandle." Like last year. Like next year.

Throughout the Pacific Northwest and across the country those reassuringly menacing pictures will appear wherever wire services reach and editorial interest exists: Seattle, Portland, New York, San Francisco, Los Angeles, elsewhere. Aryan warriors are happy. Editors are happy. Readers are happy (to be once more properly incensed). Only the TV audiences see more. But not on network news. And not till later. Only they know how close the Enemy comes to victory, to stealing the show, to transforming the notion of Aryan Might to myth and mirth.

Immigration

The way from almost anywhere to the Aryan Nations is long. Thirty-five hundred miles over the pole from Moscow, thirty-three hundred from Berlin. It's twenty-six hundred from New York, over two thousand from Selma, and nineteen hundred from Oklahoma City. My house is closer, seven hundred miles away. Each journey starts differently but most end the same, driving north on highway 95, ten minutes out of Coeur d'Alene, then east at the saloon on Garwood, and in five minutes, south on Rimrock Road. The dirt and gravel entrance with the plastic banner are easy to miss so look for the cruising cop cars, the parked team recording license plates, the media vans, and the Enemy. I spot the crowd, slow down, swing up the gravel drive. White World here I come. I'm ready, I think.

I've been rehearsing. Outfit: scruffy old camo pants and jacket, a worn American Pistol and Rifle Association (APRA) baseball cap (from another week-long adventure in Tennessee, untold in this volume), cheap hiking boots. Visage: practiced stern expression. Transport: no Peugeot this time. American iron. My twelve-year-old Ford pickup truck looks the part—dusty, dented, CB antenna waving, knobby tires, 4 × 4, canopy on the back. OK so far. But one detail puts me off by a mile. Long an opera lover, I've got Zubin Mehta and the New York Philharmonic booming "The Ride of the Valkyries" out the rolled-down truck window from my cheap but noisy tape player. I'm trying to think aryan: grand themes, titanic contests, good versus evil, conniving Albrich, powerful Wotan, the warrior maiden Walküre, winged steeds, flashing shields, giants, dragons, enchanted gold, stormy heavens. . . . I come to the guard shack. Stop. Academic fantasy meets aryan reality. Opera meets Grand Ole Opry. "The Ride of the Valkyries" draws quizzical stares and prompts a quick volume reduction. Brünhilde steps aside for Reba McEntire, the on-duty guard pair's music choice of the moment.

I show Lanky Stick and Portly Ball my credentials. They check records. I turn off Wagner. They turn up Garth Brooks, hand over a list of camp regulations, and point to the parking area. Almost in, I think. Then comes the surprise. Lanky draws his bones together and salutes. Not the military way, not like Tim. More like an actor in a deodorant commercial, the one using the "other" brand, his arm pointing straight skyward, as if to show off his damp, stained underarm. "Praise Victory," he mumbles, looking at me expectantly.

I'm supposed to do something now. But what? I try the salute. I almost get it right. I think consciously of extending the elbow, making the arm straight. But my fingers do not behave. An old habit takes over. The little finger curls into the palm and is held in place by the thumb, leaving three digits extended. The Boy Scout salute. The one I know best. Stick smiles. Ball nods and waves me through. Neither seems to notice the error.

At the top of the hill, on the right, is a twelve- by fifteen-inch sign. "Whites Only," it reads. I'm in and registered, so at least one thing is sure. I know what color I am.

When Gale's best-known spawn retired, a rumored millionaire, from the aeronautics industry in 1973, he could well afford twenty acres in northern Idaho. And Idaho could afford him. It was a less populous region then and less popular. Hayden Lake had yet to become the prosperous northern suburb of resort and retirement haven Coeur d'Alene. Butler and his odd few followers amounted to little, were tolerated or ignored. Even toward the end of the millennium, disregard for Butler was not surprising. His grandest gatherings never outnumbered the locals, loggers, and cattlemen at the Garwood Saloon on a good Saturday night. He said he was against the federal government, and who isn't? Even when his politics tarnished the region's reputation he had economic appeal, at least with neighbors. He kept property taxes down.[22]

By the 1990s, the Silverwood Theme Park a few miles farther along highway 95, not Richard Butler, was the best-known local attraction. The park's seventeen rides, restaurants, and entertainment attracted crowds in the thousands on summer days. The proprietor of the park's RV campground, a lifelong resident of the area, gave me local knowledge of the Aryan Nations. He helpfully pinpointed their camp on my map, four miles north and west (they were actually six miles south and east), told me their "big yearly get-together" would be held next month (it had started that morning), and said they were prone to fist fights requiring police intervention. He knew they were not "regular Christians" but had some kind of a church of their own, was unable to provide directions to the "Aryan Homeland," and could not recall ever having seen an "aryan" in his campground. So much for local knowledge.

Northern Idaho needs no supremacists to make it worthy. This is an attractive land, heterogeneous, stubborn, still independent. Rocky in places, unsuitable for agriculture, it is also unfriendly to those great machines that churn and homogenize the soil to the south. Spaces vary—hills, timber in groves and stands, sweeps of open ground. The trees are different here, tougher, leaner. Not the dull, dense, domesticated Douglas fir of the west. Cold and hot trees, survivors of harsh winters and dry summers, sparse and scattered, but where they are needed, for shade, to break the wind, or to frame the horizon, aspen, larch, lodgepole pine, sugar pine. Mountain trees, frontier trees. It is easy to imagine elk herds in the meadows, prosperous Indian lodges at the river bend, bronzed, laughing youth clinging to the necks of saddleless horses, racing across the rolling grasslands. Tourism and gentrification by wealthy urbanites seeking rural retreats, not aryan nationalism, are the real regional trends of the late twentieth century.[23]

Over the years, a visit to Butler's place has become de rigueur for writers and researchers claiming interest in white supremacy and other warts on American culture. Some come for news. Some have an ear for the ceremonies and speeches or for the music (for example, Aho 1990; Ezekiel 1995). Some have an eye for head counts and the program, gleaning movement politics and power shifts from attendance figures and the speakers on or off the schedule (for example, Anti-Defamation League n.d., 1995). Here is what I saw.

Butler's compound sits on twenty lightly timbered acres atop a gentle hill. Lower down, on the sun side, Butler's ranch-style home, perhaps twenty-five hundred square feet, white, tin roof facing east. On the flats above, the church. Out front, a raised platform, three flag poles, and flags that vary according to the event. On the rooftop, a guardless guard tower and public address speakers; over the front door, a small mechanically operated bell. Inside, space for possibly 200, seating for 120 (on locally rented chairs), flags, a small stained-glass window, an upright piano with cracked varnish, and one hymnal. The bulletin board just inside the door holds fading news clippings of members who have attracted attention by their public protest or clandestine pamphleteering. These features, more or less, have been reported by others. But there are more.

The clapboard, rough-hewn, styleless look of it all is not mentioned. Nor is the junk behind the bunkhouse, the rusting iron hide-a-bed, broken machinery and furniture, mildewed rug, the used lumber, dry rot down at the foundations on the north side, or rust on the tin roof. The restrooms in the church entranceway aren't mentioned either. They should be. They are important. They are not accessible at night. The other facilities lack amenities.

Arriving Thursday afternoon I park the truck behind the bunkhouse, step out, and breath in. My first whiff of the camp tells much of the weekend's story. The air smells of sweet, resinous sugar pines, ripe aryans, and fear. The indigenous pines bring well-to-do urbanites to boost the local economy, as seen all around. Ripeness and fear are camp byproducts.

Nixon had warned of the fear, the waning of aryan spirit, of the pure stock dwindling toward extinction. He was right. Few answer the call to the Aryan World Congress. Perhaps aryanism is truly on the wane. Or perhaps it is the ripeness.

Aryans ripened as the weekend progressed. The single shower stall is undesirable, seldom used. Late evenings, the church closes. Only the camp lavatory remains in service, and its toilet needs repair. The lid and seat are well enough attached to the bowl, but the bowl's bolts to the sewer pipe below are rusted through. The motions of seated users distort the appliance's wax seal. Soiled liquid flows out across the floor, past the washbasin, to the base of the sheet metal shower stall. Shoes are required. There are no open windows.

TALK, Talk, talk . . .

What went on that weekend action? Less than you might imagine. Less than many desired.

NEWS

On Friday afternoon, regional personnel provide what the program calls "reports," of progress, adventure, or hard times. Friday is also amateur actors' day. Speakers add rhetorical "refinements"—pregnant pauses, arm waving, pacing, direct appeals to the audience, Butler, or the heavens. "I was arrested *fourteen times,*" moans Canada, "I was indicted *fourteen times.*" He lists the indictments one by one on his fingers. Canada is so excited by his own voluptuous rant that when he runs out of fingers and has four more indictments to tell he stops, mute, stares at the hand that has betrayed him, and has to be coaxed by the front row into finishing the count. Wisconsin, tall, poorly connected Ichabod Crane in aryan blues, wife snooded in Mennonite fashion by his side, tells nearly tearfully of the "awful responsibility" he faced in answering Butler's call to racial leadership through his home-based ministry. Then he reads a few lines of scripture to prove he made the right choice.

Charlie Chadwick from California is the high point of the afternoon performances. Charlie is the self-appointed weekend cheerleader, adding "Hail Victory!" "Amen!" and "Heil Hitler!" to nearly everyone's presentation. When it is Charlie's turn at he podium he has little to say but much enthusiasm in saying it. He has a formula, a speech built on basics. Six words and one punctuation form is all you need. Anyone can do it.

Find three nouns, two verbs, an adjective, plenty of exclamation points, and turn up the volume. Charlie starts with the nouns, in pairs.

"*Blood* and *honor*!" he squawks. "*Honor* and *soil*!" "*Soil* and *blood*!"

Then the verbs.

"That's what we *fight* for!" "That's what we must *defend*!"

Include the adjective.

"Our honor is *sacred*!" "Our blood is *sacred*!"

Now, combine the lot.

"The honor of sacred Aryan blood upon the soil can never be removed!" "We fight for the rights of Aryan peoples of pure blood to once again defend their sacred soil!"

Finally, add the gestures. Punch a fist in the air at the end of each sentence. Add a "Hail Victory!" or a "Heil Hitler!" to every other line. Do this for ten minutes.

That is the message from California.

CAMPAIGNING

Saturday is a time for politics. Butler is ailing. There is a potential empire of followers and funds to claim. One by one the elders, not all old, appeal to the patriarch for his blessing and the crowd for its allegiance. One argues for reasoned persuasion, visits to college classrooms, honest debate to liberate the truth of racialism into the popular mind and sway the disposition of future young leaders. A second plays theologian, providing a sample reading from his magnum opus, a racially corrected Identity Bible. (No mention is made of George Udvary's Identity Bible, already home-published and in circulation for a decade.) A third devotes his time to unctuous ooze, fawning sycophantically over "our beloved leader" (much loved by the speaker), his "vision" (shared by the speaker), his "courage" (also shared, humbly, by the speaker), his "wisdom" (adopted by the speaker).[24] Butler himself is introduced with little fanfare. Butler, not vying for any job, has little to say and says it with even less style. Hardly a word is new. He gives the same speech every year. It's the same one he gave in pieces on Ted Koppel's show years earlier.

PUTTY TALK

Between (and during) speeches and meals throughout the weekend, participants gather in knots and clots for gossip and chatter. I circulate from knot to clot, listening, hello-ing, adding a word or two, filling tapes, and like the rest, killing time.

Butler and the elders stand in the shade of the church entranceway to worry about schedules and skinheads. Jim Cardinal, "Staff Leader" and "National Organizer," is in charge of scheduling, but not his emotions. His cuckolding spouse left him after a punch-up the previous night. In the morning, Cardinal and Butler fret that the program is too full, too tight to fit. There won't be time for everyone. But schedules deceive, speakers disappoint. The headliner, William Pierce, and others don't show. Those who do speak briefly, or aimlessly, or both. Presentations slated to run till seven o'clock are finished by quarter to four. Now Cardinal and Butler have another worry. Idleness. "Those skinheads [lounging near the cooking shed] are looking for trouble," Butler frets, and "dinner is not till six." The other star attraction won't be here until seven. Meanwhile, wait.

Butler is wrong about the skinheads. I sit with them, listen. They are in no mood for trouble or speeches. They had a long night, up till 3:00 A.M. They gossip a bit about romantic affairs and the t-shirt business. But last night holds most attention. Plotting revolution? Mayhem?

Drugs and drink? No. Watching CNN's rebroadcast of the congressional hearings on the Waco debacle.

The muscular, fortyish Aussie with the digger hat, across from me at the skinhead table, comments on my cap. "APRA? Isn't that a Jew organization?" he probes. "Sounds like one." I don't bother responding. He goes on about the war, Vietnam, his years in the jungle, behind the lines, in the Australian secret service. The skinheads aren't interested. He thinks I am. After a quarter of an hour he grows friendly, makes me an offer. Says he has just a few to spare, not too expensive, never used. I should have at least one. Surface-to-air missiles. No thanks. Not today.

As Butler and the elders move off, the shade of the church porch is claimed by an assorted half-dozen loungers:

A featured speaker from Portland. Bespectacled, gaunt, with a Goodwill wardrobe: yellowish green, iridescent suit, brown tie, size sixteen shirt, size fourteen neck, the lot unwashed, unironed; shop-floor shoes, thick soles, steel-toed; black socks. Carries a clipboard on which he compulsively writes and rewrites each presenter's name as the weekend schedule continually changes.

Truck driver from Queens.

Community college physics professor from Spokane, striped shirt, gray hair, beard, forty-five.

Bronx-born and -raised Italian, thirty, slight build, curly hair.

Aging Seattle-area biker.

Canada, national organizer to the north, lime green shorts, baggy t-shirt, brizzly beard.

Youthful, trim, clearly spoken, forty-four-year-old New Yorker, ex-addict, ex-inmate, and Odinist.

Me.

Aryan idle time is not easily filled. Butler's participants have few ideas of their own, few thought-out programs to promote or personal insights to share, few favored topics to animate dialogue, consolidate interest, focus attention. There is no talk of secret technology or hidden health aids, no plans for democratic reform or dietary discipline.

Transcribed and trimmed, edited and organized onto the page, aryan interlude talk may look cohesive, to the point. It was not. Talk is listless, unfocused. It comes in snippets and grunts, yeps and you bets, in brief, disconnected anecdotes that run down to stillness in a minute or two. Putty talk. It matches the surroundings and fills the cracks between silences but provides no unifying strength. My tapes are full of it—lapses, coughs, ahems, bench shifting, scratching, and remarks meant to meet civil obligations, not move or inform.

One starts, tries a topic, tells a story. Another adds a word or two. A third nods. Story ends. Wait. Wait for something to happen. Wait for someone to begin again. Listen. Forty-five minutes of tape sounds like this:

"You know those Shakers? Own all that rich farmland in Pennsylvania? Not very many of them left. They are all octogenarians, eighty, ninety years old. All gonna die pretty soon. They've been leaving that property to each other for generations and generations. Now they've only got one member that is gonna live much longer. He's forty-three, just converted to the Shaker religion."

"He's a Jew?"

"Yep. He's not dumb."

"He'll get all that land."

"You know, Jews are smart. You have to admit it."

"Not so smart as sneaky."

"Sneaky, yea, sneaky."

Pause. Scratch.

"Growing up we had Jews in our neighborhood. I don't mean it was a Jewish neighborhood, but we had some Jews there. We used to torment 'em. We'd make 'em line up against the wall, wear yellow swastikas, yellow stars we stuck on 'em."

"Yea. We used to do that, too, where I lived. We had a tough gang. We used to beat up on 'em all the time. Beat 'em up, and beat 'em up, and they'd never fight back."

"Jews and niggers, they never fight back."

Pause. Stare at the ground.

"You know anyone who practices runes and stuff? I'd like to learn some."

"I know this one guy that used to be into Satanism. It didn't work. It backfired on him. Like, he did a curse on this one guy, and a week later ten niggers jumped him on a subway.

That's black magic. He better be careful. People don't know what they are messin' with."

Pause. Cough. Crack knuckles.

"You know that black guy in the subway in New York, he killed all those people with a machine gun? He'll get off. Did you see him on TV? Defended himself. Acted real crazy. They'll let him off."

"They should put him in the chair or hang him or something."

Pause. Yawn.

"The swastika rune is the circle of seasons: fall, winter, spring, summer, all around, each returning. That's what it means."

"Really?"

"Yea, I think so."

Pause. Stare at hands.

"Preachers talk about heaven. Well, I don't know about heaven. But I like Valhalla. If you're a warrior, you go to Valhalla. I kinda like that idea of fighting and drinking and screwing all the time. Sounds like a better idea of heaven than the other one."

Pause. Scrape toe in dust.

"When did you go to jail?"

"In 1977. I was arrested because I was a drug addict. Spent nearly two years in prison.

"What kind of drugs did you do?"

"Everything. Heroin, cocaine. I did everything."

"I ran away from home when I was twelve years old, joined a gang. Some guys talk about being in Vietnam, how tough it was. They don't know what tough is. When I was living on the streets, guys were getting killed every day. They were trying to kill me all the time. One day this one guy reaches inside my car, tries to stab me four or five times, rips holes in the upholstery right next to my ribs. I grab his wrist, pull my knife out, stick it up under his throat, and say, 'One of us is gonna die.' Another time these two niggers had me in a bathtub, stark naked. One bent my neck back over the edge of the tub, put a straight razor on my throat, while the other one held my feet down."

Pause. Shift seat. Examine fingernails.

"Jews are preoccupied with sex. You know, when they were wandering out in the desert they were all sex cults."

Pause. Remove cap. Scratch scalp. Replace cap.

"Which one of those up there do you think is the FBI agent?"

"Well, the ones that are eatin' a lot."

"Yea, you can spot 'em every time. They stand around and ask all the wrong questions."

(I'm standing right next to him, asking no questions.)

"If there's about a hundred people here, I always figure about ten percent. Then again, there might not be any."

A few minutes later, we are joined by Mr. Shay.

After Robert Mathews's escapades and other law-breaking events, law enforcement and watchdog organizations paid regular though usually unobtrusive and unannounced visits to Butler's homestead, especially at larger gatherings. "Find-the-cop" is a common camp game at these gatherings. Though I cannot be sure, I believe it is not played well. I don't know who Mr. Shay really is, but I suspect he is neither "Mr. Shay" nor an advocate of the Aryan Nations.

Mr. Shay was the first to greet me as I pulled in to park on Thursday. He has a truck too, but much nicer than mine, Dodge with all the trimmings, cost nearly my year's salary, and a camper on the back, just refurbished, at a cost of twice what I paid for my truck. Says he is a contractor from the Seattle area. His waistline and vocabulary suggest otherwise. He looks the part of a fit, prosperous, punctilious, Teutonic thug. Telly Savalas turned power lifter, shiny on top, warted nose, tree stump legs, fire hydrant arms, impeccably pressed and pleated shorts, vest, shirt, expensive walking shoes, custom silver and turquoise watchband, wedding ring. Articulate, curious, mobile, yet somehow unobtrusive.

Mr. Shay and I interview each other nonchalantly. In a half hour I tell him my life story. He tells me he how much his truck cost and how long it took to drive here. I interview strangers part-time. I think Mr. Shay does it every day.

During the weekend Mr. Shay and I cross paths many times among the knots and clots, in line for chili or hot dogs, in church, and in the parking area. He leaves as I arrive; I leave as he arrives. We sign up, one after another, for splinter group newsletters. We both sit in the back of the church, both tape record the proceedings surreptitiously, both circulate, listen, encourage talk.

His front is not perfect. He gives speakers only two-clap applause and no "Heil Hitlers." And he knows and tells too much: the epidemiology and spelling of Tay-Sachs disease, the detailed financial status of the Aryan Nations, daily attendance figures at last year's congress.

I bet Mr. Shay earns a substantial salary.

I bet he has a university education.

I bet he has a weight room down the hall from his office.

I bet he is a cop.

Saving Aryanism from Itself

I bet Mr. Shay is no friend of aryanism, an enemy within even. But others, in the name of public reason, setting out to play the enemy, to critique aryanism, to reveal and unmask its dark side in candid reportage, have contrary effects, become unwitting and unwilling accomplices to the aryan cause.

Butler and the campers and groups like them elsewhere act as if they can determine their own fates, as if they can recruit, promote, and proselytize on their own merits, with their own resources. They cannot. Only outsiders can save the aryan cause and its like from their own triviality, yet consistently we do just that. The media offers up national prime-time television audiences and choreographs interviews with network news anchors; leading question provides opener for aryan sound bite then cut to commercial, repeat. Print media pose them for pictures at the gate (salutes coordinated, don't show the shoes, don't show the Enemy). Academics, with the best intentions and much skill, give them articles and chapters with teeth and horns and the vigor of youth, wrap them in smoky mists of dread and nostalgia, and create aryanism, such as it is, in spite of the ineptitude of Butler's brood.

Raphael Ezekiel, an accomplished Harvard scholar, erudite, sensitive, artful and candid in his reports, visited the camp and wrote about his experiences. His work goes courageously beyond passive description to include himself in his accounts. But therein lies part of the problem.

Butler's motley crew are nothing like Ezekiel. They are not literate, worldly in experience and outlook, or generous in their concerns for others. Nor are they organized, astute, or persuasive. They are petty, fractious, crude, ineffectual, ill organized, and clumsy.

There is nothing grand about practiced aryanism including nothing grandly sinister. To call them "Nazi," neo or otherwise, to link their haphazard gatherings to some burgeoning rein of terror such as was begun by the National Socialist German Workers' Party of the late twenties, to hear in their scratching English-language tapes of "Horst Wessel Leid" the echo of tumultuous social movements three-quarters of a century old, as Ezekiel does (1995, 38), is to legitimate aryan fantasies and fondest wishes *in direct contradiction to what they actually are and do.* There is no political cunning or sweeping fervor in Butler's aryanism, no past or pending massed marches or stirring anthems, no torchlight parades or shifting of great powers. These are the fables and fairytales, the wistful legends camp speakers spin, without conviction or proof, for their none-too-attentive audiences.

Raphael Ezekiel calls Butler's camp a "man's world." I wonder why? Ezekiel tells us "the compound in Idaho is a world of men. Women are present, as wives, girlfriends, as supportive people. Women serve the meals. Men lead the rituals; men give the speeches. No woman addresses the group" (1995, 39). From my vantage point it looks different. The importance of speeches and rituals to academics is understandable. Ideologies, belief systems, and other clues and cues to patterned behavior are all presumably readable in these events. But remember our empiricist roots. Speeches do not carry their own meanings. We must ask: How do participants *act* toward the speeches and ritual events?

What is the most obvious of actions toward speeches and rituals at Butler's camp? Avoidance. Ezekiel found the speeches titillating, "material too dramatic to be lost" filling him with "astonishment" (1995, 41). Members seem less enthralled. As noted, some leave early, some go to sleep.[25] A numeric majority never show, never come together to hear a presentation or join in an activity until Saturday night. And then the attraction is a woman, Katja Lane, new wife of former Order member David Lane. David does not join Katja. He won't be out of prison for 180 years. Katja draws an audience nearly twice the size of Butler's, second only to the weekend's star attraction. Why this disinterest?

Ezekiel and I and perhaps Mr. Shay are busy at speech time, counting, studying, tape recording, watching. For us, this is work, full, demanding work. But not for most. It is correct to say that most speeches are made by men, but it is also correct that most men do not make speeches, and only a minority of the campers listen to those that are made. A few, the regional leaders and elders, participate, get a turn at the podium, a chance to direct rituals and produce speeches. There is enthusiasm if not skill among these. But most do nothing but sit, wait, listen. Idle consumers awash in words, not engaged in deeds.

Throughout the weekend, what is practical, rational, effective, and necessary, the women do. What drifts into confusion or tedium or falls apart, these are the men's accomplishments. Women organize the registration, collect the fees, plan the commissary, calculate and order the supplies, assign jobs, feed the hungry, protect the children, create and organize the tent households, and run the t-shirt and memorabilia businesses. Butler asks the head cook when meals will be ready. She tells him. He accommodates. He never contradicts. Men are decorative, the cheerleaders and mascots.

Saturday morning is men's dress-up time. Appear "in uniform" the schedule says. Uniforms vary. The official aryan getup comes from J. C. Penney. Shirts: from the Big Mac work clothing line, long sleeved, light blue, 50/50 cotton/polyester. Features: five military creases (some already sewn in), button-down epaulets, pleated pockets with scalloped flaps and a pass-through pen or pencil compartment. Pants: Dickies brand dark blue work trousers (includes loop for carpenter's hammer). Accessories: Sam Brown belt, Aryan Nations buckle (available for purchase from Butler), clip-on tie, black boots (preferably fashionable high-tops, with pants tucked in). Rank patches with the Aryan Nations logo sewn on shirt sleeves.

Ranks vary. Butler and his aryans have an intricate stratification system with an uncomplicated base. Eleven categories of aryan supremacy are recognized, from the lowly "Schutze" ("private," pronounced "shoot-zee"), to the exulted "Obergruppenführer," ("general," use your imagination). Ranks are many but the reasons for promotion only one—recruitment. To ascend the ranks of aryan supremacy one must add to the roll call, and not incidentally, to the coffers. Each member must pay a thirty-five-dollar initiation fee and sixty dollars per year for membership maintenance. To become a lance corporal, recruit one paying member; a corporal, bring in three members; a sergeant, five members; and so forth. Butler was a general (but wore a suit), Cardinal was a colonel. Perhaps fifteen members have parts of the standard aryan outfit. Others wear less orthodox, more creative apparel.

Retro World War II regalia is in fashion. At Saturday assembly time, two surprised participants eye each other suspiciously, keeping their distance as they promenade about like socialites wearing the same designer gown at a ball, both dressed in nearly identical replicas of the Nazi naval officer's dress uniform, shiny, knee-high boots, high collars, and dress hats, all starched and stiff. Five others have less complete German military outfits. Among uniformed and costumed aryans alike, high-top boots are a fashion statement with a price. Apparently they hurt, are unsuited for movement, and so are quickly replaced with street shoes upon completion of ceremonies. Most uniforms are made up of a single clothing item or accessory. T-shirts are the favorite (and on sale at the memorabilia, clothing, and book booths). The skinheads never take their costumes off. Tattoos are permanent.

One camper, with sternum-length beard and hair, just brings a club. "Thor's Nutcracker" he calls it, a rough, eight-pound chunk of silver-painted, crude cast iron, with spikes pointing fore and aft, on a thick, twenty-inch wooden handle pushed through his sixty-inch belt. The forespike just caresses his massive, slowly oscillating midriff as he clumps along, sockless, one shoe without a heel, his XXL t-shirt still half a foot too short to span the circumference from his neck to his low-riding waistband.

Taken together, the costumed aryans create a scene like something out of Jennie Livingston's documentary of transvestite "voguing" contests, *Paris is Burning,* strutting earnestly about as if wanting to look like what they cannot ever possibly be: warriors, leaders, legends, participants in a great cause. The sporadic Hail Victory!'s sound less like an affirmations of emerging action than a declarations of dependence heard at a twelve-step recovery meeting. The whole weekend appears not much more than a pep rally for the ugly, clumsy kids who didn't get on the team. "Aryan," the ancient Sanskrit word for "noble," seems, well, excessive.

A man's world? Perhaps. Men salute, heil Hitler, mumble amen, and perform at the gate for the press. Men have the Klan robes and Nazi costumes. But women wear the pants, shoes you can walk in, and with the exception of the guards, keep the guns. Exception. A select few men do women's work: constructive, organizational, relevant. The guards have necessary things to do, check in new arrivals, maintain order. But they do not necessarily do them well.

At Butler's camp not much goes according to plan. The speakers blare in pidgin German, the schedule is maddeningly inaccurate, and rules are petty and enforced seemingly at random. Tape recording, along with interviews with media, consumption of alcohol, and disposal of cigarette butts on the ground, is forbidden. I record openly but with reserve, setting my machine down next to me on tables or nearby chairs and letting it run and record what it may. I carry a copy of Santayana's essays on aesthetics and a stainless steel thermos. A Pacific Northwesterner, I'm used to quality coffee, which I make myself in the morning.

As I leave the church Saturday afternoon, five armed, uniformed guards in assorted sizes block my way, surround me, tell me to step aside. "Let's see that thermos!" the small one in the lead insists. Flustered, confused, taken by surprise, I lose my composure, and my studied surreption. I pass the thermos to him by the strap, hooked over my extended index finger. The rest of my fingers are busy. My hand is obviously full.

"Got a tape recorder in there," a larger guard says accusingly as they gather round the suspect container, removing the cup-top, unscrewing the cap, sloshing the liquid back and forth, holding it so the sun shines in, taking turns peering. "No," I answer to the now preoccupied guards. The question summarizes the weekend: gruff, gratuitous, absurd. My full passing hand, with only a digit to spare for the thermos strap, holds my standard-size cassette recorder, in stark plain view, red light on, still running.

Ezekiel reports the lilting horror of camp music he associates, not with Reba McEntire or Garth Brooks, but with ominous Teutonic marching songs. Ezekiel, a literate man, hears with ears tuned by his deep, cosmopolitan, historically rich, multilingual memory. Likely he was in sparse company. German is not a language common to the campers. Aryanspeak is.

Yiddish is colloquial speech developed by German-speaking people familiar with Hebrew. Aryanspeak is slang invented by American-speaking people familiar with English but not German. Aryanspeak vocabulary is small, emphasis stern, volume loud. Announcements over the loudspeaker are an example. Each is prefaced by a call for attention. For this purpose we might expect something like "Attention, attention" (the calls are always in pairs). But making announcements has dramaturgic possibilities most announcers cannot resist. A little Aryanspeak is added for style. Instead of standard English we hear "Ag-tongue! Ag-tongue!" lunch is being served. Or "Ak-tongue! Ak-tongue!" dinner is ready. Or "Aug-tung! Aug-tung!" assemble at the flag stand. Tim Dalkins would have fancied a turn at the microphone here (though he would not have approved of the racism). I heard Butler addressed as "furor" and "mine hair" by low ranking camp personnel, and the Breuderschweigen were commonly rendered "Brew-der-say-why-gin."

Aryanspeak also takes written forms. A station wagon arrives from distant parts at about noon Saturday with a load of newly designed t-shirts in back and an aryan entrepreneur at the wheel. The shirt-fronts commemorate Robert Mathews and the Order with "Hail to the Order" in Gothic script around the border of a simulated medallion. In the center, one more word in script. Most apparently presume it is the German term for "freedom." But instead of freedom, "Freiheit," the medallion is centered by "F-r-y-d-u-n-g."

"That's not a German word," says the European "Ambassador at Large," likely the only German-speaking person in the camp.

"What do I know?" responds the saleswoman, tending to her first customer in a forming line. "That's how they made them for me." Someone at the print shop had made an alteration.

Soon there are a half-dozen proud new owners strutting about proclaiming their t-shirt allegiance. Privately, I cannot help but agree with the shirt's sentiments.

Hail to the Order [of] Frydung.

Hail to the Order [of] Cooked Crap.

Work

Only once in the weekend did I see the men come to life, show real interest. Late Saturday, in the still hot summer afternoon, the speaker crackles, calls attention. Calls for volunteers. Heavy work to be done. Report to the stubble grass field behind the church. Knots and clots listen, shake off lethargy, stand, trail toward the open field. Here is genuine work. Men's work. Muscle work. Work for hands on hard wood, heavy rough-skinned logs, massive, ungainly, stubborn. The first to arrive try to do the job on their own but fail. The logs are too heavy to lift, to shift, to hold. Others join. Now many backs and arms strain together. Skinheads show off their strength; older men guide, give directions, pace the work. Pull, hold against the pressing weight, hoist, push, steady, align. Feet slip, knuckles scrape, shoes are covered in dust, perspiration runs. Still more hands join. Now, strength is enough to wrap and bind firmly with the wire.

Supplies needed. Volunteers with a vehicle needed. Three clamber up into the cab of a ten-year-old flatbed Ford dualie, road lights mounted on top, a swing-out hoist in back, two empty fuel cans strapped behind the cab, and jounce down the dirt drive toward town. Half an hour later they return, cans full. The job is nearly done. Only the final siting remains.

The completed structure is circled with steel cable, attached to a small tractor, front-end loader raised high, pulling backwards, engine aroar, tires spinning. Men on the ends of strong ropes struggle to steady the mass as it slides toward its permanent location, sinks into place. More hands join on the ropes, pull with the tractor, make progress.

Slowly, the finished form rotates, rises off the ground, ascends out of the tree shadows to its full three-story height. Glistening drops of superfluous liquid drip from the stout limbs, backlit by the setting sun.

Now camp is ready for the night. Ready for the guest of honor. I know the guest. We met before at a place like this but far away, at a time like this but long ago. I remember.

Nine O'clock

Alone, two thousand miles away from home, on the third day of the Christian Patriots Survival Conference, I volunteer for guard duty. They tell us more security is needed to patrol the fifty-acre Mo-Ark Survival Base and protect the four hundred participants from spies and infiltrators.

The Klan is there with the Posse Comitatus and the rest. In the names of Reason and Patriotism and God, they urge repudiation of the national debt and race revolution, economic assistance to small farmers and genocide. Participants discuss these proposals over hot dogs and pop. Merchants sell commando knives and Bibles, powdered goats' milk and naturopathic cures for cancer. People browse. Dollars change hands.

Four of us are assigned the evening gate watch. Into the dusk we direct late arriving traffic, check passes, and get acquainted. The camp settles. Talk turns to traditional survivalist topics. First, guns: they slide theirs one by one from concealed holsters to be admired. "Mine's in the car," I lie. Then, because we were strangers with presumably a common cause, it was time for stories, to reconfirm our enemies and reiterate our principles.

We stand around a small campfire listening to distant prayers and speeches drifting from the main assembly area. Our stories go clockwise.

Twelve O'clock tells of homosexuals who frequent a city park in his home community and asks what should be done with them in "the future." His own proposal involves chains and trees and long-fused dynamite taped to body parts. Understand these remarks. They are not meant as braggadocio. We all face the "queer" problem, don't we? And the community will need "cleansing," won't it? In solemn agreement we nod our heads. Three O'clock reflects for moment, then proposes a utilitarian solution involving nighttime and rifle practice. "Good idea," we mumble supportively. Six O'clock sees a ready labor source, after some veterinary surgery. We exchange small smiles at this notion. One more car passes the gate. It grows quiet.

It is Nine O'clock. My turn. I tell a story too.

As I begin, a new man joins us from the shadows. He listens to my ideas and approves, introduces himself, then tells me things not everyone knows, about plans being made and action soon to be taken. He says they can use men like me and tells me to be ready to join. I take him seriously. Others do too. He is on the FBI's Ten Most Wanted list.

Eleven years later, after his months of running in Central America, the killings in Mexico, the extradition, the long trial, the southern jury that found him innocent, we meet again. He is Louis Beam, Butler's distinguished guest, the Aryan World Congress Saturday evening star attraction, once more my companion by the fire.

I remember well that night long ago, dozens of small fires dotting the grounds, clusters of family and acquaintances talking the evening out. Tonight, as before, we will stand and talk together in a circle. But there will be only one fire in camp. And not at our feet.

Tonight the men's afternoon work will be undone. The massive structure, burlap wrapped, kerosene soaked, ablaze over our heads, will spit and roar a searing epithet to the heavens. A great flaming cross.

If there are researchers who can participate in such business without feeling, I am not one of them nor do I ever hope to be. What I do hope is someday to forget, forget the feel of rough wood and wire in my hands, forget the smell of kerosene. And most of all forget those unmistakable sounds, my own voice, my own words, telling that Nine O'clock story.

Enemy

Not all outsiders are journalists and academics satisfied with propping up the aryan myth. Butler has enemies with power as great as his unintended benefactors. Enemies at the gate, willing to speak of the Emperor's clothes.

Actor Gene Eugene came to support the Enemy, but he is not ready. Part of his costume is missing. Today he is to act like a rabbi. His dark robes are somber and convincing, but his bare head is not. A lady in the crowd with an ample chest, generous spirit, and no unnecessary modesty understands. After some undergarment wriggling and Swiss Army knife tailoring, her endowments are less stationary, Gene's costume more complete. He is ready.

Crossing the road, facing the saluting aryans behind the barbed wire, he intones an ancient Hebrew prayer for peace.

"Sieg Heil!" "Sieg Heil!" "Sieg Heil!" the aryans chant.

"May there be peace for all of us," Gene offers.

"Sieg Heil!" "Sieg . . . "

"May there be peace for all of us."

"Sieg . . . "

Momentarily the aryans grow quiet. It could be the prayer that silences them. Or it could be the costume. Held in place with duct tape is the lady's gift, an improvised yarmulke, fashioned from one-half of her satiny, black, D-cup brassiere.

"May there be peace for all of us."

Gene has the last word. Filmmaker Michael Moore gets the last laugh. Behind Gene, the Enemy continues.

At the time, Moore was best known for *Roger and Me,* his film documentary pursuit of an interview with the president of General Motors after the auto manufacturer "downsized" Moore's hometown of Flint, Michigan. By the summer of 1996, Moore has a new project. Aryans have a new adversary. Most times the normal-news media does its part to keep up aryan appearances. They overcount participants, quote the most dramatic utterances, and push together the loose ends and fragments of aryanism into a cohesive cause. Not Moore. He is here for laughs, for material to humor and amuse and entertain his viewers. Moore, his actors, and film crew are at work on a seven-hour television series *TV Nation,* aired on the FOX network. Moore plays a joke on Butler's band. After Gene's opening act Moore sends in the Enemy.

The Enemy is an adversary genuinely to be feared by the aryan few. Not the FBI or the ADL or the police. Worse. Moore's mercenaries are not large and looming, but lithe, syncopated, cavorting to sordid song and despicable dance at the very portals of the homeland. Six females of the lowest sort, mongrels, mud people, race traitors. The mix is hard to tell at a distance but pollution is clear, perhaps one Eurasian, one black, one Hispanic, and three white women without race consciousness. This Enemy taunts, humiliates, swaying, gyrating, prancing in a chorus line as speakers blare an irksome refrain, a song recorded by black singers years before. The Supremes made the recording. The lyrics speak to the aryans directly.

"Stop! in the name of love . . . " Prance, kick, twirl.

"Stop! in the name of love . . . " Helium-filled, heart-shaped balloons bob in the gentle afternoon breezes.

"Stop! in the name of love . . . "

Here is the worst sort of foe, not a massed, armed counterforce of jack-booted repression but a dainty, lighthearted half-dozen full of ridicule and open disbelief, recording the disgrace of aryanism for a primetime nationwide audience of amused American viewers.

Aryanism meets its match. The would-be master race stands slack-jawed and mute behind the fence, can-canned into submission by six young ladies from Spokane, a dance troupe called The Class Act.

Agreed: racism is vile and repulsive.

Contested: "white supremacy" in Hayden Lake is anything more than a demographic artifact.

Exception: at Butler's, "white supremacy" is an oxymoron.[26]

• • •

The myth of antirational influences among survivalists comes to rest. Jihad languishes into a quaint curiosity. Religious fervor is slight and keeps its place. Racial identity offers little, appeals to only a few. The revolution is stillborn. But the aryans and their gateside tormentors show us a sign. Another power is sweeping through Gale's camp and across the land. While the state stands to the side another lusty, robust rationality asserts itself. No dingy, sharp-edged clanking mechanism of public order this time, no tiresome plodding bureaucracy. The new rationality appears bright, inviting, full of hope, brimming with opportunities for culturecraft. But appearances deceive, power is disguised, opportunities are hollow.

HIDDEN RATIONALITY

One more force must be reckoned, a force relatively independent of the state *and* opposed to antirationalities, to unregulated affect. This is the source of modernity's deepest influence and survivalists' most profound loathing, yet a force many pass by unnamed, unrecognized. This is the force of hidden rationality, of private, apolitical, atheistic, globalized, rational production, markets and commerce. "McWorld," Barber calls it (1992, 53). I prefer "Planet Microsoft."

Planet Microsoft is the familiar of late-stage capitalism, the contiguous force of universalizing commercialization, straining toward homogeneity, integration, uniformity. Planet Microsoft is tied together not by affective identities and tribal allegiance, but by satellite communications, cybernetic technology, and probabilistic accounting schemes. Planet Microsoft is disquieted by provincialism and commerce-disrupting conflict. Market imperatives assume a concord among producers and consumers and reinforce quests for stability if not justice. Markets are the enemies of parochialism, isolation, factions, and war (Barber 1992, 54), but they are no aid to national sovereignty.

On Planet Microsoft, frontiers run between markets and spheres of commercial interest, not along the boundaries of sovereign states (Lapham 1988, 10). International economic imperia of multinational corporations operating in transnational markets, where trade is free, banking open, currencies convertible, and contracts enforceable under international law, neither reflect nor respect national identity (Barber 1992).

These smaller but more coherent powers the likes of IBM or IT&T or Mobil Oil, focused in intent and will, consent to the fictional dominion of nominally larger, but more diffuse and constrained entities such as the governments of Venezuela or the Czech Republic, or Russia or even the United States, in return for the rights to do largely as they damn well please (Lapham 1988, 8).

Much of modern life, survivalism included, is an accommodation to Planet Microsoft. Butler's band, for example, becomes a network plaything, demonized by news reporters, caricatured on the humor channel, for the same rational, corporate reasons: entertainment, improved viewer ratings, thence increased advertising revenue. Some accommodations are obvious and intended, some reluctant, some a last resort.

While survivalists are vague or ambivalent about the global rationalization of economic interests, predicting systemic failure on structural not moral grounds, they are well enough aware of some of its specific consequences. In his own terms, Tim understands investment capital is migrating internationally in search of the highest returns commensurate with risk. He knows the mill in his hometown is not being upgraded because the owners are putting their money into a more profitable modern plant in British Columbia. Hank is aware that manufacturing is efficiency driven, that his company must compete for contracts with both automated German precision parts casting facilities and Mexican factories offering cost-effective labor resources for finishing and assembly. Nic even complains of the environmental degradation of indiscriminate timber harvest in the Amazon basin rain forest. But who is to blame? The rationalization of economy in the form of "business organization" remains value positive. So the unpalatable manifestations of Planet Microsoft as a rational *economic* entity are reassigned to a structurally similar but morally antithetical overreaching *political* entity, the hypothetical New World Order, controlled by communist ideologues not capitalist idealists.

These accounts do not stem the outflow of capital or jobs, but maintain the appearances, are a nice-sounding argument for public consumption. But what do they mean? As Weber knew would happen, charisma succumbs to method (Weber 1978, 1156), fragments into a myriad of lulling routines, shallow entertainments, ready commodities. Survivalism acquires punctuation: quotation marks and an exclamation point. "Survivalism!" moves indoors, closer to the cash register. Charismatic drama acquires a box office, prophecy simplifies to pamphlets and stock lectures, magic to sprouts, surplus, and kitsch merchandise. But as substance dwindles, appearances brighten. Planet Microsoft spreads a welcome mat. One convenient location. Handy hours. Independence and adventure in sizes to fit all. The promises ready to be realized: places for entrepreneurship, bricolage, dramatic performances, investment schemes and clever accessories; tools ready for work and tales ready to tell; equipment for mortal combat and tapes on how to do it; shelter for dollars, people, and fragile ideas—everything one could want to make a difference, be noticed, and move to the center of action. Everything—for a price.

EXPO!

On that warm, long, late-summer weekend the Seattle Center is a well-mannered, gracious hostess. The fountains are already drained for winter, but neat trees and trimmed grass stand green and lush among the parks and pathways, around the theaters and galleries, all fresh with sea breezes from the sound. Children play, parents wheel new babies, teens flirt, seniors sit on sunny benches and watch life's stages pass in review. At the Flag Pavilion the Antiquarian Book Fair entertains bibliophiles with old and rare manuscripts, maps and documents, on display and for sale. Laughing, pirouetting, preteen girls, ballet students in tights and leotards, tennies and Birkenstocks, swirl out the side door of the grand Intiman Theater, on the Mercer Street side of the Center near the fashionable Queen Anne district. Curbside, smiling parents wait for them in late-model minivans and station wagons. Harold Pinter's time-inverted ménage à trois, *Betrayal,* lights the theater marquee. Across the courtyard, at the Intiman Playhouse, the curtains open on a Saturday matinee of Tony Kushner's bawdy *Angels in America: A Gay Fantasia on National Themes, Part I: Millennium Approaches.* Worlds away, next door, fourteen steps down, at the Expo Center, a mingling throng, "survivalists" in the thousands.

It is Seattle's turn. Preparedness Expo, the traveling road show celebration of coming trouble, is in town. "Get Ready! Earthquakes. Disasters. Freedom. For Peace of Mind in Our Changing World. Emergency Preparedness—Self-Reliant Living" reads the program. Inside, three days of action: ten featured speakers, sixteen other lecturers, fifty-three exhibitors, and a snack bar. To wander and wonder among the booths and arenas come the curious, the idle, and a media contingent that calls them all "survivalists," fifteen thousand strong according to the organizers, far fewer according to the exhibitors, staff, and my ticket stub count. Still, money changes hands at the door. Visitors $6 per day; concessionaires $675 per table space, furniture and electricity extra. Most exhibitors rent two or more spaces, but skimp on the extras. Some bring tables, some chairs, one even lugs in his car battery each day to power a VCR for his exhibit.[27]

The "Seminar Stage" area, a curtained-off corner of the hall, features 450 folding chairs, dais, podium, public address equipment, and its own entranceway ticket booth; five dollars extra per lecture. All day long, featured speakers take turns at the podium, audible but not visible throughout the hall. Bulk audio and video production equipment earns more, reproducing taped speeches within half an hour; eight dollars for audio, twenty for video. Downstairs, on the "Lecture Stage," the backup team holds forth for free, to maximum audiences of eighty. Expo has more and less obvious sides, action front stage and in the wings.

Front stage

Seminar Stage, five o'clock, Friday. Don McAlvany, "a highly respected geopolitical and financial intelligence adviser," opens the show with "America in Decline—Advancing Toward the New World Order" and later, "Preparing for the Coming Economic and Political Convulsions." The McAlvany message is typical: hard times are coming, don't trust experts, and see me at my booth after the show for modestly priced "in-depth financial consultations unique to your circumstances" (gold and silver coins on sale, too). Next, retired Arizona policeman Jack McLamb lectures on "America's Move Toward a Nationalized Police Force," the timeliness of citizens' militias, and "homicides committed by Federal officers." Solution? Stop by the McLamb display for subscriptions to the "Aid and Abet Police Newsletter," memberships in the "American Citizens' and Lawmen's Association," and copies of his book, *Vampire Killer 2000.* Larry Nichols's later offering, "How You Can Take America Back!" creates momentary excitement. A heckler from another camp, the Lyndon LaRouche–Liberty Lobby booth contingent, stands and shouts denouncements. Nichols is "a spy and lying front man for the New World Order," the heckler claims. Security officers eject the heckler and later the entire LaRouche display. Undeterred, the LaRoucheites set up a card table on the sidewalk outside the main entrance, festooned with hand-lettered posters belittling their opponents,[28] and banter with passersby.

Saturday night, 7:00, prime time. Mark Koernke, a headliner, fills 350 of those five-dollar seats and gets a musical introduction. Steve Vaus, "America's leading patriot singer-songwriter," croons "We Must Take America Back," "Will You Be among the Patriots?" "I'll Remember in November," and his stock piece, the speaker's segue, "Why, Why, Why" to the accompaniment of a plug-in percussion synthesizer, first-year guitar runs, and simple C-F-G7 chord progressions. Koernke explains "The UN/Globalists' Plan for America" and "Keeping the New World Order at Bay." As "Mark from Michigan," self-proclaimed former

"U.S. Counter-Intelligence Coordinator" and ad hoc spokesperson for Michigan militiamen (his day job is different), Koernke is known for uncovering globalist conspiracies. "We all know what was going on in Oklahoma City. We all know who was behind Lee Harvey Oswald . . . er, . . . I mean, [much laughter] . . . Timothy McVeigh." The bombing was a "tactical and strategic test" to "see how much control the One World Order could manage and . . . how quickly the public would respond." The nation's militia would recognize the attack as the work of globalists and come out of hiding, ready to defend the nation. Once the militia were visibly active, United Nations troops would have an excuse to "restore order" by "moving in" and "taking over." Koernke's conjectures generate polite attention, busy after-the-speech tape sales, and half a standing ovation, but little more. His speeches are inspirational, not instrumental, avoiding all recommendations for specific action except of course to "learn more" from tape and book purchases at the Koernke table.

Get Rich, Go Free, Stay Young

Not all the action is center stage. Throughout the hall personal improvement possibilities abound. Buy this, buy that. Get rich. Go free. Stay young.

Far West Business Consulting, Financial Freedom Consultants, and the International Collectors Association handle get rich schemes with trust fund starter kits, foreign government bonds, investment and retreat real estate, precious metals, and "offshore financial services for asset protection, and privacy." Staying free poses both strategic and tactical problems, matters of "constitutional," "political," and "tax" rights, and the practical issue of providing defense and sustenance in difficult times. Strategies are proposed by the Gun Owners of America, Police Against the New World Order, the Militia of Montana (MOM), State Citizens Service Center, and numerous book, pamphlet, and tape dealers. The Javelin Press collection emphasizes "regaining your personal sovereignty," with *Good-Bye April 15th!* by Boston T. Party ringing in sales. At the Bohica Concepts book booth the proprietor looks worn. "Are you working hard?" I ask. "Yea. I do fifty shows a year," he volunteers. "That's nearly a show every weekend." I am puzzled. "How can you do it?" "I have two setups," he tells me. A helper runs the other one, mostly at gun shows. He says he makes more money at the expo, but it costs more in overhead.

Tactical advice remains thin and often specialized. Underground Shelters of America sells subcompact car-sized buriable plastic bulbs. Blow Guns offers the obvious in two-, four-, and six-foot models. Optimum

Energy, Emergency Essentials, Major Surplus, and Jungle Outfitters sell packaged food, water treatments, radios, tents, packs, stoves, and assorted "ready-to-go emergency supply kits for family, workplace, and vehicle."

Some exhibitors sell anything they can and call it "preparedness" and "self-protection" gear. Titanium Management carries a flea-market array of new, cheap odds and ends only vaguely related to survivalism. The proprietress: thin, glasses, late-thirties, nearly chinless, high cheekbones, fistful of keys on the belt loop of her baggy corduroys. Around her neck, over her tan, Winnebego-chic, poplin windbreaker, a simulated blue and white plastic "official" UN Observer ID card. "I watch the UN," it says in fine print. I admire her ID card. "Globalists are everywhere," she confirms. "Americans have to watch out." Apparently watch-out topics do not include the balance of trade.

Spread thick enough to cover the table, thin enough to reveal each item, are a miscellany of "survival supplies," gadgets, gimmicks, tools and toys for adults and children. Tiny, one-handed crossbows, targets, and darts (Korea); Taiwanese-made "Ninja" throwing stars in a segmented Tupperware box; stacks of hand and thumb cuffs (Taiwan); surgical-tape scissors and hemostats (Pakistan); leatherette tote bags (China); fanny packs (China); cheap dark glasses (China); an imitation U.S. military lensatic compass, the nearly useless kind (China); UN Observer cards (printed in Seattle); a lead-filled wooden-handled sap (Singapore); bright yellow hair combs containing hidden daggers (Mexico); a massive, crude "combat" knife like Todd wore at Gale's place, half the size of a machete (China); plastic dolls (China); and a model airplane kit (Korea). This merchandise takes up three feet of the table. Thirteen more feet of merchandise complete Titanium Management's display. There are seven similar displays in the show.

Stay young, get well, find vigor, enjoy life. Half the show's merchandisers make these promises. All use variants of a similar formula to obtain desired results: combine herbs, seaweed, algae, electricity, magnetism, and oxygen, apply topically, attach to household services, or insert into the alimentary canal at either end. Consider the last option.

Two stalls down from Koernke's, the Dr. Jensen (author of *Tissue Cleanse through Bowel Management*) "Ultimate Colon Unit" is on display, a toilet-top alternative to "eliminate laxative discomfort." The salesman explains the unit's superiority. "Five gallons of water introduced gradually into the colon and expelled cleanses all the colon, not just the fresh waste an enema expels." Two booths south, the competition advocates "Bee pollen granules, tablets, and fibre cleanse," as a "natural way for moving through the intestinal tract." Next aisle over, another cleansing story. "Arise and Shine" offers to "Lighten Your Toxic Load!" with this promotional story. "In 1986 Dr. Richard Anderson and White Medicine Crow were in the mountains living off the land, and eating only wild fresh herbs. The combination of these herbs was so powerful, it took only two large herbal salads a day for massive amounts of Toxic Bowel Accumulations (that looked similar to leather-like rope) to be eliminated from the intestines in sections of about 2 to 3 feet long with a total of about 5 or 6 feet a day." This led to development of "Chomper, the Intestinal Reamer Cleaner," the core of the "Clean-Me-Out" system. No samples or demonstrations available.

Across the aisle, more health revelations. The "Portable Phototherapy Unit . . . shines a focused beam of safe red light (LED) on irritated cells or acupuncture points" and is endorsed by "acupuncturists, chiropractors, physiotherapists, massage therapists, naturopaths, and other health professionals." At the next table the "Secret of the World's Oldest Man," a product "from Southern Pacific Islands where the inhabitants live to an average age of 106 without the normal problems of old age!" turns out to be dietary doses of coral sand. The "Life Field Polarizer" recommended by Gale's follower, Ray, "polarizes your countertops, thus clearing your food and beverages of conflicting vibrations and causing it to have better vitality and better resistance to spoiling and decay" and sorts out gender problems, allowing "the masculine/feminine polarity of the body to self-correct." Finally it "increases the biological value of tap water" in order that "you and your animals and plants all become more vital, healthier, and disease resistant."[29]

Elsewhere round the hall powdered soy, whey, yogurt, and carob drinks, juice blenders, slow cookers, coated pots, kettles, and pans, fruit and vegetable dryers, and vacuum bag sealers offer routes to regained pep and potency. The stay young through nutrition booths have the most professional appearances. Clear-complected infomercial models demonstrate products in fifteen-minute cycles of snappy, point-and-talk patter then distribute communion cup-size samples. The best food in the house.

In the Wings

Expo had rich formal front work, speeches, brochure claims, product pitches. But we can learn more by looking past public pronouncements and product packaging. Watch what participants do, or cannot do, as well as what they read and hear. Hear what salespeople say, or cannot say, about their products, what sense they make of the expo and the survival business. Consider food.

Improved health through nutrition was widely promoted at the expo but hard to practice. The food concession did not help. Instead of vigor-juice and organic sprout delights, the expo snack bar offered Babe Ruth cuisine served with K-ration finesse. On a Coca-Cola–sponsored, plastic, back-lit menu marquee, the hungry survivalist could find this limited fare: Super Dog, Polish Super Dog, Giant Pretzels, Popcorn, Peanuts, Caramel Corn, and something labeled "Sandwich" without further specification. Beverages were limited to Coca-Cola and Sprite, condiments to mustard and Ronald Reagan's "vegetable," ketchup, both in gallon-size pump dispensers, and a soup can-size shaker labeled "Salt."

Olive Drab Enterprises was the only real surplus dealer at the show. The husband-wife owners, Pete and Angie, had opinions about Expo customers and their own business. Unflattering opinions. The business, both agreed, was tedious, boring, repetitive, and showed poor profits. They had yet to break even by three o'clock Saturday. What fun they had came from merchandising, inventing packaging, concocting humorous tags, stories, and other wit to add to their dull assorted goods. Angie told sales stories. From the scrap metal dump at Boeing Aircraft they purchased barrels of fist-sized magnesium chunks for a few dollars a hundred-weight, then put pieces in a fifteen-cent plastic surplus box and sold the combination as an eight-dollar "fire starter kit." Another time they obtained, for fourteen cents each, hundreds of copper-wound electrical devices no one could identify as to function or origin. For six months these widgets sold slowly at twenty-five cents, then provided two amusements. A know-it-all customer spent some time looking over their goods, then in his best high-roller act, made an offer. Angie mimicked. "Will you gimme a deal if I buy bulk?" the high-roller pressured. Then, without waiting for an answer, he blurted gruffly, "I'll tell ya what I'll do. I'll give ya twenty dollars for thirty of 'um. Take it or leave it!" She repeated the story twice and laughed both times. When later repriced at two dollars, widget sales doubled, Angie added. More laughs.

Pete and Angie actively brought humor into the business. Attached to the display booth, and to assorted items, were incongruous labels, instructions, and sales slogans. Over the cash drawer:

> WE CHEAT OUR OTHER CUSTOMERS AND
> PASS THE SAVINGS ON TO YOU

Labels on surplus Ethicon U-10 umbilical tape read: "Ugly born at the wrong time unwanted brat umbilical cord ties, 50¢." High quality stainless steel cranial burrs, selling for $2.50, carried this "caution": "When drilling a hole in your head always put a plastic bag over the drill. Blood could splash into the windings of the drill and electrocute you."

When I chuckled at the "We cheat our other customers" sign, Angie remarked I was the first to "get it" all weekend. Most of "this crowd" do not "get it at all," either acting "confused" or worse, "asking us what the signs mean." Even low humor sailed above the expo's cultural plane, she complained. So, too, did the aesthetics of local beverages. Starbucks sponsored a small espresso booth next to the snack bar. The early twenties coed espresso maker called the expo-goers "know-nothings." "I worked all summer with tourists [to Seattle], and all day long it was explain, explain, explain, but this group is the worst I've ever seen."

Basic science also slipped by. Salespeople's renditions of their products' features were at times incomprehensible. The pond algae nutrition aid Super Blue-Green was touted as containing "all the essential amino-acids in perfect balance, almost exactly the same as the human profile, including DNA and RNA too!" With my high school biology class gnawing away at my consciousness, I had to ask the representative why "DNA and RNA too!" were claimed as bonus constituents. Was organic life possible without a chromosome structure? His response? "Well . . . there's DNA and some RNA in other products," he admitted, but "not much," not the right sort. By contrast, he told me, "Super Blue-Green has the highest concentrations of DNA and RNA ever found," and it contains "the most healthful kind."

"Reusable Laundry Disks" were "designed to activate water's natural cleansing properties" and "kill harmful bacteria" according to the flyer. How did they work? I read on. "Disks contain activated ceramics that release electrons which . . . allow ionized water to greatly increase its penetrating power into the cloth fabric [and] lift out dirt particles. . . . Scientifically explained: H_2O becomes $H+OH-$." So said the flyer. But when I asked the young salesman to explain the principle he simply grinned, pointed to half a teaspoon-worth of BB-size stones on the table in front of him and said, "See these little rocks? . . . They are inside these disks. When you put them in the wash they let off electricity that makes the dirt come out without chemicals. . . . It's electrical cleaning. . . . Dirt sticks to the electricity."

After learning that dirt sticks to electricity and hearing the DNA/RNA story, I never did find out how the Life Field Polarizer "increases the biological value of tap water." In truth, I felt I could not ask and maintain a straight face.

Health was not always evident even where it might be expected. Tall, athletic-looking Dwaine, the Aryan infomodel at Tomorrow Foods and Supplies, was a picture of virile health. Tight, trim white Dockers below, blonde chest hair curling from the unbuttoned collar of his mesomorphically bulging polo shirt above. But the picture was only paper thin. Dwaine moved slowly, pained and constrained. He sold "Japanese flexible therapeutic magnets" that at sales pitch time "cured carpal tunnel syndrome and sciatic inflammations when taped in place over irritated sites" and herbal blends for "natural healing and relief from pain." But Dwaine wore a suspendered elastic brace around his abdomen, not magnets, and popped two half-grain codeine tablets as we talked. Expo business and back pain preoccupied Dwaine's thoughts. "Expo life is wearing," he complained. Load and unload, drive for many miles between shows, crummy motels. He hurt his back lifting the boxes last summer. Tried chiropractic. Tried surgery. Neither helped. Now it is hard to drive, hard to sit all those hours in the truck. Frankie does the driving now, and the lifting. Frankie, the Sancho Panza of the pair, half a foot shorter, balding, not recently washed, shaped more like a "Stop" than a "Yield" sign, wrestled with a box of goods as we talked. Dwaine talked politics. Not New World Order politics but politics that mattered, expo politics—how to negotiate a high-traffic-flow booth location, where to get merchandise with room for plenty of markup. Surplus is good, cheap in bulk, well made, has "military" appeal. But imported products move, too—tools, knives like hollow-handled "combat" designs with accessories. Always display pepper spray prominently. That sells, and they usually buy something to go with it. OD clothing. Sometimes herbs. Have lots of small items, two-, three-, five-, ten-, fifteen-dollar stuff. You need variety. Nothing too expensive, and always remember: location, variety, markup. That was Dwaine's political advice on the sidelines.

As we chat and Frankie moves boxes, a reporter and cameraman from the local TV station work their way down the aisle then stop at Dwaine's place. Time for expo front work. Business talk turns to melodrama. The reporter asks who-from-where openers. A crowd gathers (potential customers?). Dwaine begins to answer in a diffident baritone. Then the key question. "What are all you survivalists getting ready for?" asks the media man. "What are you afraid of?" Dwaine stiffens, preparing a riposte, but disreputable-looking Frankie draws the lens. His turn to play and please the crowd. He does. It is standard fare, starting with a surly "*You* people in the media," then the usual themes: "government out of control," what the "founding fathers intended," how "foreign influence" was ruining America, the "peoples'" right to "protect themselves," what "doctors won't tell people" about alternative cures. Crowd heads nod, reporter acts alarmed, cameraman gets close-up of Frankie, "news" is created, a good time is had by all. After seven or eight minutes the TV crew moves on, the crowd moves in, and Dwaine and Frankie do a brief, brisk business. Twenty minutes later, back to normal. Frankie takes a break. I join him for coffee.

He complains steadily about his problems in America: long drives, lousy hotels, negotiating a good display space, loading and unloading merchandise. A familiar refrain. At the table beside us two women rest, eat Polish dogs, share expo experiences. Mary Poppins grown plump, pink, middle aged enthuses, "Sprouts grow so much faster in ozonated water!" Lila Kedrova in *Zorba the Greek,* painted, frail, holds up a sack of seaweed cure, proclaims it a bargain. "This is so much more expensive in California!" Mary asserts. "Larry Pratt is right on! He doesn't compromise like the NRA," Lila adds. "Linda Smith . . . We are more like her." Mary instigates rumors: "They are going to start using real silver coins to get rid of the Federal Reserve." Lila concurs: "Yea, I hear that too." Frankie listens to the neighbors, looks at me, leans forward, nodding his head slightly toward the adjacent table. "That seaweed stuff's crap," he says quietly. "No better than those sprouts we sell. . . . Taste like sawdust. . . . [I] don't see how it can do any good." We sip coffee a while more. Between the tables walks a trim, handsome, early thirties woman: dark, straight hair to her waist, two khaki-capped sons behind, and politics on her t-shirt front.

CHRISTIAN
AMERICAN
HETEROSEXUAL
PRO-GUN
CONSERVATIVE
ANY QUESTIONS?

The only question I can think of is one more for Frankie. I ask him about the episode with the TV crew, his speech and opinions. I ask the right question. A burden seems to lift from him. He brightens in recollection, unslouches, sucks in his gut, beams. Frankie thinks well of his performance. "That was fun! I had 'um going good! Did you see that reporter sweat? Sure helped business, too. Smiling broadly, Frankie goes on about his impromptu performance, recalling media encounters at other expos. "I like to get the crowd with me. Get 'um going!" These are the best of expo times for Frankie, fleeting chances to fashion drama, tell tales, hold center stage. No grand projects or encompassing causes to promote, but adventures, small and momentary, in culturecraft.

Reading the Signs of the Times

Expo headliner Mark Koernke, chubby, cherubic, with thinning brown hair and bifocals, and wearing his Sunday suit, had day-job academic connections like William Pierce, but in a different capacity. He was a janitor at the University of Michigan. Only after hours did he become "Mark from Michigan," the low power shortwave broadcaster of menaces to come and militia to follow, long of wind, short of fact, and hardly of consequence, until the Oklahoma City bombing. Suddenly survivalism mattered, to law enforcement and the media. ABC's *Prime Time* and other news seekers discovered and welcomed Koernke's radio ramblings, as did the FBI who investigated his rumored ties with Timothy McVeigh.[30] Soon, he appeared on the Expo roster, drawing cameras like Frankie and conclusions like Hank. Also like Hank, he had help. Friends and well-wishers stopped by his booth with grist for new conclusions. Some stayed for the grinding.

A crowd of five or six gathers after the Friday speech, chatters, watches *America in Peril,* part of Koernke's small stock of videos, showing on a tabletop monitor. When gossip and sales ebb, Mark plays his trump. From beneath the table he pulls an unlabeled VHS cassette. This is the "other" tape, he tells us, the clandestine one, not yet released to the public, unedited, full of damning details. "This one was made by one of *our* soldiers, one of our guys," Koernke reveals. "He wore a hidden video camera on his [combat gear] harness [at a National Guard exercise] so no one could see it." Koernke points to his shoulder where the camera would have been attached. "The stuff you see here [gesturing to the tape presently playing at the VCR station] is made from *their* material. They edited it. But on our guy's tape you can see everything, the UN insignia on the trucks and APCs. The UN flags are obvious." Grinding has begun.

Others reach into pockets and purses, bring out their own revelations, snapshots—ordinary seeming, but when understood, evidence for stories of grand and sinister plots. The group works at understanding, passing pictures to Koernke and around the circle. The group pulls together, sees things of relevance among their photos of transport and civil engineering projects, highway and rail traffic, buildings and bridges. Look for the signs. Too many trucks going north on the interstate? Trains crossing the bridge ahead of schedule? Or behind? Hauling extra cars? Too few cars? Empty, when they should be full? Full, when they should be empty? Are others on sidings? Some markings mislead. Plain, clear markings on buildings or trucks or boxcars probably indicate disguises or decoys. Interpret. "That can't be wheat. Train's going south. They don't need any more wheat down south." Missing markings hide true contents. "Looks like its regular freight but see those seals on the locks? Blue and white tags [United Nations colors]. You can just see that little white spot . . . " "Lots of UPS trucks coming west on the back roads" "They use UPS trucks now. The government controls UPS. Most of their trucks drive at night so people don't notice." "The bridge over the river on the old highway was closed three days last week," but "there were headlights on the other side moving at night, down that abandoned road along the levee" and "in the woods." "New chain-link fence around that old warehouse, barbed wire too. And it's posted, 'Keep Out.' Got night watchmen there carrying guns. They're not from around here." "Whole convoy of covered [National] Guard trucks headed south last Saturday. Drivers were all officers." And if you listened late, the last speaker told us, you could hear the powerful rotor blades across the valley. "Black helicopters," she said.

Little pictures circulate, ingenuity activates, the big picture comes into focus. Photos from the Southwest, southern California, Arizona, New Mexico, form a collective image. Koernke had predicted earlier that in Los Angeles, the Crips and Bloods gangs would be armed and recruited as first-wave assault troops with the objective of disarming the Southern California militia before the main United Nations forces lands. Here is the photographic evidence to support his predictions, evidence of troop movements, supply transfers, equipment redistribution. Active, integrating imaginations and gratifying groupthink make for a neat, logical conspiracy tale.[31] Smiles, nods, frequent praise for insights offered. Enthusiasm grows among the photo passers, perhaps even a bit of pride as their stories come together. They figured it out themselves. Who needs CNN.

Outer Limits

Koernke and his helpers make moderate sense out of little secrets: What is in the train? Who is going to the city? When will they all arrive? Down the aisle, larger secrets are being revealed. Backup speaker Phil Schneider has scratchy tapes, fuzzy photos, and quite a story. He claims to be a veteran of "seventeen years' experience working in the government 'black projects'" and "one of only three survivors" of the "now infamous Alien/Human War at Dulce, New Mexico." Al Bielek, a headliner, has even bigger secrets to tell, secrets of the universe. Al does not have pictures for support. Al does not even have his original mind.

Al's story is long and complex but highlights make the point. Al is not really Al but Ed, Ed Cameron. At least he was born Ed Cameron in 1916, earned his Ph.D. in physics from Harvard under that name, and joined the Navy in 1939. Then came the experiments, in particular the Philadelphia and Montauk experiments, that nearly destroyed the world. Piecing together his lecture with a monograph he sells, and our tableside talk, events went like this: A Navy destroyer escort, the U.S.S. *Eldridge,* was equipped with gigantic Tesla coils capable of generating an electromagnetic force field so powerful that time and space would literally be bent around the ship, rendering it invisible. On October 28,

1943, the fateful day of the first test, Ed Cameron was on board. On went the power, up rose a reported green haze of electromagnetic energy, and away went the *Eldridge*, invisible, dematerialized and teleported off to the corners of the space-time continuum. The *Eldridge* never completely got it together again but was scattered in "echoes" to the past and future, making a quick appearance in Norfolk, Virginia, and another disorganized one back at Philadelphia. The crew fared poorly. Some were burned, some phased half into the deck, some had no substance and could walk through steel walls, some disappeared to parts unknown. One, Ed Cameron, echo-bounced ahead in time to 1984. He arrived just in time. The experiment was about to be repeated, with improvements and a new name: Montauk. On went the switch, up came the haze, but now there was fundamental trouble in hyperspace. The continuum disruption effects of the Philadelphia Experiment intersected those of Montauk, opening a time-space warp vortex between the two projects. They pulled the plug at Montauk, but the powerful electromagnetic coils still generating on the *Eldridge* threatened to suck 1984 Earth through the vortex back to 1943, destroying the planet and humanity.

As with many survivalist scenarios only one response makes sense. It calls for courage, simple tools, aggressive tactics, and good timing. A volunteer must travel back through the vortex from 1984 to 1943 and destroy the generators. Ed steps forward, is issued a hammer, thanked for his bravery, and sent into yesterday. He does his job, smashing several large vacuum tubes on the *Eldridge*'s Tesla coils and saving the future from the past. (Some say aliens arrive about this time to find out who was rocking the cosmic boat.) Back in 1943, Ed Cameron is brainwashed, held incognito (literally) until 1947, then given his new identity, Al Bielek. Unknowing for many years, Al leads another life. Then memories began to well up from the depths. In 1989 he realizes what has happened, who he really is, and begins to tell his story and peddle his books on local speaking circuits and expo rounds.

That, in a nutshell, was the Philadelphia Experiment. By the end of my chat with Al, I thought I had heard everything. I had not. Three more words made the weekend truly remarkable.

Voices from the Past

Standing for the third day amid two thousand characters, gimmick peddlers, conspiracy mongers, small-time con artists, and more than one who claimed to have spoken to or fought with aliens, far from home, surrounded by strangers in every sense, talking to a man who had traveled in space and time and owned at least two identities, I hear the words. Words that do not fit, do not belong in this place, among these people. Friendly, familiar, youthful words, full of open honesty. Words from the past. Words from another world. They came from behind, without warning.

"Hi, Professor Mitchell!"

Ten feet across the aisle, waving from their own merchandise display table, smile Jackie and Jessie, my own former students, graduates in good standing from Oregon State University. Jackie ("B" in Intro, "A" in Groups and Organizations), sociology major, graduated the year before. Jessie ("B" in Intro, "B" in Criminology) received his engineering degree two years earlier but took longer than most to finish, for admirable reasons. "I stayed another year to take more social science, thirty more units, because the engineering program didn't give you enough, just technical courses." Now Jackie and Jessie, with their ten combined years of university education, are an item and in business, the modern magic business, applying the little-known benefits of ordinary technology to extraordinary uses.

The Rosetta Awarehouse table features herbs, food supplements, and improved water in several forms. There is Aqua Ginseng, Aqua Calm, Aqua Echinacea, along with Colloidal Shark Cartilage and Wild Yam Extract. The Sonic Bloom plant-growth enhancer provides healthy water and harmonies for vegetation, "opening plant pores so they can absorb nutrients from dew." It also "creates the same organic frequencies as song birds used to before the birds disappeared," Jackie explains. Jessie describes the repair and improvement of water.

The Roberts Water Activation transformer can do it all, he tells me. Technology is the secret. "It is not so much the various ingredients . . . that make [the Roberts] company and their products so great. It is their *technology*." At the heart of this "technology" is a "Micro-Activated Biosphere Delivery System which allows the body to utilize various ingredients at levels never before possible." This "water activation transformer" "turns ordinary untreated water, which has been damaged by radiation, industrial chemicals, high-pressure, electrical fluctuations, and other negative influences" and is "unbalanced and fractionated" into "living water, revitalized with concentrated natural energies." The real advantage to Roberts rejuvenated water is not its biological betterment but the neurological nudge it provides. "As thinking is only possible because of brain-water buoyancy this revitalization makes creative problem solving possible."

You are what you eat. You think what you drink.

Enough. I've had my fill of Preparedness Expo. Outside, free from the researcher role, I enjoy the fine fall evening, stop for a while at the

Liberty Lobby table and tell them what I really think of their ideas, then, refreshed and hungry, head west, slowly browsing through the Queen Anne district. My kind of neighborhood. Tower Books, open and busy till midnight. Bruegger's Bagels and the Pacific Dessert Company serve Italian sodas, French water (untreated), Washington whole-wheat pastries, and Oregon frozen yogurt. The Todo Loco Hi Energy Healthy Mex Fresh Juice and Smoothie Bar looks just right for dinner. This time I'm not surprised to find Jackie and Jessie. We sit together, reminisce over school days, then conversation turns to pyramids. I, the sociologist, remember Lewis Mumford's analysis of pyramid building—simple tools, no derrick, wheel, pulley, cart, but complex society, effective bureaucracy, and efficient civil service to organize labor and agriculture, myth of a living god. Jessie, the engineer, thinks otherwise. Pyramids have power. He saw a TV demonstration where "engineers couldn't even build a twelve-foot one exactly." And in Egypt, "all the pyramids were built at once." They must have had some secret technology, he believes, and it was unlikely to have been of human invention. Jessie and I have no common ground for pyramids. But we do agree on the food. Our burritos arrive, filled with red cabbage, tofu, cilantro, and Chinese peas, covered with a spicy yogurt sauce and served with organic brown rice and black beans. We have smoothies, too. I am a Berkeley kid, born and raised. This is excellent fare.

Heading home, the odd notions and quirky merchandise of the expo begin to slide into memory. I'm back in real America now. Listen to the radio. News. Local excitement. "Fireworks erupted inside the Kingdome an hour ago as Tino Martinez hit the game-winning 387-foot, two-run homer in the bottom of the ninth before a crowd of forty-seven thousand frenzied fans. The Mariners' 9 to 8 win against Oakland Athletics' pitcher Dennis Eckersley gave them a two-game lead over the Angels with six games remaining in the American League West pennant race." That's more like it. Normal talk. Baseball talk, not water magic and conspiracy. Onto the interstate, miles slip by. Station KOMO begins its nighttime program, Dreamland, tonight featuring author Elton Elliot. My feeling of normality is short lived.

The show takes an hour. Call-ins from listeners, reading from the guest's latest book, long pop-science explanations move things along. And then a punch line. A great tidal wave of cataclysmic change is coming, the guest tells listeners. "The only questions are just how far away the tidal wave is and how much devastation it will produce." The cause? Nanotechnology, manufacturing miniaturized to the atomic level. "Nanotechnology will reduce any manufacturing problem from constructing a vaccine that cures the common cold to fabricating a starship from the elements contained in seawater, to what is essentially a software problem . . . to designing the command set that specifies the desired atomic structure and the steps required for its fabrication and assembly." Nanotech offers nearly limitless possibilities: "cures for cancer, diabetes, all viral infections," cheap "computers and cars," and "nearly perfect recycling." The philosopher's stone, shattered into millions of fecund pieces, does the world's material bidding. Nanotech machines will assemble whatever you want from whatever you have. After all, there are plenty of atomic particles to go around. Ask precisely and receive. Here metonymy rises several orders of magnitude. Naming, in proper coded form and full detail, conjures forth being. No sorcerer could ask for more.

Of course this will be disruptive. "When the Age of Nanotechnology has dawned almost nothing that we presently value will retain its worth." Everything "will be changed almost beyond recognition." Every aspect "of our present society" will be "mutated or devalued by nanotechnology." Only those who know the codes, who learn the commands, will have power. Only the few who have prepared. As I listen, I realize Preparedness Expo may not be behind me, not over yet, not just shut up in one exhibit hall. Two days later I know for sure.

When I first heard Al Bielek's story I thought it both obscure and incredible. Back at the office, sorting through the morning mail with colleagues, I am telling them of my recent adventures in the field. I get as far as, "And this guy, Al Bielek, claims not to be himself. Says he used to be . . . " "Al Bielek?" exclaims our temporary departmental secretary excitedly. "He was in the Philadelphia Experiment! Did you *actually meet him*?"

Checkout Time

Once more we ask, what can survivalism tell us of the scope and forms rationalization will take in modern times? Which will prevail? Public rationality of the state, anarchistic antirational charisma, or private rationality obscured by guise and guile? In retrospect government proves limited and tolerant of criticism until seriously provoked, and is most evident as a rhetorical straw man to flail and deride. Charisma cools from firebrand passion to polite rounds of table-talk conjecture at Gale's, dull lecturing at Butler's, moderate applause and upswings in pamphlet sales at Expo. But hidden rationality triumphs. The Enemy turns Butler to laughing stock. Expo transforms the whole of survivalism to a commodified caricature, subject without substance, context without the content, brazen adventures in anticipatory culture crafting trivialized to indifferent mercantile routine. Newcomers and newshounds might be taken in by Koernke's mainstage rant, Frankie's public performance, and the MOM tape collection. The naive might believe all this is more than kitsch and inconsequence, petty squabbles over booth location and the cost of rental chairs, might imagine lethality in the mini-crossbows and the blow guns, cures in weed powder and ozone filters, hear portents in rambling antigovernment whining. But they would be wrong. Expo is rationalization's near triumph.

The circle almost closes. Behind Expo's false promise of freedom, independence, and self-reliance, hidden rationality recreates the conditions that first led to survivalist resistance: diminished choice among meaningless alternatives in inconsequential settings, packaged preparedness, permissible protests, elixirs and fixers, trinkets and toys, schemes and scams.

At Expo, as elsewhere, a few remnants of survival adventuring remain on the margins, but only a few. Frankie briefly conjures bogies for the media and encourages the crowd with Gale-like contagious enthusiasm. The Koernke booth crowd enjoys detective work, finding small clues to big trends in traffic patterns, building signs, and boxcar colors. Nontraditional scientists discover health and wellness in compounds of primal elements: fractionated air, ground earth, electric fire, and treated water. Pete and Angie at Olive Drab Enterprises amuse themselves if not their customers by repackaging oddments and ends, then ridiculing those who buy them. Al Bielek shares his autobiography with Ed Cameron and finds the partnership sells and tells well. But much is missing.

Expo might amuse our temporary departmental secretary and the fans of nanotech, but it is no place for Marie and Ben to barter and banter. Expo merchandise comes from wholesalers exploiting cheap foreign labor, not along chains of coincident need and negotiated worth, from personal handicrafts or hoards, via swap or barter. Expo is bottom-line business not frontline entrepreneurship. Nor is Expo a place for Nighthawk- or Ranger-style bricolage. Mechanical connections, adjustments, accessorizing, and other novel applications of material opportunity and personal skill to practical needs are already done, packaged, boxed with instructions. No tests of knowledge or talent applied. No ingenious resourcefulness required. Tepid charismatic dramas abound but only as consumables, stories to hear (for a fee), books to buy, pamphlets to peruse, mailing lists to join. In Mariposa, Gale set the table and the scene for campers' own wide-ranging interpretations of culture, their own charismatic persuasions. Expo only rents space to politically corrected speakers who entertain but assert little, represent less, require nothing.

Then has Planet Microsoft co-opted all of survivalism? Is the grand ragged experiment in culturecraft edgework at an end? No. The Expo roll call is incomplete. Ben and Marie, Tim and Nic, Hank and Penny, the Rangers and the CVF, and others are elsewhere. Shortly we will see Planet Microsoft reach them all, some with pitiless certainty. But few are taken in by Expo allure.

Modernity trades complexity and challenge for efficiency and abundance, and most are satisfied enough with the exchange. Safe, synthetic, Expo-like titillations suffice. But not for survivalists. Weber and Simmel foresaw an omnipresent order of repressive formalism against which social actors must resist to retain their identities. But the metaphor of modernity's iron-caged existence is gone to rust. Modernity's most obvious manifestation is not tyrannic restraint but Planet Microsoft. No resistance in sight. The store is open, the TV on, all welcome. The shelves and channels are full of options. Pick this, try that, they come in all sizes, all colors too, something for every budget, every taste. Modernity gives us more: more things to own and consume, more facts to analyze, more ways to communicate. But it also leaves us less: aimless, rootless, formless, meaningless, groundless, useless. Among the vaporous vagaries of Planet Microsoft neither anomie nor alienation prevail. Ennui does. In this devitalized world survivalists search and struggle *for* resistance not against it.

Survivalists don't want liberation from oppressive yokes or demystification of grand confusions. They want a place between a rock and a hard spot. A place of resistance. A firm, gritty antithesis against which to test their talents, measure their mettle, and gauge their gumption.

6 RETROSPECTS

> A country, finally, erodes, and the dust blows away, the people all die and none of them were of any importance permanently, except those who practiced the arts . . . but it is very difficult to do and now it is not fashionable.
> —Ernest Hemingway, *The Green Hills of Africa*

This final chapter turns to retrospects, looks back over the years of this project into the changing lives of survivalists we met. Eleen and I kept in touch with them. Over time, some faced new challenges, found and lost fortunes, hoped and were disappointed. Yet the spirit of survivalist adventuring proved remarkably durable. As years passed our confidence grew. Survivalists confirmed what we knew. But we had more to learn. Frank would teach us survivalism by the numbers. Thomas invited us to join his own underground New World Order. And Percy showed us how to see the stars.

CHRISTMAS CARDS

One year Hank and Penny sent computer-generated Christmas letters, dot-matrix printed, with elaborate holly border and fancy script message. Another year it was printed cards sold through their church. And another, embossed commercial cards. There is always news (but never all the news), and sometimes new family members' names or new addresses.

By the mid-1990s Hank and Penny's health, their house in the suburbs, Hank's prized Olympic Arms CAR-15, and their grandchildren, Adele and Sasha, all were gone.

The house had been a financial burden. It was "eatin' us up," Penny admitted. So was Hank's work. One card bravely reported, "Hank is still working at Specialty Cast Parts. Last November they started layoffs, but he is still working. We are very thankful for that." But their gratitude was not complete. Hank admitted he had been "waking up in the night, hollering and screaming, climbing the walls." Trying to cover the mortgage payments and other expenses and coping with his job were wearying. Work was erratic. Assignments, projects, hours, rules kept changing. Twice that year there had been down times of a week or more. The stock option plan had been withdrawn and the union "can't do anything," Hank said. Some were fired for no reason, he said. Some quit. Some were broken. The year before, a workmate, Hank's age, was felled by a fatal stroke. Hank's supervisor, five years his junior, died of heart failure. Hank cursed his job insecurity but vowed to hang on for three more years until early retirement, if something didn't get him, too.

Molten metal and heavy machinery on tight timetables with poor safety equipment and worse standards have dangerous potential. Lifting molds and cast parts weighing eighty or more pounds into carts and trucks had taken its toll on Hank. He suffered a herniated diaphragm requiring surgical repair, then needed two more operations to correct damaged wrist tendons. Still, Hank thought he was lucky. The two-and-a-half-ton rolling scrap metal cart pinned him to the tunnel wall but stopped after breaking two of his ribs and collapsing a lung. An hour passed before he was found. His calls for help reduced to gurgles as his lung filled with fluid. The cart was equipped with automatic brakes, but they had long been broken and unserviceable. That year the company's division manager received a Christmas bonus of $230,000 for operation efficiencies and cost savings. He did save money. Hank was back at work, bruised, taped, and wheezing, after five days. But two were on the weekend so the company only had to pay for three days off. Hank received a $20 Christmas bonus.

Penny's first daughter lived in the city nearby with her used car salesman husband, Marty. They owned five small houses in a working-class neighborhood near the industrial district. When Hank and Penny lost their home, Marty rented them one of the houses for one-third of Hank's take-home pay per month. The house needed work to accommodate the other family members, Socks the old cat and Kris the new dog.

Kris had an unenviable history. When Nic's dog had pups he gave one to a neighbor. The neighbor was cruel and inattentive. Retrieved by Nic after months of abuse and neglect, the undernourished, wormy, frightened pup was given to Penny. It was a Penny kind of job. With home-cooked dog meals, two expensive trips to the vet, and hour upon hour of patient currying, petting, and quiet singing, Krissie, a Bedlington terrier, was transformed into a frisky, friendly inveterate lapdog full of affection. Hank and Penny spent ten days' income and a week's labor installing three dog/cat doors and fencing around the entire rental property to give their pets a proper home. "Kris" would appear on the Christmas cards from then on, but "Adele" and "Sasha" had already been removed.

Health was a relative term those days. Penny's card reported, "Last April I had knee surgery and Hank had same surgery a week later [torn ligaments from another industrial accident]. I done pretty well, but Hank is still having trouble. I had foot surgery. I done well." There would be more. As the decade moved on Penny suffered an inflamed liver, diverticulitus, and had a cancer biopsy (benign). Hank joined Penny in becoming a diabetic. All this was OK, good enough, Penny told us on a Saturday visit. The dog and cat, snuggled improbably together in her lap for petting and scratching, tail-wagged and purred agreement. "Our nerves are a lot calmer now," she said. "Yep. They sure are," Hank concurred. His chores done, Hank luxuriated on the sofa among his favorite Jack Mormon vices, cigarettes (again) and strong instant coffee, waiting patiently for his turn to dote over the animals.

The family getaway plan had changed with their diminishing resources. Hank sold his pickup truck then bought a small, much-used trailer for $350 and went looking for a tow car. Marty sold him three: a Ford van that threw a rod, then an old Dodge station wagon, and finally an aging Chevrolet El Camino. None would pull the trailer adequately but the trailer itself sat reassuring in front of the house, filled with "bug-out" kits, sleeping bags, useless snowshoes, odds and ends of camping gear, canned food, spare clothing, backpacks. Now that he and Penny were living nearer to the factory, Hank said he could leave work and be home, hooked up, and ready to go in fifteen minutes. He did not say where to.

Weapons were economized, too. Hank sold the valuable Olympic Arms rifle to pay for Krissie's vet visits and the fencing. The street sweeper shotgun and some reloading gear went in trade for a used Ruger Mini-14; the Smith and Wesson pistol and a bit of cash fetched two Ruger .22 revolvers and a bulky but currently fashionable laser sight at the monthly gun show.

The next year Hank and Penny had other news. Tim Dalkins was back from Alaska without much money but with lots of fishing stories. He was married again, to a woman named for a weed who had a twenty-year-old son and a bullet lodged in her brain, legacies of her homicidal ex-husband. I went to visit them. They lived outside of town in a curious unfinished home, hand built by its former owner, an eccentric, impoverished artist. The home featured curving native stone walls and arched doorways, outdoor plumbing and unglazed windows on the south side. Tim writes in earnest now. Over thirty published articles fill his résumé, in his family's tradition. One late fall night, sipping coffee by the glowing woodstove, Tim told me of his relatives back east, their expectations, his motivations for writing and finishing school. Tim's dad wrote too, he admitted. Writing was part of his job. "What part?" I asked. "He's a school teacher," Tim said. "He writes articles." "A teacher?" I asked. "Where?" Tim was reluctant, then named a reputable Pennsylvania state college. "He's in the political science department," Tim confessed. "I guess I kind of disappointed him not going to college. But I do write!"

More news. After eight years, Nic finally quit his factory job when they assigned him to cleaning parts with what he knew was highly carcinogenic solvent. Cancer runs in his family. Both parents and two siblings had already died of it. He and Leanne were married in June and now live in the basement of Leanne's folks' home while she works and Nic explores his options. They have land now, a five-acre semirural lot, an "investment property retreat," on which they built a toolshed and learned some skills: carpentry, laying tile, wiring, roofing. Their other investment is firearms, lots of firearms, about two-thirds of the complete list of weaponry recommended by Mel Tappan in *Survival Guns*. It takes Nic half an hour to show me his arsenal stuffed amid thousand-round crates of ammunition and reloading supplies in a basement storage room. Finishing the recommended list is now a family objective. Performance is not. Most of the new acquisitions Nic shows me are low quality imports from China. Most have never been fired.

Hank and Nic have been trying new getaway vehicles, pack goats, envisioned as pets now and useful beasts of burden later. Maybe later. But when Hank and Nic take "Colonial" and "Jerry" to the trail head and add their packs, both animals lay down and refuse to budge for half a day. The adventure is abandoned. They're just pets now, kept at Nic and Leanne's along with Nic's other "survival" animals, the other goats and the sheep, the rabbits and the peacock.

I didn't see Ben and Marie for several years. We met again on the coast. I told them about Hank and Nic's recent adventures. They told me about theirs. They had sold and traded their boats, whole or in parts, and had given Hawaii a try. When "trouble" comes, Ben told me, "the best place to be is on the big island, away from the tourists and military," where "there's lots of stuff growing wild you can gather" and "the fishing is easy" too. Not surprisingly, they had spent several months on the waterfront working odd jobs and buying and selling old motors, rigging, pumps, and repair supplies until they came across a deal they couldn't pass up—another boat. "It was a thirty-four-footer. Got it for three thousand dollars. Had a small Honda seven-horse outboard and the rest was sail." "It needed fiberglass work," which Ben did, but as before, things did not work out the way they had first imagined. The boat was costly and cumbersome, too big to trailer. Ben complained that they "couldn't afford to get it out of the water and the port people kept raising the rent." Then Marie had a bout with cancer, and Ben hurt his back. Plans changed; they returned to the mainland.

She's OK now, she says. He's OK now, he says. Old habits return. "We never miss a [flea] market. . . . There's always some new stuff to find" and "good ideas" from other survivalists they meet. They run a little restaurant for the summer coast tourists—fish and chips. And they are working on another boat. "We will be headed for Alaska for sure when we get things settled," Ben says. "We've made some good trades . . . lots of parts and supplies." Marie beams and nods agreement. Perhaps.

The Cascade Valley Force suffered losses. On a weekend outing one member, Glen, played a "joke," throwing an M-80 military training explosive into a small pup tent amid two sleeping Force members. One tenter defecated in his sleeping bag. The other lost thirty percent of his hearing on the left side. No one laughed. Three months later Glen himself was critically burned when for some reason his automobile gas tank ruptured and ignited. His injuries were extensive. I visited him a year after the fire, but only for a few minutes. I lack Penny's training. His face was smoothed over, one-eyed and noseless, his lungs scorched, his lower legs deeply damaged, the fingers on his right hand half their former length, welded together with scar tissue.

He could not speak clearly. His bowels no longer functioned, his wife said. Perhaps it was the months of daily morphine, she said.

Cascade Valley Force has no more meetings.

Freedom Brigade no longer has a phone.

Kermit is dead.

Son-in-law Marty raised the rent on the bungalow the same month Hank's settlement came through for his knee injury. The company paid four thousand dollars. The lawyer kept all but six hundred, and as part of the settlement Hank was forced to retire. Hank had tried to prepare. He had saved into the company pension fund for nearly two decades. But twice the business had been sold, and twice the new corporate owners had raided the retirement fund. Little remained. Hank and Penny settled for a three-thousand-dollar final payout and started over again. Now they lived the survivalist life in earnest. Half the pension money went for their new home, a thirty-year-old bus, into which they arranged their few furnishings. Ever optimistic Penny, now seventy-two, beamed. "It runs real good and is cheap on gas." Off they went to the eastern Oregon mountains, to Nez Percé country, long the land of brave men and women down on their luck.

I visited for a few days last winter, a harsh bitter year in a land prosperity forgot. According to the chamber of commerce, the county where Hank and Penny settled features less than 1 percent of the state's population and has twice the unemployment rate. Household income is 18 percent under the national average; 20 percent of the population live below the poverty line. The countywide Yellow Pages list 19 pizza parlors and 2 psychologists, 1 potter, 1 poultry consultant, 3 pregnancy counselors, 19 police departments, 1 park, 1 computer store, and 123 churches.

Before heading out to Hank and Penny's, I look around in the nearby town while my old truck is repaired. The city "waiting room" downtown is clean, dry, warm, and unsupervised; a retreat in the bygone traditions of frontier hospitality. Soft sofas, toilets, and a phone, all indoors, out of the snow and wind. On a flyer rack, a booklet with the headline "The Great News!" explains "how to get rid of the peril of nuclear annihilation of yourself and your family!" How? By joining the "World Federalist Association" and supporting a "world republic."

At the Pantry Vegetarian Supply and Deli, I'm sitting in the back near the delivery room when the delivery man arrives. The owner helps unload the day's produce. Modern times. It is eighteen degrees Fahrenheit outside, yet the delivery includes fresh lettuce, sprouts, and organic carrots. The delivery man has news and views. News: A friend of his spotted an abominable snowman in the mountains over the weekend. Views: In the mountains nearby roam seven distinct species of abominable snowmen. These have been sighted recurrently by locals and have been definitively identified by scientists. "Sasquatch," as the most common species is called, translates from the local native tongue as "gentle human being." The shop owners admire the mustard greens and express mild agreement.

The delivery man leaves, and I read yesterday's copy of the only daily newspaper in the county. Political news. The owner of a prosperous restaurant in the state's distant urban center far to the west came to town on Tuesday to announce his congressional candidacy because he "senses this community is the heart of the Libertarian Party in the state." The announcement seemed odd. Not the Libertarian part, the location. The would-be congressman lived elsewhere and was contesting a seat in a district two states to the east.

Back in my truck I discover the radio is broken. I find a cheap replacement and Jack at Audio Unlimited willing to install it. Jack works under the dashboard while I sit in the back of the truck and watch his store. Teenagers wander in and out, picking through his tape and CD collection, but he is unconcerned about shoplifting. Not in this town. He brings his portable phone to the truck. It rings. The caller wants a tape. Immediately. Jack is polite. He offers to order it. The caller is irate. “Why don’t you have it in stock!” I hear her ask accusingly. Jack apologizes. The customer is always right. In the future he will try to stock her request, the official version of the theme song from the television show *The Dukes of Hazzard*. Such is life in town. But Hank and Penny can’t afford town life.

When I arrive, Hank and Penny are recently returned from the national forest clearing where they spend the summers to save rent. They are now set up at a dilapidated and nearly deserted trailer park fourteen miles from town. The owner lets them camp there for reduced rates in the winter as long as they don’t heat with electricity. So Krissie’s dog bed goes in front of the feeble propane heater while juice and medicines sometimes freeze on the kitchen table at night. Hank and Penny have a hard time keeping their feet warm because of their diabetes.

We sit in the crowded bus and sip cocoa with our jackets on, talking about the Mount Rainier Rangers. Hank shows me his guns, now stored under the bed. Hank says he doesn’t mind moving around with the seasons. He moved a lot with his mom as a child, he reminisces, sometimes three or four times a year, whenever she could find work. “What did your dad do?” I asked without thinking. “He never was around where we were,” Hank says. “He just sent cards at holidays.” There was an exception. “One time at Christmas he called, and I talked to him on the phone. He sounded nice.” Then, matter-of-factly, Hank continued. “After that call, Mom told me some more about him. He was in the merchant marine, she said. And he was a black guy. I never thought about him much.”

Come spring, things will be better, Hank tells me. “I’ll get me a new door, and we can go mining, pan for gold. Gold is gonna go up. I like panning.” A new door would help. The old one lets in the snow. A small pile of fine drift accumulates beside the driver’s seat as we talk.

“We’re on an adventure,” Penny says. “Most of our married life has been an adventure. You get out of life what you put in.”

Chief Joseph, buried nearby, could have told her otherwise.

• • •

"I will fight no more forever," the great Nez Percé warrior declared after he had done all he could to save his people. There was nothing more for him to do. But how do *we* know when to quit? When is the fieldwork done? When can we turn away? And how? Is leaving the field merely a matter of rearranging schedules and priorities, a shift in rational routines? Or are we, like the great chief, sometimes pursued by our own relentless enemies, enemies of the mind, haunting memories, even when action is long past?

Practical answers to the ending question treat fieldwork as rational labor, effort to accumulate data broad and deep enough to justify reliable and valid commentary. Warranted assertions derive from Bernoulli's law of large numbers applied to social action (Miller 2000). The categories of grounded theorists achieve theoretical saturation when continued observation yields no more information applicable to concepts or hypotheses being developed (Glaser and Strauss 1967, 61). Quit when events become familiar, routine. But fieldwork is more than a change in venues for interaction, more than a method for finding and observing and asking and recording until the categories are full or the numbers large enough. Researchers who would understand social life in its fullness must be more than technically competent, more than merely methodical or artful. They must enter into cathected intimacies, open themselves to their subjects' feeling worlds, be those worlds congenial to them or repulsive, clear or confusing, open or hostile. They must confront the duality of represented and experienced selves simultaneously, both conflicted, both real. On either end of research, coming or going, the notion of the researcher role as an autonomous self-directed creation should not be overstressed. Fieldworkers do not "enter" or "exit" the field as through revolving doors at commercial establishments. They do not "claim" or "assume" or "take" their research roles with the vigor or assurance these active verbs might suggest. Qualitative investigators are well aware the roles they play in the field and beyond are not strictly and exclusively of their own choosing. Much is made of overidentification with research subjects, the notion of "going native," of losing the distinction between "us" and "them," in affirmative and uncritical embrace of the subjects' worlds. But there is an alternative. What if some subjects taint and besmirch, revolt and repel? What if after our times in the field we are left like Lady Macbeth, stricken by a compelling urge to unremember, to wash and wash and wash our forever unclean hands?

How do we bring closure, expunge doubt, rid ourselves of disruptive retrospection, find the limits of concern? Perhaps we don't. Perhaps we realize the informed researcher's voice no longer provides an authoritarian monologue but contributes a part to dialogue. When researchers immerse themselves in vital lived experience they realize they are no longer distanced from the action, the discourse, but unavoidably implicated in its production. The social scientist joins Camus's list: the artist, writer, dramatist, and other interpreters of culture who discover they are as much defined by their work as it is defined by them.[1] Finally and fundamentally, fieldworkers may understand. In action of consequence there is only an imaginary frontier between appearing and being (Mitchell 1993).

Do we visit the field one last time to acquire final facts? Or is it to liberate ourselves from unquiet memories?

THE LAST INTERVIEW

When I saw Nixon again I came full circle and knew it was nearly time to quit. I'd seen enough, heard enough, been at this long enough. Perhaps too long. Survivalism was wearing upon me.

This time the advantage of surprise was mine. I stopped by his shop unannounced, and as before, used a magazine to start our conversation. After neutral greetings I gave him a copy of the lead article from the May 1995 issue of *Atlantic Monthly,* "The Diversity Myth: America's Leading Export."[2] There was a message in this gift; I was not an ordinary coin shop customer. Nixon could tell I knew something about him, but what? Was I friend or foe? (I was not sure either.) Our long time apart had dimmed recollections for both of us. As Nixon leafed through the article he probed, "Uh, do you live around here? Have we talked before?" I affirmed both questions with a few details, and like the proud parent I am, I showed him a picture of my six-year-old, blond, blue-eyed daughter. That was enough. Friend.

Nixon became amiable and as before, instructive. The years had done nothing to diminish his eclectic literacy and eccentric zeal. He was soon launched into an impromptu lecture full of new facts and familiar themes. He warned again of the "spreading tentacles" of egalitarianism spawned by Franz Boas and the Columbia school of anthropology that continue to ensnare intellectuals and politicians. He offered biographical particulars of friends and enemies. With an occasional reference to an article in *Insurrection,* Nixon repainted Shakespeare's picture of black people and miscegenation. He quoted the Bard on the "abhorred union" of Othello and Desdemona. He noted one of Portia's suitors in *The Merchant of Venice* was black, inept, and quickly dismissed, and identified Aaron, the villain of *Titus Andronicus* as Shakespeare's expression of "the Devil incarnate." Next, Nixon turned to the Rockefeller dynasty, starting with the patriarch, John D.'s father, "a bigamist and a charlatan" who traveled the byways of Pennsylvania and the East "fathering at least ten illegitimate children" and peddling raw petroleum as an elixir. The Rockefellers' interest in oil had its roots in this crude patent medicine, he told me, for "this stuff was just bubbling out of the ground, and nobody knew what to do with it, so they developed pharmaceuticals" and as a result, "90 percent of pharmaceuticals are petro-based." Nixon also saw a link between Rockefeller and the "high rates" of "mental defects and insanity and violence" among black people. "They may not have the genetic resistance of whites" to the "poisons and heavy metals" that Rockefeller's "petrochemical-pharmaceutical combines are spewing into our air and food and water." He went on about the changes he had seen lately, the signs, "even things appearing in the legitimate press that prove we are heading in the wrong direction." The *Atlantic* article was of a type. He spoke of Edward O. Wilson's work in sociobiology, of Herrnstein's *The Bell Curve,* even an article from *Society,* "The Seeds of Racial Explosion" (Kuran 1993). Nixon continued for ten more minutes. As before, he seemed enthused by his topics and pleased with his audience.

There was something different about this visit. I felt more at ease, in control. Nixon's ideas were strange, to be sure, but not unprecedented. In the past years I'd heard the likes of them more than once. I was on familiar ground. Half-attention was all I needed to follow his arguments. I listened but looked, too, around the shop. Things had changed. A few years ago he moved his business downtown, across from the county courthouse where he could "keep an eye on things better." (The police chief later told me this surveillance worked both ways.) Nixon was visibly older. His hair was still thick but near white. His waist was still thin but so, too, were his arms. The furniture had been rearranged. Nixon's desk—and his gun—were now in an adjacent room, nearly out of sight, nearly out of reach. We talked standing at the counter and this time I noted I was three or four inches taller than he. Judging from the posters on walls and windows Nixon was more active in community theater and music than politics these days.

It was late afternoon, time to close. The comforting institutional shadow of the courthouse crept up Nixon's storefront. Bidding him goodbye, I walked toward home, calm and satisfied with the results of day. All had gone well. I had found new data and no real danger. Yet my composure was not full depth. It never was in those days. Over time I'd grown uncertain, apprehensive. I wondered, had I done everything necessary for the future, for the next interview? New tape recorders run silently. And with a permit, I could carry a gun.

It was time to leave survivalism behind.

RECONSIDERING MODERN TIMES

Let's summarize. For all the bright hopes of the Enlightenment, with Solomon's Houses of cumulating wisdom built and bustling in Berlin and Beijing and Berkeley, for all the work of thousands of scholars stored up in great libraries and whisked about the globe on hurrying electrons, for all the manifold masteries of the material universe, there is yet doubt that the best of all worlds has been achieved. Ready-to-go rationality abounds. Election-year politicians and Big Macs, on-line stock trades and Dial-a-Prayer, lifestyles, liver-spot removers, and roll-on luggage, all publicly done up in bright packaging and privately tallied in the ledgers of Planet Microsoft. Wants and needs of every kind made and met. What could be missing?

In ancient times there was a name for it. *Techne*. *Techne* stood for living knowledge, for understanding, being entirely at home with something, enjoying a sense of familiar expertise (Roochnik 1996; Heidegger [1952] 1977). *Techne* lies behind all that is crafted, imagined, invented, negotiated in human relationships and accomplishments. It is the will to create culture beyond reflex and instinct, to "reveal whatever does not bring itself forth," as Heidegger ([1952] 1977, 13) turns the Aristotelian phrase. *Techne* is not simply a practical way of doing things but a simultaneous synthesis, envisioning, and revelation of concrete material, imagined form, telic purpose, and agency of the creator,[3] the elements of causation long distinguished by philosophers. Rationalized, differentiated, industrial society pries *techne* apart, fragments human agency, separates the knowledge of mind from the knowledge of eye and hand; the knowledge of doing from knowledge of design. Spontaneity and insight in imagining forms succumb to method (Mitcham and Mackey 1972, 3–4). Diverse purposes shrink to efficiency and effectiveness (see Bittner 1983). Kinesthetic relations with materials and instruments are standardized and incorporated into machine operations (Feibleman 1966, 320).

Techne goes unrequited. Most of what can be known and done by social actors in crafting culture (see Heidegger ([1952] 1977, 7) narrows to task-specific routines. Economics, science, politics, and other prime venues for human effort specialize, formalize, aggregate into ever larger organizations beyond the reach of individual influence.

What then? The fate of Deirdre Robertson awaits.

Messengers and Troubadours

Remember Deirdre Robertson? No? Most do not. Remember her words? Ah, yes. Who of adult age in the late twentieth century could forget? The nation stood still to hear them. Tens of thousands of police and National Guard stood combat-ready as she spoke. Her pronouncements were carried via satellite links to most of the television- or radio-accessible world. Those who did not understand her native tongue heard nearly instantaneous translations into Spanish, Arabic, Russian, Chinese, Japanese, Hindi, and probably other languages. Within seventy-two hours at least one major newspaper in every nation in the United Nations quoted her. More people listened to Deirdre Robertson than watched the last Olympics at its peak. But hardly anyone remembers Deirdre, for there was nothing of Deirdre in what she did. No place for Deirdre. No interest in Deirdre. Only the words. Only two words, really. She went to the office, did her job, said the words, returned home, and was within hours or days forgotten. Modern work. Deirdre was just a clerk reading the executive summary of a committee report on a fall day in 1995. Deirdre? Clerk of the Los Angeles County Superior Court. The committee? The jury deciding the fate of Orenthal James Simpson, "O.J." for short, the football legend accused of killing his wife. The words we remember? "Not guilty."

There have long been unremembered messengers, bearers of precious cargo and portentous news, about whom we knew little. Pheidippides we remember for his fatal run from Marathon, mythical Mercury because messaging was his job, and perhaps Montjoy from Shakespeare's *Henry V,* but most remain obscure.

Contemporary life encourages obscurity, makes messengers of many. Words and works pass through us, but are not marked by us. We redirect information, goods, and services. We do not create them. We ladle out the textbook content, bolt on the replacement parts, assemble the units manufactured elsewhere, dispense someone else's pills, enforce rules not of our own making on peoples not of our choosing. And repeat others' words. We do not construct culture. At best we maintain it. But it has not always been so.

In earlier times messengers had imaginative competition. Troubadours and storytellers lyricized the news, popularized it, gave substance and an edge to heroism and hard times, shared the details and the drama of daily life. Their stories were less linear guides to policy, but more fervent and provocative. They stirred inspiration and memory, sympathy and awe, gave life a tempo and a tune. Storytellers and troubadours were invited to stay for dinner, to eat at the head table, while messengers who kept their heads were sent off to the kitchen or barracks for plain fare.

Survivalists are messengers longing to be troubadours, individuals longing to stand center stage amid grand events and sing of epic deeds. Survivalism, like art, promises what rational life does not, grandiloquent symbolic means of making a difference, personally and morally, in modern times. But how? On Planet Microsoft costumes are plentiful but competition for stage time is keen.

Making Selves

Recall from chapter 1 Gubrium's and Holstein's essential point (2000). The self evolves and is expressed in and through the modern institutional order, not in spite of it. But this is no passive process. Identity is negotiable, a show and tell creation full of artful amendments to appearance and biography, some helped, some hindered by the conditions of modernity.

Show. Goffman made it obvious. We posture and pose, put on airs and wigs, throw parties and fits, polish our teeth and shoes, images and wits, learn to speak with an accent or without one, change our names, noses, nationalities, or even our sex in efforts to manage impressions. Planet Microsoft helps, providing a plethora of cosmetics, camouflage, and sign equipment for dress-up, show-off, play-acting front work. But not all are satisfied to be known merely by what they own, wear, control, and imitate. Some seek to create identities in more integrating and holistic ways.

Tell. The self is also a story, a transcendent scenario, a proffered set of narrative frames within which appearances and attributes may be interpreted. "A man [or a woman] is always a teller of stories," Sartre insisted. "He lives surrounded by his stories and the stories of others, he sees everything which happens to him through these stories; and he tries to live his life as if it were a story he was telling" (Sartre [1938] 1949, 56). As Gubrium and Holstein (2000) note, ready-made story lines proliferate in the modern institutional order: in the dominant reality of vocation, the world of work (Schutz 1962, 226–29), in public agencies of correction, amelioration, and control, in self-help programs, and other venues. Choices abound, but ready choices, stories with known plots and predictable epiphanies, tightly scripted stories, easy to tell but hard to change, encompassing stories that once begun, once named, envelop the teller in rigid expectations.[4] There is comfort in these ready-made self-tales for those bothered by change and uncertainty. But for others there is diminishment and constraint. Survivalists need to locate themselves in more flexible self-narratives. Survivalists need room to ad-lib and improvise, to recast the bit player as hero or heroine, to change plots and add unexpected outcomes. Stories closely linked to current events and the existing institutional order resist revision, so survivalists look elsewhere and when.

Identities are easier to negotiate when claims of who we are and what we will become are ambiguous or unavailable for direct inspection. Claims relocated back in time to honorific ancestry, antecedent ethnic achievements, and other exalted origins, or forward to readiness and effective action in the face of future urgencies, are amenable to presentations for affect. Here is the stuff of grand storytelling, stirring epics of past prowess and noble lineage or pending bravery in the face of as yet unforeseen exigencies, set safely away from disconfirmation to there-and-then, not here-and-now. All these stories need for starters is a little trouble and a chance to tell about it. But here modernity is less an aid than a hindrance. There is powerful competition in this storytelling arena. Others with their own vested interests vie for control of trouble narratives.

Newscasters, entertainers, and would-be experts of Planet Microsoft create Huberty dramas, drowning out the likes of Hank's simple stories and distorting his motives. Assorted intellectuals go farther, claiming their own privileged possession of trouble narratives, finding much to doubt in themselves and others.[5] Doubt becomes a virtue. Grim forebodings delegitimate the very possibilities of others' knowledge, truth, senses of history. Jacques Derrida argues against the "metaphysics of presence," discrediting immediate, here-and-now experience as the foundation of sociological knowledge (Sarup 1989, 35; see also Fuss 1989, 114). Jean Baudrillard tells us we are living in an end-time. He predicts the "death of the social," the displacement of meaningful symbolic representation with nostalgic imitations, referentless signs (1983, 65–67). Jameson takes this farther, declaring with Derrida the death of history. Variants of postmodernism cast in doubt nearly all forms of knowledge upon which science, art, and the humanities are built, leaving only their own *nouvelle vague* (Lyman 1997) to ponder.

Against this chorus of elites' trouble tales, survivalism holds little appeal. There are bigger things to worry about, more fashionable anxieties to host. Hank's awkward and unglamorized stories go unnoticed, unheard, or unconsidered except by a few. Disregard is acceptable. Survivalists can organize and tell among themselves satisfactorily. Survivalism is no movement for the masses, no attempt to shift power, sway the polity, or rearrange national priorities.

Survivalism is neither intentional protest nor practical readiness for coming uncertainties. For all its apparent calculation and utility, it is primarily resistance to rationalization, to fixed meanings and predictable process, an encompassing game of make-believe. But this is not to suggest it is trivial experience. Survivalist scenarios are like Spinoza showed the Bible to be, deliberately metaphorical, allegorical, given to color and ornament, exaggerated descriptive expressions designed to convey by arousing imagination. And with imaginations aroused there is room for adventure, places where culture raw and vibrant can be wrested by strong arms and agile wits from the exigencies of pressing urgency. When survivalists play out their distopian creations, they are not far from the powerful imaginative actualizations of sacred performance in archaic culture (see Huizinga [1944] 1949, 1–27) or millenarian rituals of more modern times (see Wilson 1973; Worsley 1957; Linder 1982). Personal worth is reaffirmed, overawing belief once more within reach.

The much touted troubles of millennium transition have come and gone with little more than fireworks and speeches. Is survivalism therefore on the wane, a passing fad diminished by lack of confirmation, a burgeoning economy, and brighter futures? No. Survivalism persists. There are yet among us those who make what they can of small troubles in order to make something of themselves. Few, but all around us, individuals yearning to puzzle and wonder, tinker and putter, test and explore the possibilities of culturecraft imagine themselves amid might-be action in could-be worlds. As the future darkens the present brightens, fills with tentative titillation, rich discoveries aglow on the horizon. Survivalism is a search for *techne* in a world of technicians, playful drama and narrative invention amid the piled up emperia of form and facts. The whole stands as a well-wrought defense against the diminishments of rationality.

Survivalists' endgames are temporary enchantments, times when worlds that never were nor could have been nor ever will be in the obdurate reality of everyday existence are crafted and momentarily admired. Life is transformed, idealized, simplified. Imaginary sides are drawn, rules set, action consequent and lasting. The complex modern world of competing ideas and alternative life stratagems distills to a few simple principles, the right tools, and a will to work. And there is work to be done, just right work, for the skills at hand and the resources ready for use.

Listen to Frank and Thomas and Percy as we end our exploration of survivalism the way it began, not with judgment and analysis but a story. Listen to the tale of three survivalists with work to do and how they sought to do it. See the meaning that fills their lives as they ready for the end of the world, as they go dancing toward Armageddon.

NORTH

A gathering of sociologists once more brought me back to survivalism, to Frank and Thomas and Percy and their quests for knowledge, common language, even the very possibility of human existence. Their stories and our acquaintance began long before.

I always asked when I traveled. On a year away, in the country to the north, I received this advice: "You want to meet survivalists? Call Frank. He'll talk to you." I did. He did.

Knowing Things

Frank Hearne was born on the plains of Saskatchewan but moved at a young age to a small town in southern Ontario, where he grew up "fundamentalist." "We had a fundamentalist household, went to all kinds of fundamentalist churches, were steeped in fundamentalism," Frank recalled. Later Frank's fundamentalism was tempered with other curiosities, in his teens—science, nature, other religions—then on to college, graduate studies. Now he is married, established in the community, his daughter and three stepchildren grown and gone to live in Toronto and Vancouver. Frank says he is the survivalist in the family, though his wife is "open minded" about his ideas.

For Frank, survivalism is about knowing things. Not utilitarian knowledge like how to lay bricks or generate electricity or handle firearms but more fundamental knowledge. Why do things happen as they do? Where do I fit in? How can we tell what lies ahead? Some have a knack for knowing, Frank told me, some have a gift.

Consider this. Nuclear war could start unintentionally. The Russian missile control system is run by antiquated, unreliable computers programmed by ill-trained and disgruntled workers. "No one does their job in Russia anymore," except "the KGB, which is everywhere," Frank told me. "People think the world is at peace," but "there is more nuclear destruction potential in one Russian submarine today than there was in the whole world during the Cuban Missile Crisis." However, there are ways of knowing when trouble is coming, Frank argued. Some have the knack. "I know this fellow, a computer engineer. He used to work for the government. He can call this secret number at the defense network. They have a code—beeps and tones. And depending on the response to the phone call, he knows what is happening. He says that if there is a breakdown, if the computers start to malfunction, they will tell him a couple of days in advance."

"What's the number?" I asked. "I don't know," Frank admitted. That is the knack, knowing things like where to call. Others have gifts.

Some knowledge is all around us, ripe for apprehension. "One thing I've learned from my study of religion and science is that thoughts are energy. No thought is ever lost because matter and energy are always conserved. The record of every thought, every idea, past and future, is out there. It's just a matter if receiving them. Soon we will be able to build a machine, like a thought radio, that will let us tune in to thoughts, or what I call 'impassioned records.'"

A few can tune in now, without the radio. "Did you ever hear of Edgar Cayce?" Frank asked. "He died in 1945. He was the U.S.'s foremost psychic of the century."[6] Cayce found out as a child he was gifted. His teachers said he was stupid but he slept with his books under his pillow and could remember everything, every word, every map, every formula. Later they found he had other potentials. "He could go into a deep hypnotic state, and they would ask him complex questions, predictions." He also "gave medical diagnoses that were amazingly accurate, better than the doctors', and he'd use all the correct terminology, technical and scientific terms. His predictions have come true just like he said." Cayce's hypnotic utterances are a matter of record, "all documented at Virginia Beach" by his life-long secretary who took down every word in shorthand. "He could do readings of people on the other side of the world. They didn't have to be in the same room. He would give their name, location, tell everything about them."

Frank's knowledge of Cayce's work was literally encyclopedic. "I found one of his books sixteen years ago," Frank recalled. "Since then I've read everything he wrote, collected all the stories about his predictions, found out what happened when he predicted something. I know his works as well as anybody." Frank's claim was substantiated by a ring-bound, annotated volume, over five hundred pages thick, which he pulled from his briefcase to show me—"The Edgar Cayce Encyclopedia," by Frank Hearne.

Others have continued Cayce's tradition of "tuning in" to the knowledge around us, Frank told me. "Ross Miller, he did exactly the same as Edgar Cayce"; he provided personal readings, made predictions. "I found Miller's book in 1977 and wrote him right away. I went to see him. Now I go about every three years." "What does he tell you?" I asked. "Everything," Frank claimed. "I ask him everything and he tells me. I ask him questions about knowledge, understanding myself, about life, but also about physical things. My daughter, her eyesight was bad. So I asked him what she should do. First of all he x-rayed her with his eyes and his mind. Then he said all these technical things. I wrote it all down, took the technical statement to my chiropractor and said, 'Would you x-ray my daughter and let me know if there is any truth in this [diagnosis]?' He did everything and then he said, 'I don't know where you got this analysis, but it is exactly correct.'"

"Has your daughter's vision improved?" I inquired. "Yes, some," Frank equivocated, "but the doctor told me I needed to get more information. I'll ask [Miller] more next time."

Trips to visit Miller in northern Michigan are not distant, but they are expensive. "He charges four hundred dollars an hour; it used to be three hundred dollars." Prices have gone up because of Miller's personal problems, Frank reflects. "He is an alcoholic and everything, and he's had eight, no, nine wives."

"What is the connection between psychic understanding and survivalism," I asked Frank. Practical facts were one benefit. Except for Miller's revelations, Frank said he would not have known about Havblum, "an organic spray they developed to put on buildings to keep the radiation out." But Frank has not been able to find it in any scientific catalogs. Frank also learned what he claims others will realize after the war. "There is going to be a great new understanding of the benefits of radiation. Because radiation—the right kind of radiation in the right amounts—can be rejuvenating. Lots of things are going to be rejuvenated" from nuclear explosions.

So psychics provide specific knowledge of use to survivalists. But Cayce and Miller did more for Frank than inform him. They inspired him. By searching for nonordinary ways of understanding, "It helps you live you life more constructively, more usefully. That's the whole point of survival—learning how to be useful, constructive. Constructive's the word. When the war is over we are all going to have to be more constructive."

"I'm getting ready myself." "How?" I asked. "I've made a special study of numbers. Numbers can tell you a lot. But you've got to know what they mean. Every number *means* something. When you talk about seven years you have to look at the meaning of 'seven.' It has nothing to do with seven *years*. It's the meaning of the number that matters. The body rejuvenates in seven years, for example, it's a seven year *cycle*. The whole universe is based on number cycles. Every number *means* something. Like when Miller says that in *eighteen* months certain prophecies are going to happen."

Frank was now on familiar ground. We sat in a small coffee house and bookstore. Polite young people nodded as they passed by or stopped briefly to say hello. Most addressed him by his title. He pushed aside our pie and coffee dishes, pulled a blank sheet of paper from his briefcase, and began drawing—numbers, formulas, connecting lines, circles, and other shapes, pointing here and there on the page as he continued to explain. "'Eighteen' is like 'nine'; 'eighteen' is always a period of completion. The number 'nine' is relative to a period of *completion*. 'Two' is a *separation*, that's where you start with the 'one,' and there's a *division* . . . "

And so it went for half an hour and three more paper sheets. Frank did not have a bomb shelter or guns or much stored food,[7] but he had a new and novel way of understanding things. "You've got to look at these numbers differently. You can only understand them if you study these things. I have studied numbers for years. Numbers are my specialty."

Others would probably agree. The coffee house in which we sat was two blocks away from a small but well respected local university. Frank worked there. He was a full professor, and at that time acting chair, of the Department of Mathematics.[8]

Not long after that I met the man who introduced Frank to survivalism, the one with the knack, the one Frank said had secret phone numbers. He never told me about his phone numbers, but he did have big plans and a modest helper who made them possible. We spent time together in those days. I watched, listened, then moved away. Ties thinned, projects came and went. Nine years later came a chance to revisit the past, to remember.

Words and Deeds

The American Sociological Association is meeting in Toronto, making "Bridges for Sociology." I leave the bridge building to colleagues and join the urbanite Sunday drivers heading north through the carefully regulated Canadian farmlands, inflating real estate prices and the market for roadside curios as we go. Bustling highway slows to ambling byway. Corn and alfalfa fields stand ripe and still in the muggy August sunshine. Recumbent Guernseys rest, reconsider breakfast. Gentrified villages half an hour apart slow traffic with tourist-friendly shopping fairs and festivals, sidewalk ice cream, crafts, pottery, antiques. Claybourne holds its annual fiddle contest next week at the fairgrounds. The mini-tractor pull is later today. Pony rides are five dollars. So are the popular emu and ostrich burgers. One last turn, no more traffic, a quarter-mile down the hill, lies the village of Franklin's Fork, population two hundred. The scattered homes of Franklin's Fork line the bottom of a hollow that today holds summer heat, in winter shelters from the chill Lake Ontario storms, and for a century and a half has been home to Thomas Sands's wife and her ancestors. Midtown on Main Street, a small dusty white cottage, old Toyota in the driveway, grass growing in cracks of the little used street, sits the Sands residence since 1970. Percy's place is a few miles away, out of town, on a dirt road, in more open country. His wife came from far away.

Thomas expects me. Percy does not. These are different men.

WORDS

It is easy to say things about Sands for he has much to say about himself. Sands is a man of words, generous in his production of texts, pronouncements, predictions, explanations of view, lectured, semisermonized, authored, in self- and unpublished flyers, pamphlets, magazines. He has written book-length manuscripts and lesser tracts recounting his roots and references, discussing his credentials and vision. Recently he has developed a Web page. Streamlined, his story goes like this:

Sands's childhood began and was spent in conservative, small-town, big-family Kansas, where many of his relatives still live. He claims to have attended eleven colleges and universities,[9] earning a bachelor's in "Bible, religion and philosophy" from the family alma mater, Southwestern College in Kansas, and a master's in "economics and political science" from Texas Christian University. He traveled to China and throughout Latin America on business as a computer consultant and sales representative. He also taught for short periods at small colleges in the southern United States and northern Canada,[10] invented a chess teaching machine "sold in several countries," and authored "a number of books in the computer sciences."[11]

During the 1970s Sands promoted construction of *Canada Tomorrow,* a ocean-going research ship designed to develop techniques for robotic undersea mining and recovery.[12] He also owned one-third of World Discovery Corporation, the firm that conceived and built the robotic arm used to recover the space shuttle *Challenger.* Neither of these projects finished well. The ship fell into international legal wrangling and remained unused in a Chilean port for much of the 1980s, eventually being sold into receivership without ever beginning its exploratory tasks.[13] The robot arm company went bankrupt without further accomplishments, though its most famous product found its way to the Smithsonian.

Sands held other jobs, as chauffeur to Ezra Benson, U.S. Secretary of Agriculture ("drove him all around Iowa just when they were harvesting corn, and to the Chicago Stock Exchange"), and as a U.S. Air Force control tower operator in the Arctic for a year.

Sands says he is "greatly interested in religion" of all forms, and aside from religious works, lists as his favorite books *Zen and the Art of Motorcycle Maintenance*; *Flatland*; *Gödel, Escher, Bach*; *Varieties of Religious Experience*; and "many works by J. S. Mill." He denies any musical or sports talents but says he was "once an exceptional speed reader." He is married to "a woman everyone says is a saint" and describes his progeny collectively as a "total of twenty children and grandchildren."

These things and more Sands says about himself. He also has things to say about the world at large. "I am an optimist about the long-term future of mankind," Thomas told me, "but a pessimist about the immediate future." His pessimism stems from two sources: the failure of the world's peoples to communicate and the threat of nuclear oblivion. Sands has partial correctives for both.

The World Language Program, of which Sands is the "coordinator, founder, and initial vision holder" is a thirty-year effort to discern, develop, and disseminate the "Angel Tongue" (more correctly spelled "Anjel Tung"), a modern-day version of the Biblical lingua franca rendered rational: phonetic, androgynous, freed of homonyms and synonyms, and soon, Sands says, to be tested on Spanish-speaking prison inmates in Florida. "I wrote a book, *The Restoration of the Angel Tongue*," Sands says. "I haven't published it or anything, but I wrote it." Over the years Sands has invested much effort in promoting the World Language Institute as an antidote to many of the world's ills. But some trouble transcends talk. When the nuclear bombs fall, as well they may, Sands has other plans. He wrote another book about that problem, a book with many subtitles. "The Recovery of the Titanic (America): A View across the Chasm: A Vision of the Nuclear Holocaust and The Path to Civilization's Recovery."[14]

Look backward two decades to the beginning of that book, and the project it inspired. Sands and those times are different.

Ronald Reagan has captured the hearts and befuddled the minds of U.S. voters. There is a palpable, popular schism between East and West, Communism and Democracy, spelled with capital letters in black and white. Inflation is raging, Thomas's customary suspenders are red, his beard is short, and he has more money, hair, and people responsive to his whims. The little house at Franklin's Fork is not domestic, dusty, or quiet. It is command central.

The room behind the garage with the big glass windows looking out on the garden bustles with people amid the loud staccato of muscular line printers driven by the desk-sized dedicated word processors of that era. Small work stations round the walls, phones everywhere, ringing, busy writers talking, taking messages, passing drafts and outlines back and forth. On one wall a bulletin board with lists of things to do organizes the work. The World Language Program is in full swing, beside other Sands business ventures, applying for grants and making proposals, producing sample teaching materials and promotional flyers. Sands oversees the lot, makes the lists, scribbles notes, gives orders, then in a hurried moment, as if it were one more detail, puts in a phone call. Amid all the words, the magazines and flyers and glossy brochures, there is a deed to do. Someone must be found to do it. It is one of the most important calls of his life. Sands gives it thirty seconds.

Three rings.

"Hello?"

Thomas goes straight to business.

"Are you Percy Kent?"

"Yes," replies the callee.

"This is Thomas Sands. I want you down at my office at nine o'clock tomorrow morning."

"Do I know you?" the callee asks warily.

"No. But you are going to." Sands asserts.

"Sorry buddy," comes the reply.

Then a dial tone. Sands sits a moment, calls again. Less brusque this time, he introduces himself. "I was given your name. They say you are a good man. I have a little project you might be interested in." They arrange to meet.

DEEDS

On that Ontario spring day when they met, Percy Kent was different from Thomas Sands—ten years older, fifteen years less formally educated, and walrus strong. He had scars on his hands from work and on his chest from war. He wore an olive mackinaw and a long ponytail tucked under his watch cap. His great bushy eyebrows, Edwardian sideburns, and mustache were all unkempt salt-and-pepper steel wool. He needed no suspenders, but thick boots, to stand and carry more than his own weight. At the edge of the noisy clerical bustle he waited.

Percy recalls: "This guy I've never seen before comes up to me and says, 'Are you Percy?' Yeah, I'm Percy, I say. He grabs a piece of paper and sits us down at a table. In about half a minute he makes this little sketch, no details or anything, just a box with an arched top, then pushes it over to me. I look at the sketch. 'Make the top arched, bury them in the ground, cover them with concrete,' he says. 'Make them in units.' How many? I ask him. 'Ten, maybe fifteen. I'll pay you handsomely.'"

"Did he?" I asked.

"No, not really, but we came to terms. He gave me one of those little desks, in with the writers, a phone, and told me 'Round up whatever you need, materials, equipment.' Then he says, 'Flo, put Percy on the payroll.'

"'I want something that will take care of a couple of hundred people,' he says. What's it for? I ask him. 'A bomb shelter, for nuclear war,' he tells me, then walks out of the room. I didn't see him again for a month. I thought he was an absolute crackpot."

It took seven years to build.

Percy

"It was a challenge. I always like a challenge. It makes your mind work. There are still some of us who want to discover for ourselves, make our own mistakes. All the time knowledgeable people are coming along and telling us, 'You can't do that.' 'It won't work.' 'It's already been tried.'

That might be, but we want to see for ourselves. You never know everything you can do until you try."

Percy did not talk about himself without prodding. His accomplishments stood for themselves. His opinions kept to themselves. So I prodded.

Percy's story differed from Sands's. Born in the early 1920s to a large impoverished working-class family on the outskirts of Manchester, England, Percy had a short, hard upbringing. School ended for him at age "fourteen and one week" when his father signed him over to became an indentured refinery fitter's apprentice. "You did not receive a man's wage until your apprenticeship was up—seven years," Percy recalled. But "it was learning work and I liked it."

> The way they did it was great. They divided the year into six-month periods. You'd work six months in the fitting shop, then for the next six months you'd go with the fitter out in the field. The same with the blacksmith, the tool maker, the lead burner, thc welder, and so on. And at each and every one of these steps you'd progress in maturity. So now you're fifteen, you can swing a hammer. Now you're sixteen, you can cut pipe.
>
> The most interesting time I had was with the boiler maker. At that time they didn't weld a patch on a boiler. They did it all cold. And this guy didn't rivet. I know because I drilled every bloody hole and tapped every thread. It was drill and tap, and every hole matched, and the threads were all hand corked on the boiler shell. Every boiler tube had to be cut out with a cutting chisel and new ones had to be expanded by hand.
>
> I learned a lot in those days.

Then came another lesson. War. At sixteen and a half Percy joined the infantry. He fought on three continents for five years, always in the front lines. They gave him tin medals in a box for his efforts, an official hero. Percy's war tales were seldom told and not about medals. They were what you would expect of real war. Unspeakable. Sometimes he ran. Sometimes he watched. Sometimes he hid. Sometimes he killed. He survived. He came home.

He and Rose married and in time had three daughters, the centers of their lives, around whom they centered their lives for a quarter of a century, until all three were fine and strong and happy and respected in their professions.

The family moved to Canada in the mid-1960s when the coin came up heads. (Australia was tails.) There were private cars instead of busses, houses made of wood instead of the fourteenth-century stone of their Derbyshire cottage, and Percy's skills were in high demand. Fraser Steel was happy to get him. He worked all his skills into the job, sometimes on double shifts. Percy was a problem solver, and there were problems aplenty in building postwar Canada.

He also built things for himself.

> A guy I knew at Fraser was having a house built, invited me down to take a look. There were workers busy all over. I looked at the blueprints—this was my life, you know, blueprints—and my chum Ray said, "What do you think?"
>
> I said, "What do you want all those guys for? All you need is a hammer, a square, a level, and choke line, and you're in business. Oh, and of course a saw."
>
> "Ha, ha, ha," he said. "You're living in a dream world."
>
> So my first house I built in Canada I used a handsaw. I cut everything with a flipping handsaw. And I built a 2,300 square foot colonial home. Anybody can do it.
>
> "But he had to fit it in," Rose added. "He was working full time, so he built the house evenings, weekends."

It took fifteen months to build the house.

As the years passed Percy's responsibilities grew. He taught welding to crews of a dozen or more immigrants who sometimes spoke no common language. "I traveled in the military. Round the world. I had seen terrible poverty. I knew how those fellows felt being here in Canada, making a living wage. We got on. They worked hard." Later, "I was the layout man for 130 fitters. I made all the jigs and forms and templates for the shop. We made road graders, mining machinery, heavy equipment and like that."

Then with the children gone, Percy and Rose decided to try one last adventure, a move to the country to make one more new start. Percy told me why. "Rose and I, we both retired, retired early. There's a reason for it. I felt that I should do now what I've always wanted to do while I'm still able to do it. Work on my own project on my own time. Do something memorable. This is my sabbatical."

Not long after the move, Sands called. Percy had the sabbatical project he wanted.

Though Sands often took credit for creating the shelter, his claim was based on entrepreneurship and ownership, not craftsmanship. Percy described the shelter's development.

> Thomas was busy. He never paid more than a few minutes attention at a time to the whole project. I pretty much did it on my own. We would talk about a problem for a bit, then he'd break off in mid-sentence, be gone for three hours, or three days, then pick up right where he left off. I

said, "I've got these prices," as he would go walking by. "Oh, good," he says. "Get it done." So I made arrangements, set up orders. There was never any problem with money. I tried to keep prices down, but whatever I ordered they paid for right away. I said, "We need a hole dug." He said, "Find a digger." That's all, for nearly a year.

Then one day he came by and said, "I've had some thoughts. I think we need to expand our operation." And without blinking an eye he says, "Double everything. Make it twice as big. And draw some plans so I can see what it looks like. I don't have much time. I've got to go." So that night I worked late and finished a whole set of drawings.

When I went to his office the next morning they told me, "Thomas is in Japan." So I just went ahead and started ordering what we needed.

Excavation began in 1980. Sands had expanded the project again, added more units, enough for "up to five hundred people," he said. The result was an underground structure of ten thousand square feet built into a hillside hole 120 feet square and up to fourteen feet deep, cut into a twelve-acre plot of land Sands's wife and her family had owned for a century. Once the units were in place, they were connected, reinforced with steel, then entombed in twenty-five hundred tons of concrete. "Framework should last a thousand years," Percy said.

It was a bargain, but not cheap: $1.2 million Canadian, Sands said. "It would've cost $20 million if the government built it," Percy said.

As the project neared completion Sands began running ads in Toronto newspapers to attract future denizens. He organized discussion meetings, printed and distributed thousands of information sheets. The ads ran for a year. The largest meeting attracted under fifty people. Visitors came to look, among them Frank Hearne, but as often as not they were cranks or newspeople looking for a story. No one moved to be nearby.

Tour

By 1989 the shelter's main systems are in and running. After looking at drawings and pictures for so long, Eleen and I are ready for our first inside tour. The main gate, steel barred and padlocked, is free of the drifting snow that covers the surrounding fields. Underground it is always the same, forty-two degrees Fahrenheit year round. Thomas and Percy are our guides. Sands points to things. Percy explains them. Percy built the shelter. Sands promoted and labeled it.

The units are modular, connected to form corridors and side alcoves. Most are empty, but signs are everywhere. Thomas is fond of signs. "Gas Surgery" says the entrance to one empty alcove; "Local Surgery" is the label for another. Clocks are everywhere, too, "to prevent disorientation," Thomas says. "Library" proclaims the sign over one more vacant unit. Those inclined to pray can go to the "Chapel."

Two large washrooms are simply labeled "Men" and "Women." These signs do not tell it all. This is Percy's domain. Beneath the shelter spreads a sophisticated septic system, a pit under the pit, carefully graded, properly drained, with oversized feed pipes, environmentally safe, big enough to last for two years of underground life, Percy tells us with pride.

"What's in here?" I ask. The sign reads "Privacy Room." "That's, ah, for couples," Sands hesitates, "to be, ah, intimate. . . . They can take turns." The unit is dark. He does not show us the inside. Instead, he slides the "Vacant/Occupied" marker by the door back and forth several times to underscore its function.

The "Commander" has his own unit, a bit more spacious, sparsely furnished, and off limits. "A shelter is much like a landlocked submarine," Sands explains. "The rules of the sea apply." Shelter life "is not run as a democratic society." On shipboard and in a shelter "you have the bridge and you have to have permission to enter the bridge. If you enter the bridge without permission, we shoot you on the spot. That's just the way it is." The lieutenants have space of their own, less than Sands, more than others. Who these lieutenants might be in the future is unknown. No one is here yet. Nor does Sands yet have a gun.

There are shadow members of the shelter community, persons Sands identifies as sympathetic to the effort and who he expects will be active when the time comes: the local chief of police, the fire marshal, and a "Board of Directors," which includes persons of prestige and learning, we are told. Sands identifies one of these as the shelter's "staff psychiatrist," who inspired a special unit, the "Flotation Room," an immersion tank to "desensitize people with cabin fever."

As we move further into the complex, signs are less frequent. The units and then the corridors begin to fill with equipment. In the "Kitchen" four huge commercial stoves are in place, fully plumbed and vented, along with vast, though empty, cold and dry food storage facilities. Fresh potable water from an underground spring flows directly to subshelter storage in a twenty-thousand-gallon stainless steel tank from a milk truck. Farther along, a three-decade-old, carefully rebuilt diesel generator stands by to provide power. Beneath it, down in the bedrock below, sits a fuel tank large enough to keep the generator running for three months. In "Communications," ancient Canadian Air Force radio transmitters sit shielded (hopefully) from electromagnetic pulse by the natural Faraday cage of the units themselves and a double-bladed, two-handed knife switch big enough to disconnect a city.

As we penetrate the deepest interior, Sands drops back to chat with a helper who is along to do some touch-up painting, leaving us alone with Percy. Percy tells us about the connections, the functions, the capacities, the personalities of his machines. His fingernails hold a sensible amount of grease, but his tools and work are spotless. Everything here is strong, firmly mounted, ready, and when Percy explains it, easy to understand.

I ask him about survivalism, expecting talk of portents and hazards on the horizon. He seems surprised by the question.

> Survivalism? I guess there are many aspects of survivalism. The old-age pensioner is surviving when she walks around the supermarket saying, "I can't afford that. I'll get by with this." That's her way of surviving.
>
> A survivalist is basically an independent person who cannot in his mind see the status quo remaining. He does not have faith that the powers-that-be will take care of him in all situations. That's all. It's like being your own insurance. If there is a windstorm and your house gets damaged, you don't wait for the government to come and help. You start to rebuild right away with what you have and do the best you can.

Confused by this generic response, standing as we are in the innermost reaches of one of the largest individually owned bomb shelters in North America, I ask, "But what about nuclear war?"

"Yea, Thomas talks about it. But as far as I'm concerned there probably won't be one in my life time. Probably never will be one."

Still uncomprehending, I'm silent for a moment. Then Percy answers the question I am trying to ask.

"Why all this?" he gestures with a freshly wiped screwdriver. "Life's no good without something to work on, is it? I really enjoy doing this shelter. I really got into this because it was innovative. I've had a free hand. Nearly everything in here, everything you see is secondhand. I hunted in scrap yards, tracked down parts and materials from all over. I got a kick out of doing it. I don't care much for new technology. I prefer something that's simple, easy to maintain, and practical. That's the way I built this place."

I was beginning to understand Percy's sabbatical project.

Along the corridors at various locations are exercycles with plumbing extensions and belt drives off the front wheels. Percy explains while Thomas sits on one to have his picture taken. These human-powered multipurpose devices can generate electricity, grind grain, and recirculate air in the shelter ventilation system. I try one. They also offer an aerobic workout.

Shelter sleeping is segregated activity. The dormitories are basic triple-decker bunks sufficient to simultaneously bed 178 persons. A larger shelter population would work and sleep in shifts. By necessity sleeping accommodations are divided among several units. By Sands's design they are intricately segregated according to age and sex: male adults, female adults, male teens, female teens, male children, female children, male infants, female infants—all have separate sleeping facilities marked off from each other.

We near the entrance again, past the "Engineering" and "Conference" units, an old dental chair, and surplus radiation detection equipment. We emerge into the sunset, time travelers back from a possible future.

As Eleen and I drive south into the evening we compare impressions and feelings. It had been a strange experience for us, hours underground, cool, damp, oddly lit by flickering sixty-watt bulbs. Yet we agree. It was also strangely familiar. We had been in these curved-top spaces before, long ago. We met there often with friends, sharing laughter and secrets and days long and full of life's adventures. We carried our own supplies then, food and drink and tools for our work, and we spoke a simpler language of fewer words, but it served us well, not to conceal but to say what we meant and felt.

Sands's ark to the postapocalypse had already safely carried precious cargo for the future. The whole complex honeycombing the hillside, unit by unit welded together, entrance to entrance, back to front, right and left, was made from forty-two wheelless, cement-encased, faded yellow school busses, ready for one last hopeful trip toward a better tomorrow.

Modern Times

I'm remembering Percy and Thomas and the shelter they built as I park my rented car on Franklin's Fork's main street and walk to the kitchen door where familiar guests enter. I'm still familiar even after years away. I'm greeted, shown in. The house has changed. In the late 1970s the room off the garage was the center of action, full of busy Percy and the writers. By the late 1980s the writers were gone. The filing cabinets are still full, but seldom opened. The aging computers and the model of Sands's research ship project stand as mementos on display, reminders of former enterprise. As the century nears completion, the space is a spare bedroom, temporary home to Sands children who come to help care for him. Sands has changed, too.

We settle, I on the sofa, Thomas in a tilting padded office chair centered in the cluttered small living room, his office for the late '90s. His chair is unpartnered by desk or table, but on a knee-high shelf beneath the front window sits a wire-caged fan, a rotary dial phone, and a low-end personal computer with a grainy fourteen-inch screen displaying the local Web server home page.

Thomas Sands is sixty-four. Part of this age shows. His blond-turning-white hair is sliding downward off his head, leaving a shiny bald pate and brow above, long tresses down past the collar behind, and a beard Santa Claus would wear in summer below. Suspenders, now wide and brown, keep his gray flannel pants waist centered on a stomach that declines in circumference above and below. One eye sees, the other stares, sightless but animate, eclipsed by a stroke four years ago.

Sands sees both ways—backward into memories and history, ahead into the new millennium. Hindsight gives him comfort, foresight gives him things to do. These days Sands is balanced between remembering and doing. And he has found new candor.

We chat for a time of world affairs and change. Of course I ask of the shelter and its prospects in these times, the same questions I've asked before. When will the shelter be ready? When will it be needed? This time Sands laughs, I think partially at himself, tilts his chair back, and speaks up toward the ceiling, as if others were listening.

> You've heard me say it before. I've always known when the shelter would be needed. That would be in about two years. The truth is, it is *always* going to be needed in about two years, no matter when you ask me. [Laughs again.]
>
> I had not analyzed it last time you raised the question, but I finally did. Why is it always this two-year period—and not just with myself, but probably with all other shelter builders? Because we want to believe there is something we can do that matters. If you think your shelter won't be needed for twenty years or fifty years, then there is no sense acting now. And if you think that you will need it immediately, then there is not much you can do. So it is always two years from now or whatever time someone thinks it will take to act meaningful. See, we want to make a difference, do something that will count.

Sands's shelter is a grand and obdurate thing, but it does not now hold his first attentions, nor was it ever intended to stand alone. "I'm not a survivalist, I'm a reconstructionist," Sands says. The shelter was not intended to preserve a few deserving individuals to continue on as they were in times ahead. Without other changes the shelter is of no worth. The shelter offers only a temporary respite from human folly or error. Always, salvation is in words. "We can learn to understand each other now," Sands warns, "or we can use the shelter and try again in hope that it will preserve not the worst but the best of human possibilities." From this homunculus of a new global civilization will come the final solution to humanity's most vexing obstacle to unity, the babble of disparate tongues.

Sands's vision is neither paltry nor lightly developed. He has read Chomsky and Whorf, speaks critically of "irresponsible scientism" used to gloss over differences in the world's language forms in attempts to justify arguments for some primogenitive Indo-European tongue. He talks of paradigm shifts in the sciences both social and physical, and by name speaks of the decline of logical positivism. That done, he succumbs as many of us do, to a fascination with rational systems of our own derivation, to the allure of culturecraft.

The possibilities of a universal auxiliary language are vast, he enthuses. "This new language will be taught to children in their schools throughout the world. A universal language will help promote world peace and understanding." It will also help world commerce by giving "economically deprived individuals in developing countries an opportunity to learn to speak English as a second language so that they may improve their economic situation." His plans are comprehensive, and bright.[15] First, research, an effort that has gone on for three decades. Then basic pedagogical materials: instructional videos, teacher's guides, practice workbooks. These are in the garage file cabinets awaiting editing and publication. Now the vision expands, beyond the garage and living room, beyond the present.

Next will come a forty-thousand-word simplified phonetic dictionary, a captioned animation series, comic books based on this series, large-type phonetic books of classic literature and basic sciences. And the "future dream" list: "publishing of an international newspaper or magazine in simplified phonetic" form, "training and sending out the first one thousand teachers" coordinated globally over the Internet, "establishing schools and classes throughout the world," forming "institutions for further research and development," and finally, a television network broadcasting around the globe with programming captioned in the phonetic Anjel Tung from the "Universal Language Institute at Bahji du Canada," that is, Franklin's Fork. Sands hands me an illustrated flyer with an architect's rendering of the Institute and its soaring broadcast antenna on its cover.

In spite of his mild protests, Sands is a survivalist. A skeptic, a critic of the status quo like many, he also offers alternatives, scenarios of radical transformation through which profound change may be realized. That he locates himself in the center of these transformations is not incidental but neither is it self-aggrandizing. The center bears the weight and responsibility, provides the inspiration and impetus. The center is a busy place, and that is were Sands and other survivalists want to be, busy among compelling challenges and consequent action. When he was younger and had more resources, he built a shelter. Now he builds language for the world's peoples with what he has, a fifteen-dollar-per-month Internet access fee.

"Today, no, just this afternoon, I had offers come in to help me from Germany and Australia, this is just this afternoon, and from a woman that helps me with programming from California. And a lady sent me files that she edited from New Jersey, and another fellow sent files that he edited from British Columbia. So it's just marvelous to have that kind of a resource!"

Sands is eccentric, no doubt. He writes books he has no intention of publishing then sends them out for review. He keeps the often critical response letters in plastic sleeves and three ring binders he handles with respect and shows solemnly to visitors.[16] He bars the front door of his home and sends guests through the kitchen so the old upright piano will fit in the diminutive living room, on hand to be played badly by visiting grandchildren. He is a staunch vegetarian, the only one in his large family, and when Eleen and I last dined with him he had just finished a nineteen-day dawn-to-dusk fast. It was mid-March, a special occasion, the spring equinox; he called it New Year's Day. The Hare Krishnas were coming over the next Saturday for a "big party" to celebrate.

By every account Sands is also a man of stubborn principle. Percy provided a neat example.

> Thomas? I think he would have made a good old-time pirate because he thinks authority is something to be challenged. He is stubborn. He will bother a thing if it takes him ten years. He'll just keep going at it. If there is some rule or law he thinks is wrong he stands up and says so. Like the time he got the speeding ticket driving to Toronto. Now this was maybe a twenty-three-dollar ticket. But Thomas doesn't speed. So he goes to his hearing. They say, "We got you on radar. You were exceeding the speed limit." He says, "But I was not." "You can take it to court if you want. It's your prerogative," they tell him. "OK," he says.
>
> When it came time for his court appearance he flew in the inventor of that radar gun all the way from California. He had all the specifications, tolerances, error ranges of the machine that policeman was using. Spent three days submitting evidence, and won the case. That's the kind of guy Thomas is.

We are called to supper. Thomas's daughter Alice has prepared simple fare, baked fish and potatoes, iceberg lettuce and bottled dressing, coffee for me, and cookies for all. Vegetarian Thomas uncomplainingly skirts the fish. Alice is gentle with him, putting food on his plate, a napkin in his lap, condiments close at hand. Sands's world is smaller now. His dream of a proud research ship only memories and a plastic model sitting on a shelf by the table. The World Language Program home page he had been showing me is up on the computer, visible through the doorway. He is dressed for dinner, a long sleeved striped dress shirt, buttoned to the top, but he wears no socks, no shoes. These days felt slippers take him everywhere he needs to go.

Two miles away the shelter rests and rusts. After years of disuse, without funds to run the heating system, decay has begun. There is dry rot in the floors over the bus wheel wells and walkways. Vandals have broken in twice to steal tools and building materials. The doors and hatches were reinforced but to no avail. They came again. Now the valuable equipment has been removed, taken away to places paradoxically safer than a steel and concrete bunker built to withstand the blasts of apocalypse. From the shelter entrance looking west, one can just see the urbanites arriving after all these years, staking their own claims to the future in Franklin's Fork, on Scenic Ridge Development's one-half and two-acre home sites.

Sands is eccentric, stubborn, perhaps misguided, and one other thing. He is content. As we bid each other farewell he reminds me, "Man is more than a rational being. He is also a mystical being. He must live his days in hope. I lead a very active life, working fourteen to sixteen hours a day. I have a loving wife and children who look after me, and my grandchildren all bring me great pleasure. I am truly a happy and joyful person, a claim that I wish that more people could make in this technologically illustrious and spiritually dark age." This he says with a smile as genuine and original and full as his mouth of yellow teeth.

Visit to Percy

Our year away is nearly over. Eleen and I are saying good-bye. Out of town, up the hill, down the short, dirt road we go to visit Percy and Rose for our first and last time in their home.

It is still winter. We arrive at dusk. The snow has stopped; the clearing clouds reveal the moon ten days old and Orion well up in the southern sky. Short, energetic Rose shoos us straight into the comfortable armchairs near the roaring cast iron stove. Percy putters in the kitchen making tea, serves us all properly, cups with saucers and a few cookies, too, then sits snug next to Rose on the sofa. Percy follows my gaze around the room, explaining as I look.

Percy's living room is his office, too. The sofa and coffee table in front of us are surrounded with piles of magazines and books. "I read a lot," he confesses, *Popular Science, Science Digest, Popular Mechanics,* auto racing and design magazines, "mostly what they call junk stuff," he says. (An open, bent-backed copy of Graham Greene's *The Power and the*

Glory is on the cushion next to him.) A cardboard box at the sofa's end is filled with instruction manuals of machines and equipment Percy has built or repaired over the years. "I like to see how they say they work after I get through with them," he explains. There are paint cans and brushes by the kitchen door and work in progress—a wood-braced framework, tarps, and scaffolding high over our heads—that need explaining too.

Never a loud man, Percy is now even quieter. "Well, see," he begins, "we don't have TV out here," gesturing gently behind us, "but Rose, she likes to see the stars."

Eleen and I turn, begin to understand. Behind the tarps and framework, soaring from the A-frame's foundation to its peak two stories above, rises a great glistening window, huge glass panels recycled from a department store front, just installed, still partly covered, still untrimmed.

Smiling a shy walrus smile down at Rose, Percy finishes, "So now, come evenings, I can sit here with her while she watches."

Percy is older now. In his seventies. There is little left to be done at the shelter, or at least little left to do it with. Sands's money is gone. Percy's sabbatical is nearly over. It is dark and cold when we leave. Percy and Rose shake our hands and say come back, but we never do. Now we cannot.

One day, down by the shelter, as I watched him work, Percy told me how he got on in life.

> I've done a little bit of everything, you know. I feel good about knowing I'm a jack of all trades but master of none. You understand that? I can do electrical work, plumbing, welding, fitting, rigging, house building, anything—fix cars, trucks, bulldozers, build a fence, dig a hole, set stone, lay bricks. I like stonework and bricklaying. They tell me Churchill used to really relax when he was laying brick. I do too. I like doing it all.
>
> The youngsters today in school so often get sidetracked by ambition and humdrum, trying to get ahead, but never really doing anything they care about. They have to get out, break free. We should teach them to use all their God-given talents, their minds and hands and crafts together.

Percy was a modern man, not a postmodern one. He was a maker of things, true objects molded into better if not perfect forms with what means he could muster and craft. Percy's sight was keen and straight but seldom past the horizon. The future never bothered him much, nor did the past. The past was done with, just the facts of life. The future would get here on its own. Percy lived life today, right here, an arm's length away.

When last I spoke with Rose she told me about Percy's eyes, how they looked at noon on that cold February day. In the back yard, behind the house he was always building, next to his tractor that might work next summer and the truck that ran until fall, Rose found a neatly stacked pile of freshly cut hardwood logs ready for the stove. Beside the stump lay one last log, cleaved neatly in two. She remembered the scene well. Two unstacked pieces beside the stump, and Percy, boots on, bare callused hands gripping the oak axe handle, eyes focused six feet away, just where the sharp splitting maul would have hit the log, on his back, face up, dead from his third heart attack.

• • •

What the future will bring I do not know. Perhaps peace. Perhaps plenty. But of this I'm certain. If this world ever ends and there is a next one, it won't run without Percy's kind, or at least it won't start. Or if it does, somehow automatic and autonomous, I don't think I want to be there.

And one more thing. To endure, tomorrow's societies must offer more than security and comfort. They must answer the survivalists' question, "Who shall create?" in ways as generous and inclusive as justice and equity are now sought. Ways must be found for people of varied means and imagination to craft culture as well as consume it. For to be sure, ways will be found, licit and welcome or otherwise. Some may be inconsequential and some a boon, and some may bring genius and depravity together.

APPENDIX

OFFICIAL VIEWS

Even in the early 1980s it seemed that law enforcement and civil defense planners would be concerned with potential survivalist activity in the near or postdisaster future. I examined the law enforcement view first.

A call to the National Criminal Justice Reference System (NCJRS) was disappointing. The researcher with whom I consulted was unable to locate relevant references and asserted that if their database contained no mention of survivalists, the extent of the "survivalist problem" was probably insignificant and therefore undeserving of independent consideration. This seemed improbable. Surely some information was to be found in the NCJRS's vast repository of law enforcement research. To see for myself, in those pre-Internet days, I arranged a personal trip to Washington, DC, and the NCJRS library. With direct access and the assistance of a competent librarian using the institute's then state-of-the-art bibliographic retrieval program, we searched every term, phrase, activity, group, and individual name I suggested, for two and one half hours. The result: nothing. In should be noted that another author did find a single a government document entitled "Illegal and Unauthorized Activities on Public Lands—A Problem with Serious Implications" containing this comment, "the presence of survivalists is becoming more apparent" (J. Mitchell 1983, 19), and noting survivalist activities in national forest lands in southern Oregon. The publication source, however, was the U.S. General Accounting Office, not the Department of Justice.

I returned to Oregon intending, with help, to take a more direct approach. Perhaps survivalism was too new a phenomenon to have generated written reports, incorporated into the NCJRS files. But what of the law enforcement agencies in areas where I suspected, from field contacts, that concentrations of active survivalists were to be found?

A local sheriff's department heard of my research and offered assistance. As an official police inquiry, thirty-two law enforcement agencies in seven states were contacted via interagency teletype regarding survivalist activities in their areas.[1] Information was also solicited from the regional offices of the FBI and from law enforcement officials with the U.S. Forest Service. The Law Enforcement Data System (LEDS) was also searched for possible leads. Results? A few agencies alleged experience with survivalists. An armed group dressed in military garb was reported to have frightened hikers in northeastern Washington. A forest service officer was threatened by apparent survivalists building a retreat on public lands. Knowledge of one organization, the Posse Comitatus, was sketchy but widespread. (Gordon Kahl's killing of two federal marshals in a North Dakota shootout was highly publicized a few months before this phase of my inquiry began.) With these and a few other exceptions, responses were of the "Yes-No-Yes" variety. Paraphrased: "Yes, there is some sort of survivalist activity going on in our jurisdiction. No, we don't know much about it. Yes, we think it is important and would like to learn more."

Responses, but little information, trickled in for months. One conscientious sheriff's deputy, also a student of mine, with whom I often discussed my research and field activities, made a sustained and vigorous effort to help. After eight months of searching he located and forwarded a copy of a newsletter put out by a survivalist group he thought might be active in his area. Indeed it was. My enthusiastic law enforcement informant wrote an eighteen-page report on his find: where it came from, what the news items probably meant, who was likely in the group, what they were planning. I thanked him for his good works and invited him to coffee where we looked over his report and the newsletter together. "Survival Times" it was called, published [photocopied] by the Mount Rainier Rangers. I asked him if he recognized the editors listed under the newsletter title. He looked, then said no. "Edited by Richard Mitchell and Eleen Baumann," it said. I asked him to look again. The third time he got it.

The full-time civil defense coordinators and directors in five southern California counties were interviewed by a colleague, Rick Peterson. These officials had only vague, media-fostered images of survivalists, virtually no professional contact with them, and were generally indifferent toward them and their activities. As one civil defense director put it to

Rick: "[Survivalists] don't come to us, and we don't know much about them" (personal communication with the author).

During a trip to the British Isles I interviewed the Assistant Director of Civil Defense for the Greater London Council. I described survivalism in the United States, as I understood it, and asked if a comparable movement might be afoot in England. "Not in London, certainly," he told me, and "not at all likely in Great Britain." Survivalism "seems more an American sort of thing," he offered assuredly. Civil defense in the nuclear age requires optimistic assumptions (or rosy ignorance), and here was another example.

As the assistant CD director continued to chat about London's readiness for nuclear war, I glanced through the copy of *Protect and Survive Monthly* I had brought with me. The magazine was what I by then recognized as typical survivalist fare, featuring articles on rural retreats, fallout shelter concealment and defense tactics, and the selection of survival combat firearms (scoped, military assault rifles in .223 caliber with thirty-round magazines, backed up by .38 special/.357 magnum revolvers, was their recommendation). Typical, perhaps, but not American. The magazine's publisher was Protect and Survive, Ltd., Fleet Street, London. "What about this?" I asked, passing the magazine across the desk to the assistant director. I suggested he look at page 21 for a discussion of a survivalist organization claiming groups in fifteen of the London boroughs and fifty other towns and cities throughout Great Britain. (I later interviewed a member of this organization in Crainlairch, Scotland.) The assistant director was puzzled. He recalled vaguely having "seen issues of the magazine once or twice before" but was unaware of its contents or of the groups mentioned. I was puzzled, too. I had come across *Protect and Survive Monthly* only half an hour before this interview. I found it atop a pile of such magazines on a table in the dusty waiting room outside the office in which he and I now sat. The copy the assistant director held came from his own subscription.

From these several experiences, dependence on official views of survivalism seemed unwarranted. Other research was needed.

SELF-DESCRIPTIONS

Data reported here are derived from content analyses of documents collected from a variety of sources including personal correspondence, short introductory statements in group newsletters, and other naturalistic bases. All are voluntary and autobiographical. Data derive from 304 separate reports of 248 discrete persons (N = 248) appearing in five sources. Information regarding some individuals appeared in more than one source.

Table A.1. *Major Survivalist Locales*

	PERCENTAGE OF SAMPLE	N
California	19.0	47
Illinois	10.1	25
Texas	5.2	13
New York	4.8	12
Ohio	4.8	12
Total	43.9	109

Note: Survivalists reside primarily in urban or suburban areas (89.3 percent of sample). All fifty states are represented in the source materials.

Table A.2. *Demographics*

AGE	
Mean	39
Range	19–75
Percentage[a]	81.0 (n = 201)
SEX (%)	
Male	89.3
Female	10.7
Percentage	87.1 (n = 216)
RACE (%)	
White	96.8
Nonwhite	3.2
Percentage	61.7 (n = 153)
MARITAL STATUS (%)	
Married	74.2
Single	16.7
Other	9.1
Percentage	53.2 (n = 132)
CHILDREN (MEAN PER FAMILY)	2.2
Percentage	30.6 (n = 76)
FORMAL EDUCATION (%)	
Less than twelve years	3.1
High school graduate	23.1
Some college	21.5
B.A. or B.S.	26.2
M.A. or M.S.	10
Ph.D, LL.D., or M.D.	16.2
Percentage	52.4 (n = 130)
MILITARY SERVICE (%)	
Not reported	79.8
Reported[b]	20.2
Percentage	20.2 (n = 50)

[a] "Percentage" refers to the percentage of the total sample that voluntarily offered this attribute as a self-description.

[b] Most reported military experience was in noncombat capabilities.

Table A.3. *Future Crisis-Time Scenarios*

	PERCENTAGE OF SAMPLE	N
Nuclear war	50.4	125
Economic collapse	37.5	93
Alien invasion	14.1	35
Civil unrest	12.9	32
Political collapse	11.7	29
Monetary collapse	11.3	28
Unspecified collapse	10.9	27
Social collapse	10.5	26
Authoritarian state	8.9	22
Pollution, resource depletion	6.9	17
Natural disaster	6.9	17
Moral collapse	6.9	17
Vulnerability of cities	6.0	15
Famine	4.0	10
Fulfillment of biblical prophecy	4.0	10
Overpopulation	2.8	7
Rampant crime	2.8	7
Unspecified cause	2.8	7

Note: One hundred percent of the sample mentioned one or more of the scenarios listed.

Table A.4. *Future Crisis-Time Preparations*

	ALREADY MADE		IMPORTANT TO MAKE SOON	
	PERCENTAGE OF SAMPLE	N	PERCENTAGE OF SAMPLE	N
Locate retreat	12.1	30	20.2	50
Store or find water	2.4	6	22.2	55
Store food for more than one year	.4	1	19.0	47
Store food for less than one year	2.0	5	21.8	54
Medicine	2.4	6	12.5	31
Miscellaneous supplies	2.8	2	24.6	61
Alternative energy	6.9	17	9.7	24
Communications	1.2	3	3.2	8
Livestock	.8	2	2.8	7
Literature	.4	1	19.4	48
Special vehicle	2.4	6	9.7	24
Farmland	5.6	14	10.1	25
Develop relocation plans	.4	1	10.9	27
Join survival group	4.8	12	3.6	9
Acquire firearms	63.7	158	.4	1
Other weapons	0	0	1.6	4
Locate natural food supply	0	0	2.4	6
Fallout Shelter	7.3	18	10.5	26

continued

Table A.4. *(Continued)*

	ALREADY MADE		IMPORTANT TO MAKE SOON	
	PERCENTAGE OF SAMPLE	N	PERCENTAGE OF SAMPLE	N
Move to rural area	6.9	17	20.2	50
Be totally self-sufficient	8.1	20	2.4	6
Store supplies for others	1.6	4	7.7	19
Find spouse			5.2	13

Note: One hundred percent of the sample mentioned one or more of the preparations listed.

Table A.5. *Reported Survival Skills*

	PERCENTAGE OF SAMPLE	N
Construction (carpentry, plumbing, wiring, welding, masonry, etc.)	29.8	74
Hunting, fishing, trapping	25.4	63
Commercial services for other survivalists	22.6	56
Emergency medical (CPR, first aid, emergency medical technician, etc.)	20.6	52
Agriculture, animal husbandry	18.1	45
Martial arts, self-defense	15.3	38
Combat, special weapons use	14.5	36
Wilderness travel (backpacking, camping)	10.5	26
Radio communication	10.1	25
Home economics (food preparation and storage, soap making, weaving, sewing, etc.)	9.3	23
Leadership, organizational ability	6.0	15
Gunsmithing	5.2	13
Total	85.9	213

NOTES

CHAPTER ONE

1. The root term, *survival,* is derived from the Latin *vivere,* to live on, to go on living, whence the French *survivre,* to survive, and thus to *survival* and *survivor* (Partridge 1983, 785). *Survival* connotes continued existence and viability through trying circumstances. Species struggle for eons in vast Darwinian conflicts over resources and adaptability. The lost hiker shivers through the long night hours to dawn, light, and hoped-for rescue. Both quest for survival. "Survival" is also an everyday exaggeration, hyperbole used to describe degrees of toleration for quotidian social tedium. The bureaucrat who weathers successive changes in administration and policy is dubbed a "survivor." Snobbish pseudosophisticates may speak of "surviving" the boredom of obtuse bridge or cocktail party companions, long lines at the supermarket, and protracted waits at their analysts' offices. In these senses the notion of survival is comfortably distant and depersonalized, or unproblematic and familiar in modern industrial society. But in other senses of the word, it is not always so.

2. Measured at the center, some survivalist attributes are unremarkable (see appendix). In a sample of 248 individuals who volunteered comparable self-descriptive data, nine out of ten were male, three-quarters were married, and all but one were white. They averaged two years of college, thirty-nine years of age, and 2.2 children. Only one in five reported prior military service, nearly all in noncombat capacities. *American Survival Guide* (Gallant and Eisen 1997, 41) reports similar characteristics among readers responding to a survey regarding gun ownership and regulation. These are hardly distinctive characteristics. With the exception of education these data would probably fit other commonplace groups—a Midwestern state college department of sociology, for example.

3. Donald Levine makes clear the French preoccupation with quite another issue in contradiction to Simmel's view, threats to the social order posed by what

French liberals and conservatives alike view as the "noxious growth of individualism" (Levine 1995b, 169).

4. This is Hegel's first usage of *Entfremdung*. See Schacht 1970.

5. Hegel's second usage of *Entfremdung*. See Schacht 1970.

6. The characterizations here are Herbert Marcuse's "one-dimensional man" (1964), David Riesman's "other-directed personality" (1950), William H. Whyte's "organizational man" (1957), and Jay Lifton's "protean man" (1993). "Man" is used here and elsewhere in its gender-neutral sense and in consonance with the cited authors' terminology.

7. Jim Jones, personal communication with the author.

8. Survivalists are not alone in anticipating troubles. Toward a myriad of untoward eventualities ordinary people take joint and separate action. Together, they buy life, health, home, and collision insurance and enroll in the automobile club. They support firefighters and law enforcement, join environmental and peace activist groups, and march against drunk driving. Individually, they wear seat belts, carry spare tires, buy guns and alarms for home protection, get a second medical opinion, and listen to weather forecasts for warning of tornadoes and high water. In the 1960s they built bomb shelters at President Kennedy's urging. At century's end they submitted to airport security screenings and organized their neighborhoods against crime. Many pray regularly for personal salvation, while a few prepare in other ways for imminent supernatural transformations (Lofland 1966; Festinger, Riecken, and Schacter 1956). Nonsurvivalists are rewarded for these preparations with increased security and reassurance; survivalists by the attractions of cathected problem solving.

9. Survival scenarios exhibit four essential criteria: they posit conditions that are *global, caused,* amenable to *technique,* and susceptible to *individual* solutions. It is the combination of these elements that characterizes survivalism and distinguishes it from nonsurvivalists' worldviews.

Survival scenarios build on plights that are *global,* not individuated. They entail events and conditions, such as nuclear war or alien invasion, that are expected to affect many if not most persons rather than more selective hazards such as automobile accidents or street crime. Survival problems are not merely circumstantial or random. There are logical, secular reasons for these problems. Survivalism is not action toward manifestations of inscrutable divine will or inexorable historical process. The problems confronted are *caused* by agents, agencies, and processes survivalists may discover and understand with appropriate effort and access to relevant information. Once understood, survival problems are amenable to *technique*—combinations of resources, rational procedures, and standardized practices potentially at hand. Finally, the solution to survival problems lies with individuals and small groups, not collectives. Survivalism is the exercise of *individual* skill and will, the expenditure of personal effort and possessions, not political activism, community organization, or a social movement.

10. See the classified section of almost any issue of *Soldier of Fortune* or the "Survivalist Directory" section in *American Survival Guide* for examples.

11. Similarly Timothy McVeigh became a "militia" member as the media sought an inclusive label for events leading to the Oklahoma City bombing (see Mitchell 2000).

12. Joel Best's "Rhetoric in claims making: Constructing the missing children problem" (1987) and Eleen Baumann's "Research Rhetoric and the Social Construction of Elder Abuse" (1989) point precisely to the inaccuracy of such preemptive judgments.

13. Edward Meyers (1982, 15) correctly predicted that survivalist secretism would severely limit both the possibility and validity of traditional surveys. As would-be researchers discovered, even when reasonable samples could be located, outsiders' attempts to conduct survey research among survivalists proved largely unsuccessful. Tom Tyler and Kathleen McGraw (1983, 31) sought responses from the members of the Chicago division of Live Free, Inc. Even with the direct assistance of that organization's founder and president, Jim Jones, who personally vouched for and participated in the research, only twenty surveys were returned of the seventy-five distributed. Tyler and McGraw obtained minimal and perfunctory answers to some questions and incomplete responses to numerous others. Stephen Linder (1982, 209) experienced similar disappointments.

14. When material derives from nontraditional sources, group newsletters, photocopied flyers, and other low-volume publications not publicly archived or accessible, attempts are made either to indicate the origin in a note or refer to it directly in the narrative. In most instances, when no source information is provided, quoted material derives from field notes, personal communications, or both, the forms of which are indicated in context when practical, e.g., "Jim and I chatted on phone the following week . . . " or "One correspondent with whom I often exchanged short notes wrote . . . " Some quoted material derives from more than a single source. For example, in one instance group leader Jim Jones and I chatted on the phone regarding a topic about which Jim later wrote to me in a letter and, later still, commented on in his newsletter. In these instances I use the first source, that which was obtained in the most naturalistic context.

15. Identities of specific individuals, locales, and other identifiers are, when necessary, obscured with pseudonyms and by other means, with the exception of public figures and those who have repeatedly sought public attention.

16. The quote (or, more correctly, paraphrase) is perhaps unfounded. Richard Koffler at Aldine said he heard Norman Mailer quote Gide to this effect.

CHAPTER TWO

1. See Wilkinson 1997; Spolar 1997; Smale 1997.

2. These monographs were available from Survival Books, North Hollywood, California.

3. In the face of plague and marauding enemies, feudal lords of medieval Europe shut themselves in towers and turrets, behind moats and walls. Ronald Reagan's Deputy Undersecretary for Defense, Thomas K. Jones, offered a simpler solution to the perils of nuclear holocaust. Dirt. "Everybody's going to make it [through a nuclear attack] if there are enough shovels to go around. Dig a hole, cover it with a couple of doors and then throw three feet of dirt on the top. It's the dirt that does it" (Scheer 1982).

4. Regions of Arizona, Arkansas, Montana, Idaho, and elsewhere are similarly labeled. Consider the Oregon case typical.

5. Like other places in America, southern Oregon is largely populated by

nonsurvivalists. Most residents of the region work in agriculture or an ailing timber industry and worry more about incursion of Japanese lumber products and the gypsy moth than Russian spies, foreign invasions, or the New World Order.

6. If southern Oregon has character, it also has characters. Former California radiovangelist Ray Masters came in the 1980s with a handful followers and his ongoing message. Human love is "the root of all human misery," Masters warns. Husbands beware. "Every woman instinctively inherits this black widow spider knowledge, tempting her man and sucking out his life juices" (Eure 1995, A1). Jim McKeever, author of *Christians Will Go through the Tribulation* (1978), is a southern Oregon resident, as is Neal Donald Walsch, host of "Radioactive Talk," a local radio show. Walsch not only predicts God's will, he claims to have spoken with her, from 4:15 to 4:30 a.m. daily for three years while she guided his hand in transcribing his Putnam publication *Conversations with God* (1996), which rose to number fourteen on the *New York Times* best-seller list thirty days after its release. Walsch's editor at Putnam remarked that Walsch's bad credit, his nine children from five marriages, and his missed child-support payments are assets. They show he is a regular guy (O'Keefe 1996).

I never met Masters or McKeever or Meyer or Bach, but I did get some southern Oregon advice one Sunday morning at Buzz's Wheel-In Cafe, off I-5 in Merlin. At ten o'clock Buzz's was two-thirds full of regulars. The toast was Williams "brown" or "white" in the age of whole grains; the coffee, Framer Brothers in the era of imported espresso. Three-quarters of the customers actively smoked and half of those had their hats on (all bills forward). Across the street, at the Merlin Community Park, the Lions Club horseshoe tournament clanked and shuffled along in the fall sunshine. The permanent junk shop "flea market" down the road was closed, but drivers-by still stopped to look over the fence at the clothing and utensils left on display.

As I nursed my hash browns and eggs, listening to local talk, my countermate struck up a conversation about comfortable topics—trucks, deer-hunting season, guns, the weather, government conspiracy—and offered this advice: "Wrap all your letters in aluminum foil." This tactic would keep them from being read by the "X-ray machines" he assured me had been installed in all the local post offices.

7. Prices began at $9,000 to $17,000 in the early '80s depending upon road access, sun exposure, timber density, and the view. By the summer of 1986, 45 parcels had been sold, 18 plots were improved with buildings, 10 were owner-occupied. By 1998, 170 lots had been sold (or resold) for around $20,000 each. Eighty people were in residence by 2000.

8. Sources: advertising materials for the Terrene Ark and interviews with L. Lane Blackmore, president of the Ark's development company, Winter Rose Corporation, LaVerkin, Utah.

9. Missile sites available for purchase advertised in *American Survival Guide* 20, no. 1 (1998): 16–17.

10. "The French Connection: Sailsafe," *American Survival Guide* 7, no. 6 (June 1985): 34–37. The "what you have is what you will need" theme is well illustrated by survivalist boaters. Bill Shannon, who is single, thirty-six, and lives in a southern California beach community, not surprisingly invested in "a well-stocked sailboat" ready to waft away and "anchor . . . by an offshore island." On

the other coast Ralph Zumbro and his wife adapted a Key West-based, sixty-foot power cruiser, the *African Queen,* into a what they call a "floating survival retreat" (Zumbro 1982, 28; also see Bradley 1981, 22, 24). Following a catastrophe "the nation's transportation network will be choked with panic-stricken refugees and would-be survivors," Zumbro argues, but "if you have chosen a water [escape] route you have the option of firing up and cruising off. You could be one hundred miles away from trouble in a matter of hours, safe in some secluded cove, your antenna quivering with bad news" (Zumbro 1982, 28).

11. During my early undergraduate days I sold Mercedes Benz automobiles part time. In North America, the Mercedes is considered an expensive "luxury" car, partly because of marketing image management and partly because only the most expensive models are imported. But in many places around the globe, the Mercedes is appreciated more for its durability and efficiency. Mary Ann's car was a taxi-cab model, stripped to the running gear essentials and powered by an extremely efficient, albeit underpowered, 1.9 liter diesel engine capable of consistently obtaining high fuel mileage in my own driving experience. Given open roads, a delicate foot on the accelerator, and a little help from the wind, Mary Ann's model might just make the Oregon-Texas trip without refueling.

San Luis Obispo, California, residents Dave and Verna Wescott have a similar problem. Their retreat is a "twelve-acre mountain cabin . . . stocked with a year's supply of everything." They also have a camper fitted with extra gas tanks, spare parts, and the travel supplies needed to get there. But under crisis conditions the trip would likely be challenging. The cabin is in Montana.

12. Recent samples include *America in Depression*—"fact based trend analysis shows depression is on its way" (1993), *Chaos in America*—"learn how to survive and prosper despite the chaos with investments, real estate, food, energy" (1995), *The Secrets of the Federal Reserve*—"find out who really owns the FED and how our economy is being decimated" (1995), *How to Survive and Profit in the Clinton Crash of 95–96* (1995), and *Final Warning*—"how to protect yourself from stock market crashes and dangers of hyper-inflation" (1996). These pulp monographs, often without authors or ISBNs, are distributed and sometimes produced by such small-scale outlets as America West Distributors, Bozeman, Montana, and the Nitro-Pak Preparedness Center, Herbner City, Utah.

13. Matthew 19:30.

14. Over the years of this research nearly one in two of the survivalists I met claimed access to "bulk," "wholesale," "dealer," or "distributor" deals and discounts. The attraction of these contacts seemed less the price break, not significant when compared with conventional sources such as the community food co-ops, than being in the action, a part of the exchange process, a "dealer."

15. I discovered with my first subscription to a survivalist magazine that subscription lists quickly find their ways into the hands of marketeers eager to include survivalists in their promotion efforts as "investors," "partners," or "sales representatives," allowing them to obtain the marketed product at reduced cost. This form of marketing has the double advantage of appealing to price-conscious shoppers and including the buyer in the exchange process.

16. Marx borrows this expression from Shakespeare (*Timon of Athens,* act 4, scene 3). Here Kant and Marx might agree. Money contravenes the categorical imperatives, transforming persons to means. Vocational commitment is

corrupted into self-abnegation. Prideful work-identities, crafted from effort, artistry, and imagination, are depersonalized and objectified, appraised and sold for alienating wages.

17. Note this is not specifically a coincidence of wants, the ostensible weakness of barter economy to which neoclassic economists point critically. Survivalist buyers and sellers may engage in the discourse of valuation, even buy and sell, without any strong perception of objective need for proffered goods or the remunerations they bring.

18. On April 8, 1997, ABC News reported the sale at auction of a single silver Liberty dollar, one of fifteen still in existence, for $1.8 million.

19. Not incidentally, nearly all the experts could provide "direct" sales of the recommended commodity at "substantial savings" from a "trusted" source.

CHAPTER THREE

1. Stephen N. Linder used this phrase first in describing his own contacts with survivalists in the Southwest. A decade later James Gibson would support this less sinister view in his descriptions of the fantasy-play of many middle-aged North American males in *Warrior Dreams: Violence and Manhood in Post-Vietnam America* (1994).

2. Watkins and Strong 1984, 40, 41.

3. Ibid., 42, 43.

4. Nic's politics were enigmatic, too. He called himself a "moderate Democrat who is bullish on some social programs." His reading of history (another major he would enjoy) leads him to offer that "our society is in some ways on the decline . . . but in others we are enjoying a renaissance in some of the personal freedoms." "I kind of like blowing that stereotype of lower-middle-class, whitey, prejudiced survivalist. Survival is not a white, Anglo-Saxon game. If I can be here, anybody can."

5. Ron Goodman was a high school senior with a toothy grin and close-cropped hair, his own Colt M-15 rifle, a summer's worth of experience in Army Reserve boot camp, Civil Air Patrol training, and a desire to make a career in police work or military life. As Nic predicted, when Ron later applied to join the CIA, it was necessary for him to sever connections with active survivalism, downplay his Ranger affiliations, and conceal his participation in Operation Aurora Borealis and its sequels.

6. Not exactly. Eleen and I both whispered to each other that proceeding a *very* long way around, over several distantly visible hills, seemed eminently practical. We were, after all, fit mountaineers, not fearless warriors. Long hikes seemed far preferable to even short shootouts.

7. Unlike the *American Survival Guide* account of the weekend's activities, the troops moved infrequently and little. According to my reading of the U.S. Geological Survey topographic map of that area, B-team progressed no more than five-eighths of a mile the entire first day, including the ridge walk, and less than that the second day. The action was perhaps dramatic but certainly not far ranging.

8. Bluntly put, the Reagan pony could be glimpsed only if you stood in the horse shit.

9. These early survival tales proposed an invading Soviet force in various

guises. Since the collapse of the Soviet Union, the "Soviet" antithesis in warrior tales has been augmented, though not entirely replaced, with United Nations troops under the direction of the New World Order. Hollywood has not yet found this to be a profitable film theme.

10. Weber stresses that the struggles between ultimate value-orientations in the modern world are not contests between solitary communities of commitment and belief, one against the other, but evermore struggles between small groups and sects, and ultimately, a struggle of individuals (see Weber 1978, 148–56; cf. Weber [1946] 1989, 282).

11. Society stands in judgment of the bricoleur whenever she or he performs. The bricoleur has no recourse to ready accounts for failure. The engineer's complaints of misfollowed instructions or faulty supplies do not apply. Unsuccessful attempts at bricolage have no excuse; the project works, and is given its due, or the bricoleur is demoted to tinkerer, putterer, unhandyman or woman.

12. Alternatively "surprise" attacks occur only after their possibility has been well considered and contingency plans are in place.

13. As with much of survivalism, even Hank's exotic garment succumbed to market pressures. By the late 1990s, custom-fit and standard sized ghillie suits could be mail ordered.

14. The group was atypically large that day, with eight members and nine guests.

15. NIC, Inc., Law Enforcement Supply could have made this work easier. They sell a "Militia Kit" advertised as "perfect for all militias," including a "Citizen Soldier Manual," two ID cards, two uniform patches, and two four-color stickers for your vehicle or home which "allow you to easily identify your members"—$19.95 per kit.

16. It took Nic two hours and six full disassembly/assembly cycles to demonstrate this process to me with any learning effect, although he described each motion and sequence nearly verbatim as reported here. Nic could show and tell clearly and well, but I could not do well at all (the recoil spring *did* go flying across the room).

17. If crisis struck evenings or weekends, then it would be three from the north, four from the south.

18. Three men in their early twenties and two girlfriends comprised Freedom Brigade. In side conversations with Eleen, roommates Tammy and Wanda spoke of the group's recent adventures. The men (John excluded) had brandished their assault rifles to end a party down the block from Tammy and Wanda's apartment when the party givers turned out to be "radicals" (hippie-types, apparently). Tammy, Wanda, and their boyfriends had begun working on handcuff escapes a month prior and had been practicing hand-to-hand combat for the past two weeks. They were all slightly bruised from training in a nearby park two days earlier. The move to the park was a domestic improvement. The week before they had practiced in the apartment, but amid their gyrations Wanda's boyfriend put his foot through the television screen, and Tammy and her combatant fell on and shattered the coffee table.

19. Published by Omega Group, Limited, publishers of *Soldier of Fortune,* since late 1981.

20. Published by the McMullen Group, who also publish *Biker Lifestyle, Truckin', Custom Rodder, Street Chopper,* and *Street Rodder,* since 1979.

21. The sample spanned the years 1983 to1990, with a less systematic but complete reading of all issues from 1991 to 1998.

22.

Table 3.1. *Article Types,* American Survival Guide, *January 1990–March 1991*

TYPE	TOTAL SIZE (SQ. IN.)	PERCENTAGE OF TOTAL
Contributed articles	5,330	66.3
Editorials	834	10.2
Product reviews	1,879	23.5
Total	8,043	100

In my interview with *American Survival Guide* editor Jim Benson (July 27, 1992), we discussed the requisites for contributed articles. Four times in eight minutes he mentioned visual appeal as the most crucial factor in determining an article's acceptance and subsequent reader appreciation, using the phrases "eye-catching," "quality photos," "good graphics and artwork," and "quality pictures." He discussed his attempts to change the paramilitary appearance of the magazine by removing the photos of firearms that characteristically occupied the front cover. The two-month experiment produced a 12 percent drop in counter sales and an estimated 10 percent reduction in subscriptions. After this experiment, firearms continued to figure prominently on the cover until the late '90s, when more neutral cover topics were again attempted.

Table 3.2. *Article Content,* American Survival Guide, *November 1981–June 1987*

TOPIC	TOTAL	PERCENTAGE OF TOTAL
Weapons	58	48
Food, medicine, energy	27	23
Preparation for general/future threat[a]	20	17
Preparation for specific/immediate threat[b]	15	13
Total		100

[a]Threats such as currency collapse, environmental destabilization, crop failure.

[b]Threats such as lightening strike, criminal invasion of home, auto wreck in remote area.

23. These constitute roughly 20 percent of the articles in one sample year.

24. These tales circulate in the manner of urban legends, never being entirely believed, never entirely discredited. Over a decade later, Mark Koernke would make nearly the same claim regarding the Oklahoma City bombing, attributing it to CIA operatives plotting to expose secret militias, thereby legitimating government repression (see chapter 6).

CHAPTER FOUR

1. See Dan Glaser's discussion of "possession imagery" in his analyses of twentieth-century deviance theory (1972).

2. Metonymic ("other name") magic works by reducing things to objects, specifically words which when invoked, have telling consequences. Knowing the

name of a thing and uttering it in proper ritual form gives power over that object to the speaker (or writer). Donald McClosky reminds us that the notion is one of long standing in literary criticism. Russian poet-critic Andrey Bely put it this way nine decades ago: "The process of naming . . . is a process of invocation. Every word is a charm. By charming a given phenomenon I am in essence subjugating it. . . . For living speech itself is unbroken magic" (Bely [1909] 1985).

The objectification of word power reaches its apogee when books and pamphlets themselves are put on display as samples of captured exotica the likes of illicit goods found in a police raid. The trend is common among journalists but can be found on occasion even in careful scholarship. One otherwise thorough and thoughtful book devotes thirteen pages to *photographs* of published materials. Pictures of mimeographed correspondence, flyers, even conference registration notices and a brochure advertising beverage mugs, baseball caps, t-shirts, and belt buckles are displayed with redundant captions identifying flyers as "flyers," posters as "posters," letters as "letters"—dead text but with an aura of lingering danger (Aho 1990, 229–41; see also Lamy 1996; Ezekiel 1995, iii; Parfrey 1990).

3. Survivalist common sense is generous and inclusive. Siberian ponies *might* carry heavy loads, and who knows how dense the jungle is on the Yucatan peninsula or how many enemies could hide there? The jungle and the ponies are real enough, as are the numbers of Asians and Latinos of unknown allegiance in Chicago and New Orleans and Florida. It *could* happen as Hank tells it, and that is sufficient to move the story along if not prove its final veracity.

4. The Hunt brothers with their plans to rebase the U.S. economy on their private silver hoard are the limiting case but one still predicated on world economic turmoil. The Cascade Valley Force's crisis-time escape tactics are more typical—specific to time and place, beneficial only to friends and family.

5. This was not Gale's only vehicle. To maintain the tax-free status of the ministry, Gale lived a short distance away in a thirty-two-foot motor home with a room full of computers, ham radio equipment, antenna controls, and lately, oxygen bottles. He owned other rolling stock: a Dodge pickup truck, an International Scout with a new engine, two more Volkswagen vans, a Karmann Ghia, and a thirty-foot Silverstreak trailer.

6. See Aho 1990 and Coates 1987a, 77–103. These may be contrasted with members' perspectives in Udvary 1982, Sacred Truth Ministries n.d., and especially the collection of pamphlets authored by Wesley Swift and E. Raymond Capt.

7. Thanks to Michael Ondaatje from whom this description of Uncle Terry borrows a few words and large dollop of inspiration (see Ondaatje 1992, 265).

8. In 1950, Identity was ascendant. Washington, DC-based "anti-Zionist" (don't call him anti-Semitic) Willis Carto and his Liberty Lobby glared the weekly Spotlight to a nationwide circulation of 150,000. The Holocaust never occurred, he told his readers. Ann Frank's diary is a forgery, and most missing children disappear during Jewish holidays when they are secretly sacrificed (see Coates 1987, 51). Gerald L. K. Smith, Identity's ailing North American progenitor, a forty-year veteran of racist sermonizing and author of the long-running "The Cross and the Flag," came to southern California. So did his progeny. Smith's former attorney, Bertrand Comparet, joined the Identity action, as did

San Jacinto Capt. At the center stood Smith's favorite, his ex-chauffeur and a former opening act at the Los Angeles Foursquare Church for headliner Aimee Semple McPherson, Wesley Swift. Into this congregation came Gale and others, who joined, recruited others for Smith, and then found followers of their own.

The alignment of these Identity characters was loose. They knew each other by name and often face, united in some efforts, competed for funds and devotees in others. But together they created interest in this new testament. Some preferred weeknight discussion groups and prayer sessions, others, Sunday services. Still others called for spreading the word cross-country. A handful urged action. All got what they wanted.

9. Gale ran for governor of California in 1958 on the Constitution Party ticket, endorsed by the States' Rights Party. In 1964 and 1968 he entered the Republican primary for California's Twenty-seventh Congressional District.

10. Gale's Midwest preaching destinations included the Christian Conservative Churches of America in Missouri, a forerunner of John Harrell's Christian Patriot's Defense League.

11. In 1989 Morris Dees and the Southern Poverty Law Center [SPLC] filed suit against Tom Metzger and W.A.R. after three members of a Portland, Oregon, skinhead group, the East Side White Pride, beat an Ethiopian immigrant to death with a baseball bat. The SPLC suit contended that the murder was an outgrowth of training and direction the skinheads received from an associate of Metzger's who had his full and express approval. In 1990 a jury assessed damages of $12.5 million against Metzger, his son, and W.A.R. (Dees 1996, 101).

12. In the first manual for the Posse, Beach and Gale wrote: "In some instances of record the law provides for the following prosecution of officials of government who commit criminal acts or who violate their oath of office. . . . He shall be removed by the posse to the most populated intersection of streets in the township and, at high noon, be hung by the neck, the body remaining until sundown as a example to those who would subvert the law" (Coates 1987, 105). Here Coates cites an IRS report, but Gale made essentially the same remarks repeatedly during our weekend seminar. Threatening to implement this sentiment would eventually cost Gale his freedom, and indirectly, his life.

13. Instead of a state-issued vehicle identification, Thomas's motorcycle bore custom embossed plates (he changed them from time to time) expounding what he called essential precepts: e.g., "Work," "Birthright," and "Pray to God."

14. This "letter" attributed to Mathews was probably written by Louis R. Beam. Beam is former Grand Dragon of the Alabama-based Knights of the Ku Klux Klan. A Vietnam veteran, Beam was active in recruiting for the Klan among military personnel after return to civilian life. He ran a paramilitary training school for Klan members in rural east Texas during the 1980s, is alleged to have harassed Vietnamese refugee fishermen, and served as an Aryan Nations "Ambassador at Large." Beam was certainly responsible for the letter's wide circulation via newsletters and electronic bulletin boards to which he contributed under several pen names, most often Nathan Bedford Forest.

15. How much of *The Turner Diaries* derives from *The John Franklin Letters* can only be surmised. Side-by-side comparison of the texts reveals numerous similarities. One library copy, checked out only four times in thirty-eight years,

was from the history section of Milne Library at Oregon State University, William Pierce's former employer.

16. Both Orders began with words. In *The Turner Diaries* the would-be worthies gathered upstairs in a warehouse. "And then we swore the Oath—a mighty Oath, a moving Oath, that shook me to my bones and raised the hair on the back of my neck" (Macdonald 1978, 73).

Mathews led his gang to the second floor of what he called the "Bunker," a building he had constructed adjacent to his rural home. Lit candles surrounded a blanket. Mathews told the recruits to circle the blanket, hands joined. One man placed his six-week-old daughter in the ring's center. Then, following Mathews, the men repeated this oath:

> I, as an Aryan warrior, swear myself to complete secrecy to the Order and total loyalty to my comrades.
>
> And furthermore . . . let me bear witness to you, my brothers, that if I break this oath, let me be forever cursed upon the lips of our people as a coward and an oath breaker. (Dees 1996, 140)

At the trial of the Order more than one hundred witnesses swore oaths, too.

CHAPTER FIVE

1. Academic arguments against achievement of federal policy stress two conservative themes: a preference for private over public, and local over national, collective action. There has long been a tradition of antigovernment, probusiness ideology in the United States (Lindbloom 1977). Government programs are assumed to be inefficient and ineffective; public rational actors, bureaucrats in the pejorative sense, are presumed to be incompetent, slothful, and self-aggrandizing. By contrast, even repeated and large-scale failures of private sector enterprise at the hands of corporate bureaucrats is seen as anomalous, atypical (Downs and Larkey 1986). Similarly, there is an expressed preference for proxy policy implementation, for charging local governments rather than federal agencies with practical achievement of policy objectives, even when local entities are demonstrably lacking in competence or will (Pagano and Bowman 1989; Conian 1988; Wright 1988; Nathan et al. 1987; Peterson, Rabe, and Wong 1986).

2. Desai (1992) notes the career-enhancing advantages of finding policy faults, and Mazmanian and Sabatier underscore the desire among academics "to investigate the anatomy of failure" (1983, 5).

3. Until the passage of the Brady Handgun Violence Protection Act in 1993, ownership of sound-suppressed or fully automatic weapons and other currently banned munitions was not illegal in the United States, only costly and procedurally cumbersome. Pistol-caliber submachine guns the likes of Uzis and Mac-9s and 10s, and full-sized .223 and .308 caliber assault rifles such as M-16s and M-14s, could be obtained by payment of a substantial tax and completion of some additional paperwork, though this process was only slightly more procedurally daunting than other weapons purchases, for example, handguns in states like New York or later California or Oregon. It should be noted that among most survivalists, submachine guns were novelties at best, "gangster guns" in less flattering terms, weapons largely useless in imagined future combat.

4. Survivalist imagination is tempered by military experience, especially that

derived from the Vietnam conflict, experience that demonstrated the tactical and logistic *dis*advantages of fully automatic fire in standard field weapons. Again, survivalists favor appearances of practicality, preferring sign equipment built around "real war" tactics and tools.

5. Popular culture, too, offers fictive heroines and heroes caught up in affect-dominated lives, perpetually consumed by disorienting "love" or driven by insatiable "rage" over passion or dishonor. However, in neither the popular nor the academic instances are these ideal typifications empirically demonstrable.

6. This is little more than the "great man/woman" theory of leadership, largely found to be insubstantial both in terms of "leader"-trait correlations within studies and between trait lists from one study to another (Stogill 1948; Mann 1959; cf. Borgatta, Bales, and Couch 1954). What matters is an individual's ability to help group members achieve their goals, which is nearly as Weber puts it (1958a, 248–49). Those persons with task-relevant information and resources are attributed leadership over those with artful presentational style.

7. In popular usage charisma is even more diffuse, a "bargain word" expression requiring little or no thought "that can be used with an air of expertise" yet signifying little or nothing (Kaufman 1970, xlix). Charisma has become a catch-all for excesses of unconventional enthusiasm summoned from followers by charismatic leaders divisible according to the moral worth of their appeals. "Bad" charisma is all about the dominance and possession of wills, lumping together "bogy men and demons" (Simi 1997) the likes of Hitler, the Ayatollah Khomeini, and Saddam Hussein with other undesirables such as leaders among opposition political parties and unappreciated religious persuasions. "Good" charisma is about the realization of collective and personal potential, ascribed indiscriminately to "saints" and "visionaries" akin to Winston Churchill and Mahatma Ghandi together with rock stars, health gurus, and feel-good motivational speakers on the business lunch circuit. All these are "charismatics" in popular usage.

8. Henry V also used his archers, the boggy fields, and the morning fog to his advantage.

9. As Weber puts it:

> Pure charisma does not know any "legitimacy" other than that flowing from personal strength, that is, one which is constantly being proved. The charismatic hero does not deduce his authority from codes and statutes, as is the case with the jurisdiction of office; nor does he deduce his authority from traditional custom or feudal vows of faith, as is the case with patrimonial power.
>
> The charismatic leader gains and maintains authority by proving his strength in life. (1958b, 248–49)

10. Magic and technology often vie for legitimacy. Charismatics claiming for uncustomary methods, vested authorities for conventional means. Intellectuals have sided with convention, seeking to discredit magic. Millenarian magic, for example, is explained away by anthropology as simply bad technology, ignorant attempts by tribal peoples to redress perceived inadequacies born of thoroughly Western motives. Contact between technologically unequal cultures engenders deep feelings of inadequacy for which magic seeks to compensate (see Barkun 1974, 4). As Wilson puts it, "all [millenarian] movements must be

considered . . . attempts to explain and/or amend the disparity of wealth, power and status between themselves and the [superior] Europeans" (Wilson 1973). Magic is reserved for ignorant and deprived savages abroad and the materially and intellectually impoverished at home (see also Lipset and Raab 1960, 61–62).

11. All agreed. The Republicans and Democrats aren't any good. They've all been bought off by the rich. Nothing novel about that idea, I thought. But the evidence offered to support this claim struck me as sophisticated. Zillah spoke in detail of the behind-the-scenes management of Gary Hart's bid for the presidential nomination. Cliff analyzed trends in Carter's committee assignments when he was governor. Bob critiqued the Libertarian impact in splitting the conservative vote in two California congressional districts. Zillah found fault with the Libertarian embrace of unrestricted free enterprise. "Free enterprise by itself is not good," Zillah offered, "because without regulation, big multinational companies will bring cheap foreign labor in or have their products made abroad with cheap labor, then sell in the U.S. and undermine Americans' jobs." Bob and Tina, union supporters that they were, agreed, as did most others.

12. "Can you do that?" Todd asked. "Won't they come and get you?" Tom admitted it got complicated at times. "I've got two cases in the courts right now. The Universal Life Church helped us with one." I later asked Tom what he expected to come of these cases. "I don't know, really. We're gonna go as far as we can in the courts, appeal it and the whole route, delay it as long as we can." "How about the other members of your group? What are they doing?" I asked. "There's not any group, really," Tom admitted, "just me and a couple of guys scattered around. The closest one to me is Jay, and that's the only two right here [south San Francisco Bay area] around us. My wife isn't into it as much as me. She has her job at Lockheed, so I do most of the survivalist stuff."

13. In popular culture, rock concerts, televangelism, and soap opera heartthrobs may be well crafted and choreographed, but they are also ephemeral and segmented from daily life. Such pseudocharisma offers no solution to pressing problems, no more intimacy than a pledge card or fan club magazine, and produces little more change in behavior than increased viewer attention to interludic commercial messages, the real appeals to action.

14. Recall that Winston Churchill, prime minister from 1940 until the end of World War II, rallied war-torn Britain but was defeated when he stood for reelection in peacetime 1945. Hitler's Nazi Party attracted a broad cross-section of Germans during the economic deprivation of the 1920s and early 1930s, but by 1933, as national economic conditions improved, party membership began a steady decline (Burnstein 1996).

15. In modern infamous instances, such as Jim Jones's "Jonestown" and Marshall Applewhite's "Heaven's Gate," members' allegiance was not held with fine speeches and high ideals alone. Members did not come and go daily from ordinary lives of family, work, and other diffuse associations, but lived among and entirely dependent upon the subcommunity, having transferred their stocks, savings, and real estate to collective control. Jones's and Applewhite's rhetoric may have been inspiring, but they also controlled the payrolls, property deeds, and bank books.

16. Dan Glaser's useful sociological axiom is to the point here. Social separation leads to cultural differentiation, not the other way around. Alternative

identities seldom arise from sheer force of will, but from change in associations with significant others over time. Charismatic influence is manifest when followers have few personal, social, and economic resources still in their control. The Mariposans were more influenced by Gale's inducements than the mail-order members. Value orientations follow the adoption of new action forms. Belief follows action.

17. Investigators did indeed seek to locate tapes specifically pertaining to the organization and activities of the Committee of the States.

18. Butler claims six thousand adherents in the United States, according to the Anti-Defamation League of B'nai B'rith (n.d., 56).

19. Dennis Hilgoss, the Aryan Nations State Coordinator, Oregon, made this statement in a newsletter sent to Oregon members.

20. Bill Morlin, "Kicking up a furor." *Spokane Spoksman-Review,* 22 July 1995 (Saturday), A1, A8.

21. Social facilitation is evident. Like photophobic cockroaches caught in the glare of bright lights and audience stares, the aryans do what is most familiar to them.

22. Peter Simi interviewed a Butler neighbor who expressed this specific gratitude, pointing out the rapid increase in taxation rates in surrounding areas (personal communication with the author).

23. Not far away from Butler's place was property for sale, a "North Idaho Executive Retreat" featuring "134 acres with lighted airstrip, creek, pond, 8,800 sq. ft. Tudor home with gym, full bar, 2 greenhouses, 2,000 sq. ft. master suite plus 5 bedrooms, 4 full baths, 3 half baths, separate caretaker's quarters." The corporate owner would consider partial trades but the price, in the millions, was firm.

24. This one got the job.

25. At the opening session of the 1997 Aryan World Congress, Peter Simi reports even more dulling discourse. "Of the thirty-six people in the audience, I counted thirteen who had fallen asleep at one time or another, including myself" (Simi 1998, 2).

26. At the beginning of the new millennium, Butler would suffer one final disgrace. Other enemies would put an end to the Aryan Nations. When overzealous volunteer camp guards mistook auto backfire near the gate for invaders or foul play, they shot at, pursued, and cornered a passing vehicle, then roughed up its occupants, Victoria Keenan and her son Jason. In a civil lawsuit against Butler brought by the Southern Poverty Law Center, the Keenans were awarded $6.3 million in compensatory and punitive damages. Butler lost everything—his property was deeded to the Keenans, even his interest in the name "Aryan Nations," which Butler was prohibited from using henceforth. Butler moved to a small home in suburban Coeur d'Alene, purchased for him by a sympathizer, Vincent Bertollini, an evangelist for "The 11th Hour Remnant Messenger." The aryan nation shrank from global cause to regional irritant to a seldom-used renamed Web page.

27. Preparedness Expo is a production of Preparedness Shows, headquartered in Salt Lake City. Like a traveling carnival, the show, and many of its key participants, crisscross the country to locations in Seattle, Denver, Salt Lake City, Phoenix, Dallas, and elsewhere, organizing approximately one show per month.

28. These include "Larry Nichols is a British-directed Oliver North, Bush,

Drug Running Assassin for the New World Order," and "Newt Gingrich is Out to Lunch! And You are On the Menu."

29. If polarizing does not solve your problems, try ozone. "Sterilize/Re-Oxygenize the Air You Breath, Purify the Water You Drink and Bathe in. The O_3zonator produces a powerful Cold Corona arc which turns oxygen into its more potent allotropic form, Ozone (O_3). This super-activated oxygen then . . . oxidizes many contaminants. . . . With the O_3zonator System in your home and workplace, you can enjoy the healthful benefits of a sanitary environment and additional oxygen which your body craves."

30. Timothy McVeigh ostensibly served as one of Koernke's "bodyguards" at a speaking engagement. When questioned by law enforcement, Koernke had no recollection of McVeigh.

31. I had friends in the 1960s who studied shipping manifests and corporate reports in order to ferret out the reach and sinew of the "military industrial complex" with equal enthusiasm.

CHAPTER SIX

1. In mind here is Camus's essay "Absurd Creation" in *The Myth of Sisyphus,* though he makes the point elsewhere. Sartre concurs, as does Gide, that "feeling is formed by the acts one performs" (Sartre 1967).

2. Schwartz 1995.

3. Material. Concrete and cognitive cultural artifacts alike are crafted from resources: matter, raw materials, and energy. The sacred chalice derives from silver ingots and casting molds, heat and hammers. The book of poems emerges from paper, ink, and printing presses, from pens, notepads, and perhaps computers. Materials cannot be excised from the creative process. While Smith convincingly traces the origins of fired pottery, copper smelting, bronze casting, and other means of making to artists in search of new means of aesthetic expression, not practical manufacture, he notes, "Art is born along by the very matter it is sworn to repudiate. . . . [T]he whole quality of a line and surface depends upon both the material and the tool as well as the artist's hand" (1971, 132–33). Survival scenarios are artful creations conditioned by resource at hand and inspired by material possibilities.

Form. Cultural artifacts emerge in forms, take shape, are given organization into scene, architecture, design, plan. In its earliest usages *techne* denoted grand and fateful planning. In the *Iliad* (23.415) Antilochus plans to win the chariot race and fame by a clever contrivance [techno[e]somai] to pass at the narrow place. In Hesiod's *Theogony* Earth devises "a crafty wile" [*techne*] (line 160) to combat the vicious Sky, and Cerberus employs an evil and devious *techne* by which he welcomes souls to Hades but never frees them (line 770) (see Roochnik 1996, 23). Much of survivalism is grand plan making.

Purpose. Cultural artifacts embody telos: intents, purposes, goals. When these are intrinsic to the action, what Weber called wertrational acts, right performances are ends in themselves. In religious ritual performed without procedural error the gods are glorified. When acts intend subsequent consequences, zwecktrational, results are what matter. Souls must be saved, demons exorcised (see Brubaker 1984, 51–53). Survivalists craft scenarios that reconfigure social relationships to newfound purposes.

Agency. The integrating and directing actions exercised by artisans, craftpersons, leaders, and administrators in bringing cultural artifacts into being constitute the final element of cause. Survivalist agency is evident in skill tests but in the prechaotic present can only be imagined in broader contexts.

4. The reciprocal embrace of these encompassing prescripted stories of self is what Sartre called "bad faith" (see Sartre [1943] 1966, 86).

5. Intellectual crises, ever popular among out-of-favor intellectuals (see Kolakowski 1990, 32–43), proliferate as the humanities are eclipsed by the physical sciences in practical success and popular favor (see Schneider 1997).

6. See, for examples, Cayce 1968, 1969, 1972, 1975, 1976, 1978, 1981, 1989.

7. "What preparations have you made?" I asked Frank. "Nothing really," he said. "I keep a little extra food in the house. I have a cold cellar that I might stay in for a while. But my studies will help. I look at the world situation, and I have my intuition and my studies. I feel I have a little time so I'm not hurrying things."

8. *The Bible Code,* released by Simon and Schuster and touted to be more popular than *The Celestine Prophecy,* is based on an article in *Statistical Science* titled "Equidistant Letter Sequences in the Book of Genesis" (Witztum, Rips, and Rosenberg 1994).

9. Sands clarifies his college study this way: "I didn't attend them all physically; I took courses from them—University of California, a course in criminology; Southwestern College in Kansas, that's where my father, aunt, and uncle graduated from; University of Wichita; University of Chicago; Brigham Young University; MIT; University of Georgia; University of Maryland . . . "

10. During the 1960s "I taught in black colleges in the U.S. (Morgan State and Jarvis Christian College in Hawkins, Texas)," in computer science at the University of Oregon, and in Canada's "Northern College System (in Sault Ste. Marie, Kirkland Lake, and Kapuskasing)" in the 1970s.

11. As of the publication of this volume, no books by Sands were found in *Books in Print* or in the extensive collections of the combined University of California libraries. This should not be taken as a conclusive contradiction to Sands's claim. He has published numerous flyers, pamphlets, and short monographs at his own expense and prepared at least one book-length manuscript pertaining to survivalism. Likely, the computer publications to which he refers were produced by private organizations for limited circulation or were self-published in small numbers.

12. Funding for *Canada Tomorrow* came in part from a twenty-two-million-dollar grant from Canada's Scientific Research Tax Credits.

13. In October of 1997 I asked Sands what had become of the ship. His answer came back in an e-mail note: "The short story: Sold by the Court. And I don't know where it is. I consider that part of my past life. Thomas."

14. The title continues: "A book that may give new meaning to the word controversial: a book that describes your, your children's, and your grandchildren's future, by Thomas M. Sands, Copyright 1988 by the Author."

15. Sands seemed genuinely unaware of the colonizing effects of such a language effort. He speaks of streamlining language to a few action words, easily taught, even to the illiterate, in a few short sessions. "We can give them the

content later," he adds. But the examples of content suggest a theme, words for cooking or equipment maintenance or food service or the performance of other menial tasks. The babble of tongues reduced to the sonorous hum of happy, minimally informed workers, efficient in their task performances. I am convinced Sands missed these implications. When I pointed them out he seemed disturbed, made several notes, said he must talk to others about this, calling it "a real problem . . . I hadn't anticipated."

16. As we spoke of "The Recovery of the Titanic," his treatise on nuclear holocaust, sheltering, and recovery, he sat on the sofa beside me turning pages, pointing out letterheads, titles, signatures of those with whom he had corresponded concerning the manuscript. "I've had fourteen professors review it, or professional people at least—economists; physicists; ministers; the people in Ottawa [national civil defense personnel]; a Mormon bishop; a Christian Science teacher—that's their rank above practitioner; a very fundamentalist minister—he wrote all the way through it. I sent a copy to Dr. Mayhew, president of the American Association of Economists, if that is the right name.

APPENDIX

1. It should be unequivocally stressed that in contacts with law enforcement and other agencies of social control, information was solicited *from,* but under absolutely no circumstances was it provided *to,* these agencies in accordance with my own view of the ethical constraints of my profession. Agencies contacted were those in whose jurisdictions I believed survivalist activities to be extant—for example, the area in Missouri where the Christian Patriots Defense League held its conference. Respondent agencies were asked to report on specific criminal activity, if any, associated with survivalists and to provide "individual profiles of members, goals and objectives of the group, type of training members receive, types of weaponry that group may have access to and their philosophy toward civil disobedience." Letters and, when necessary, telephone calls followed these teletypes. Sixteen responses were obtained from these teletype inquiries.

REFERENCES

Aho, James A. 1990. *The politics of righteousness: Idaho Christian patriotism.* Seattle: University of Washington Press.

———. 1994. *This thing of darkness: A sociology of the enemy.* Seattle: University of Washington Press.

Anti-Defamation League. n.d. Aryan Nations: A theology of hate. In *Hate groups in America: A record of bigotry and violence,* 54–58. New York: Anti-Defamation League of B'nai B'rith.

———. 1983. *Extremism on the right: A handbook.* New York: Anti-Defamation League of B'nai B'rith.

———. 1995. Aryan Nations. In *Paranoia as patriotism: Far-right influences on the militia movement,* 9–11. New York: Anti-Defamation League of B'nai B'rith.

Barber, Benjamin R. 1992. Jihad vs. McWorld. *Atlantic Monthly* 269 (March): 53–65.

Barkun, Michael. 1974. *Disaster and the Millennium.* New York: Harper and Row. Quoted in Stephen Norris Linder, *Survivalists: The ethnography of an urban millennial cult* (Ann Arbor, MI: University Microfilms, 1982), 41.

Bates, Tom. 1995. Extreme thinking—a culture wars sampler. *Oregonian,* 30 October.

Baudrillard, Jean. 1983. *In the shadow of the silent majorities; or, the end of the social and other essays.* Trans. Paul John Foss and Paul Patton. New York: Semiotext(e).

Baumann, Eleen A. 1989. Research rhetoric and the social construction of elder abuse. In *Images and issues: Typifying contemporary social problems,* ed. Joel Best, 55–74. New York: Aldine de Gruyter.

Bely, Andrey. [1909] 1985. The magic of words. In *Selected essays of Andrey Bely,* trans. S. Cassedy, 93–104. Berkeley and Los Angeles: University of California Press. Quoted in Donald N. McCloskey, *If you're so smart: The narrative of economic expertise* (Chicago: University of Chicago Press, 1990), ADD PAGE.

Best, Joel. 1987. Rhetoric in claims-making: Constructing the missing children problem. *Social Problems* 34, no. 2: 101–17.

———. 1990. *Threatened children: Rhetoric and concern about child-victims.* Chicago: University of Chicago Press.

———. 1997. Society for the Study of Symbolic Interaction Distinguished Lecture, Toronto.

Bittner, Egon. 1983. Technique and the conduct of social life. *Social Problems* 30, no. 3: 249–61.

Blau, Peter M. 1970. Weber's theory of bureaucracy. In *Max Weber,* ed. Dennis Wrong, 141–45. Englewood Cliffs, NJ: Prentice Hall.

Blumer, Herbert. 1969. *Symbolic interactionism: Perspective and method.* Englewood Cliffs, NJ: Prentice-Hall.

Borgatta, E. F., R. F. Bales, and E. S. Couch. 1954. Some findings relevant to the great man theory of leadership. *American Sociological Review* 19: 755–59.

Bradley, Dick. 1981. Running scared. *Motor Boating and Sailing* March: 22, 24.

Brubaker, Rogers. 1984. *The limits of rationality: An essay on the social and moral thought of Max Weber.* London: Allen and Unwin.

Burnstein, William. 1996. *The logic of evil: The social origins of the Nazi Party, 1925–1933.* New Haven, CT: Yale University Press.

Callinicos, Alex. 1989. *Against postmodernism: A Marxist critique.* Oxford: Polity.

Camus, Albert. [1942] 1975. *The myth of Sisyphus.* Reprint, Middlesex, England: Penguin.

Carr, Joseph J. 1996. When money has to be real. *American Survival Guide* 18, no. 7: 29–30.

Carruthers, Bruce G., and Sarah Babb. 1996. The color of money and the nature of value: Greenbacks and gold in postbellum America. *American Journal of Sociology* 101, no. 6: 1556–91.

Casey, Douglas. 1981. *Crisis investing.* New York: Pocket Books.

Casson, Mark C. 1982. *The entrepreneur: An economic theory.* Oxford: Martin Robinson.

Catton, William R. 1984. Probable collective responses to ecologic scarcity: How violent? *Sociological Perspectives* 27, no. 1: 3–20.

Cayce, Edgar. 1968. *Edgar Cayce's story of Jesus.* Ed. Jeffrey Furst. New York: Coward-McCann.

———. 1969. *A commentary on the book of the Revelation: Based on a study of twenty-four psychic discourses of Edgar Cayce.* Virginia Beach, VA: A.R.E.

———. 1972. *Edgar Cayce's story of attitudes and emotions.* Ed. Jeffrey Furst. New York : Berkley.

———. 1975. *The early Christian epoch.* Comp. Readings Research Department. Virginia Beach, VA: Association for Research and Enlightenment.

———. 1976. *Dreams and dreaming.* Comp. Marilyn Lindgren Miller. Virginia Beach, VA: Association for Research and Enlightenment.

———. 1978. *Edgar Cayce's photographic legacy.* Comp. David M. Leary. Garden City, NJ: Doubleday.
———. 1981. *Daily living: Meeting life's challenges.* Comp. Readings Research Department. Virginia Beach, VA: Association for Research and Enlightenment.
———. 1989. *Egypt at the time of Ra Ta.* Comp. Ann Lee Clapp. Virginia Beach, VA: Association for Research and Enlightenment.
Center for Environmental Quality and Department of State. 1980. *The global 2000 report to the president.* Washington, DC: U.S. Government Printing Office.
Charmaz, Kathy, and Richard G. Mitchell Jr. 1996. The myth of silent authorship: Self, substance, and style in ethnographic writing. *Symbolic Interaction* 19, no. 4: 285–302.
Chester, Conrad V., Dale Torri-Safdie, George A. Christy, Hanna B. Shapiro, and Carl Taylor. 1984. The home as a haven. *Survival Guide* 6, no. 9: 24–27.
Churchman, Deborah. 1984. Survivalist literature popular again. *Christian Science Monitor,* 2 March, B6.
Cipollini, Peter J. 1983. The Midas touch. *Survive* 3, no. 1: 40–41.
Coates, James. 1987. *Armed and dangerous: The rise of the survivalist right.* New York: Hill and Wang.
Conian, Timothy. 1988. *New federalism: Intergovernmental reform from Nixon to Reagan.* Washington, DC: Brookings Institution.
Conti, William J. 1983. Are you a combat survivalist? *New Breed* October: 8–11, 68, 70.
Corcoran, James. 1990. *Bitter harvest: Gordon Kahl and the Posse Comitatus—Murder in the Heartland.* New York: Viking.
Couch, Carl. 1989. From hell to utopia and back to hell: Charismatic relationships. *Symbolic Interaction* 12, no. 2: 265–79.
Dahms, Harry F. 1995. From creative action to the rationalization of the economy: Joseph A. Schumpeter's social theory. *Sociological Theory* 13, no. 1:1–13.
Daniels, Jessie. 1997. *White lies: Race, class, gender, and sexuality in white supremacist discourse.* New York: Rutledge.
Dawe, Alan. 1978. Theories of action. In *A history of sociological analysis,* ed. Tom Bottomore and Robert Nisbit, 362–417. New York: Basic Books.
Dees, Morris. 1996. *Gathering storm: America's militia threat.* With James Corcoran. New York: Harper Collins.
Desai, Uday. 1992. Implementation of public policy: Note on the American experience. Paper presented to the National Endowment to the Humanities summer seminar: Social Construction of Social Problems, June, Southern Illinois University, Carbondale, IL.
Deutscher, Irwin, Fred P. Pestello, and H. Frances G. Pestello. 1993. *Sentiments and acts.* New York: Aldine de Gruyter.
Douglas, Mary. 1982. *In the active voice.* London: Routledge and Kegan Paul.
Dow, T. E., Jr. 1968. The role of charisma in modern African development. *Social Forces* 46 (March): 328–38.
Downs, George W., and P. D. Larkey. 1986. *The search for government efficiency: From hubris to helplessness.* New York: Random House.

Dyer, Joel. 1997. *Harvest of rage: Why Oklahoma City is only the beginning.* New York: Westview Press.

Ellis, Carolyn. 1995. *Final negotiations.* Philadelphia, PA: Temple University Press.

Erickson, Kai. 1984. Presidential address to the seventy-ninth annual meeting of the American Sociological Association, San Antonio, Texas.

Eure, Rob. 1995. Josephine County residents join forces against racism. *Oregonian,* 25 February, 4th ed., A1.

Ezekiel, Raphael S. 1995. *The racist mind: Portraits of Neo-Nazis and Klansmen.* New York: Viking.

Feibleman, James K. 1966. Technology as skills. *Technology and culture* 7, no. 3: 318–28.

Ferris, Timothy. 1997. The wrong stuff. *New Yorker,* 14 April, 31.

Festinger, Leon, Hank Riecken, and Stanley Schacter. 1956. *When prophecy fails.* New York: Harper Torchbooks.

Fine, Gary Alan. 1992. *Manufacturing tales.* Knoxville: University of Tennessee Press.

———. 1996. *Kitchens: The culture of restaurant work.* Berkeley and Los Angeles: University of California Press.

Fiocco, Giorgio, Daniele Fua, and Guido Visconti. 1996. *The Mount Pinatubo Eruption: Effects on the atmosphere and climate.* New York: Springer.

Freed, David. 1984. Gunman kills twenty in San Diego area. *Los Angeles Times,* 19 July.

Fuss, Diana. 1989. *Essentially speaking: Feminism, nature, and difference.* New York: Routledge.

Gallant, Paul, and Joane Eisen. 1997. ASG gun-owner survey. *American Survival Guide* 19, no. 12: 40–41, 66, 90.

Garfinkel, Harold. 1964. Studies of the routine grounds of everyday activities. *Social Problems* 11: 225–50.

Geertz, Clifford. 1973. *The interpretation of cultures.* New York: Basic Books.

Gergen, Kenneth J. 1991. *The saturated self.* New York: Basic Books.

Gibson, James W. 1994. *Warrior dreams: Violence and manhood in post-Vietnam America.* New York: Hill and Wang.

Glaser, Barney G., and Anselm L. Strauss. 1967. *The discovery of grounded theory: Strategies for qualitative research.* Chicago: Aldine de Gruyter.

Glaser, Daniel. 1972. Criminality theories and behavioral images. In *Symbolic Interaction,* 2d ed., ed. Jerome G. Manis and Bernard M. Meltzer, 442–62. Boston: Allyn and Bacon.

Goldhammer, John. 1996. Beware all destructive group dynamics. *Oregonian,* 31 May.

Gubrium, Jaber F., and James A. Holstein. 2000. The self in a world of going concerns. *Symbolic Interaction* 3, no. 2: 95–115.

Gusfield, Joseph R. 1989. Constructing the ownership of social problems: Fun and profit in the welfare state. *Social Problems* 36, no. 5: 431–41.

Hacker, Andrew. 1981. Popular culture in America. National Public Radio series OP-780406.01/01-C 1981.

Harper, Douglas. 1987. *Working knowledge: Skill and community in a small shop.* Chicago: University of Chicago Press.

Heidegger, Martin. [1952] 1977. *The question concerning technology and other essays.* Trans. and with an introduction by William Lovitt. Reprint, New York: Harper Torchbooks.

Herrnstein, Richard J. 1996. *The bell curve: Intelligence and class structure in American life.* New York: Simon and Schuster.

Hilbert, Richard A. 1987. Bureaucracy as belief, rationalization as repair: Max Weber in a post-functionalist age. *Sociological Theory* 5 (spring): 70–86.

Hochschild, Arlie. 1983. *The managed heart.* Berkeley and Los Angeles: University of California Press.

Hofstadter, Richard. [1965] 1996. *The paranoid style of American politics.* Reprint, New York: Knopf.

Horstman, Barry M. 1984. Killer called "angry at world." *Los Angeles Times,* 21 July.

Hubble, Edwin Powell. 1936. *The realm of the nebulae.* New Haven, CT: Yale University Press.

Hughes, Everett C. 1984. Going concerns: The study of American institutions. In *The sociological eye: Selected papers,* 52–64. New Brunswick, NJ: Transaction Books.

Hughes, Langston. [1953] 1994. That powerful drop. In *Production of reality,* 2d ed., ed. Jodi O'Brien and Peter Kollock, 40. Reprint, Thousand Oaks, CA: Pine Forge.

Huizinga, Johan. [1944] 1949. *Homo ludens: A study of the play element in culture.* Reprint, London: Routledge and Kegan Paul.

Hurt, Harry, III. 1981. *Texas rich: The Hunt dynasty from the early oil days through the silver crash.* New York: W. W. Norton.

———. 1988. The real Hunt brothers story. *Newsweek,* 5 September, 50.

Iannaccone, Laurence R. 1994. Why strict churches are strong. *American Journal of Sociology* 99, no. 5: 1180–211.

The John Franklin Letters. 1959. New York: n.p.

Kanter, Rosabeth M. 1973. *Commitment and community: Communes and utopias in sociological perspective.* Cambridge, MA: Harvard University Press.

Kaplan, Marshall, and P. Cuciti, eds. 1986. *The great society and its legacy: Twenty years of U.S. social policy.* Durham, NC: Duke University Press.

Kaufman, Walter. 1970. The inevitibility of alienation. In *Alienation,* ed. Richard Schacht, xii–lvi. Garden City, NJ: Doubleday.

Kettl, Donald F. 1988. *Government by proxy: (Mis)managing federal programs.* Washington DC: CQ Press.

Kifner, John. 1995. Green Beret newsletter gives window on extremist activity. *Oregonian,* 15 December.

Kogelschatz, Deane. 1982. *Everyman's guide to financial survival.* Denver, CO: Paladin Press.

———. 1983. Survival treasure chest: Today's pieces of eight make sterling investment. *Survive* 3, no. 1: 38–39, 41–42.

Kolakowski, Leszek. 1990. *Modernity on endless trial.* Chicago: University of Chicago Press.

Kuran, Timur. 1993. Seeds of racial explosion. *Society* 30, no. 6: 55–67.

Lamy, Philip. 1996. *Millennium rage: Survivalist, white supremacist, and doomsday prophecy.* New York: Plenum.

Lapham, Lewis H. 1988. Leviathan in trouble. *Harpers* 277, no. 1660: 8, 10–11.

Larsen, Jim. 1984. "Mathews' final letter reveals his ideas." *South Whidbey Record,* 12 December, 1.

Lee, Byron. 1997. Ultimate off-road sporter: Four tons of armor and engine. *American Survival Guide* 19, no. 10: 48–49, 54–55.

Lehman, Nicholas. 1990. *The promised land: The great Black migration and how it changed America.* New York: Knopf.

Levine, Donald N. 1995a. Sociology and the nation-state: Will they survive? Alpha Kappa Delta Distinguished Lecture, August, Washington, DC.

———. 1995b. *Visions of the sociological tradition.* Chicago: University of Chicago Press.

Lévi-Strauss, Claude. [1962] 1966. *The savage mind.* Reprint, Chicago: University of Chicago Press.

Lifton, Jay. 1993. *The protean self: Human resilience in an age of fragmentation.* New York: Basic Books.

Lindbloom, Charles E. 1977. *Politics and markets: The world's political-economic systems.* New York: Basic Books.

Linder, Stephen Norris. 1982. *Survivalists: The ethnography of an urban millennial cult.* Ann Arbor, MI: University Microfilms.

Lipset, Seymour M. 1960. *Political man: The social bases of politics.* New York: Doubleday.

Lipset, Seymour M., and Earl Raab. 1978. *The politics of unreason.* Chicago: University of Chicago Press.

Lofland, John. 1966. *Doomsday cult.* Englewood Cliffs, NJ: Prentice-Hall.

Lyman, Stanford M. 1997. *Postmodernism and a sociology of the absurd and other essays on the nouvelle vague in American social science.* Fayetteville, AR: University of Arkansas Press.

Macdonald, Andrew. 1978. *The Turner Diaries.* Washington, DC: National Alliance.

Majone, G., and A. Wildavsky. 1979. Implementation as evolution. In *Implementation,* 2d ed., ed. Jeffery Pressman and Aaron Wildavsky, 177–94. Berkeley and Los Angeles: University of California Press.

Malamud, Bernard. 1961. *A new life.* New York: Avon.

Mann, R. D. 1959. A review of the relationship between personality and performance in small groups. *Psychological Bulletin* 56: 241–70.

Marcuse, Herbert. 1964. *One dimensional man.* Boston: Beacon Press.

———. [1858] 1973. *Grundrisse: Foundations of the critique of political economy.* New York: Random House.

Marx, Karl. 1963. *Karl Marx: Early writings.* Trans. and ed. T. B. Bottomore. New York: McGraw-Hill.

Mazmanian, Daniel A., and Paul A. Sabatier. 1983. *Implementation and public policy.* Glenview, IL: Scott, Foresman.

McAlvany, Don, and Duncan Sellers. 1982. Hard assets for hard times. *Survive* 3, no. 2: 26–27, 53–56.

Mead, George Herbert. 1934. *Mind, self, and society.* Chicago: University of Chicago Press.

———. 1938. *The philosophy of the act.* Chicago: University of Chicago Press.

Mesarovic, Mihajlo D. 1974. *Mankind at the turning point: The second report to the Club of Rome.* New York: Dutton.

Meyers, Edward. 1982. *The chosen few: Surviving the nuclear holocaust.* South Bend, IN: And Books.

Miller, Dan. 2000. Mathematical dimensions of qualitative research. *Symbolic Interaction* 23, no. 4: 399–402.

Mitcham, Carl, and Robert Mackey. 1972. Introduction: Technology as a philosophical problem. In *Philosophy and technology,* 1–30. New York: Free Press.

Mitchell, John G. 1983. "Waiting for Apocalypse" *Audubon,* 18 March, 20–22, 24–25.

Mitchell, Richard G., Jr. 1983. *Mountain experience: The psychology and sociology of adventure.* Chicago: University of Chicago Press.

———. 1993. *Secrecy and fieldwork.* Newbury Park, CA: Sage.

———. 2000. Militia. In *Encyclopedia of criminology and deviant behavior,* ed. Clifton D. Bryant. London: Taylor and Francis.

Mitchell, Richard G., Jr., and Kathy Charmaz. 1996. Telling tales, writing stories: Postmodernist visions and realist images in ethnographic writing. *Journal of Contemporary Ethnography* 25, no. 1: 144–66.

Nathan, Richard P., Fred C. Doolittle, and associates. 1987. *Reagan and the states.* Princeton, NJ: Princeton University Press.

Nichols, Jeffrey. 1992. *How to profit from the coming boom in gold.* New York: McGraw-Hill.

Nietzsche, Friedrich. [1888] 1968. The twilight of the idols; or, how to philosophize with a hammer. In *The twilight of the idols/The anti-Christ,* 21–112. Reprint, London: Penguin.

Nisbet, Robert. 1980. *History of the idea of progress.* New York: Basic Books.

NOAA—National Geophysical Data Center. 1992. *Mount Pinatubo: The June 1991 eruptions.* Boulder, CO: U.S. Department of Commerce, National Oceanic and Atmospheric Administration, National Geophysical Data Center.

O'Keefe, Mark. 1996. "Pen sketching a different deity—*Conversations with God.*" *Oregonian,* 29 November.

Ondaatje, Michael. 1992. *The English patient.* London: Bloomsbury.

Oppenheimer, Michael, and Robert Boyle. 1990. *Dead heat: The race against the greenhouse effect.* New York: Basic Books.

Pagano, Michael A., and Ann Bowman. 1989. The state of American federalism 1988–1989. *Publis* 19, no. 3: 1–17.

Parfrey, Adam. 1990. *Apocalypse culture.* Portland, OR: Feral House.

Parsons, Talcott. 1951. *The social system.* Glencoe, IL: Free Press.

Partridge, Eric. 1983. *Origins: A short etymological dictionary of modern English.* New York: Greenwich House.

Peachey, D. E., and M. J. Learner. 1981. Law as a social trap: Problems and possibilities for the future. In *The justice motive in social behavior: Adapting to times of scarcity and change,* ed. M. J. Learner and S. C. Learner, 439–61. New York: Plenum.

Persons, S. 1958. *American minds: A history of ideas.* New York: Hank Holt.

Peterson, P., B. G. Rabe, and K. K. Wong. 1986. *When federalism works.* Washington, DC: Brookings Institution.

Polanyi, Karl. 1957. *The great transformation*. Boston: Beacon Press.
Read, Richard. 1995. The patriarch of paranoia. *Oregonian*, 23 July.
Rempel, William C., and Larry Green. 1983. Ultraright group arms to fight final holy war. *Los Angeles Times*, 17 July.
Richardson, Laurel. 1994. Writing: A method of inquiry. In *Handbook of qualitative research*, ed. Norman K. Denzin and Yvonna S. Lincoln, 516–29. Thousand Oaks, CA: Sage.
Riesman, David. 1950. *The lonely crowd*. New Haven, CT: Yale University Press.
Roochnik, David. 1996. *Of art and wisdom: Plato's understanding of techn[e]*. University Park: Pennsylvania State University Press.
Ruff, Howard. 1979. *How to prosper during the coming bad years*. New York: Time-Life Books.
Sacred Truth Ministeries. n.d. *Your inheritance: The best kept secret in the world*. Hayden, ID: Church of Jesus Christ Christian.
Sartre, Jean-Paul. [1938] 1949. *Nausea*. Trans. Lloyd Alexander. Reprint, New York: New Directions.
———. [1943] 1966. *Being and nothingness*. Reprint, New York: Washington Square Press.
———. 1967. Existentialism and human decision. In *Introductory philosophy*, ed. Frank Tillman, Bernard Berofsky, and John O'Connor, 694–704. New York: Harper and Row.
Sarup, Madan. 1989. *An introductory guide to post-structuralism and postmodernism*. Athens: University of Georgia Press.
Say, J. B. [1803] 1964. *A treatise on political economy; or, the production, distribution, and consumption of wealth*. Reprint, New York: Augustus M. Kelley.
Schacht, Richard, ed. 1970. *Alienation*. Garden City, NJ: Doubleday.
Scheer, Robert. 1982. Interview with Thomas K. Jones. *Los Angeles Times*, 16 January.
Schneider, Mark. 1997. Social dimensions of epistemological disputes: The case of literary theory. *Sociological Perspectives* 40, no. 2: 243–63.
Schumpeter, Joseph A. [1912] 1934. *The theory of economic development: An inquiry into profits, capital, credit, interest, and the business cycle*. Trans. R. Opie. Reprint, Cambridge, MA: Harvard University Press.
Schutz, Alfred. 1962. The problem of social reality. Vol. 1 of *Collected Papers*. Ed. Maurice Natenson. The Hague: Martinus Nijhoff.
Schwartz, Benjamin. 1995. The diversity myth: America's leading export. *Atlantic Monthly* 275, no. 5: 57.
Schwarz, John E. 1988. *America's hidden success: A reassessment of public policy from Kennedy to Reagan*. New York: W. W. Norton.
Seymour, Cheri. 1991. *Committee of the states: Inside the radical right*. Mariposa, CA: Camden Place Communications.
Sica, Alan. 1993. Does PoMo matter? *Contemporary Sociology* 22: 16–19.
Silk, Joseph. 1980. *The Big Bang: Creation and evolution of the universe*. San Francisco: W. H. Freeman.
Simi, Peter George. 1997. Dangerous liaisons: Participant observation and the white supremacist movement. Paper presented at the annual meeting of the Midwest Sociological Society, April, Kansas City.

———. 1998. Shaved heads, white-sheet demons, and the bogeyman: Ethnographic fragments of a white supremacist. Paper presented to the session "Extremism and extremists on the right" at the annual meeting of the Pacific Sociological Association, April, San Francisco.
Simmel, Georg. [1903] 1971. The metropolis and mental life. In *Georg Simmel on individuality and social forms,* ed. Donald N. Levine, 324–39. Reprint, Chicago: University of Chicago Press.
———. [1907] 1978. *The philosophy of money.* Trans. Tom Bottomore and David Frisby. Reprint, Boston: Routledge.
———. [1908] 1950. *The sociology of Georg Simmel.* Ed. and trans. Kurt H. Wolff. Glencoe, IL: Free Press.
Smale, Alison. 1997. Ruins of factory symbolize Albania's shattered dreams. *Oregonian,* 7 June.
Smith, Cyril Stanley. 1971. Art, technology, and science: Notes on their historical interaction. In *Perspectives in the history of science and technology,* ed. Duane H. D. Roller, 129–65. Norman: University of Oklahoma Press.
Smith, Jerome. 1981. *The coming currency collapse and what you can do about it.* New York: Bantam.
Souchik, Greg. 1987. All that glitters: How to protect yourself from swindlers when you buy precious metals, gems. *American Survival Guide* 9, no. 10: 64–67.
Spolar, Christine. 1997. Triana quiet after police hand out more guns. *Oregonian,* 16 March.
Starr, Mark, et al. 1985. Violence on the right. *Newsweek,* 4 March, 23, 25–26.
Stogill, R. 1948. Personal factors associated with leadership: A review of the literature. *Journal of Psychology* 25: 35–71.
Stryker, Sheldon. 1980. *Symbolic interactionism: A structural version.* Menlo Park, CA: Benjamin/Cummings.
Swerdlow, Joel L. 1998. Making sense of the millennium. *National Geographic* 193, no. 1: 1–33.
TACDA. n.d. *The American Civil Defense Association.* P.O. Box 1057, Starke, Florida, 32091.
Tappan, Mel. 1976. *Survival guns.* Rogue River, OR: Janus.
Theroux, Paul. 1982. *The mosquito coast.* New York: Penguin.
Thomas, W. I., and Florian Znaniecki. [1918–20] 1958. *The Polish peasant in Europe and America.* Reprint, New York: Dover.
Tinker, Jon, ed. 1985. *Acid Earth: The global threat of acid pollution.* Washington, DC: International Institute for Environment and Development.
Tyler, Tom R., and Kathleen M. McGraw. 1983. The threat of nuclear war: Interpretation and behavioral response. *Journal of Social Issues* 39, no. 1: 25–40.
Udvary, George. 1982. *Identity Bible reference manual.* Waynesville, NC: New Beginnings.
Van Mannen, John. 1988. *Tales of the field.* Chicago: University of Chicago Press.
Veblen, Thorstein. [1899] 1967. *The theory of the leisure class.* Reprint, New York: Penguin.
Vonnegut, Kurt. 1952. *Player piano.* New York: Dell.

Walsch, Neal Donald. 1996. *Conversations with God.* New York: Putnam Press.

Watkins, James, and M. E. Strong. 1984. Operation Azimuth Bearing. *American Survival Guide* 6, no. 4: 40–43.

Weber, Max. [1946] 1971. Religious rejections of the world and their directions. In *From Max Weber: Essays in sociology,* ed. H. H. Gerth and C. Wright Mills, 323–59. Reprint, New York: Oxford University Press.

———. [1946] 1989. The sociology of charismatic authority. In *Max Weber on charisma and institution building: Selected papers,* ed. S. N. Eisenstadt, 18–27. Reprint, Chicago: University of Chicago Press.

———. 1958a. *From Max Weber.* Trans. and ed. H. H. Gerth and C. Wright Mills. New York: Oxford University Press.

———. 1958b. *The Protestant ethic and the spirit of capitalism.* Trans. Talcott Parsons. New York: Scribner's.

———. 1964. *WirtSchaft und Gesellschaft, Studienausgabe.* 2 vols. Ed. Johannes Winckelmann. Köln: Kiepenheurer and Witsch.

———. 1978. *Economy and society: An outline of interpretive sociology.* 2 vols. Ed. Guenther Roth and Claus Wittich. Berkeley and Los Angeles: University of California Press.

Weiss, Leonard W., and M. W. Klass, eds. 1986. *Regulatory reform: What actually happened.* Boston: Little, Brown.

White, Terri Lyn, and Jim Larsen. 1984. Fiery ending followed thirty-four hours of stand-off. *South Whidbey Record,* 9 December, 8.

Whyte, William H. 1957. *The organization man.* Garden City, NJ: Doubleday.

Wilkinson, Tracy. 1997. Chaos rules amid gunfire in Albanian capital. *Oregonian,* 15 March.

Williams, Jeffrey. 1995. *Manipulation on trial: Economic analysis and the Hunt silver case.* Cambridge: Cambridge University Press.

Wilson, Bryan R. 1973. *Magic and the millennium: A sociological study of religious movements of protest among tribal and third-world peoples.* New York: Harper and Row. Quoted in Stephen Norris Linder, *Survivalists: The ethnography of an urban millennial cult* (Ann Arbor, MI: University Microfilms, 1982), 36.

Witztum, Doron, Eliyahu Rips, and Yoav Rosenberg. 1994. Equidistant letter sequences in the book of Genesis. *Statistical Science* 9, no. 3: 429–39.

Worsley, Peter. 1957. *The trumpet shall sound: A study of "cargo" cults in Melanesia.* London: Macgibbon and Kee.

Wright, Deil S. 1988. *Understanding intergovernmental relations.* 3d ed. Pacific Grove, CA: Brooks/Cole.

Wright, Will. 1975. *Sixguns and society: A structural study of the Western.* Berkeley and Los Angeles: University of California Press.

Yeats, William Butler. 1920. *Selected Poems and Four Plays.* 4th ed. New York: Scribner, 1996.

Zelizer, Viviana. 1987. *Pricing the priceless child: The changing social value of children.* New York: Basic Books.

Zellner, William W. 1995. Survivalists. In *Countercultures: A sociological analysis,* 47–75. New York: St. Martin's.

Zumbro, Ralph. 1982. Waterway getaway. *Survive* May/June: 28–29, 56–59.

INDEX